THE REBELLION OF THE DAUGHTERS

JEWS, CHRISTIANS, AND MUSLIMS FROM
THE ANCIENT TO THE MODERN WORLD

*Edited by Michael Cook, William Chester Jordan,
and Peter Schäfer*

A list of titles in this series appears at the back of the book.

The Rebellion of the Daughters

JEWISH WOMEN RUNAWAYS IN HABSBURG GALICIA

RACHEL MANEKIN

PRINCETON UNIVERSITY PRESS

PRINCETON & OXFORD

Published by Princeton University Press
41 William Street, Princeton, New Jersey 08540
6 Oxford Street, Woodstock, Oxfordshire OX20 1TR

press.princeton.edu

Library of Congress Cataloging-in-Publication Data

Names: Manekin, Rachel, 1948– author.
Title: The rebellion of the daughters : Jewish women runaways in Habsburg Galicia /
    Rachel Manekin.
Identifiers: LCCN 2019059670 (print) | LCCN 2019059671 (ebook) |
    ISBN 9780691194936 (hardback) | ISBN 9780691207094 (epub)
Subjects: LCSH: Jewish women—Conversion to Christianity—Poland—Kraków—
    Biography. |
Christian converts from Judaism—Poland—Kraków—Biography. | Conflict of
    generations—Poland—Kraków. | Felician Sisters. | Kraków
    (Poland)—Biography.
Classification: LCC HQ1172 .M36 2020 (print) | LCC HQ1172 (ebook) |
    DDC 305.48/8924043862—dc23
LC record available at https://lccn.loc.gov/2019059670
LC ebook record available at https://lccn.loc.gov/2019059671

British Library Cataloging-in-Publication Data is available

Editorial: Fred Appel and Jenny Tan
Production Editorial: Debbie Tegarden
Jacket Design: Layla Mac Rory
Production: Erin Suydam
Publicity: Kathryn Stevens and Kate Hensley
Copyeditor: Karen Verde

Jacket art: Mark Kadyson / Polona.pi

CONTENTS

ILLUSTRATIONS

ACKNOWLEDGMENTS

I ACKNOWLEDGE with gratitude the institutions that supported and enabled the research and writing of this book: The University of Maryland granted me a Research and Scholarship Award for Spring 2018 that allowed me to devote all my time to the project, as well as a leave of absence for the following academic year to complete it. A fellowship at the Israel Institute for Advanced Studies in 2015, as part of the research group, "Galicia: Literary and Historical Approaches to the Construction of a Jewish Place," motivated me to think of literary representations of the stories of runaways, which I later included in the book. I am particularly grateful to the leaders of the group, Ariel Hirschfeld and the late Alan Mintz, for the challenging discussions on Agnon as a "historian" of Galician Jewry. A fellowship at the Herbert D. Katz Center for Advanced Judaic Studies at the University of Pennsylvania in 2010, as part of the research group, "Secularism and Its Discontents," enabled me to continue my research on Michalina Araten. I would like also to acknowledge the support of the Littauer Publication Fund of the Joseph and Rebecca Meyerhoff Center for Jewish Studies at the University of Maryland.

I would not have been able to conduct my research for this book without the help of the Interlibrary Loan Services of the University of Maryland, the National Library of Israel in Jerusalem, the library of the Supreme Court in Vienna, the library at the YIVO Institute for Jewish Research in New York, the Central Archives for the History of the Jewish People in Jerusalem, the National Archives in Kraków, the Central Archives of Historical Records in Warsaw, the Central State Historical Archives of Ukraine in Lviv, the Austrian State Archives in Vienna, the Vienna University Archives, and the *Ginzach Kiddush Hashem* Archives in Bnei Brak. My deepest thanks to all of them.

I would like to express my gratitude to the many individuals who offered advice, comments, and assistance: Michel Araten, David Ashboren, Liat Bauminger, Robert Bogusz, Dariusz Dekiert, Eugeniusz Duda, Glenn Dynner, Norman Eisen, Robert Fradkin, Lili Haber, Lindsay Kaplan, Shnayer Leiman,

Yael Levi, Benyamin Lukin, Gilad Malach, Ruth Malach, Eluzer Mermelstein, Agnieszka Meller, Eyal Miller, Stanisław Obirek, Iris Parush, Eugenia Prokop-Janiec, David Rosen, Giorgio Rowinski, Krzysztof Rowiński, Simah Schreiber, Naomi Seidman, Avishalom Westreich, and Jolanta Żyndul. Special thanks to Ela Bauer for the many discussions during the different stages of writing this book; to Gerda Dinwiddie and Mark Shraberman for their help with translations; to Zuzanna Kołodziejska-Smagała, who introduced me to the works of Aniela Kallas (Korngut); to Joanna Lisek, who made Sarah Schenirer's handwritten Polish diary available to me before its publication; to Alicja Maślak-Maciejewska, who answered numerous questions and helped me locate materials in Poland; to Reuven Mohr for his help with transcribing German handwritten documents, and to Arielle Rein, who read several chapters and offered feedback and advice. My thanks also to the anonymous readers of the book manuscript for their helpful comments and suggestions.

Material from my article, "The Lost Generation: Education and Female Conversion in Fin-de-Siècle Kraków," *Polin: Studies in Polish Jewry* 18 (2005): 189–219, is reproduced with permission of Liverpool University Press through PLSclear.

Special thanks are due to Fred Appel of Princeton University Press for his graciousness, encouragement, and interest in the project from the time I submitted the book proposal; to Jenny Tan, for her editorial coordination; to Debbie Tegarden, the production editor, for her care and attentiveness; and to Karen Verde, the copyeditor, for her accuracy and attention to details.

To my children Devorah, Mikhael, Elisheva, Avigail, and their spouses, Elon, Yael, Amitai, and Elitsour: thanks for your encouragement, patience, humor, and love.

Charles (Bezalel) Manekin accompanied the writing of the book from its inception, read its chapters, offered comments, and served as a critical sounding board. To him I dedicate the book.

ABBREVIATIONS

AGAD   The Central Archives of Historical Records, Warsaw

CAHJP   Central Archives for the History of the Jewish People, Jerusalem

HHStA   Haus-, Hof- und Staatsarchiv, Vienna

TSDIAL   Central State Historical Archives of Ukraine, Lviv

RGBl   *Reichs-Gesetz-Blatt für das Kaiserthum Oesterreich*

NOTE ON TRANSLITERATION
AND TERMINOLOGY

HEBREW TERMS, whether in Hebrew or Yiddish documents, have been transliterated according to the 1973 *Encyclopedia Judaica*'s general rules for transliteration for Hebrew and Semitic languages, with certain modifications. That is not how the terms would have been pronounced by the people of the period, but after some hesitation and for the sake of uniformity, I have adopted it. Thus, "Beit Yaakov" rather than "Bais Yaakov," "Beth Jacob," or "Beys Yankev"; "Agudat Yisrael," rather than "Agudas Yisroel," "Agudath Israel," etc.

Place names are according to contemporary usage, with their current names following in parentheses. The phrase "Habsburg Empire" refers here to the Austrian part of the Austro-Hungarian Empire (Cisleithania).

Throughout the book the terms "Orthodox" and "traditional" are used interchangeably. There is an extensive literature that distinguishes between the two terms, but I have not seen fit to introduce the distinction in this book. On rare occasions I use the term "ultra-Orthodox," the meaning of which can be understood from the context. The term "Neo-Orthodoxy" refers to the religious worldview of the the German rabbi, S. R. Hirsch, and his followers, as will be made clear.

Unless otherwise stated, text in square brackets ("[ ]") represents my additions. References appear in shortened form in the notes, with the exception of archival sources or newspaper/magazine articles; the expanded forms are provided in the bibliography.

THE REBELLION OF THE DAUGHTERS

Introduction

To the Österreichisch-Israelitischen Union, Vienna,

My husband died thirteen years ago, and I was left behind with three children, among them a daughter, Lea, who was then four years old. I ran an inn in Czchów and worked hard in order to feed and educate my children. My children grew and thrived, and I had my joy in them; they were my bliss, my pride, my solace. Particularly close to my heart was my only daughter Lea, who after completing the primary school was assisting me in the inn and at the counter. She was already 17 years old. She was well-behaved, hardworking, and diligent. Then the misfortune happened! On November 12, 1907, at 7 o'clock in the evening, my daughter disappeared from our home. All the searches were in vain. [. . .] I asked the police for help, but the answer they received after calling the convent about my daughter was that Lea Gänger was not there. Only when a police commissioner appeared personally in the convent was my daughter found there [. . .]

Czchów, December 8, 1907
Mirla Gänger[1]

---

1. "Interpellation des Abgeordneten Dr. Straucher und Genossen an Ihre Exzellenzen die Herren k. k. Minister des Innern und der Justiz, betreffend geeignete Massnahmen zur Hintanhaltung von Kinderraub, beziehungsweise Mädchenentführung," 130. Sitzung der XVIII. Session am 29. Jänner 1909, *Stenographische Protokolle* (1909): 14617–14633, esp. 14626–14627. Lea (Leonora) Gänger converted to Catholicism in 1908. See the National Archives in Kraków, Magistrat miasta Krakowa, Kr 144–31804/08.

IN JANUARY 29, 1909, Benno Straucher (1854–1940), the Bukovina Jewish delegate in the Austrian parliament, submitted an interpellation to the Ministers of the Interior and Justice in which he described the disappearance of thirty Galician Jewish minor girls, including Lea Gänger of Czchów. The girls were subsequently discovered in the Felician Sisters' convent in Kraków, where they prepared themselves for baptism, but most of them refused to return to their parental homes. Straucher characterized these stories as "kidnappings" and accused the convent and the local authorities of disregarding the parental custody over their underage daughters.

The allegations in Straucher's interpellation were not new to the Austrian parliament members or to the broad public. Between the years 1873 and 1914, hundreds of Jewish girls disappeared from their homes, found shelter in the Felician Sisters' convent in Kraków, and converted to Roman Catholicism. Stories about these women, most of them minors according to Austrian law, were often published under sensational titles in the Viennese press, Jewish and non-Jewish, as well as in the major Hebrew newspapers. The liberal press blamed the Catholic Church for allowing such a phenomenon to take place, explaining that this was happening specifically in "backward" Galicia, where clericalism ruled the day. The Catholic and conservative press claimed that the girls were not abducted but rather abandoned their parental homes and freely chose to be baptized. Each of the two narratives found support in legal arguments, adding fuel to the anti-Semitic atmosphere in the Habsburg Empire during that period. Many of the parents enlisted the help of the Österreichisch-Israelitische Union, the Viennese Jewish organization that was established in 1884 to fight anti-Semitism. But despite legal intervention, parents were generally unsuccessful as the courts sided with the convent and the girls, who declared that they had entered the convent of their own free will.

What makes the phenomenon of the runaway girls especially noteworthy is that it was particular to Galicia, the southeastern part of the Polish-Lithuanian Commonwealth, which was annexed to the Habsburg Empire in the first and third partitions of Poland in 1772 and 1795. Unlike in other Habsburg crown lands, a majority of Galicia's Jewish population was Orthodox, many of them Hasidim.[2] Indeed, most of the runaways came from traditional homes. There were many converts from Judaism in other Habsburg provinces, including in Vienna where their numbers were particularly high,

---

2. See Wodziński, *Hasidism*, 151. Based on a variety of sources, Wodziński concludes that "slightly above 50%" of Galician Jews were Hasidim.

but the essential feature distinctive to Galicia—large-scale **disappearance** of female minors from Orthodox homes—was unheard of in any other Habsburg territory.

The few scholars who have noticed the large proportion of Jewish females among the converts in Kraków have tended to view these converts within the broader context of Jewish conversion in "Eastern Europe," namely, Imperial Russia, ignoring the specific conditions in Habsburg Galicia.[3] True, there were some common aspects between female conversion cases in both Imperial Russia and Kraków, such as the abduction narrative.[4] Likewise, conversion of underage girls occurred also in Imperial Russia, where age fourteen was considered the age of majority for the purpose of conversion of Jews.[5]

But despite these similarities, the Galician runaways and the subsequent conversion of many of them demand a separate historical treatment because the Galician context differed significantly from that of the Russian Empire. For example, school attendance was mandated by law for all children in Galicia and, indeed, throughout Cisleithania (the Austrian half of the dual monarchy), but such a law didn't exist in Imperial Russia.[6] Galician Jewish girls didn't abandon home in order to marry a gentile peasant or a soldier passing by, as in many of the Russian cases. Regardless of the economic status of their families, Galician Jewish girls experienced a growing gulf between their dreams and aspirations as educated young women and their parents' traditional norms and expectations. When parents arranged a match for their educated daughters with a Hasid who lacked a modern education, a family crisis often ensued. Strong-willed daughters rebelled, and some ran away to a place that would offer them shelter for a few months, such as the Felician Sisters' convent in Kraków, which acquired a reputation for harboring female Jewish runaways.

How was it possible for such a phenomenon to take place in Habsburg Galicia? As citizens of a constitutional monarchy since December 1867, a *Rechtsstaat*, Galician Jews enjoyed equality before the law, and freedom of

3. Endelman, *Leaving the Jewish Fold*, 123, 135–137; Hyman, *Gender and Assimilation*, 72–75.

4. Schainker, *Confessions of the Shtetl*, 105–106, and Freeze, "When Chava Left Home," 153–188, esp. 156.

5. Schainker, *Confessions of the Shtetl*, 38; Freeze, "When Chava Left Home," 155, n. 11, 169, 186.

6. See Adler, *In Her Hands*. Adler shows that as a result of private initiatives by Jews, many private Jewish schools were established for girls in the Russian Empire, something that didn't exist in Western Galicia prior to World War I, where almost all Jews sent their daughters to public or private non-Jewish schools. After the 1867 *Ausgleich*, the Hungarian Ministry of Education issued its own laws regarding education mandating in 1868 six years of primary school.

movement, domicile, assembly, religion, expression, occupation, and association, as well as access to public offices. Although in practice the extent of these rights in their application to Jews was sometimes limited, such rights were something Jews in the bordering Russian Empire could only imagine. As we shall see, the answer lies in the peculiarity of the Habsburg legal situation that allowed minors to convert while still under the custody of their parents. That is one reason why the issue of the Galician female converts has to be researched within the Galician and Habsburg contexts rather than in a general (and often vague) "Eastern European" context.

Although several important contributions to the study of Galician Jewry have appeared in the past few years in the English language, they have focused almost entirely on the experience of males, whether in politics[7] or the 1898 anti-Jewish riots in Western Galicia.[8] The increased tension between Jews and Christians during and following those riots did not stop young Jewish women who lived in Western Galicia from running away and preparing themselves for baptism. The attraction of Catholicism for some Galician women from Orthodox Jewish homes calls for explanation, and the present study attempts to provide one. More broadly, it attempts to provide insight into experiences of what was called the "lost generation" of Galician Jewish women.[9] It does not, however, discuss the phenomenon of prostitution or sex trafficking ("white slavery"), which in most cases affected young women from very poor families and thus requires a different type of analysis.[10]

This book focuses on Western Galicia, specifically Kraków, because it was the main arena in which the stories of the runaways took place. That the majority of female Jewish converts to Catholicism were from villages and small

7. Shanes, *Diaspora Nationalism*, is devoted to Jewish national politics, politics being a sphere from which women in the Habsburg Empire were legally barred. A volume of the annual *Polin* that concentrates on Jews in Galicia has twelve articles, none of which deals with women, see *Polin: Studies in Polish Jewry* 12 (1999).

8. Unowsky's *The Plunder* analyzes the background and describes in detail the riots against Jews in Western Galicia at the close of the nineteenth century. Unowsky mentions also the involvement of women in these series of attacks, both as perpetrators and as victims, but their testimonies are rather brief and limited.

9. In 1925, R. Tuvia Horowitz used this phrase when lamenting the "neglect of the lost Jewish generation [*ferloyrenen yudishen dor*] that was torn from the body of the Jewish people"; see Horowitz, "What Do Jewish Daughters Lack?" 75.

10. For scholarly works on this topic see Stauter-Halsted, *The Devil's Chain* and Bristow, *Prostitution and Prejudice*.

towns in Western Galicia is not surprising. First and foremost, Polish Catholics constituted the absolute majority in rural and urban areas in Western Galicia, including in Kraków, the most important city of the region.[11] Kraków was the center of religious, intellectual, and cultural life in Western Galicia, with an elite class that included conservative academics, high-ranking church and state officials, authors, and artists. By contrast, the population in Eastern Galicia, whose capital was Lwów (Lviv, L'viv, Lemberg), was composed of a majority of Ruthenians (Galician Ukrainians) with Polish, Jewish, and Armenian minorities. In addition to being multi-ethnic, it was multi-religious, with Christians of different denominations in addition to Jews, all living in close proximity to each other.[12] In contrast to the distinctly Polish and Catholic character of Kraków, Lwów, the seat of the Austrian central administration in Galicia, had a long legacy of German culture, and its atmosphere was more tolerant and cosmopolitan.[13] School education in Western Galicia was marked by its emphasis on Polish language and history and the cultivation of a strong Polish identity, of which Catholicism was an essential part.

Of course, most young Jewish females in Western Galicia did not vanish from their homes and enter convents. But the fact that more than three hundred of them—according to the records I found; there likely were more—formally declared their intention to convert set off alarm bells among the Jewish population and generated a debate on the causes of this problem. Jewish publicists claimed that even young women who remained Jewish had to find ways to reconcile their wishes as modern educated young women with the expectations of their parents, who in most cases subscribed to traditional ways of life. *The Rebellion of the Daughters* looks at the challenges young Galician Jewish females experienced during this period and highlights the growing family conflicts in the face of a new reality—compulsory education, Polish acculturation, and the growth of feminism—that was alien to their parents' generation. It is based on archival police investigations, court records,

11. In 1910, Roman Catholics constituted 88.5% of the population in Western Galicia, Greek Catholics—3.24%, and Jews—7.92%. See Mark, *Galizien unter österreichischer Herrschaft*, 85.

12. In 1910, Roman Catholics constituted 25.3% of the population in Eastern Galicia, Greek Catholics—61.68%, and Jews—12.36%. See Mark, *Galizien unter österreichischer Herrschaft*.

13. In 1910, Roman Catholics constituted 51% of the population in the city of Lwów, Greek Catholics—19.1%, and Jews—27.8%, ibid., 100. By contrast, Roman Catholics constituted 76% of the population in the city of Kraków, Greek Catholics—1.1%, and Jews—21.3%. See Mark, *Galizien unter österreichischer Herrschaft*.

government correspondence, Polish, German, and Hebrew press reports, parliament protocols, law codes, and scholarly literature.

To be able to understand the world in which the runaway young women lived, it is crucial to chart the opportunities and challenges created by the new laws enacted by the Austrian government and carried out by the Galician administration. Chapter 1 traces the imperial legal context of both compulsory education and religious conversion and their selective application in Galicia. It presents the necessary backdrop against which the stories of the runaways in the following chapters unfold. The chapter considers also the new cultural and intellectual opportunities for females in Kraków, as well as the spread of feminist ideas with which the highly acculturated Orthodox women would be familiar. An analysis of archival records on Jewish conversion provides data such as the age and geographical origin of the female Jewish converts, as well as the time period when their baptism took place. The last section of the chapter discusses the lack of rabbinic response to the growing phenomenon of the female runaways.

The next three chapters reconstruct the histories of three runaways: Michalina Araten, Debora Lewkowicz, and Anna Kluger. Araten came from an affluent Hasidic home and enjoyed an education in a private prestigious primary school in Kraków. Attracted to Catholicism while in school, Araten initiated an acquaintance with a military officer who lived across from her home. The acquaintance was short lived, but when informed by her father that she was about to be engaged to a man of his choice, she ran away and entered the Felician Sisters' convent and later disappeared. The Araten affair was broadly reported in the Habsburg press as well as in major newspapers outside Austria. The second young woman, Debora Lewkowicz, a daughter of a village tavernkeeper, completed her primary school education in the city of Wieliczka in Western Galicia. She had a close relationship with a young Pole, as a result of which her father quickly arranged for her to marry a Jewish man. Debora ran away on the eve of her wedding and entered the Felician Sisters' convent, where she stayed for several months. She was subsequently baptized there and prepared for the profession of governess. Finally, Anna Kluger, a daughter of an affluent family in Podgórze and a direct descendant of R. Hayim Halberstam, the founder of the Sandz Hasidic dynasty, was sent to one of the best private girls' schools in Kraków. She had a passion for learning and received her gymnasium matriculation certificate as an external student, since her parents expected her to marry and stop her schooling after completing primary school. Kluger continued her studies at the university in secret after getting married and finally ran away from home to pursue her dream. Kluger did not convert but rather hid in a convent while trying to be released of her father's custody. (Her religious marriage was not officially recognized.) All these cases were brought to court, with the parents demanding that the state authorities help them bring their underage daughters back home.[14]

Chapter 5 interrupts the historical narrative with a short literary interlude that identifies and discusses works of contemporary fiction in German, Polish, Yiddish, and Hebrew, that were inspired by press reports of the Galician female Jewish runaways. It shows how different authors—males and females, Jews and non-Jews—interpreted the predicament of the contemporary young Galician Jewish women.

Paradoxically, the devastation of the war years bore the first initiative for a change in the traditional practice of female education. While spending time as a refugee in Vienna, Sarah Schenirer, a young woman from Kraków, was inspired to establish a religious afternoon school, a plan she carried out when she returned to her hometown. This breakthrough subsequently paved the way for the creation of the Orthodox Beit Yaakov female school network. As shown in the book, while the Beit Yaakov movement introduced formal religious education for Orthodox girls, it also controlled and filtered their exposure to secular studies. The school and the home in effect became partners in an effort to preempt the allure of secular culture and to tame potentially rebellious daughters. The last section in the chapter looks at the model of Orthodox female education developed in Kraków, where the teachers' seminary, rather than the gymnasium, was adopted as the highest learning institution for young Orthodox women.

This book places particular emphasis on the voices of the women recorded in a variety of sources. Since female voices documented in real time, especially of traditional women, are quite rare for this period, these sources offer us a glimpse into the life of young women as *they* experienced it at that time. I have included within an appendix some of their letters and statements. As is the case with ego-documents, the records of these voices should be read and

---

14. The explicit expressions of emotions such as insult, anger, loneliness, shame, and shock in all three cases by the daughters, as well as by the parents and even some state and church authorities, might be further examined in the context of the history of emotions in an attempt to understand how they shaped the ensuing events; however, this is beyond the scope of this book.

analyzed in light of the specific conditions under which they were written, and which are discussed in the relevant chapters.

————

A concluding word concerning the origin of this book: In 2002, while conducting research in the National Archives in Kraków on another project, I stumbled upon several files that included copies of hundreds of notifications about Jews, mostly female, intending to convert to Christianity. The copies were sent to the Kraków rabbinate by the office in charge of Jewish records in the Kraków magistrate; the originals had been sent to the Bishop's consistory in Kraków. Since the phenomenon of female conversion had gone virtually unnoticed in histories of Kraków Jewry, I slowly began to collect materials on such conversions on subsequent research trips. I also began to search for relevant news items in the contemporary press. I learned quickly that the stories of young Jewish women runaways who found shelter in a Kraków convent had often involved police investigations, court cases, ministerial intervention, and parliamentary debates. Press reports of "kidnappings" of young Jewish women in Kraków appeared throughout the world.

That all this occurred in Habsburg Galicia, where Jews enjoyed, at least in principle, full and equal rights and privileges of citizens, was intriguing; that the runaway young females were coming from Orthodox homes even more so. As I started analyzing the sources I collected, I soon realized that the runaway phenomenon touched upon several internal and external aspects of Jewish life that were unique to Galicia during this period, and that attempting to explain the phenomenon would require examining the broader social, religious, political, and legal contexts. Since these aspects were not addressed in the scholarship, I began to research and publish several preliminary studies that touched upon the broader phenomenon, and that included the basic outlines of the stories of several young women.[15]

The decision to include within this book an account of the beginning of formal education for Orthodox Jewish women reflects my view that a main cause of the rebellion of the daughters was the cognitive dissonance they experienced as a result of their Polish acculturation and their lack of formal

15. See Manekin, "'Something Completely New'"; "The Lost Generation"; "Orthodox Jewry in Kraków"; Manekin, "Tehilla's Daughter and Michalina Araten," *Haaretz*, Literary Supplement, June 27, 2003 [Hebrew].

Jewish education. But equally interesting was the much-delayed Orthodox response, which was to create the Beit Yaakov school network. That the first Orthodox school was established by a young Kraków woman, Sarah Schenirer, and that later the flagship educational institution of the movement was built in Kraków, are both critical points for understanding the path female Orthodox Jewish education took in subsequent years.

Schenirer has been portrayed in traditional Beit Yaakov literature as a pious Jewish seamstress who spearheaded an educational movement designed to attract young assimilated Jewish women back into the Orthodox fold. This was the portrait of her that I received from my teachers when I was a student at the Beit Yaakov school and teachers' seminary in Tel Aviv. Recent academic studies have tended to portray her as a woman learned in Jewish religious texts who, despite significant male opposition, launched an educational movement for young Orthodox women that aspired for, and achieved, excellence in both Torah study and secular subjects.[16] Both these analyses tend to view Schenirer through the prism of later concerns rather than in her immediate historical context. Neither sufficiently take into account the problems of using internal sources, which in many cases are the only sources we have about the life of Schenirer and the beginning of Beit Yaakov.

I have grappled with the often tendentious and promotional nature of these sources by looking carefully at the context in which they appeared, seeking conflicting narratives and evaluations (especially in memoirs), and balancing them with external sources, when available, and internal sources that were not intended to be made public (such as protocols of faculty meetings). In this manner, I have tried to establish the most plausible account given the specific historical context of the Orthodox Jewish community in prewar Galicia and interwar Poland. As a result, Schenirer is portrayed in this book as neither female saint nor scholar, but rather as a learned religious enthusiast and Orthodox ideologue who sought to rescue the daughters of her contemporaries by providing them with an emotional and intellectual allegiance to Orthodox Judaism that their mothers lacked. The physical walls of the Felician Sisters' convent that had sheltered some of the rebellious daughters, and the Polish

16. The traditional portrayal appears in publications and memoirs of Beit Yaakov administrators, teachers, and students, and in the Beit Yaakov journal (which was published beginning in 1923 and ending in 1939). Recent scholarly works include Weissman, "Bais Ya'akov"; Oleszak, "The Beit Ya'akov School in Kraków"; Seidman, "A Revolution in the Name of Tradition" and Seidman, *Sarah Schenirer*.

acculturation that had been the hallmark of others who remained Jewish, were replaced by religious commitments and restraints inculcated by the first female Orthodox Jewish educational movement, one that created a neo-traditional model of female Jewish piety. The ideological founders of the Beit Yaakov movement hoped and believed that through indoctrination and education, and employing the tools of contemporary youth movements, the daughters of the "lost generation" of Orthodox Jewish women would proudly and enthusiastically embrace their Orthodox identity.

1

The Origins of the "Daughters' Question"

AT THE END OF the nineteenth and the beginning of the twentieth centuries, hundreds of young Jewish women ran away from their homes and found shelter in a Kraków convent, where many of them subsequently converted to Roman Catholicism. The runaway phenomenon attracted the attention of the press, as well as that of the Austrian and Galician authorities. Particularly noteworthy was that most of the women were legally minors from Orthodox Jewish homes. Nothing like this appears to have occurred in other places where Jews converted to Christianity.

The runaway phenomenon presented the most extreme example of a more widespread problem referred to at the time as the "Daughters' Question," a predicament in Galician Jewish society that resulted from the clash between familial expectations and female aspirations during this period. The runaway phenomenon exposed the failure of traditional Jewry to adapt itself to a world in which young women underwent a process of Polish acculturation with little religious Jewish education that often left them frustrated and unwilling to adopt their mothers' lifestyles. Of course, the overwhelming number of young Galician Jewish women did not run away from their homes, much less convert; they accepted their roles as Orthodox wives and mothers, sometimes after some resistance. But all young women were affected by the political and cultural changes in Habsburg Galicia, though they reacted differently to them, as we shall see in this and subsequent chapters.

A detailed examination of the stories of some of the female runaways, together with what can be gleaned from press reports, official correspondence, police investigations, and court cases, reveal three important factors responsible for precipitating the crisis in Galician Jewish society: the rise in attendance of girls in school coupled with the dearth of Jewish education, the spread of cultural activities intended for young women, and the practice of parentally arranged marriages at an early age. These factors do not explain why hundreds of runaways chose the city of Kraków as their destination, or how they were able to convert despite their status as minors. For this we need to introduce two other factors: the Kraków convent that sheltered these women and facilitated their conversions, and the peculiar legal status of the runaways who were still legally under the custody of their Jewish parents.

Compulsory Education in Habsburg Galicia

In the last quarter of the nineteenth century, Orthodox Jewish girls in Galicia, including daughters of Hasidic families, started attending public and private primary schools in unprecedented numbers. To be sure, this was not the first time Galician Jewish girls had attended schools. Already in the late eighteenth century, the Austrian administration appointed the Bohemian-born Jewish Maskil (enlightener) Herz Homberg (1749–1841) to establish and supervise German Jewish elementary schools composed of one to three grades to teach Jewish boys and girls the rudiments of reading and writing in German as well as basic arithmetic.[1] Attendance was mandatory, but many in the Jewish community opposed the schools. When the schools closed in 1806, Jews were allowed to attend Galician public schools (which were not many), although they had to sit on separate benches.[2] Neither Christians nor Jews welcomed Jewish attendance at these schools, and since attendance wasn't enforced, only a small number of Jewish children enrolled. The Austrian administration did retain a 1789 requirement that Jewish brides and grooms present a school diploma or pass an examination on basic school subjects in order to receive a marriage permit,[3] abolishing the requirement only in 1859.[4] But this was of little consequence, since most Galician Jews preferred to avoid the legally required marriage procedure and to marry only according to Jewish religious law. The imperial policy designed to "civilize" Galician Jewry, viewed as culturally backward and religiously superstitious by the Austrian administration, failed to achieve its stated goal.

1. Sadowski, *Haskala und Lebenswelt*.

2. Austria, *Politische Verfassung der deutschen Volksschulen*, §476e, 268.

3. Karniel, "Das Toleranzpatent Kaiser Josephs II.," §13, 77.

4. "Nr. 217. Kaiserliche Verordnung vom 29. November 1859," *RGBl* (1859): 605–606.

In subsequent years a considerable number of Galician Jewish children, including girls, attended the schools established by the Jewish communities in Tarnopol, Brody, Kraków, Lwów, Bolechów, Przemyśl, Andrychów, as well as in some smaller communities. Since the curriculum for boys in these schools deviated significantly from that of the traditional ḥeder, which was restricted to traditional Jewish texts,[5] the schools attracted children from the Jewish acculturated and professional classes, and not from the Orthodox Jewish population. The latter also did not send their children to non-Jewish schools, a practice that became increasingly prevalent among non-Orthodox Jews beginning in the mid-nineteenth century.

Instead, Orthodox Jewish families with the wherewithal hired private tutors to teach their daughters to read Jewish prayers, and occasionally works like *Że'ena u-re'ena*, the popular seventeenth-century Yiddish compilation that included a selection with a commentary of translated scriptural texts read in the synagogue on the Sabbath,[6] or Jewish ethical works translated into Yiddish. Affluent families often provided their daughters private lessons in foreign languages and classical literary works.[7] Secular education was not provided according to a well-organized curriculum but depended on the availability of local tutors.[8] Girls generally learned about women's religious obligations from their mothers.

This situation began to change after several laws were enacted that obligated parents, under threat of punishment, to send their children to school. Since Galician Jews, as Austrian citizens, were subject to the same laws as were Christians, it is important to see how these laws came about, how they gradually took hold in Galicia, and what became the educational options for Galician Jewish children. In particular, it is important to see how the new compulsory education law affected the vastly different educational experiences of Orthodox Jewish boys and girls, thus giving birth to the "Daughters' Question" and the runaway phenomenon.

After passing the fundamental laws about the rights of citizens in December 1867, Austrian liberals began taking steps to curtail the power of the Catholic Church. On May 25, 1868, the two houses of the Austrian Parliament approved the three so-called May Laws that abolished the control of the Roman

5. On the ḥeder, see Zalkin, "Ḥeder."

6. See Faierstein, *Ze'enah U-Re'enah.*

7. See Parush, *Reading Jewish Women*, 71–96; Stampfer, "Gender Differentiation."

8. Bergner, *On Long Winter Nights*, 46.

Catholic Church in matters of matrimony and education and regulated the interconfessional relations between citizens based on equal treatment of all recognized churches and religious societies.[9] Prior to the promulgation of the May Laws, education in the Habsburg Empire had been the exclusive province of the Roman Catholic Church, as agreed upon in the 1855 concordat between Austria and the Holy See. The Catholic consistories together with the district administrations also supervised the small number of Jewish schools in Galicia, except for the study of the Jewish religion.

The Catholic Church fought vehemently against the new laws, but the liberals persisted in their anti-concordat legislation. The clashes between the Austrian Catholic clergy and the state turned into what was referred to at the time as a culture war (*Kulturkampf*), although it was much milder than the parallel German case. After all, Austrian officials were mostly Roman Catholic themselves, but what they refused to do was grant the Church exclusive authority and control in public life.

The May Law regarding schools established principles pertaining to all public schools, especially the relations between school and religion.[10] It stipulated in its first clause that supervision of matters of teaching and education belonged to the state. While the teaching of religion was to remain under the control of the religious establishments, all other school subjects were to be independent of any influence of churches or religious societies. Still, the law allowed churches and religious societies, if they so wished, to establish private parochial schools at their own expense; however, such schools needed to be subject to the laws governing teaching. Attendance in schools established for a particular religious faith could not be denied to students of another faith, and teaching positions in public schools were to be open to all citizens with the appropriate skills regardless of their religious faith. Religion teachers and religious subjects, on the other hand, needed approval from the relevant religious communal institutions.

On May 14, 1869, after a series of contentious parliamentary debates, the emperor signed the compulsory primary education law, which put into practice the principles outlined in the 1868 education May Law.[11] Its first clause stipulated that the purpose of the primary public school was to provide

9. Judson, *The Habsburg Empire*, 281–288.

10. "Nr. 48. Gesetz vom 25. Mai 1868," *RGBl* (1868): 97–99.

11. "Nr. 62. Gesetz vom 14. Mai 1869," *RGBl* (1869): 277–288 (henceforth: primary education law).

children with an ethical-religious education, develop their mental abilities, equip them with knowledge and skills necessary for further learning in life, and lay down the foundation for developing individuals who would be capable members of society. The law listed the required school subjects, with religion appearing first, and explained issues pertaining to teachers, class size, and establishing schools. In addition, the law mandated school attendance for boys and girls between the ages of six and fourteen. A girls' school had to be established in locales where at least eighty girls were enrolled. In addition to the required subjects, the school had to teach girls "female handicraft" as well as housekeeping. The law exempted those who attended private schools or were home schooled from compulsory attendance in public schools.

Like the 1868 May Laws, the 1869 compulsory school law aroused fierce opposition among clericals and conservatives who believed that the state control of education "violated the natural rights of parents, of nationality, and of Church" and viewed it as "a plot to denationalize and dechristianize the children." They joined hands for this purpose with landowners who opposed the eight years of compulsory schooling, believing that "farmers needed their healthy lads for the unending toil of the agricultural routine, while their wives needed the girls of the family for household chores. Why distract these plain but honest children with a medley of academic subjects of no further use to them after they had arrived at their twelfth birthday?"[12] Children's school attendance from ages six to twelve was already established in cities by Maria Theresa's 1774 school ordinance and was since then considered the ideal norm, at least theoretically.[13]

Government coalition considerations later led to the exemption of several Austrian provinces, including Galicia, from the eight years of compulsory schooling. On May 2, 1873, a special law was promulgated for Galicia requiring school attendance only from ages six to twelve and granting more authority and control to the Galician school council.[14] Since the 1869 Austrian law defined two categories of primary schooling, *Volksschule* (elementary school

---

12. Jenks, *Austria Under the Iron Ring*, 122–140, esp. 124.

13. Felbiger, *Allgemeine Schulordnung*, §12, 21–22.

14. "Nr. 250. Gesetz über die Errichtung und Erhaltung der öffentlichen Volksschulen und über die Verpflichtung zum Schulbesuche," *Landes-Gesetz- und Verordnungsblatt für das Königreich Galizien und Lodomerien sammt dem Grossherzogthume Krakau* (1873): 181–192, esp. §40, 190. The law required Christian pupils to attend an additional two years in a Sunday religious school.

generally composed of five grades) and an optional urban *Bürgerschule* (a middle school composed of three grades following the five-grade elementary school) designated for students who didn't plan to continue their studies but wished to advance their education for the purpose of employment, the Galician 1873 version defined a parallel system of *szkoły ludowe pospolite* (common elementary school) and *szkoły wydziałowe* (middle school, literally: department school) which was composed of three or four grades following the four grades of a common elementary school. The Galician law required that at least one of the latter types be established for every two school districts,[15] thus giving an option to parents in urban areas to provide their children with a more advanced education. The *Bürgerschule* and its Galician equivalent didn't treat boys and girls equally. Unlike the primary public school, the *Bürgerschule* and the *szkoły wydziałowe* were not allowed to be coeducational, and the curriculum for girls had fewer hours devoted to arithmetic, geometry, and drawing in order to allow for time to teach female handicraft.

The parliamentary debates continued following the promulgation of these laws, becoming fiercer after 1879, when liberals lost the majority in the lower house. Conservatives and clericals demanded strengthening the religious character of schools and accused the school law of "producing youngsters, who frequented skittle alleys, played cards, and swaggered about the streets smoking cigars instead of going to church and learning the precepts of Christianity."[16]

On May 2, 1883, after much pressure, an amendment to the 1869 compulsory education law was approved which introduced several changes (*Schulnovelle*). The most controversial change was the clause requiring that headmasters of public schools be competent to teach the religion of the majority of the students.[17] While this provision was intended to exclude Jews and Protestants from the position of headmasters in schools where most of the students were Roman Catholics, Galicia was exempted from compliance.[18] As one of the Galician representatives explained, Poles didn't want Jewish headmasters in urban schools where the majority of students were Jewish.[19] Other provisions for Galicia included the reformulation of the first aim of the school—instead of an ethical and religious education, a special 1885 law for Galicia reversed the

---

15. Ibid. §5, 182.

16. Jenks, *Austria Under the Iron Ring*, 127–128.

17. "Nr. 53. Gesetz vom 2. Mai 1883," *RGBl* (1883): 199–206, esp. §48, 204–205.

18. Ibid., §75, 206.

19. Jenks, *Austria Under the Iron Ring*, 131.

order and stipulated that the public school's purpose was to teach children the tenets of religion and ethics.[20] The required number of weekly religion classes remained two, but religion teachers were allowed to teach more weekly religion classes if they wished, for which they received compensation.[21] These changes reflected the central role of religion and tradition in Galician society.

Galician Poles were able to receive preferential treatment because of the pressure exerted by the Polish Club (the Polish Galician party in the Austrian parliament composed mostly of conservatives and Polish nationalists) aimed at securing a privileged status for Poles in Galicia. The Polish Club agreed to support major government legislation in exchange for the Polonization of the Galician administration, court system, and the schools, which included making Polish the instruction language at the universities of Lwów and Kraków. By 1870, the Austrian government granted Poles the autonomy they desired despite the opposition of the Ruthenian minority.[22]

These developments impacted all Galicians, including the Jewish population. Transferring local decisions on education policies to the Galician school council, in which all members were Poles (the first Jew, Leon Sternbach, became a member in 1905), not only resulted in the Polonization of almost all Galician public schools, but ensured that their character remained distinctly Christian. It is important to emphasize that despite the fact that the formal religious instruction was restricted to special classes for that purpose, Galician public schools were not *secular* institutions leading to the secularization of their students, especially since Polish national identity had been closely linked to Roman Catholicism.[23] This was not much different in the Habsburg Empire in general, as evidenced in the failure of the Freie Schule association in the early twentieth century to establish a private *secular* school without religion classes in the curriculum. Appeals to the Supreme Court presented by the Jewish socialist lawyer Julius Ofner were rejected even when it was promised

20. "Nr. 27. Gesetz vom 2. February 1885," *Landes-Gesetz- und Verordnungsblatt für das Königreich Galizien und Lodomerien sammt dem Grossherzogthume Krakau* (1885): 85–96, esp. §1, 86.

21. "Nr. 81. Gesetz com 22. Juni 1899," *Landes-Gesetz- und Verordnungsblatt für das Königreich Galizien und Lodomerien sammt dem Grossherzogthume Krakau* (1899): 199–200, esp. §1, 199.

22. Bled, *Franz Joseph*, 163–167; Kolmer, *Parlament und Verfassung*, vol. 1, 213–214; 334; 351–354; 365–367; 397–398; vol. 2, 34–36.

23. Dziadzio, "Weltliche oder konfessionelle Schule?" 43–44. See the description of the gymnasium in Brody, Eastern Galicia, in Sadan, *Mi-meḥoz ha-yaldut*, 243–255.

that parents would provide their children with home religion classes.[24] According to the Court, the teaching of religion was specifically required in the law. Similarly, children of parents with no religious affiliation who studied in public schools were required to attend religion classes.[25]

How did the leaders of Galician Orthodox Jews react to the compulsory education law? Surprisingly, unlike non-Jewish conservative and clerical groups, Orthodox Jews did not conduct a public struggle against any element of the compulsory education law. Galician Orthodox Jews organized politically in 1879,[26] but compulsory education was not on their political agenda; moreover, there is no evidence of any private attempts by rabbis or Hasidic leaders to use influential individuals to lobby the authorities on their behalf.[27] Still, this doesn't mean that they were not apprehensive about the possible repercussions of the new law, specifically its effect upon the ḥeder education system for boys. Indeed, their apprehension was not unjustified, at least initially.

Compulsory Education and Orthodox Jewish Boys

Unlike in other provinces of the Habsburg Empire, most Orthodox Jewish boys in Galicia continued to be educated in the traditional ḥeder even during the late nineteenth century. The first sign of a potential threat to this practice appeared after the publication of the Galician version of the compulsory education law. Following a directive of the Minister of Religion and Education from June 1874, special instructions were forwarded in August by the Galician governor to district education councils requiring that ḥeder teachers apply for a license in order to be able to continue their operation. The requirement for receiving the

24. On Ofner, see Wistrich, *The Jews of Vienna*, 315–318.

25. Dziadzio, "Weltliche oder konfessionelle Schule?" 43–45. According to Dziadzio, "The religious education of the youth was generally regarded as a remedy against the increasing social and political decay of the state."

26. See Manekin, *Yehudei Galizyah*, 122–162.

27. The Hebrew newspaper *Ha-Magid* reported about the May Laws and the Catholic opposition to them, expressing relief and joy that the Roman Catholic Church would no longer control marriage and education. It didn't raise any question regarding the possible effects of the laws on Jews, see "Letters from Vienna," *Ha-Magid*, June 10, 1868, 178–179; "Political News," ibid., June 17, 1868, 185–186; "Political News," ibid., July 1, 1869, 201–202; "Political News," ibid., July 29, 1868, 233–234 [Hebrew].

license included appropriate sanitary conditions,[28] a curriculum that included such subjects as arithmetic and reading and writing in Polish, and the payment of a special tax. Ḥeder teachers who intended to teach only religious subjects had to register in the local Jewish community councils, which were responsible for inspecting the sanitary conditions of the place according to public school guidelines.[29] Attending a ḥeder that taught only religious subjects did not exempt one from the required compulsory schooling.

Following the 1874 directives and similar regulations published in subsequent years, a growing number of teachers did register their ḥeders, mostly as strictly confessional schools. Some ḥeders were closed by the authorities due to bad sanitary conditions. In Kraków, as in some other places, there were also several local initiatives to establish private Jewish schools for boys that would conform to school regulations; however, most of their teachers were not competent enough to teach in Polish and so those schools were mostly unsuccessful. The Jewish school in Kazimierz (where most Kraków Jews lived), which was established by the local senate in the early nineteenth century and funded by the budget allocated for the Jewish community, became in 1871 a Polonized Jewish public school financed by the municipality. Since this was a public school and not a Jewish school associated with the values of the Hebrew Haskalah (Jewish enlightenment), the number of Orthodox Jewish female students in it kept increasing. No similar trend occurred with regard to boys.[30] In 1904 the Jewish community in Kraków opened a school that further contributed to the decline of the Jewish private schools.[31]

Galician Jewish parents who sent their sons to ḥeders that taught only religious subjects could supplement their studies with private lessons in the state-required school subjects. Another option included supplementing or replacing ḥeder study with enrollment in the Baron Hirsch schools that were first

28. For the sanitary and other conditions for receiving a ḥeder license, see "Regarding the ḥeders," *Gazeta Narodowa*, February 11, 1890, 2 [Polish].

29. In the 1883/84 school year, 17,251 school-age boys studied in 1,000 licensed ḥeders, out of which only ten taught secular subjects in addition to Jewish ones; see "Ḥeders in Galicia," *Kurjer Lwowski*, November 21, 1885, 1 [Polish]. Of course, those numbers reflect only registered ḥeders.

30. For example, in the school year 1869/70 there were 288 boys and 346 girls in the school. The next year the numbers were 331 and 522, and in the following year, 286 and 551 respectively; see Żbikowski, *Żydzi krakowscy*, 244. See also Friedmann, *Die galizischen Juden*, 31–32.

31. For the education initiatives in Kraków see Samsonowska, "The Hebrew Secondary School," 16–23; Żbikowski, *Żydzi krakowscy*, 241–268.

established in Galicia in 1891 and were designated almost exclusively for boys. The schools were financed by a special foundation established by the philanthropist Baron Moritz von Hirsch (1831–1896) aimed at promoting Jewish education.[32] Most of the Baron Hirsch schools offered the minimum required secular education and focused mostly on teaching boys skills that would enable them to make a living as artisans or craftsmen. They also provided two weekly hours of religious studies. A small number of them, especially in big cities, offered a parallel curriculum to the public schools. In order to make the Baron Hirsch schools attractive, many of them provided their students clothing and free meals.[33] The Orthodox opposed the Baron Hirsch schools, accusing them of carrying out a calculated plan aimed at destroying the ḥeders altogether,[34] and so their press continued to praise the study in the ḥeder, denouncing all other alternative options.[35] While the number of Jewish boys in public schools and the Baron Hirsch schools kept rising, attracting mostly the poor or middle-class families who were not staunch Hasidim, the education of boys from Hasidic families remained restricted to ḥeders, with the rich sometimes providing their sons private lessons in skills needed for commerce or other urban professions. Still, those private lessons were quite limited because of the long daily hours spent in the ḥeder.

Parallel to the government regulations imposed on ḥeders, liberal and progressive Jews attacked the ḥeder system and called for its total abolishment.[36] Other attacks were voiced by Teofil Meronowicz, one of the most notorious Galician anti-Semites. Meronowicz viewed the ḥeders as privileged anti-Polish institutions and submitted several petitions to the Galician Sejm (state

32. Those schools also accepted Christian boys. For a report on the schools, see "Baron Hirsch's Projects," *Ha-Magid,* July 26, 1900, 349–350; August 2, 1900, 362 [Hebrew].

33. Thon, *Die Juden in Oesterreich,* 89. For a vivid memoir of the schooling experience of a Galician boy at the time, which describes all the available options, see Brawer, "Memories of a Father and Son."

34. "The Situation of Our Brothers in Galicia," *Kol Maḥazikei Ha-Dat,* August 11, 1892, 1–3 [Hebrew].

35. See for example *Kol Maḥazikei Ha-Dat,* June 18, 1880, 5–6; February 17, 1887, 1–3; March 3, 1887, 3–4; January 26, 1888, 1–2; August 11, 1892, 1–3; January 20, 1899, 1–2 [Hebrew].

36. In a long talk in the Galician Sejm in late 1882, the president of the Jewish community council in Lwów, Filip Zucker, suggested closing all the ḥeders. He asked the Galician school council to give more thought to the education of Jewish boys, claiming that the compulsory education law exists only on paper and the ḥeders continue to operate as before, see Manekin, *Yehudei Galizyah,* 232–234.

council) calling to outlaw them. Meronowicz was not successful. The political support that organized Orthodoxy promised to the Poles beginning in 1879 paid off, and his petitions were rejected. Responding to Meronowicz, the conservative Kraków organ *Czas* claimed that it was not the ḥeders that endangered the Polish society, but rather the secular pro-German Jewish liberals.[37] Another Polish newspaper, *Zgoda*, argued that it was better that Jewish children *not* attend public schools but remain in their ḥeders. Their high proportion in the population, especially in cities, would make Jewish students the majority in schools if they all go there, and that would subsequently lead to the de-Christianization, Judaization, and the weakening of the Polish national spirit not only in schools but also in society. Moreover, when those Jewish students would graduate, they would become the dominant sector in the country's economy and corrupt its ethics. The paper suggested considering the ḥeders as private schools, placing them under the supervision of the education council and requiring them to teach the Polish language.[38] Interestingly, a few years later the Orthodox newspaper *Kol Maḥazikei Ha-Dat* expressed similar views, explaining that if the ḥeders would be abolished, tens of thousands of Jewish boys would flood the public schools, and when those boys, descendants of Talmudists and rabbis, would wish to earn a living, they would push the Christians outside the job market. According to the newspaper, this had already happened in Germany and Hungary, antagonizing the Christian populations.[39] Clearly, Orthodox Jews and conservative Poles (who constituted the major political power in Kraków) had a mutual interest in keeping Jewish boys in ḥeders, far from the Polish public schools. The various directives from the Polish authorities were effectively ignored, and the ḥeders were allowed to function without major disturbances.[40]

Throughout this period the Orthodox in Kraków allied with conservative Catholics who prioritized the place of religion in education. In January 1888, for example, the Catholic conservative member of the Viennese parliament, Prince Aloys von Liechtenstein, submitted a law proposal to re-confessionalize the public schools.[41] Some Kraków liberals worried that it might also

---

37. "Kraków November 21," *Czas*, November 22, 1879, 1 [Polish].

38. "Petition in the Sejm on the Abolition of the Ḥeders," *Zgoda*, October 12, 1883, 1 [Polish].

39. "The Labor of the Torah," *Kol Maḥazikei Ha-Dat*, January 1887, 5–6, esp. 6 [Hebrew].

40. Samsonowska, "The Hebrew Secondary School," 18.

41. *Stenographische Protokolle*, 490 der Beilagen (1891): 1–4.

institutionalize the ḥeder system which Galicia had incorporated within its school system "as a result of much pressure."[42] But *Kol Maḥazikei Ha-Dat* praised Liechtenstein's proposal as in accord with its own view that ḥeders were central in the education of boys.[43] The Polish Club did not support Liechtenstein's proposal, but not because it opposed more religion in schools. On the contrary, one of its members said openly in the parliament that the Catholic Church built a powerful bulwark for Polish nationalism, Polish culture, and Polish language.[44] The Poles preferred that the issue of public education be left to the Galician Sejm rather than be imposed by the Austrian government. Transferring responsibility for education to the Polish school council in Galicia was ultimately beneficial to the ḥeder system, because of the political alliance of the Orthodox with the Polish conservative Catholics.

Compulsory Education and Orthodox Jewish Girls

The discussions and administrative directives in the 1870s and 1880s concerning compulsory education for Jews were limited exclusively to the ḥeder system and the education of boys. Little mention was made either by Jews or non-Jews about the education of Jewish girls, which was also compulsory. The Galician press noticed that the number of Jewish girls in public and private schools rose disproportionally to the number of Jewish boys. It cited the statistics published by the Galician education council for the school year 1874/75, namely, just one year after the publication of the Galician version of the compulsory education law, according to which 6,582 Jewish boys and 9,555 Jewish girls attended public and private schools, including Jewish schools and licensed ḥeders. A decade later, in the school year 1883/84, those numbers grew to 14,821 boys and 24,884 girls. The gap between school attendance of boys and girls kept widening in the following years, for example, in 1890, the numbers

42. "The Request of Priest Liechtenstein and Its Application to the Ḥeders," *Kurjer Lwoski*, March 10, 1888, 1 [Polish].

43. "Ascribe unto the Lord Glory and Strength," *Kol Maḥazikei Ha-Dat*, February 24, 1888 [Hebrew].

44. Kolmer, *Parlament und Verfassung*, vol. 4, 178–191.

rose to 15,497 Jewish boys and 29,573 girls, and in 1900 to 22,666 Jewish boys and 43,855 Jewish girls.[45] While there was clearly an upward trend for both boys and girls, it was much more accelerated for girls.

The concern that many Galician Orthodox Jewish parents expressed for protecting their sons from state-mandated education stood in marked contrast to their lack of concern with respect to their daughters. How does one account for their willingness to break from old norms and send their daughters to non-Jewish schools? A Polish newspaper commented that the gap between the number of Jewish boys and Jewish girls attending school resulted from the fact that the Orthodox "hide" their sons in ḥeders to protect them from outside influence, while at the same time they send their daughters to public schools because they look down upon the position of women in society.[46] A Jewish liberal newspaper, however, wrote that Orthodox Jews sent their daughters to schools because they were "less prejudiced" regarding girls.[47] Whatever the answer, or answers, to these questions, it should be emphasized that there was no tradition or ideology in Galician Jewish society of educating girls in a certain way, or for that matter of educating girls at all. In general, where neither Jewish law nor custom forbade a practice, rabbinical leadership was unwilling to take a stand, lest it be disputed, or ignored, especially when the law of the land required it.

Jewish religious legal sources were of little help in this matter. The paucity of sources concerning the status of women's secular education stands in sharp contrast to the well-known exemption, not to mention the prohibition, of fathers teaching their daughters Torah, as reflected in the oft-cited Mishnaic dictum, "Anyone who teaches his daughter Torah it is as if he is teaching her *tiflut* (*Sotah* 3: 4)."[48] This prohibition provided for some a legal justification of barring women from formal Jewish education, but it only referred to Torah education. Regarding the study of secular subjects by women, the only Talmudic reference is attributed to the early fourth-century Palestinian Amora, R. Abbahu, who taught in the name of R. Joḥanan that "a man is permitted to teach his daughter Greek because it serves her as an ornament," and he did so

45. Thon, *Die Juden in Oesterreich*, 82–84.
46. "National Affairs (Ḥeders)," *Gazeta Lwowska*, December 4, 1885, 1–2 [Polish].
47. *Izraelita* (Polish supplement of *Der Israelit*), December 25, 1885, 1–2 [Polish].
48. *Tiflut* is often understood either as frivolity or licentiousness.

with his own daughter.[49] The young woman's knowledge of Greek, it seems, was considered an embellishment, an adornment reflecting the family's high socioeconomic status.

The first to make use of the Talmudic precedent in the Galician context that I know of was Ahron Marcus, the Hamburg Jewish author who moved to Kraków following his embrace of Hasidism.[50] According to Marcus, worried Kraków Jews approached him following the 1873 Galician compulsory education law and the 1874 special regulations for ḥeders and asked him for his advice. Marcus first pointed out the legal option of hiring private tutors instead of sending their sons to public schools. But to those who lacked the financial means to hire tutors, he suggested a somewhat surprising solution. Since there were not yet enough public schools at the time to accept all school-age children, Marcus suggested that parents send their *daughters* to the schools, thus "protecting their brothers" who because of the girls would have no seats left for them. Marcus gave three justifications for this policy: (1) Rich and respected Hasidim had for several years sent their daughters to non-Jewish schools, including convent schools (perhaps starting after the promulgation of the 1869 Austrian compulsory education law). (2) Teaching girls secular subjects was not prohibited by Jewish law as evident in R. Abbahu's saying cited above, and even if it should be prohibited, the practice had already taken root; hence, it was better that parents sin inadvertently rather than deliberately (i.e., were rabbis to forbid it publicly). (3) Proposing that daughters attend public schools was not problematic because according to government legislation, textbooks and classes in subjects other than religion were supposed to be devoid of any religious references.[51] We have no evidence that his advice was followed by Kraków Jews, but in any event, after several years, more schools

---

49. Palestinian Talmud, Pe'ah 1,1 (15c); see parallels P. T. *Sotah* 9, 15 (24c); P. T. *Shabbat* 6,1. Saul Lieberman argued that the term "Greek'" in this statement refers to Greek literature and not the vulgar Greek of the lower classes, because only "Greek literature [. . .] could serve as an ornament to young ladies of social standing such as the daughter of R. Abbahu." Lieberman, *Greek in Jewish Palestine*, 23–24; 27. R. Simeon bar Abba doubted the attribution of this to R. Joḥanan, saying that "because he wants to teach his daughter (Greek) he ascribes it to R. Johanan," ibid., 24. According to Grossman, *Pious and Rebellious*, 156, Simeon bar Abba's position "did not leave an impression upon medieval Jewish society, and in many places, we find testimony of women who acquired general education for purposes of their economic activity as well."

50. On Marcus see Shanes, "Ahron Marcus."

51. Ahron Marcus, "Peace Be on Israel and the Rabbis!" *Ha-Mizpeh*, June 28, 1912, 1–2; July 5, 1912, 1–2 [Hebrew]. See also Manekin, "'Something Completely New'," 69–72.

were built providing enough seats for everyone. It should be noted that Marcus's own granddaughters attended public school.

Primary and Secondary Schools for Girls

The schools to which Marcus referred were primary schools. Until the 1870s there were no public secondary schools for girls in Galicia.[52] The first post-primary option for females was the teachers' seminary, three of which opened in 1871 in Lwów, Przemyśl, and Kraków. The seminary did not prepare women for higher learning and accepted female students who had graduated primary school and had reached the age of fifteen. In the early twentieth century, the lyceum, a new type of secondary school for women, was introduced in Galicia. The curriculum included modern languages, Polish literature, history, and home economics, among other classes. Latin and Greek were not offered, much less required, as was the case of the classical gymnasia, and minimal time was devoted to math and the sciences. The course of study lasted six years. Despite opposition to post–primary schooling for women, the first genuine gymnasium for women in Galicia opened in Kraków in 1896. It was a private institution, and it followed the very recent examples of Prague and Vienna. By 1914, there were already nine private gymnasia for women in Galicia but no public one because of the resistance of the Austrian government and the general public. Statistics cited in the early twentieth century on Jewish secondary school attendance reflect the lack of such public institutions for young females rather than a lack of interest.[53]

The typical public primary school in rural areas had one or two grades with boys and girls of different age groups in one classroom. The course of study in each grade lasted two or three years. Urban areas that were stronger financially established public schools composed of three to five grades in which boys and girls generally studied together because of limited financial means and a lack of trained teachers. District cities could generally afford establishing separate public schools for boys and girls composed of five and even six grades. In Kraków there were several schools of the four-grade type in which the course of study in the third and fourth grades lasted two years each, but there were also schools composed of one, two, and three grades. Conservative Poles who dominated the Galician Sejm decided in the 1890s that schools in rural areas

52. Czajecka, "*Z domu w szeroki świat . . .*," 50.
53. Thon, *Die Juden in Oesterreich*, 82–84; cf. Stampfer, "Gender Differentiation," 86.

would operate under a more limited curriculum in order to preserve the social structure and allow the youth in villages enough time to help their families with their agricultural work. At that time there were 3,726 public primary schools in Galicia (of all types), 127 of them for boys, 121 for girls, and the rest, gender-mixed. Lwów and Kraków stood out in their developed public school system, with Kraków having ten schools for girls and nine schools for boys.[54]

Following a decision of the Galician Sejm in 1886, public middle schools for girls (*szkoły wydziałowe*) were organized in several Galician cities, including Lwów and Kraków. At the end of 1898 there were already twenty-six of these schools for girls in Galicia. Each school was composed of three or four grades (following four years of primary school) and also taught female handicrafts and home economics. While the curriculum was more advanced and rigorous than in a regular primary school, the middle schools were intended to teach skills that would help female graduates earn a living.[55] Hasidic girls throughout Galicia for the first time attended public primary schools and some continued to private finishing schools or middle schools.

The most prestigious public middle school for girls in Kraków, and one of the best in Galicia, was św. Scholastyki school. It was established in the 1870s and soon developed into an eight-grade school. In 1886 it became a four-grade middle school connected to a four-grade elementary school. Św. Scholastyki possessed the best female teachers, some of whom came from outside of Kraków. It also offered four courses on practical "female handicraft" for girls who completed the elementary school and two courses teaching commercial skills to middle school graduates.[56] Although Antoni Gettlich, the school's director, was a Jew who had converted to Catholicism, św. Scholastyki attracted girls from Hasidic homes. Ahron Marcus related that a young female "heretic" once asked him: "What are you unfortunate Hasidim doing? My Hasidic friends go with me to study at the [school of the] apostate Gettlich, and he argues against them daily and humiliates the Torah of the Jews. With me he barks, but his voice is silenced because I know how to give him a conclusive answer. But what are the unfortunate domesticated animals (*behemot*), who are dumbfounded like a sheep before its shearers, to do?" Marcus added: "I had no answer to give her."[57]

54. Czajecka, "*Z domu w szeroki świat . . . ,*" 50–53.
55. Ibid., 54–56.
56. Ibid., 58–61.
57. Marcus, "Peace Be on Israel and the Rabbis!" *Ha-Mizpeh*, June 28, 1912, 2 [Hebrew].

A rare testimony from one of the pious Hasidic girls who attended a public primary school is found in the Yiddish memoir of Sarah Schenirer (1883–1935), the woman responsible for establishing the first religious school for Orthodox Jewish girls in Kraków. Schenirer writes:

> My father, may he rest in peace, had invested all his might in the education of his children, educating them to be Jewish and religious. He was an enthusiastic Belz Hasid, and indeed a regular at the older Belzer Rebbe, may his memory protect us.
>
> I went to a primary school (*povshechne shule*)[58] for eight years, where also Christian children studied. Already at age six, I was called in school by the nickname "chusetka" [female Hasid]. I also remember that I was especially strong and distinguished in the study of religion. When children were questioned about [what was studied in] religion [classes], many didn't know the answer, and so the [female] teacher was always praising me with these words: "Why does she know?" "Children," she would add, "you should be diligent in religion, because religion is a holy matter."
>
> I did not have difficulties in studying, and that is why I was a diligent student. Each year I moved up to a higher grade with good marks, and at the same time I was also excellent in handicraft. When it was time for me to move up to the seventh grade, they [my parents] wanted to pull me out of school, so I could start earning money. But I pleaded with them and I remained in the seventh grade. I successfully completed primary school.[59]

While Schenirer praised her Hasidic father for investing all his might in the Jewish education of his children, she writes with pride about her education in public school. She does not mention the name of her school, but she indicates that she went to school for eight years, which clearly exceeded the six-year compulsory schooling in Galicia. (As noted above, her parents initially wanted to pull her out after the sixth grade.) We can identify the school based on Schenirer's handwritten Polish diary where she mentions meeting her former school principal "Pogonowska"[60] as well as her former teacher "Kopcińska."[61]

---

58. After the First World War, this term was used in Poland to designate a full-fledged primary school instead of the different categories used in Galicia, see Juśko, "Organizational Structure of Primary Schools," 122–123.

59. Schenirer, *Gezamelte shriftn*, 5–6. Her schooling may have included a preparatory year.

60. See Dekiert and Lisek, eds., "*Żydówką być to rzecz niemała*," entry for June 17 [1910].

61. Ibid., entry for April 20 [1913].

Joanna Pogonowska was the principal of the girls' school Stanisław Konarski ("Konarskiego pod Zamkiem") which by 1896 had seven grade, and Walerya Kopcińska was one of the teachers there.[62] The fact that even pious Hasidic parents like the Schenirers, who were of limited means, allowed their daughter to attend the seventh grade, something not required by law, is testimony to the value Hasidic parents in Kraków assigned to their daughters' education. For her part, Schenirer wished to complete the seventh grade and continue her education despite her religious piety and commitment to the Hasidic way of life.

In her Yiddish memoir, Schenirer referred to her Jewish religion teacher as a female, but public schools had no female teachers of Jewish religion at the time.[63] The Jewish religion teachers at the school were all males,[64] and to receive such a position they needed to have the ability to speak the Polish language. Male teachers of Jewish religion were generally considered heretics by the Hasidim, who would not welcome them into their homes. By the time that Schenirer wrote her Yiddish memoir she was a revered Orthodox educator, and perhaps she altered the gender of her religion teacher in order to conceal this fact. In any event, religion classes were obligatory for all pupils, including Jewish religion classes for the Jewish pupils. Generally, schools had to have at least eighty students of a given religion in order to offer classes in their religion. However, in rural areas and small towns, schools often couldn't find teachers for the Jewish religion with the appropriate qualifications. In some cases, the local rabbi provided a certificate to the school attesting that a pupil passed the required examination in the subject of religion so the teacher could fill in a grade for this required subject.

The statistics on Jewish attendance in public schools cited above did not differentiate between rural and urban schools, although rural schools were limited in the number of grades and teachers. Still, even girls living in rural

---

62. *Kalendarz Krakowski* (1895): 112; *Kalendarz Krakowski* (1896): 144. See also Martin, *Jewish Life in Cracow*, 130–131. According to Martin, in 1900/1901:

> [T]he proportion of Jewish girls in the school was approximately 50 percent [. . .] it offered a wide range of activities to its students, including participation in the city-wide School Theatre (*Teatr Szkolny*) programme and involvement in the commemoration of national holidays and the funerals of Juliusz Słowacki and Karol Szymanowski. (ibid.)

63. According to Majer Bałaban, the first public school female teacher for the Jewish religion was appointed in 1903, quoted in Łapot, "Female Teachers of the Mosaic Religion," 411.

64. *Kalendarz Krakowski* (1889): 161, and all subsequent years.

villages were required to attend school, where their intellectual abilities could be appreciated and their desire for learning could be ignited.

One such girl was Hinde Bergner (née Rosenblatt, 1870–1942), the mother of the Yiddish poet and writer Melech Ravitch, who grew up in the village of Radymno (district of Jarosław) and who helped her family manage its farm and fields. Bergner reached schooling age in 1876, when the new compulsory education legislation was beginning to have its effect in Galicia. Bergner describes in her memoirs how she used to wake up very early in the morning to get ready for school, although her father told her that "a big girl ought to have business on her mind rather than confusing herself with such foolishness." But Hinde wanted to learn:

> I was very industrious. I believed then that I could become something extraordinary . . . I both studied and watched over the storehouse, and I was awarded prizes in school.[65]

Hinde's parents did not share her hopes for the future:

> When I finished primary school, Mother wanted to tie me down to housework immediately, while father wanted me to become involved in his business. But I had a powerful young will to learn. I fought with my parents until I was allowed to realize my dreams. My father loved me very much, but he did not want to hear any more about my going to Yerslev [Jarosław] to study.[66] I pleaded with him, I embraced him, I kissed him, but it was useless. My mother might have been persuaded, but she was something of a religious zealot, and she feared that if I experienced life in a modern city, I would not grow up to be a pious woman. But I remained focused on a single thought—how to devise a plan to steal off to Yerslev.

One winter day at dawn Hinde heard a carriage outside of her home, and she spontaneously ran out and paid the coachman to take her secretly to her aunt's house in Yerslev. The city school was more developed than the one in her village and she was clearly aware of it:

> I stole away from home with the intention of realizing my dream to learn, to become educated, and to take piano lessons. This was my lofty ideal. And

65. Bergner, *On Long Winter Nights*, 31.

66. In 1870, Jarosław became the seat of the district school council; see "Nr. 137. Verordnung des Ministers für Cultus und Unterricht vom 1. December 1870," *RGBl* (1870): 295–302, esp. 298.

even if I was very young at the time, I remember promising myself that I would never impede the desire of my own children to learn!

Upon hearing of my escape to one of my mother's sisters, my Aunt Shtern in Yerslev, Father quickly figured out that I was planning to enroll in school there. He immediately came after me and pleaded with me, both gently and angrily. He argued: "Yerslev, Shmerlev . . . What's the point? You have the point? [. . .] I'm begging you, come back, let's go home. And if you want to, we shall pay a visit to the *rebbe*, Bunem-Mendel, so that he can recite a blessing over you to obey your parents.[67]

Hinde couldn't face her father's tears, and so she returned home with him. She was allowed to take private French lessons, but her tutor soon left the village and that was the end of it. It is important to note that Hinde's parents did not oppose her attending the village school; they complied with the law and did not seek ways to minimize its impact. What they feared was education in the big city and the lack of parental supervision. Indeed, the big city offered not only advanced schools but also cultural events designed specifically for women.

Cultural Activities for Kraków Women

In the late nineteenth century Kraków became a center of feminist activities, albeit with a Polish patriotic tone.[68] Because the law barred women from involvement in political associations, those activities were limited to the cultural and educational spheres. One such center was the Reading Room for Women (*Czytelnia dla Kobiet*), an association formally approved in 1895. The reading room had a library stocked with books and periodicals, many of them promoting feminist ideas. (After 1910 its direction became more conservative.)[69] It also organized public lectures for women delivered by university professors and literary figures. Another institution geared for women was the Baraneum. It was an institution of higher learning for women established in 1868 by Adrian Baraniecki, three decades before Austrian universities accepted women as regular students. Its faculty included university professors, and it often offered lectures by famous poets and literary figures. The Baraneum did not grant academic or other degrees, but it provided access to knowledge on a high

67. Bergner, *On Long Winter Nights,* 44–45.
68. Czajecka, *"Z domu w szeroki świat . . . ,"* 8.
69. Dadej, "The Reading Room for Women in Kraków," 32–38.

level not available to women at this time in any other place. It offered courses in literature, science, and the arts, for which students had to register and pay tuition, in addition to free public evening lectures.[70] Between the years 1901 and 1924, a total of 691 Jewish women were enrolled for courses there compared with 3,023 Catholic women.[71] The courses in the Baraneum attracted mostly women from the intelligentsia, including Jewish women from acculturated families, but the evening lectures attracted women from all social classes.

Even Jewish women from Hasidic homes took advantage of the public lectures offered in such institutions, as we can learn from the Yiddish memoir of Sarah Schenirer:

> I used to sit every night with my work until a late hour, and after that I busied myself with . . . I remember that my father of blessed memory had once purchased Ḥok le-Yisrael with a Yiddish translation, so I took upon myself to go over the teachings of the Pentateuch, Prophets, Mishnah, and Gemara every day and I drew from this a great pleasure.[72] Other than that, I also had a strong interest in general scientific issues, and from time to time I used to attend lectures in a Christian women's association.
>
> The truth is, that I had great regrets after each attendance in that place, but at that time there was no other place [for Orthodox Jewish women] to go to and listen to an academic (visenshaftliche) talk.[73]

Schenirer is probably referring here to the Reading Room for Women, which was indeed a women's association. Her desire for advanced knowledge was not something promoted in her home but rather at school. Schenirer added that there were several Jewish organizations for young females that offered lectures, but she soon discovered that those were not appropriate for her. She recounted how once she accompanied a cousin of hers on a Friday night to a lecture at the Ruth Zionist association and quickly realized that not only was the

70. Czajecka, "Z domu w szeroki świat . . . ," 138–139.

71. Kras, Wyższe kursy dla kobiet, 79.

72. Ḥok le-Yisrael is a late compendium of texts from traditional Jewish sources, arranged according to the weekly readings of the Torah (Pentateuch) in the synagogue and divided into daily sections. Each section includes the relevant Torah portion, passages from the Prophets and Writings, Mishnah, Talmud, Zohar, and some Jewish laws and ethics. It was very popular among Hasidim, and several editions included a popular Yiddish translation and commentary of some of the sources (excluding, for example, the Zohar), which is what Schenirer was able to read and comprehend.

73. Schenirer, Gezamelte shriftn, 7–8.

Sabbath desecrated there, but also that the lecture, on Spinoza, was full of heresy. The Friday night lecture was attended by daughters of Hasidic parents at the same time that their fathers were busy with their Talmud and their mothers with their Yiddish translated Pentateuch.[74]

In her handwritten Polish diary, Schenirer provides more details about the different lectures she attended with friends and cousins, with topics ranging from the latest Polish literature, to issues of women's health, raising children, the power of self-control, and education. She also discloses that her friends dragged her to the theater on the occasion of her betrothal to see *Gody życia* (Life's Feast) by the modernist playwright Stanisław Przybyszewski (1868–1927), a play about a woman who leaves her husband and child to live with her lover. When the woman tries to reconnect with her daughter, she is rejected, and after returning to her lover, is raped by his friend. She seeks absolution through attempting to immerse herself in a fountain high up in the mountains, where she slips and plunges to her death. Przybyszewski was one of the central figures in the Young Poland movement, and his compositions were considered avant-garde. His books and personality contributed to the development of a cult of admirers around him, especially those who were attracted to Polish literature. Schenirer was apparently aware of Przybyszewski's other works, for her comment on the production was, "It's good, but like Przybyszewski, some disgust."[75] Still, she was not deterred from attending the production, albeit at the initiative of her friends. Reflecting on what she saw, she connected the play with a *midrash* she had read on the Sabbath and lamented that it was better to spend time on a thorough examination of one's destiny rather than go to the theater.[76] Schenirer, a devout young woman from a Hasidic family, appears to have been conflicted at this stage of her life by her love for Jewish religion and her cultural and educational activities. She wrote in her diary:

> [A]nd again these thoughts, perhaps I should not, maybe a true Jewish girl should not go there [to lecture halls] . . . but what should I do . . . where should I go—when there is no association for Jewish girls?[77]

74. She reveals the subject of the lecture in her Polish diary. See Lisek, "Sara Schenirer: Diary (excerpts)," 68–70, esp. diary entry for September 9, 1910, 68. Schenirer eliminates this detail in her published Yiddish memoir, see Schenirer, *Gezamelte shriftn*, 8.

75. Lisek, "Sara Schenirer: Diary (excerpts)," diary entry for October 17, 1910, 69.

76. Ibid. In her Yiddish memoir Schenirer refers to the *midrash* but leaves out the part about her going to see a play by Przybyszewski, see Schenirer, *Gezamelte shriftn*, 13.

77. Lisek, "Sara Schenirer: Diary (excerpts)," diary entry for September 9, 1910, 68.

Attending public lectures for women, as well as the theater, contributed to the awareness of young women of the feminist themes of the day, such as the value of education, women's bodies, and self-fulfillment. It was also a social activity unique to women that promoted female friendship and solidarity, something not available for isolated Jewish women living in villages.

Schenirer's personal piety, close family ties, and thirst for Jewish knowledge anchored her within the Orthodox world. But there were other Orthodox Jewish girls who lacked that anchor. As members of a minority in schools that glorified all things Polish, including Catholicism, and as bereft of a mature understanding of their own religion, young Jewish women were often indifferent toward or contemptuous of their religion. Moreover, the excitement of attending school was something most Orthodox girls could not share at home because their parents had never experienced life in a Polish school. Like children of immigrants,[78] young Jewish women in Galicia lived in parallel worlds: the world of their traditional Orthodox homes and that of their Polish schools, the gateway to modern social and cultural activities. As daughters, however, it was presumed that they would acquiesce to the expectations of their traditionalist parents, which was to complete school and to enter into an arranged marriage with a young Orthodox Jew, often a Hasid, whom they did not know, and with whom they had nothing in common intellectually or spiritually. This constituted the breaking point for some of these young women.

Arranged Marriages

The phenomenon of the Jewish female runaways is a complex one that defies simple generalization, yet one common theme runs through the stories: the young woman's desire to avoid an incompatible marriage arranged by her parents when she is very young. The historian of education Zvi Scharfstein, who spent the years 1900–1914 as a teacher in Western Galicia, described vividly the plight of Galician Orthodox Jewish families during this period.

> The tragedy commences when it is time for a betrothal agreement. The father wishes for his daughter a young man with side-locks, somewhat of a Talmudic scholar, a Hasid; in short: somebody similar to him. The daughter

---

78. There is a vast literature on conflicts in immigrant families between parents and children, especially daughters. For a review of some of this literature, including a historical perspective, see Foner and Dreby, "Relations Between the Generations in Immigrant Families."

objects, fights—but in vain. She is compelled to be given to a man that she despises in her heart, she is compelled to cut all her hair, and she is compelled to cover her head. If she is weak, then with time, she gets accustomed to this life. But if she is strong-willed, then there is no end to the many frictions and conflicts that fill the house, and those frictions ultimately cause each spouse to lead his or her life, live in his or her own world, think his or her thoughts, and act as he or she wishes.[79]

Also problematic was the economics of arranged marriages, according to which a young woman with meager means, hence with a lower market value, was matched with a man who had some money but whose religious education was limited and who may have possessed other deficiencies. Such was the case with Sarah Schenirer, whose family was not rich. In her handwritten Polish diary she revealed her torment after not being able to disobey her parents, who wished her to meet somebody in whom she was not interested. The man was clearly not a Torah scholar, but his family owned a house, and he had money. Although her parents arranged for her to meet him before the final decision, she already knew that she didn't want this match.[80] It is clear from what Schenirer writes that she considered a Torah scholar as the ideal match for her, but she lacked the courage to say "no" and agreed to the match against her own wishes.[81]

79. Zvi Scharfstein, "From the Life of Our Brothers in Galicia: The Education of Daughters," *Ha-'Olam*, September 29, 1910, 11–2, esp. 12 [Hebrew]. In his biography of the eminent Galician rabbinical authority, R. Shalom Mordecai Schwadron (1835–1911), Moshe Chaim Bloch recounts how Schwadron tried to arrange a match between Bloch and his granddaughter, but the latter was not interested because Bloch wore Hasidic garb and lacked secular knowledge. See Bloch, *Maharsham—ha-posek ha-aḥaron*, 4, cited in Manekin, "'Something Completely New'," 79. In his 1900 talk, the aforementioned Julius Ofner made a similar observation about the different education of boys and girls in Galicia, where boys are sent to ḥeder and girls to public school, as a result of which "a spiritual and cultural gap opens between the two, which is of tragic consequences," see "Kinderraub in Galizien: Rede des Landtagsabgeordneten Dr. Ofner," *Dr. Bloch's Oesterreichische Wochenschrift*, November 2, 1900, 784.

80. See Dekiert and Lisek, eds., "*Żydówką być to rzecz niemała*," entries for September 9 [1909? 1910?] and October 1 [1909? 1910?].

81. In the Kraków census for the year 1910, Schenirer is listed as married to "Samuel Nussbaum, unemployed." Her first name appears as "Salomea," her birth date as April 12, 1883, and her address as Krakowska 43. See *Spis ludności miasta Krakowa z r. 1910*, vol. 16, entry nr. 569, 116–117. In the 1900 census her first name appeared as "Salka," a diminutive of "Salomea." See *Spis ludności miasta Krakowa z r. 1900*, vol. 15, entry nr. 1372, 276–277 (her birth date appears there as July 3, 1883). Calling a girl by these names was apparently not uncommon (as in the case

Alarm at the prospect of an arranged marriage was not restricted to acculturated Jewish women living in the cities. Girls from villages outside the cities also struggled with their parents over marriages that would put an end to their hopes and aspirations. As Hinde Bergner recounts in her memoirs:

> Matches were proposed for me only, even though one of my brothers was two years older. Once, returning home from the granary, I managed to overhear my father say: "Yes, I can immediately offer a dowry and even arrange a wedding within two weeks . . ." When I learned of Father's decision to finalize an engagement for me so soon, I did not enter the room but went to the children's bedroom instead. Unable to hold back the tears that were choking me, I burst out crying. I was maybe eleven years old then, and I was still used to stealing away to my schoolmates' home to play. Even though my father kept me busy working for him throughout my childhood I nevertheless managed to borrow German and Polish books in secret so that my mother wouldn't find out. I read them at night in bed by the light of a wax candle. And all of a sudden, here came this scarecrow of marriage raising its terrifying head. Inconceivable—I imagined my husband's beard and long *peyes* [side-locks], while I pictured myself wearing a *shaytl* [a wig, according to the religious requirement for married women to cover their hair] instead of my beautiful long, blond braids. Wringing my hands, I mourned my lost dreams and my ambition to acquire a higher education so that I would surpass all my girlfriends.[82]

Bergner did not run away from home, much less convert. She avoided marriage at an early age, and after she married at the age of twenty-one, she did not wear a *shaytl*.

Indeed, most educated young Jewish women did not convert, but rather found a way to live their lives without taking the difficult step of breaking their ties to family and community. The number of Jewish women converts who grew up in a city like Kraków was relatively small. Jewish girls who had lived their lives in Kraków had friends with similar backgrounds and similar experiences. They could also provide each other with a sense of solidarity and social cohesiveness by attending theater and lectures together, as even a pious woman like Sarah Schenirer did. Kraków had a visible Jewish community with

---

of the Galician-born actress Salka [Salomea Sara] Viertel), but Schenirer later became known only as Sarah, probably by her own choice.

82. Bergner, *On Long Winter Nights*, 47–48.

Jewish neighborhoods, synagogues, shops, and markets. By contrast, in villages and small towns Jewish life was mostly confined to family life indoors. When a young Jewish schoolgirl walked out of her house, she was already on the boundary between the Jewish and non-Jewish worlds. This seems to be the principal reason why most of those who converted in Kraków came from the surrounding small towns and villages.[83]

The frustration of these Jewish women at home was best described in a critical review of Bertha Pappenheim's treatise, *Zur Judenfrage in Galizien*, published in 1900, in which the Jewish Frankfurt feminist had criticized the Baron Hirsch foundation for establishing schools in Galicia for boys and not for girls, with predictable results:

> If [...] a pupil of the foundation schools remains in the country and establishes a family with a wife under the spell of Hasidism, who remains in the grip of an absolute ignorance and lack of culture, then the laborious sowing of the school will certainly yield meager fruits.[84]

Pappenheim assumed that educated boys from the Baron Hirsch schools would be mismatched with unschooled and ignorant Hasidic women. The reviewer of the treatise pointed out that the opposite was true. Most Galician girls, including those from Hasidic families or from rural areas, were better educated than their brothers. The problem was that their educations were vastly different:

> Imagine: A girl who has benefited from a school education for many years, who has become acquainted with a different life than that in the parental home, and through reading modern books has been made acquainted with modern ideas—*and there are masses of such girls nowadays in Galicia*—is tied to a young savage infinitely beneath her, of terrifying appearance, tongue-tied, with no manners and so on for her entire life! The

83. See Manekin, "The Lost Generation," 211.

84. Pappenheim, *Zur Judenfrage in Galizien*, 7. Despite her visits to Galicia, Pappenheim viewed young Galician Jewish women through the lens of poverty and prostitution, displaying a bias not atypical of western Jewry. After she spent an entire week observing the Beit Yaakov teachers' seminary in Kraków in November 1935, she continued to focus on establishing an educational institution to teach girls' practical professions such as handiwork, taking care of the sick and the poor, and housekeeping. See Pappenheim, *Zekhutah shel ishah*, 52–53, 73, 398–403. See also Keren Hathora-Zentrale, *Programm und Leistung*, 277–281; cf. Seidman, *Sarah Schenirer*, 39–40, 174–175.

consequences are not hard to gauge. From time to time a cry of distress reaches public attention, from time to time such an unfortunate creature escapes into the bosom of the Church, which willingly receives her. [85]

In Kraków, the Church was indeed willing to receive the Jewish runaways: the Felician Sisters' Convent, close to the city center, provided them with shelter, room, board, and some vocational training, in addition to preparing them for their baptism. Even when young women were irresolute in their decision, the convent offered them a refuge from their struggles, albeit one with strings attached.

The Felician Sisters' Convent in Kraków

Although the phenomenon of Jewish female conversion occurred throughout Galicia, its epicenter was Kraków, and within Kraków, the Felician Sisters' convent. The Congregation of the Sisters of St. Felix of Cantalice was founded in Warsaw in 1855, but it moved to Kraków following the failed 1863–1864 Polish insurrection. After receiving permission from the Austrian authorities, the sisters built the convent on Smoleńsk Street, where it stands to this day. In 1870, the sisters established a catechumenate. The other convents in the area lacked a place for the preparation of converts, and so the Felician Sisters' convent on Smoleńsk became the address for the shelter and conversion of most Jewish female runaways.

According to the history published by the order, the catechumenate was a shelter where women who wanted to convert to Catholicism could live and be taught the catechism, Bible, and biographies of saints. In exchange for education, room, and board, the women were expected to help in the kitchen, the laundry room, and the garden. The goal was to plant and develop within the women "a truly Christian spirit of love and peace." Almost all the young women who sought shelter in the convent were Jewish, and before they were allowed to become baptized, they had to give up their "sinful habits, among them swearing, lying, and laziness." Running the catechumenate posed a great challenge since one was at risk of "attacks by Jews who tried to release their daughters or cousins with the use of force." Since the motives of the girls were not always sincere, "it was not unusual for those who were disappointed after

85. "Zur Judenfrage in Galizien," *Dr. Bloch's Oesterreichische Wochenschrift,* July 27, 1900, 549–551, esp. 551. Italics added.

FIGURE 1.1. The Felician Sisters' convent on 6 Smoleńsk Street, Kraków. Courtesy of the Historical Museum of the City of Kraków, Department of Kraków Photography, sygn. MHK-1309/K. Photograph taken by Natan Krieger, circa 1890.

baptism to return to their homes."[86] For the runaways, the convent offered shelter, safety, and refuge from their families. Where else would they have been able to go?

Almost all young Jewish females who converted to Catholicism in Western Galicia did so in the Felician Sisters' convent in Kraków. Their names can be found in several sources: copies of notifications about Jews intending to convert to Christianity sent to the Kraków rabbinate by the office in charge of Jewish records in the Kraków magistrate,[87] protocols signed in the Kraków magistrate by individuals preparing to convert,[88] and baptism books of All Saints in Kraków, which recorded not only births but also baptisms of converts.[89] The first two sources include the paperwork required by the civil authorities as stipulated in the 1868 interconfessional May Law and 1869 amendment, while the baptism books are church records, also required by the civil authorities. According to these three sources, between the years 1873 and 1914, there were 340 conversions to Catholicism of individuals staying in the Felician Sisters' convent, 14 of them of non-Catholic Christians and the rest Jews. Among the Jews, there were 2 males and 324 females.[90] These are the recorded cases available to researchers today; there may have been unrecorded ones.

What stands out in the data of the converts is the young age of the girls; at least 199 of them were ages 14–20 when they converted, and seventy-nine were ages 21–30. A small number of women were older than thirty, and no age was provided for twenty-five of the girls.[91] As for the geographical origin of the

86. SS. Felicjanki, *Historja Zgromadzenia SS. Felicjanek*, vol. 2, 220–221. I have not seen any reports in the press, or anywhere else, on attacks by Jews on the convent using force, but this assertion may have been based on a story that circulated during the Araten affair.

87. The National Archives in Kraków, Pełnomocnik ds. metryk izraelickich przy Magistracie miasta Krakowa, PMI 52–60.

88. The National Archives in Kraków, Magistrat miasta Krakowa, Kr 3, 12, 13–16, 23, 37–39, 41, 54–55, 65, 99, 114, 129–130, 144–146, 218–219, 240, 242, 246–247, 271–275, 301, 303.

89. The National Archives in Kraków, Akta stanu cywilnego Parafii Rzymskokatolickiej Wszystkich Świętych w Krakowie, 29/332 for various years.

90. See Bogusz, "The Felician Sisters' Convent in Kraków," 153. When I first came across the archival material concerning Jewish converts in 2002, I engaged Mr. Bogusz to help me identify more sources and make copies of them for me after I left Kraków, which he did. His article is based largely on the material he found. See also Kutrzeba, "Jewish Converts in Kraków," 203–214.

91. Five of them were 14 years old, nineteen were 15, thirty-five were 16, thirty-seven were 17, fifty-two were 18, twenty-six were 19, twenty-five were 20, seventeen were 21, eighteen were 22, eight were 23, fourteen were 24, four were 25, seven were 26, seven were 27, one was 28, one was

girls, nineteen were from the city of Kraków, including Podgórze, and seventeen from the Kraków district. The rest of the girls came from different places: 211 from all over Galicia, fifty from the Polish parts of Imperial Russia, and a few from Germany, Austria, and Hungary. Most of the Galician converts came from villages and small towns, but some came from Tarnów, Lwów, Wieliczka, Dębica, and Nowy Sącz. The first conversion of a Jewish girl in the Felician Sisters' convent occurred in 1873. Altogether, eighteen girls converted between 1873 and 1879, ninety-seven between 1881 and 1889, forty-five between 1890 and 1899, 115 between 1900 and 1909, and forty-one between 1910 and 1914. There was no conversion date recorded for the rest of the girls.

Until 1906 most of the protocols signed in the Kraków magistrate by potential proselytes recorded the profession of the parents. From this data we learn that the two most common professions of fathers were tavernkeepers and merchants.[92] But there were also bakers, shopkeepers, ḥeder teachers, kosher slaughterers, alcohol producers, and owners of farms or other properties. A small number of the girls were maternal or paternal orphans. Most of the Galician girls' signatures on the protocols were written in a steady, fine hand. All this suggests strongly that the young women who converted during this period came from lower-middle-class and middle-class backgrounds.

No available data exist on young Jewish women who chose conversion in order to marry a Catholic lover. It should be emphasized that in the Austrian half of the dual monarchy during this time, conversion was not a necessary condition to marry a Christian in all cases. Although the 1811 Austrian Civil Code (ABGB) required an appropriate religious marriage ceremony and prohibited marriages between Christians and non-Christians,[93] legal changes introduced in later years allowed civil marriages in limited cases, which made such mixed marriages possible without conversion. Change began with the May Law on matrimony, which stipulated that when a priest refuses to conduct a marriage because of a reason not recognized by the state, the couple is free to marry by the secular state authorities (*Notzivilehe*, emergency civil marriage).[94] But this civil marriage option was relevant only to Christians. A

29, three were 30, four were 31, two were 33, one was 38, one was 39, one was 42, one was 46, and one—71 years old. The rest of the data didn't include the age of the converts.

92. This is not surprising since many Galician Jews in villages and small towns were indeed tavernkeepers and small merchants. See Unowsky, *The Plunder*, 13–17.

93. Ellinger, *Handbuch des österreichischen allgemeinen Zivil-Rechtes*, §64, 43.

94. "47. Gesetz vom 25. Mai 1868," *RGBl* (1868): 93–97, esp. Art. II, 94.

broader consideration that applied to individuals who were not members in a legally recognized church or a religious association was introduced in an 1870 law. A marriage of such an individual with a Christian could be conducted in a civil ceremony at the office of the district authorities or a magistrate and would subsequently be registered there.[95] A few months later a special ordinance instructed the civil authorities to write down in the religion rubric of marriage, birth, and death registers the term *confessionslos* (unaffiliated with any religion) for the spouse who was not a member of a religious community.[96] Thus, after 1870 the road was open for a civil marriage of couples provided that one spouse declared himself or herself as not affiliated with any church or religious association.[97] Of course, one had to first remove himself or herself from any formal membership in a religious community. I have not come across data on confessionless persons for Galicia, and it is unclear how many couples chose this option instead of conversion. Compulsory civil marriages were introduced in Austria only in 1938.

Jakob Thon, in his 1908 work on the Jews of Austria, cites conversion data in different Austrian crown lands for the years 1887–1902. He noted that 302 out of the 444 Jewish converts in Kraków during those years were females. In comparison, the conversion data for Lwów for the years 1897–1902 revealed an almost equal number of male and female converts; seventy-seven males and eighty females. In Vienna, which had the highest number of Jewish converts in the Habsburg Empire, the ratio for the years 1868–1903 was 5,097 males versus 3,988 females. Thon didn't attempt to explain the high number of female converts in Kraków, but rather observed that compared to Vienna, the average annual number of Jewish converts in Lwów and Kraków was small, if one considers the size of the Jewish population in Galicia of about 800,000.[98]

Three years after Thon's book appeared, the statistician Jacob Lestschinsky published a series of articles about conversion of Jews. He too noted the large percentage of Jewish female converts in Kraków and offered no explanation. He argued instead that the fact that many of the converts there came from

---

95. "51. Gesetz vom 9. April 1870," *RGBl* (1870): 83–84.

96. "128. Verordnung der Minister des Innern, des Cultus und der Justitz vom 20. October 1870," *RGBl* (1870): 277.

97. See Harmat, "'Till Death Do You Part,'" 109–128.

98. Thon, *Die Juden in Oesterreich*, 69–80. Thon's brother, R. Joshua Thon, was the preacher of the Kraków temple at the time. On conversion from Judaism in Vienna, see Rozenblit, *The Jews of Vienna*, 132–146.

outside of Kraków, and even the country, "proves that the Jewish influence in Kraków, which is not such a large city, is still effective on the city dwellers and prevents them from betrayal. But it is not strong enough to influence the foreign Jew who comes from another country or even another city."[99] Neither Thon nor Lestschinsky explained why women fled to Kraków to convert, and why the majority of converts were young women.

The Peculiar Legal Status of Converts

Although the Felician Sisters' convent received Jewish girls with open arms, the civil procedure of religious conversion in the Habsburg Empire, like education, was regulated in the 1868 May Laws, specifically the law on the interconfessional relations of citizens.[100] In its second section the law detailed the procedure required for every religious conversion. According to article 4 in that section, anyone who had completed fourteen years, regardless of gender, had the free choice of a religious confession according to her conviction, and if necessary, the authorities needed to protect this choice. At the time of making this choice, an individual could not be in a mental condition or a state of mind that inhibited free decision. Article 6 stipulated that in order for the withdrawal from a church or religious association to take place, the individual had to report the intention to convert to the political authorities (the district administration or the magistrate) which on its part had to notify in writing the lay head or religious leader of the abandoned church or religious association. The entry into the newly elected church or religious association needed to be declared personally to the respective heads or religious authorities.

This law was further clarified in a regulation of January 1869 that stated that upon the declaration of the convert, the political authorities needed to write down such data as the address of the convert at the time (i.e., the convent's address), place of origin, name of parents, etc., in a protocol and have the convert sign it. The authorities had to check whether the convert was already fourteen years old or whether the individual was in the required mental condition and state of mind only if there was a reason for suspicion.[101] All these steps

99. Jacob Lestschinsky, "Apostasy in Different Countries," *Ha-'Olam,* February 8, 1911, 6; February 15, 1911, 4 [Hebrew].

100. "Nr. 48. Gesetz vom 25. Mai 1868," *RGBl* (1868): 99–102.

101. "Nr. 13. Verordnung der Minister des Cultus und des Innern vom 18. Jänner 1869," *RGBl* (1869): 83–84.

were supposed to ensure that the conversion was not conducted in secret or by coercion and that the civil authorities had all the relevant information. The civil law didn't intervene in the religious rituals of conversions, and those were recorded in the books of the relevant churches or religious associations. In the case of Jewish conversion in the Felician Sisters' convent in Kraków, the required information was recorded in the Kraków magistrate, and was then notified by its office of Jewish records to the Kraków rabbinate. This made the Kraków rabbinate aware in real time of all reported conversions. Clearly, the Kraków rabbinate was also aware of the fact that the address of most of the female converts was the Felician Sisters' convent on Smoleńsk Street.

What made the conversion of the female runaways particularly noticeable was their young age. Before the promulgation of the May Laws, the legal age of conversion was eighteen and up. (There were separate laws regarding the age of children in the case of conversion of their parents.) When the interconfessional law was promulgated some Jews even welcomed it. In Vienna, according to one report, four baptized Jews quickly embraced Judaism in the Viennese Temple under the guidance of the preacher Dr. Adolf Jellinek. During the Sabbath celebration for this occasion, Salomon Sulzer and his choir performed hymns of thanks.[102] Little did they know that this same law would facilitate the baptism of hundreds of young Jewish women in Galicia.

Determining the age of fourteen to be the age of religious majority (*annus discretionis,* the age at which a child is capable to decide which confession he wanted to belong to) was not an invention of the Austrian parliament. Since the sixteenth century the age for religious majority kept changing, ranging from ages fourteen to twenty-one, and despite a few voices questioning the 1868 decision on the age of religious majority, the draft law was approved.[103] But age fourteen was the age of majority only for the purpose of religious conversion. The Austrian Civil Code considered twenty-four to be the age of majority for all other cases, and an individual younger than that age was considered a minor and under the father's custody (as the head of the family).[104]

102. "Letters from Vienna," *Ha-Magid,* August 5, 1868, 242–243 [Hebrew]. Like the exodus from Egypt, the author wrote, "Thanks to God, we too emerged from slavery to freedom and from darkness to light, and here we dwell under the freedom of the new laws." Ibid., 243.

103. Hauptmann, "Die Entwicklung der Religionsmündigkeitsgrenze," 162–165. During the debate over this law some claimed that a fourteen-year-old is arguably still a child, but the majority of deputies approved this article.

104. The law defined three categories of children: *Kinder*—those who had not reached the age of seven, *Unmündige*—those who had not reached age fourteen, and *Minderjährige*—those

Accordingly, paragraph 145 of the Civil Code stipulated that parents were entitled to search for their missing child, to demand the return of a fugitive child, and to bring the child back home with the assistance of the authorities.[105]

But what about a daughter younger than twenty-four who ran away from home and entered a convent with the intention to convert? There was a contradiction here, because the convent was allowed to keep the girl if she reached the age of religious majority and if she had prepared for baptism although she was still a minor according to the civil law. Parents who tried to have their daughters returned home continued to seek legal help citing paragraph 145, but this was ineffective because of two precedent rulings of the Viennese Supreme Court.

The first case entailed a Jewish couple, fruit sellers from Tarnów in Western Galicia, who approached the local court in June 1880 and demanded the return of their eighteen-year-old daughter from the Blessed Sacrament Sisters' convent in Lwów, citing paragraph 145 of the Civil Code. In the police investigation, the daughter said that she attended a public school in Tarnów, where she also participated in the Catholic religion classes and decided to become Catholic. She approached the Catholic archbishop in Lwów, and he suggested the aforementioned convent, where she was baptized in 1879. Since then she had been studying home economics (household management) and wished to remain there. The Tarnów court asked the judge in Lwów to demand that the convent return the minor girl to her parents. The convent superior appealed this decision, asking that the Tarnów court further investigate the case.

In September 1882, after more investigations, the Tarnów court argued that paragraph 145 stipulated to return missing children to their parents so the latter could fulfill their obligations as outlined in paragraph 139 of the Civil Code, namely, to care for their children's health, provide them with skills to develop their physical and mental potential, and to give them the basis for a prosperous life through the teachings of religion and practical knowledge. The investigation revealed that the girl left her home for religious reasons, was baptized, and enjoyed a religious and especially a practical education suitable for her inclinations and skills. She would not have been able to enjoy this at her father's home, because according to the certificate issued by the Tarnów magistrate, the parents were poor people and could barely provide for their own needs.

who had not reached age twenty-four, see Ellinger, *Handbuch des österreichischen allgemeinen Zivil-Rechtes*, §21, 25.

105. Ibid., §145, 76.

The daughter, who by that time was twenty-one, had been preparing herself for a future occupation and refused to return home. The court decided that she should be allowed to remain in the convent according to paragraph 148 of the Civil Code. This paragraph stipulated that a father may educate his child who had not yet reached the age of fourteen for an occupation he thought was appropriate for him. Beyond that age, if the child failed in his request from his father to learn another occupation that was more appropriate for his inclinations and skills, he could approach the court with this request. The court would make its decision based on the financial means and arguments of the father. Based on all that, the Tarnów court rejected the parents' request.

The parents appealed to the Viennese Supreme Court, which concluded that the parents had not provided any reason to support their request that their baptized daughter should return home other than their antagonism against Christianity. Should she return home she would only encounter hostility there. The girl was older than fourteen, her baptism was legally valid, and she declared that she refused to return to the home of her Jewish parents. She had been preparing for an occupation that was appropriate for her and that her father could not afford to grant her. According to paragraph 148, the regular court was to reach its decision based on the father's financial means, which in this case were clearly lacking. Bringing the daughter home would surely aggravate her situation. Based on all this, the Supreme Court affirmed on April 24, 1883, the decision of the Tarnów court against the return of the daughter to her parental home.[106]

The second precedent involved a daughter born in 1865 who converted to Catholicism in 1882, when she was seventeen years old. In 1883, she left her parents' home in Kraków and moved to a Catholic educational institute in Breslau (now Wrocław). In 1885, she approached the local court there requesting they release her from her father's custody and appoint a guardian for her. The Kraków court that was approached on this issue summoned the father, who rejected the request and demanded that his daughter be returned to her parental home. Both courts accepted the request of the daughter. The father appealed to the Viennese Supreme Court against that decision and requested the return of his daughter. The Supreme Court revoked the decisions of the

---

106. "Nr. 9399," *Sammlung von Civilrechtlichen Entscheidungen des k. k. obersten Gerichtshofes* 21 (1888): 204–206. For the quoted paragraphs from the Civil Code, see Ellinger, *Handbuch des österreichischen allgemeinen Zivil-Rechtes*, §139, 73; §§145 and 148, 76. Names are eliminated in the published decisions of the Viennese Supreme Court.

lower courts regarding the custody of the father but dismissed the father's request that his daughter be returned to him. The reason it gave for rejecting the request to revoke the father's custody was that the daughter claimed her father mistreated her at home and that was the reason that she ran away in 1881 (when she was sixteen years old) and decided to convert to Catholicism. She was afraid that if she returned home her father would try to alienate her from the Catholic faith through persuasion and moral coercion. This request, according to the Supreme Court, was not supported by the law she cited, namely, paragraphs 176 and 177 of the Civil Code, which listed abuse as one of the reasons for revoking a father's custody. The Supreme Court cited paragraphs 414 and 415 of the Penal Code, which stipulated that mistreatment of children by their parents should be reported to the court, which for its part first warned the parents not to repeat their behavior, and if this occurred a second time, they were threatened with losing custody of their children. In this case, no complaint was filed in the court by the daughter or a third party, and since this happened in 1881, the statute of limitation prevented its consideration five years later.

As for the request of the father to have his minor-age daughter returned to him, the Supreme Court argued that the daughter had been in Breslau for two years, learning the profession of a domestic (*Kammerjungfer*, chamber maid), and asked to remain there. According to the protocol of the Breslau court the girl was perfectly capable of making her own decisions. As such, she could not be considered as a runaway for the purpose of paragraph 145, and according to article 4 of the interconfessional law she was entitled to judicial protection in her free choice of changing her religious confession. The decision was made on October 20, 1885.[107]

The arguments of the Supreme Court in both cases constituted a far-reaching interpretation of the law and cleared the way for convents to keep runaway girls within their walls provided that the latter were at least fourteen years old and declared their desire to convert out of their own free will, and especially if they were preparing themselves for a future profession, which they generally did. In fact, paragraph 145 regarding the return of missing children was of no use in any of the hundreds of cases of girls who fled their homes and

<hr>

107. "Nr. 10753," *Sammlung von Civilrechtlichen Entscheidungen* 21 (1888): 532–533. For the paragraphs cited in this decision, see Ellinger, *Handbuch des österreichischen allgemeinen Zivil-Rechtes*, §§176–178, 88; "Nr. 117. Kaiserliches Patent vom 27. Mai 1852," *RGBl* (1852): 493–591, esp. §§414–415, 569.

entered a convent. There was only one law that could apply to such cases, and it had to do with a third party. According to paragraph 96 of the Penal Code, aiding a minor child to flee the parental home, either by force or by deceit, was considered kidnapping (*Entführung*) and listed under the crime of disturbing the public peace. The punishment for such an act consisted of severe imprisonment for five to ten years if the minor was not yet fourteen years old, and from one month to one year if the runaway minor was at least fourteen years old and had given consent.[108] But even in such cases, the convent, which provided the shelter for the runaway, was not implicated and was not required to release the girl.[109]

In a talk he gave 1900, the Viennese jurist Julius Ofner, who was involved in providing legal help to Galician parents of runaways, criticized both decisions of the Supreme Court, arguing that they reflected the clerical spirit that had taken hold in Austria since the promulgation of the 1883 and 1885 amendments to the compulsory school law. He mentioned a decision of the Austrian parliament from late 1867 recommending to the Ministers of Justice and Religion that they ensure that minor girls or women who run away from their parental or husband's home should not be given shelter in convents. The courts were then instructed to rely in such cases on paragraphs 145 of the Civil Code (in addition to paragraphs about married women) and paragraph 96 of the Penal Code when applicable.[110] But that was of course in the liberal era of the fundamental laws, before the clerical and conservatives gained the upper hand in the Austrian parliament.

Interestingly, in both cases brought before the Supreme Court, the girls fled from home because of dissatisfaction with their life. The first girl became attracted to Catholicism in the public school she attended, and the second claimed that she was mistreated by her father. Both prepared themselves to be independent economically by seeking appropriate education. They were both

108. Ibid., §§96; 97, 515.

109. Several cases of imposing punishment on Polish young men who were found guilty of aiding Jewish girls to run away from their homes and enter a convent were reported by the Galician governor to the Minister of the Interior in response to the 1909 interpellation submitted by Benno Straucher in the Austrian parliament. The punishment consisted of imprisonment of fourteen days to two months in rare cases. See Central State Historical Archive of Ukraine, Lviv (TsDIAL), f. 146, o. 4, s. 5067, in microfilm copy in the Central Archives for the History of the Jewish People, Jerusalem (CAHJP), HM2/9440.7, 15–51.

110. "Kinderraub in Galizien," *Dr Bloch's Oesterrechische Wochenschrift*, November 2, 1900, 780–785, esp. 784–785.

city girls, products of female empowerment through education, a path that was rather new.

Rabbinic Inaction

Throughout the entire period of the Jewish runaway phenomenon in Galicia there was no formal response from the Jewish rabbinic leadership. It should be noted that the problem was primarily an Orthodox one, since the smaller liberal Jewish population experienced none of the dissonance brought about by the disparate educational and cultural experiences of boys and girls. The rabbinical leadership knew of the problem in detail since the appropriate rabbi had to be notified of every conversion. Indeed, following the Araten affair (discussed in chapter 2), the Jewish runaway phenomenon in Galicia was known even to rabbis outside Galicia. At the 1903 rabbinical assembly in Kraków, R. Menachem Mendel Chaim Landau of Nowy Dwór (district of Warsaw) spoke about the flawed practice of female education, namely providing them with teachings of literature and the languages of the nations while neglecting their Jewish education:

> The terrible outcome is already staring us in the face, in the many cases of Galician girls who are leaving the Jewish religion. As for the one who doesn't actually leave her people, her heart is in practice already estranged from them. One cannot expect that the generation she raises will be educated in the Jewish spirit.[111]

The laxity in religious observance, "even in the case of the daughters of the ultra-Orthodox, since they lack any comprehension of Judaism," demanded that they be educated in the knowledge of Torah, he announced.[112] One of the local participants, Meir Rappaport, proposed in response to those remarks the establishment of Talmud Torahs (Jewish religious schools) for girls in every

111. Landau, *Mekiz nirdamim*, 51. See also Manekin, "'Something Completely New'," 76–78. Apparently Landau's book, which chronicled the debates in the 1903 rabbinical assembly, was not well received by many in the Orthodox society because of Landau's criticism and suggestions to change accepted educational practices, see Verdiger, ed., *Sefer Zekhuta de-Avraham*, 179–180.

112. Reacting to the rabbinic dictum "Whoever teaches his daughter Torah is as if he teaches her *tiflut*," quoted by the opposing rabbi, Landau explained that this prohibition was true in earlier times when Jewish women were isolated from the outside world, "but now that they teach them all sorts of frivolities themselves why should [the place of] Torah study be missing from the other studies?" Landau, *Mekiz nirdamim*, 55.

city, where they would be taught prayers, blessings, and the laws pertaining to Jewish homes, as well as "the language and writing of the nations," so they would not be tempted to attend non-Jewish schools. The reaction of one of the participants, R. Eliyahu Akiva Rabinovich of Poltava (Ukraine), an Orthodox zealot, was harsh: "Even this custom they wish to bring upon the Jews— Talmud Torahs for young women! God forbid! Such a thing never was, nor never will be!" As a result, Rappaport's proposal was rejected.[113]

A Galician rabbi, Pinchas Ha-Levi Horowitz of Bohorodczany, suggested publishing appropriate books for the girls, especially in Galicia, where fathers were obligated to send their daughters to school. He also called for a special rabbinical advisory meeting to discuss how to instruct girls in order to make them God-fearing, and to provide them with appropriate books that would arouse their hearts and motivate them to fulfill the religious commandments. It should be emphasized that Orthodox Yiddish literature started appearing in the Orthodox press in Poland only in the interwar period, while German language books had been published by the Orthodox press in Germany already in the 1860s.[114] Indeed, Landau commented that there were already appropriate books for that purpose, namely, *Horeb* by R. Samson Raphael Hirsch of Frankfurt,[115] which should be distributed in several languages, and the novels for the youth written by the rabbi of Mainz, Dr. Meir Lehmann.[116] Although those works were not designated for a specific gender, they assumed knowledge of non-Jewish culture, especially literature, and thus could be recommended in the Galician case for young women. Landau also suggested the establishment of Jewish schools for girls. The specific suggestions were postponed to another session after the loud opposition expressed by R. Eliyahu Akiva Rabinovich, but they were never discussed again. Instead, the assembly voted for a general statement calling upon the parents to also educate their daughters in faith, Torah, and modesty.[117] This was clearly an empty decision,

113. Ibid., 56.

114. On the Orthodox literature in interwar Poland, see Lang, "Orthodox Yiddish Literature in Interwar Poland."

115. On Hirsch, see Isidore Singer and Bernard Drachman, "Hirsch, Samson Raphael," *Jewish Encyclopedia* http://www.jewishencyclopedia.com/articles/7741-hirsch-samson-raphael. *Horeb* discusses the religious commandments and was written for "thinking young men and young women."

116. On Lehmann, see Hess, *Middlebrow Literature*, 157–200; Lezzi, "Secularism and Neo-Orthodoxy."

117. Landau, *Mekiz nirdamim*, 52–57.

as it didn't outline any practical steps to be taken and left all the responsibility for female education to the parents, where it had rested for a long time.

In the years following the 1903 rabbinical assembly, some new educational initiatives were introduced, but none of them were successful. The first was the establishment of a religious gymnasium for boys in Kraków by the rabbi of the Moravian town Ungarish-Brod (today, Uherský Brod), Dr. Meir Jung. Because of pressure exerted by Orthodox zealots, as well as by Jewish assimilationists, Jung was forced to close his school after a few months.[118] The second initiative was the establishment of an association in 1904 named Agudat Yeshurun that was aimed at revising the education of boys and girls. According to the religious nationalist newspaper *Ha-Mizpeh*, the association leaders were R. Shalom Mordechai Schwadron (known as Maharsham), one of the greatest Talmudic authorities in Galicia, and R. Dr. Yosef Zeliger (1872–1919). The association's public appeal said, among other things:

> How long will we suffer in silence our youth growing up without Torah and commandments, without religion and aspiration, without craft and manners, without *derekh erez* (mores, lit., "the way of the land") and taste [. . .] A Jewish daughter learns Polish language and literature, German language and literature, French language and literature, etc. Does she have any conception of Judaism? Will this be a Jewish mother who will bestow Jewish life and spirit upon her suckling? Will not this bitter and evil situation lead Judaism (*yahadus*), our people and our Torah together, to the bottom of Sheol and abject failure?[119]

The association selected a committee of thirty-six members and planned to convene meetings of rabbis and "God-fearing and Torah knowledgeable" individuals in the hope of composing an educational plan that would "raise our sons and daughters for Torah with *derekh erez*, so they don't wander like sheep without a shepherd."[120] The secretaries of the association explained to *Ha-Mizpeh* that, judging from the fact that the association's leaders were a respected rabbi and a European-educated individual (Zeliger received his PhD in Switzerland), one should gather that its purpose was not to introduce

118. See Manekin, "Orthodox Jewry in Kraków," 192–197. The son of Meir Jung, R. Dr. Leo Jung, was later involved in the establishment of the Beit Yaakov teachers' seminary in Kraków.
119. "Agudat Yeshurun," *Ha-Mizpeh*, June 17, 1904, 1 [Hebrew].
120. Ibid., 2.

innovations into religion, nor to breach its boundaries, but rather "to pour old wine into new bottles."[121]

However, the association's plans were never implemented, perhaps because of the opposition voiced by the Orthodox newspaper *Kol Maḥazikei Ha-Dat* (associated with the Belz Hasidic dynasty) which, while expressing respect for R. Schwadron, viewed the endorsement of the moderate *Ha-Mizpeh* as a reason for rejection. The different factions in Galician Jewish society, especially those that published their own newspapers, made it difficult to suggest any innovation without being publicly attacked. This had a chilling effect on individuals who otherwise would have been willing to introduce changes in the practice of Jewish education. Schwadron apparently learned his lesson, and when Meir Jung suggested to him in 1907 to establish an Orthodox association in Galicia, he responded that, while he liked the idea, the Orthodox in Galicia are divided, and what one builds the other destroys, as his experience with Agudat Yeshurun proved. Schwadron's advice was to seek the approval of the leader of the Belz Hasidic dynasty, because nothing would materialize without the latter's support.[122] Schwadron was referring to R. Yissachar Dov Rokeach, who not only was known as a religious zealot but was also the son of R. Yehoshua Rokeach, who was instrumental in the founding of the Orthodox political association Maḥazikei Ha-Dat established in 1879.[123] The newspaper of the association, which bore its name, served also as an attack platform, as was the case with Agudat Yeshurun.

The issue of female conversion in Galicia was raised again in 1912, this time during the founding conference of the Agudat Yisrael Orthodox party in Kattowitz (Katowice). Ahron Marcus, who was a delegate from Kraków, asserted that one of the main questions in which Agudat Yisrael must intervene is the issue of girls' education in Galicia:

> The Galician rabbis have so far failed in this question, and it is a burning scandal, a desecration of God's name (*ḥilul ha-Shem*) of the worst kind, when one watches how our daughters are being led toward baptism, in violation of state laws, and without one of our rabbis lifting a hand.[124]

121. Ibid.

122. See Leiter, "A Few Aspects of the Figure of the Maharsham," *Or ha-Mizraḥ* 3–4 (1964): 10–15, esp. 14 [Hebrew]; Manekin, "'Something Completely New'," 78–80.

123. Manekin, *Yehudei Galizyah*, 122–162.

124. Agudat Yisrael, *Agudas Jisroel, Berichte und Materialien*, 97.

Marcus blamed schoolbooks that included what he called "propaganda" for the Catholic Church, which was expressly prohibited by the civil law:

> While the boys from Hasidic circles do not attend school, the girls grow up in the atmosphere of these Catholic school books without any Jewish religious education. Gradually, they become hostile to Jews and Judaism, and the consequences are devastating for the whole future of the Torah-true Jewry in Galicia. I have held it to be my duty to raise this disgrace on this platform of world Orthodoxy already today and request taking remedial actions for [solving] it.[125]

Although Marcus won much applause for his appeal, nothing was done.

This lack of action stood in stark contrast to the attitude of the Church, which became extensively involved in the education of girls through local convents. Christian girls, just like boys, were traditionally taught the catechism, so no religious or traditional norms were crossed here. Kraków convents were particularly active in female education at all levels, establishing thirteen private primary schools of different types (Lwów had eight primary convent schools) as well as two private teachers' seminaries.[126] While all private schools needed the approval of the Galician school council, not all of them were recognized as compatible with public schools. In all cases they had to follow the 1869 compulsory education law, especially its section on private schools.[127] Convents cast their educational net wide, establishing vocational schools, secondary schools (without matriculation examinations), and teachers' seminaries. Kraków was the most dominant in the number of its convent schools, as the religious, intellectual, and cultural atmosphere in the city viewed such institutions favorably.[128]

Writing in 1925, R. Tuvia Horowitz from Rzeszów, central Galicia, tried to explain why he and other rabbis had been silent in the face of the great numbers of conversions:

> The heart bleeds at the realization that a long list of accusations can be made against us, accusations of neglect of the lost Jewish generation that

---

125. Agudat Yisrael, *Agudas Jisroel, Berichte und Materialien*, 97–98.

126. Czajecka, "Convent Schools in Galicia," 285–291.

127. Some convents opted for more freedom and less government intervention, see ibid., 236–237. For the regulation concerning private schools, see the compulsory education law, §§68–73, 286–287.

128. Czajecka, "Convent Schools in Galicia," 284.

was torn from the body of the Jewish people. It is true that from the standpoint of the Torah the question of the education of young women is very
sensitive and complex. It is true that for the sincere holy modest Jew of the
previous generation, entering the "women's gallery" was a difficult decision.
But we should have adopted the scriptural verse as our example: "Thus shall
you call upon the house of Jacob and tell the sons of Israel" (Exod., 19:3),
that when it concerns the holy Torah, and when it concerns Judaism in its
entirety, one must call upon women first. Hence, we cannot say that "our
hands have not shed this blood" (Deuteronomy, 19:3). Now that we have
taken up the difficult question of women's education, we must confess that
it is too late [for the lost generation]; what we have already lost on account
[of that neglect], we cannot regain. "None that go unto her return" (Pro-
verbs 2:19) was speaking of the former regime of neglect.[129]

Horowitz gives two reasons why Galician rabbis were hesitant to take a stand.
First, Jewish education for women was complicated "from the standpoint of
the Torah." He may have been referring to the Talmudic statement that whoever teaches one's daughter Torah is as if he taught her *tiflut* and its subsequent
codification within Jewish law. In any event, traditional Jews had never insti-
tuted formal Jewish education for their daughters, and such an innovation
might be associated with reformers or enlighteners, i.e., modernity. The question of formal religious education soon became politicized, with some hardlin-
ers opposing any change in the traditional norms, and no one willing to take
the first step.

Horowitz's second explanation for rabbinic inaction was that it was difficult for Jewish men of the previous generation to enter the women's gallery.
Galician rabbis, many of whom were Hasidic leaders, grew up and lived their
lives in a gender-segregated society, never addressing a female audience.
Such rabbis did not teach or deliver sermons to women, whether in the
synagogue or in any other venue. Horowitz writes that the rabbis should
have taken their cue from the Divine command that Moses was to speak first
to the "the house of Jacob," which the rabbis in antiquity had interpreted as
meaning the women. Yet, though this rabbinic interpretation had appeared
in exegetical and homiletical literature, it had not been cited in the context
of the permissibility or desirability of formal religious education for Orthodox women.

129. Horowitz, "What Do Jewish Daughters Lack?" 75.

In the following chapters we shall examine in detail the stories of three runaways: Michalina Araten, Debora Lewkowicz, and Anna Kluger. These young women shared much in common: all were educated in Galician schools and all received at best a rudimentary Jewish education at home; all were unhappy with arranged marriages; all fled their homes and sought refuge in a convent. Morover, all were the subject of police investigations and court cases. But, as we shall see, their experiences also differed in significant ways.

2

Religious Ardor

MICHALINA ARATEN AND HER
EMBRACE OF CATHOLICISM

WHEN ISRAEL AND CYWIA ARATEN returned home from morning Sabbath services on December 30, 1899, their housekeeper informed them, to their surprise, that their oldest daughter Michalina had gone into town.[1] When after many hours she had not returned, her Hasidic parents searched for her but could not find her. After the conclusion of the Sabbath, Israel reported her missing to the police. The next day, Israel and an accompanying police guard inquired at the Felician Sisters' convent on Smoleńsk Street whether she was there, and they received an affirmative response. A week later Israel made a formal request of the police commissioner, Dr. Leo Tomasik, to speak with his daughter. In the convent Michalina explained to commissioner Tomasik that she was of legal age to convert to Roman Catholicism, that she had left her parental home voluntarily, and that she entered the convent without any external coercion. She also declared that she would not see her father. This did not deter Israel, who for the next three weeks attempted to see Michalina and extract her from the convent, but to no avail. On Monday, January 29, the young girl disappeared from the convent, with the nuns claiming to have no knowledge of her whereabouts.

Thus began what became known as the "Araten Affair," in which Israel Araten claimed that Michalina had been kidnapped by the Church and secretly transferred from convent to convent to elude the efforts of the police to find her. The claim was accepted by the Viennese and Galician liberal press, some

1. In different archival documents, she is also referred to as "Michaline" or "Mechla." I will use "Michalina" throughout this chapter.

Jewish organizations, and anti-clerical politicians. As the search for the girl continued, reports about the case appeared in dozens of newspapers in the Habsburg Empire and also around the world. The *Times* of London summarized the story in an article entitled, "Religious Kidnapping in Galicia," viewing it as reflecting "the influence exercised by the clergy in certain parts of the empire."[2] The London *Spectator* described the Araten affair as a "new Mortara case," referring to the famous 1858 seizure of the six-year-old Edgardo Mortara from his home in Bologna.[3] The Australian *Bible Echo* gave its report the title: "Convent Imprisonment."[4] And writing for the *American Jewish Yearbook*, Henrietta Szold listed the Araten affair among the leading events of the year 1900.[5] The conservative and Catholic press in Galicia and in Vienna rejected the claim of abduction and insisted that Michalina entered the convent of her own free will. They blamed the father, Israel Araten, for feeding the press false information, and the liberal press for presenting a one-sided picture of what happened. Conservative and anti-Semitic politicians also blamed the father's heavy-handed attempts to remove his daughter from the refuge to which she had voluntarily escaped, thus fanning the flames of interreligious discord.

Although in the last two decades of the nineteenth century a growing number of young Jewish women from Western Galicia fled their homes and entered the Felician Sisters' convent in Kraków, this phenomenon did not attract any significant public attention, Jewish or non-Jewish, prior to the Araten case.[6] Why did the story of Michalina Araten become such a cause célèbre? The first to raise this question was the Galician publicist Shimon Menachem Lazar. Writing in *Ha-Magid* a month after Michalina's disappearance, Lazar speculated that Michalina's story aroused public interest because her father

2. "Religious Kidnapping in Galicia," *The Times,* May 22, 1900, 7.

3. "A New Mortara Case Occurred in Austria," *The Spectator,* May 26, 1900, 726. See also the short report in a Zagreb (Agram) newspaper titled "Eine polnische Mortara-Affaire," *Agramer Zeitung,* February 14, 1900, 5. For the Mortara case, see Kertzer, *The Kidnapping of Edgardo Mortara.*

4. "Convent Imprisonment," *The Bible Echo,* June 4, 1900, 373.

5. "A List of Leading Events in 5660," *The American Jewish Yearbook 5660* (1900): 642. See also "The Araten Affair," *Public Opinion: A Comprehensive Summary of the Press Throughout the World* 28 (1900): 755.

6. I was able to find only a single article on the matter before 1900, see "Rebellious Girls Traversing Their Ways," *Ha-Magid,* December 9, 1897, 395 [Hebrew]. The writer reports that an average of 35 Jewish girls convert in Kraków annually, most of whom come from villages and small towns in the area. He blames the flawed Jewish education of females for this problem.

claimed that she was not yet fourteen, the legal age for religious conversion. Lazar also noted that her father and grandfather were men of considerable means, which they used to garner public sympathy for their struggle to return the young girl to her home.[7] Michalina's father was indeed a wealthy property owner, but Lazar neglected to mention that he was also a prominent Hasidic Jew, a member of the inner circle of the leader of the Ger (Gur, Góra Kalwaria) Hasidic dynasty, Yehudah Aryeh Leib Alter (1847–1905, author of the *Sefat Emet*), which added a certain notoriety to it.[8] Michalina's case was also more dramatic than the previous cases as she subsequently vanished from the convent, leaving no trace of her whereabouts. These sensational elements made the Araten case a riveting newspaper story, especially since it involved religion, and, as we shall see, a clandestine relationship with a Christian military officer.

Most of the dozens of press reports about the Araten affair provide very little information about the girl herself and say nothing about such issues as her upbringing, her relations with her parents, her social network, or her character. Perhaps unsurprisingly for that period, they focus almost exclusively on Israel Araten's ongoing search for his daughter and on his account of how he was treated by the convent and the local Galician authorities. They help reveal the working of Habsburg and Galician bureaucracies in the struggle over the young girl's fate and the tensions between liberals and conservatives, and between Jews and Catholics, at a time of heightened political anti-Semitism.[9] Indeed, parties to the debate used the Araten affair to advance their own agendas. But none of the press reports about the Araten case help us understand Michalina's actions from her perspective. Fortunately, the extant police and court files documenting the investigation of her case provide us with a wealth of material that enables us to reconstruct the life story of the most famous young Galician Jewish female runaway. Although the documents do not contain a summary statement by Michalina at any point in the affair, they include copies of some of the letters she wrote, as well as statements made by

7. Shimon Menachem Lazar, "Precious Out of the Vile," *Ha-Magid*, March 1, 1900, 100–101 [Hebrew]; Lazar, Galizische Zustände," *Allgemeine Zeitung des Judenthums*, March 16, 1900, 126–127, esp. 126.

8. Araten et al., *Ha-Shevet li-Yehudah*, 10–11. Araten traveled to R. Alter's court several times a year, spending a few weeks each time. He was granted a seat at the table of the rebbe, an honor bestowed only on a small number of followers.

9. See also Buchen, *Antisemitismus in Galizien*, 300–317; Buchen, "'Herkules im antisemitischen Augiasstall." Buchen's focus is on the Araten affair within the context of anti-Semitism.

individuals whose lives crossed hers. From these documents we can infer a great deal about Michalina's motives and aims.

Michalina's Education

Israel and Cywia Araten moved in 1895 to Kraków from the Łódź area in Congress Poland (within the Russian Empire at the time) with Michalina and her four younger siblings.[10] We do not know what kind of schooling Michalina received before the family moved to Galicia, but presumably she received a general education that enabled her to start the fourth grade in a prestigious Kraków school for girls. Providing such an education for girls was a common practice among affluent Hasidic Jews in major Polish cities; private tutors were employed for their daughters to teach them languages and classical literature. One memoir recounts:

> Reb Jacob [Engelman] maintained among all the teachers and scholars two or three male and female teachers to "polish" his daughters and give them a smattering of aristocratic culture [...] They read Schiller and Mickiewicz and went for walks in the outlying fields beyond the whole Hasidic and scholarly bedlam around Reb Jacob's residence. There, in the fields, Reb Jacob's daughters walked amid the wheat and rye and declaimed Schiller's poems. All this lasted until their wedding days, when the girls were harnessed into the yoke of Judaism. In Reb Jacob's house there were never any tragedies. And Schiller's poems evaporated together with the girls' youth.[11]

Since there was no compulsory education law in Imperial Russia, employing private tutors for Jewish girls avoided the effects of socialization with non-Jewish school friends.

The Kraków school that the Aratens chose for their daughter was the school of Gertha Rehefeld, a private eight-grade girls' school for daughters of upper-class Polish families. The advertisement for the school in Polish newspapers

---

10. According to the 1900 Kraków census Israel was born in Warsaw on November 3, 1867, and Cywia, Michalina's mother, was born on November 3, 1865. See *Spis ludności miasta Krakowa z r. 1900*, vol. 14, entry nr. 2080, 418–419. According to the 1910 census Israel was born on November 17, 1867, and Cywia's birth is erroneously recorded as May 17, 1886 (making her younger than fourteen in January 1900; perhaps the reference is to 1868). See *Spis ludności miasta Krakowa z r. 1910*, vol. 13, entry nr. 738, 156–157.

11. Trunk, *Poyln*, 131–132.

said that it was a "German school," but it also included one line in English: "English School for Young Ladies," thus clearly marking it as a finishing school. The school taught drawing, painting, embroidery, and music, as well as German, Polish, French, and English. It also claimed to care for the physical and spiritual development of its students.[12] The school did not conform to the official public school regulations; thus its diploma didn't grant automatic entrance to an upper school. The aim of the school was to prepare the girls for their future roles as educated bourgeois wives and mothers. Rehefeld, a Protestant and single woman, was originally from Germany,[13] but since the school was geared toward the local elite families who were mostly Catholic, the teaching staff included Józef Tomasik, a priest catechist who taught the tenets of Roman Catholicism.[14] Religion classes were mandatory according to the law, but Jews were not obligated to attend classes on the Christian religion. It is unknown whether Michalina left class during catechism lessons, but even if she did, the atmosphere in Polish schools was distinctly Catholic. Textbooks contained many images and stories about Christian saints; school trips included visits to local historic churches; and Christian holidays and other religious events were marked in school.[15]

At that time a Hasidic daughter was provided with a very rudimentary knowledge of prayers and other Jewish observances incumbent upon women. According to one report in the Galician Orthodox press by an author claiming to be a visitor in the Araten household, Michalina had been given the best traditional Jewish education "according to the spirit of the time and place," and that "from the time she learned to read, she never refrained from praying the morning and evening prayers and reciting the *Shema Yisrael* prayer and the Grace after Meals." The problem, according to this author, was that she had been "stuffed" with foreign subjects and languages that were superfluous for Jewish daughters and that inclined her to "follow strangers" and to cleave to their

12. See advertisement for the Rehefeld School in *Nowa Reforma*, August 29, 1889, 4.

13. *Spis ludności miasta Krakowa z r. 1900*, vol. 3, entry nr. 160, 32–33.

14. For the staff of the school see *Szematyzm Królestwa Galicyi*, vol. 2, 538. Roman Catholics constituted 70% of the city's population at the time and Jews, 28%. See Wood, *Becoming Metropolitan*, 37.

15. The insertion of religion into the curriculum via textbooks and school trips was criticized by some Jews, claiming that it was against the law, see Aaron Marcus, "Peace Be on Israel and the Rabbis!" *Ha-Mizpeh*, June 26, 1912, 1–2 [Hebrew]. See also Zvi Scharfstein, "From the Life of Our Brothers in Galicia: The Education of the Daughters," *Ha-'Olam*, September 29, 1910, 11–12 [Hebrew].

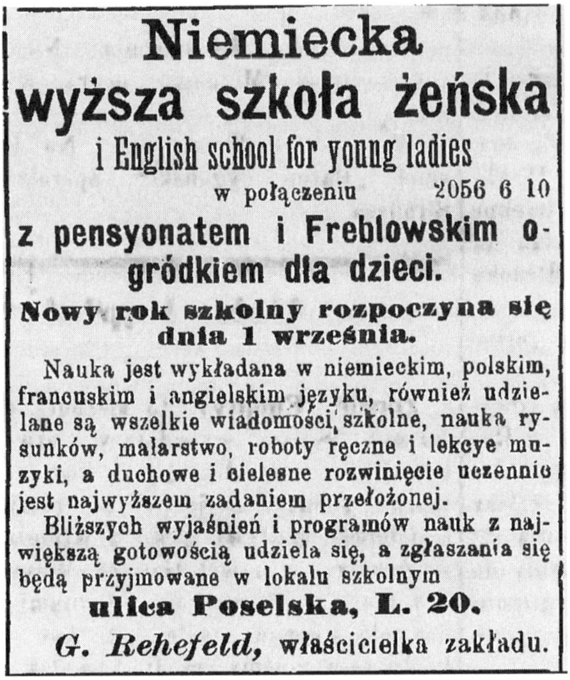

Niemiecka
wyższa szkoła żeńska
i English school for young ladies
w połączeniu   2056 6 10
z pensyonatem i Freblowskim o-
gródkiem dla dzieci.

Nowy rok szkolny rozpoczyna się dnia 1 września.

Nauka jest wykładana w niemieckim, polskim, francuskim i angielskim języku, również udzielane są wszelkie wiadomości szkolne, nauka rysunków, malarstwo, roboty ręczne i lekcye muzyki, a duchowe i cielesne rozwinięcie uczennic jest najwyższem zadaniem przełożonej.

Bliższych wyjaśnień i programów nauk z największą gotowością udziela się, a zgłaszania się będą przyjmowane w lokalu szkolnym

ulica Poselska, L. 20.

G. Rehefeld, właścicielka zakładu.

FIGURE 2.1. Advertisement for the Rehefeld School. *Nowa Reforma,* August 29, 1889, 4 (enlarged).

"immoral views."[16] Even according to this testimony, her Jewish education was nowhere near the level of her Polish education.

As for her social life in Kraków, it appears to have been rather limited. Anna Araten, Michalina's twenty-two-year-old aunt who lived with them, related that Michalina had a close relationship only with Regina Horowitz, a classmate of hers.[17] According to Regina, a merchant's daughter,[18] she and Michalina were close friends and occasionally visited each other, although Michalina never disclosed to her anything beyond their daily routine.[19]

16. "The Tongue that Speaks Proud Things," *Maḥazikei Ha-Dat,* March 23, 1900, 2–3, esp. 2.

17. The National Archives in Kraków, Sąd Krajowy Karny w Krakowie (SKKKr) 409 (henceforth: Araten court file), 203.

18. *Spis ludności miasta Krakowa z r. 1900,* vol. 13, entry nr. 51, 12–13. Regina Horowitz was born in 1886, thus she was younger than Michalina.

19. Araten court file, 206.

FIGURE 2.2. Photograph of Michalina Araten.
Courtesy of the Central Archives of Historical Records
in Warsaw (AGAD), sygn. f. 305, s. 287.

The Military Officer

Michalina attended Rehefeld's school for three years and left on June 30, 1898, after completing the sixth grade.[20] Although this would fulfill the mandatory education obligation in Galicia, it is not clear why she was removed from the school at this time; perhaps her parents were not happy with the school's influence on their daughter. Spending three years in the company of rich Catholic Polish girls under the responsibility of highly educated teachers had surely

20. The Central Archives of Historical Records in Warsaw (AGAD), f. 305, s. 287 (henceforth: Araten Warsaw file), 45. This file contains the correspondence of the Austrian Justice Ministry with the Kraków public prosecutor and other local authorities.

affected Michalina's sense of identity, both religious and social, especially since she was new in town and naturally eager to be accepted. A clash between her life in the Polish-speaking school and life in her Yiddish-speaking Hasidic home was inevitable. Her grandfather related that she was educated, spoke German, Polish, and French well, and pronounced very well the letter r, unlike the Jewish guttural way.[21] After leaving school and spending most of her days at home, Michalina apparently experienced a growing sense of alienation from the life she was confined to.

Matters took a sharp turn about a year later, when she spotted from her window Dr. Philipp Müller, a physician in the third division of the artillery regiment stationed in Kraków, who lived across the street from her home.[22] In a written statement that Müller later submitted to his regiment, he explained the nature of their relationship. Since it is the only source detailing the trajectory of that relationship, it is cited here in its entirety:

> I met Miss Michaeline Araton [sic] in the month of October [1899], namely in the [following] manner: First, I saw her standing often for a long time in the window across from my apartment, observing my apartment. Having become aware of this, I wrote a letter, the first and at the same time the last one—in which I expressed the wish to get to know her and to have an opportunity to see and talk to her. This letter was picked up by a girl sent by Miss Araton. My wish was fulfilled, and on the same afternoon I was able to talk with her, that is, on the street and in the company of a second girl.
>
> A few days later Miss Araton notified me in writing that she would expect me in the Rynek [market square] tramway station, and this time too she appeared in the company of a young lady. The three of us, in the presence of other people whom we did not know, rode in the tramway to the Podgórze Bridge.[23] That was the second and last time that I got together and talked with Miss Araton. There was never any talk of love or marriage between us.

21. See the grandfather's testimony from March 1, 1900, Araten court file, 134. He described his granddaughter as tall for her age with a mound of light brown hair.

22. Müller is listed in *Schematismus für das kaiserliche und königliche Heer*, 1068. He was a holder of a Jubilee Commemorative Gold Medal. His age is not indicated in the 1900 census, see *Spis ludności miasta Krakowa z r. 1900*, vol. 14, entry nr. 2241, 452–453.

23. The tram was drawn by a horse at this time, and only in early 1901 was it operated electrically, see Wood, *Becoming Metropolitan*, 32.

A few days later I was notified by Miss Araton through a woman, that her parents, who had been informed by somebody of our meeting, and of my letter, had beaten and abused her. From that moment on I avoided any opportunity to approach the young lady. I never wrote to her, and I even did not appear in my window in order to not give her parents any further occasion to abuse her.

I did not reply to her messages that were brought to me by a woman, nor did I respond in any way to her letters, nor give her any sort of answer. In this manner three months passed from the time of our meeting up to the time the young lady left her parents' home, during which time I neither saw nor wrote to her, nor conveyed any message.

Not until January 1, 1900 (or December 31, 1899) did I learn that Miss Araton had disappeared. I gave the girl's father and grandfather, who appeared in my apartment, the assurance that I neither knew where the girl was nor even knew that she had disappeared.

For quite a while I did not know what had happened to the girl. I only found out from my brother, whom the parents had contacted through a lawyer, that Miss Araton was in a convent and that there she supposedly was claiming that she would not leave the convent, because she wanted to get baptized in order to be able to marry me.[24]

Through this lawyer as well as through a different facilitator later—a physician—the parents demanded that I should go to the convent and convince the girl to leave the convent, for which they were inclined to pay me 5000 fl. With the assertion that this entire affair had nothing to do with me, I rejected these offers.

I must correct the erroneous allegation in the newspapers that the girl was only 14 or even only 13 years old. The father of the girl himself corrected that statement in saying that already in December of last year she had completed her 15th year.

In the above statement I have truthfully, completely, and totally described my connections to this girl.[25]

---

24. This allegation of the parents' lawyer might have been based on the suspicion of the parents, however they never raised it during the investigation. The father later claimed that Michalina was only thirteen years old when she entered the convent.

25. Araten Warsaw file, 2524–2526. Müller handed the letter to the investigative judge during his interrogation, ibid., 2536. He was first investigated by the military, which found no reason for a criminal investigation, ibid., 2517–2518.

It was quite common for Austrian officers to flirt with younger women and have occasional love affairs,[26] but Müller emphasizes in the above statement that this was not a relationship of that sort, although he subsequently described her as "a young pretty adult female."[27] Müller admitted that he took the initiative to invite Michalina for a walk, but he maintained that they were accompanied by a third person. For her part, Michalina was clearly not shy or inhibited, and she accepted Müller's invitation knowing full well that such conduct contradicted Orthodox Jewish norms held by her Hasidic family and community and would be considered scandalous. Taking a walk with Müller in the open street would be correctly viewed in itself as a rebellious act against her family. According to Müller's account, his relationship with her fell apart rather quickly. Whether Müller indeed felt sorry for Michalina after learning of her mistreatment by her father, or whether he realized that she was not the simple *Süße Mädel* (lit. "sweet girl," a fin-de-siècle Viennese phrase denoting a young female from the lower classes available for a sexual relationship) that soldiers regularly flirted with,[28] he decided to distance himself from her.

Müller and Michalina were assisted by several people in their efforts to communicate with each other, and their accounts shed light on what transpired between the two. The girl who picked up the letter that Müller threw down from his window was Regina Sattler, a fifteen-year-old girl who lived in the same building as Michalina.[29] Sattler related that Dr. Müller often used to communicate with Michalina from his window in sign language. Once he informed Michalina that he was throwing down a letter for her, and upon the request of Michalina and a promise of a five-florin reward, Sattler had brought the letter to her and watched her covering it with kisses. Michalina told her that she was kissing the letter as if it was the man himself.[30] Sattler recounted that when Israel Araten heard about Müller's letter, he grabbed Michalina by the hair, slapped her on the face, and beat her with a belt. The beating lasted a long time.[31] After that incident, Araten limited Michalina's freedom and didn't allow her to receive guests at home or go out without being accompanied by a house

---

26. István Deák, *Beyond Nationalism*, 142–145.

27. Araten Warsaw file, 2535.

28. Wood, *Becoming Metropolitan*, 39.

29. *Spis ludności miasta Krakowa z r. 1900*, vol. 17, entry nr. 729, 146–147.

30. Araten Warsaw file, 2436.

31. Apparently, beating teenage children with a belt was not unusual at this time, even among families of the nobility, see Tarnowski, *The Last Mazurka*, 52.

maid. Sattler also emphasized that the Araten family was Hasidic.[32] Discovering his eldest daughter's relationship with a non-Jewish army officer must have come as a shock to Israel Araten, but his anger and physical abuse only further alienated his daughter from the family.

The woman who brought messages to Müller from Michalina was Anna Klimas, a forty-three-year-old washerwoman who worked at the Araten home. In the court investigation Klimas first denied knowing Dr. Müller, speaking to him, or transmitting Michalina's letters to him. She claimed that she was too busy working and had paid no attention to what was going on around her, and in general, people in Jewish homes never spoke to her. She said that Araten alleged that she led his daughter to the convent and kept harassing her even at night, threatening that neither she nor her daughter would see the end of the year. As a result, she was frightened especially since her daughter was seriously ill. Because of Araten's allegations against her (i.e., that she had enticed the girl to go to the convent), the police questioned her many times as if she had committed some crime. But when she was confronted with Dr. Müller, Klimas admitted that she recognized him, explaining that she didn't know his name, and when she saw him at his home, he was dressed in civil clothing rather than in military uniforms. She related that the cook at the Araten home told her that the Araten couple beat their daughter, but all she was concerned about was doing her work and going home. Klimas then admitted that she once delivered a letter to Müller's home without knowing his name. The letter was not written by Michalina, but rather by her own daughter Stanisława, who asked her to take it over to the gentleman who lived opposite the Aratens on the first floor. Since she could not read or write, she had no idea what was written in that letter, so she handed it to Müller and told him that Michalina was beaten at home. Müller took the letter but did not answer it.[33] Klimas insisted that she knew nothing about Michalina's escape from home or of who might have helped her with it.

Stanisława Klimas, the seventeen-year-old daughter of Anna Klimas, occasionally helped her mother with the laundry at the Aratens and got to know Michalina. She spoke very little with her because she was too busy with her work, and because of the presence of Michalina's family. On one occasion

32. Araten Warsaw file, 2445, where the word is transcribed "*hussitisch*" because of the girl's Galician Yiddish accent. The reference means *ḥasidish*, with the *d* pronounced as a *t*; ibid., 2605. Apparently, Israel Araten learned about the letter from his neighbor Adolf Schönberg, who heard about it from one of his guests who had meanwhile immigrated to America, ibid.

33. Araten Warsaw file, 2457; Araten court file, 98–106.

Michalina complained to her that she had been beaten and asked her to write a letter in her name to the doctor living opposite from her home, telling him that he should have pity on her and write a few words back, otherwise she would commit suicide. When Stanisława asked her why she wanted to kill herself, Michalina said that she could no longer live among the Hasidim. Stanisława was moved by what Michalina said and wrote the letter in her name, then handed it to her mother to take it over to Müller's apartment. Stanisława claimed that she didn't know anything about Michalina's relationship with Dr. Müller or of her escape.[34]

Was Michalina deliberately looking for contacts with a Christian man as an exit path from her religion? Was she romantically inclined toward the Austrian officer, or did she view him as a dear friend? Michalina clearly had strong feelings for Müller, but we don't know what her expectations were of their relationship. Alienated from her Hasidic home, she had no one else to turn to but this gentile military physician, a confidant whose life couldn't have been more different than hers.

The "Wax Doll" Bridegroom

After receiving no response from Müller to her first call for help, Michalina wrote him a couple of months later, on December 10, 1899.[35] Since Müller was not a native Pole, she wrote him in German, addressing him as "Highly honored Sir" (*Hochgeehrter Herr*). She explained that she had not written for a long time because she was closely watched by her mother. Once when she walked to her music lesson accompanied by her aunt, her mother saw Müller watching at his window and later forbade her to go out for a whole week. Feeling miserable and isolated, Michalina confessed that many times she contemplated killing herself by jumping out the window, but "the Almighty God, who does not leave His children when they are in danger, watched over me too." In her pain, she reached out to somebody she still hoped would understand her. But then she disclosed the real reason for writing the letter. Her father had informed her earlier that day that since in ten days she would be fifteen years old, and since at that age all her cousins were already married, a bridegroom had been chosen for her. The engagement was scheduled to take place in two weeks. She pleaded with her father not to carry out his plan, but to no avail.

34. Araten Warsaw file, 2457–2458; Araten court file, 112–115.
35. For the copy of the letter see Araten Warsaw file, 2540–2541.

She then asked a person she trusted, a thirty-four-year-old woman, what she should do, and the woman recommended that she should ask Müller's advice since he was older and more experienced. Michalina didn't reveal in the letter who this trusted woman was; it may have been her music teacher, whom she saw regularly. She concluded her letter explaining the urgency of her situation: "I am turning to you with folded hands and with tears in my eyes to please help me a little. I must leave the paternal home at any price, for I cannot possibly become betrothed to this wax doll (*Wachspuppe*) that my father had presented as my bridegroom to whom I am to be betrothed."

Michalina does not indicate the identity of the "wax doll." While it is possible that she used this word in the letter simply as a pejorative, the reference may also have been to Moshe Waks, the son of the famous R. Haim Elazar Waks (1822–1889), the Hasidic author of *Nefesh Ḥayah*. In his youth, Israel Araten was a close disciple of R. Waks,[36] who had seven daughters and one son, Moshe.[37] Moshe later married the daughter of the affluent businessman, Jacob Engelman, mentioned at the beginning of this chapter.

Incidentally, we learn from the letter that according to Michalina, she was born on December 20, 1884.[38] She closes it with "Yours, constantly thinking of you, Michaline A." Michalina could not have been completely surprised by her father's rush to marry her off; arranged matches at her age were the norm in Hasidic families. But when an actual bridegroom was selected for her, and the date for the engagement set, it was too much for the young girl to bear. She contemplated an escape from her home, but she desired Müller's counsel on how to manage it. Michalina mailed her anguished cry for help to Müller from the post office, perhaps to ensure that it was not intercepted by her family. Müller sent no reply.

Running Away from Home

According to Michalina's letter to Müller, her engagement was to take place on Sunday, December 24, 1899. On the following Sabbath, December 30, she ran away to the convent. In an effort to clear Müller of any connection to her

36. See Araten, *Ha-Shevet li-Yehudah*, 9.

37. Ibid., 131.

38. Her parents were married on April 9, 1883 (March 28 in Russian old style), so her birth as the first child on December 20 makes perfect sense. For her parents' marriage registration, see Łódź PSA Birth, Marriages, Death 1878–1905, Łódź Piotrków Gubernia, f. 1568, a. 60, marriage of "Izrajel Aroten" and "Cywiia Wajs."

decision, she told commissioner Tomasik that she didn't know Dr. Müller closely enough and had met him only twice: once in the city park and once in the tram. She declared that she would not return to her home because of fear of retribution and wouldn't meet her father or grandfather. She was willing to speak with her mother and aunt if they came to the convent. Commissioner Tomasik read the protocol of his meeting with Michalina to her grandfather, but not to Israel Araten "in consideration of his condition (he fell into a faint)."[39]

Indeed, Tomasik had gone with the grandparents of Michalina to the convent, and after both he and Kazimerz Rzeszódko, the notary of the Bishop's consistory,[40] spent a long time persuading her to meet with them, she finally agreed. Rzeszódko related that Michalina, who looked to him to be sixteen or seventeen, revealed to him her firm decision to change her religion. She declared that even if she were removed from the convent by force, she would not return to her parents' home. He also indicated that it frequently happened that girls in the catechumenate changed their minds and left the convent, and that the nuns did not interfere with this choice. He insisted that no persons under the age of fourteen were admitted to the convent, which strictly complied with the law.

This did not deter Araten from seeking his daughter's return home. On January 11, 1900, Araten presented medical documentation according to which his wife had been stricken with a mental affliction and requested that his daughter be taken home to visit her mother, escorted by the police. However, Michalina refused to go home regardless of the medical certificate presented to her, stating that she would speak with her mother only inside the convent. The next day a meeting took place between Michalina and her grandparents, whom she met again on January 20. On January 23, Michalina met in the convent with her grandfather and with two aunts in the presence of the superiors of the convent and Rzeszódko and declared firmly that she would not return to her parents.[41] Her father came to the convent ten times but was unsuccessful in his efforts to see her.[42]

39. Araten Warsaw file, 2436.

40. Kazimerz Rzeszódko is indeed listed as the notary of the Bishop's consistory, see *Szematyzm Królestwa Galicyi*, vol. 1, 408. According to the convent regulations, each such meeting had to take place in the presence of representatives from the police and the consistory.

41. Araten Warsaw file, 2605–2607; 2435–2436; 2618–26211.

42. Ibid., 2606.

Honorata Kummer, the Vicar General of the Felician Sisters' convent, re-lated in the initial investigation that the catechumenate, administered by Sister Rosalia Zagrabińska, numbered on average between eight and twenty girls. She emphasized that girls under the age of fourteen were not accepted on principle. Each admittance of a girl was notified to the consistory and the police directorate as required by law. The freedom of the girls was not at all restricted, and anyone could leave the convent as they wished. Cases of girls leaving the convent without a prior notification or farewell were not uncom-mon. As to Michalina, she approached the gatekeeper Magdalena Kozek at noon on December 30, 1899, and asked to be admitted; she was initially re-jected, however, because the catechumenate was overcrowded at the time. When she didn't want to leave and kept crying and begging to be admitted, the gatekeeper reported this to Kummer, who subsequently talked to the girl. Michalina told her that she had turned fifteen in December 1899, and that she had been contemplating conversion to the Church for four years, from the time she started school. After learning that Michalina had left her parental home of her own free will, she was admitted to the convent. When the next day Israel Araten showed up at the convent with the police guard, they were told that Michalina was there. Kummer added that when the Araten family later claimed that their daughter was not yet fourteen years old, and she told Michalina that she would have to be returned to her parents, Michalina re-plied: "As I have come, I will disappear; I will not return home."[43]

During the initial investigation it was not determined when and whether the Felician Sisters' convent reported to the police that Michalina had been admitted, or whether Kummer's claim that every time a girl was admitted to the catechumenate it was reported to the police, was true.[44] In response to a question of the Austrian Justice Ministry, the police investigated this issue and found out that the Felician Sisters' convent neither reported Michalina's ad-mittance to the police nor registered her name in their books. The police learned of her stay in the convent after her father and the police guard inquired whether she was there.[45] This was clearly in violation of the law. However, the investigation did not reveal anything that would suggest that the convent was notified by a third party that Michalina would be arriving there.[46]

43. Ibid., 2442; 2537–2539.
44. Ibid., 2431–2432.
45. Ibid., 2539.
46. Ibid., 2537; 2539.

Rosalia Zagrabińska related that during Michalina's stay in the convent a
gentleman in official uniform appeared in the convent, introducing himself as
"Dębowski" from the embassy in Rome. Another time someone calling himself "Lewicki," allegedly a court official, showed up there. Each of them demanded the release of Michalina for a few hours, but when Michalina was told
about this, she rejected their request. Both were apparently disguised Jews.
Zagrabińska explained that Michalina did not want to see her father because
she loved him the most and wanted to spare him the pain of hearing his own
daughter telling him that she wanted to be baptized. But according to
Zagrabińska, Michalina was especially agitated by another issue, namely, the
various medical examinations conducted by doctors sent to the convent by
her father under the pretext that she suffered from all kinds of illnesses.[47]

Indeed, Araten sent to the convent Dr. Karol Żuławski, a professor of psy-
chiatry at the Jagiellonian University and the director of St. Lazarus mental
hospital, to visit his daughter. This hospital also served as the address where
registered prostitutes had to be regularly checked for venereal diseases.[48]
Żuławski examined Michalina on January 20 and found her in perfect health
mentally. She told him that she had left her parents' home of her own accord
and fled to the convent because she wished to convert to the Catholic religion.
He estimated that she was fifteen years old.[49] Another doctor Araten sent to
visit his daughter in the convent was the court physician, Dr. Anton Filimowski. Araten first came to see him in his office with a man he introduced as
Michalina's bridegroom. Araten said that she was suffering from her heart, and
the bridegroom said that she was "insane and syphilitic." Filimowski examined
Michalina in the convent and found her perfectly healthy except for some ane-
mia. He estimated her age as about sixteen and said the impression she gave was
of a "smart, educated, serious, tactful, and energetic girl."[50] A third doctor sent

47. Ibid., 2443. Relying on Israel Araten, the liberal press claimed the opposite, namely, that the
father sent doctors to the convent because Zagrabińska claimed that Michalina couldn't see him
because she was sick, see "Die Krakauer Klostergeschichte," *Neue Freie Presse*, February 14, 1900, 5.

48. See Wood, *Becoming Metropolitan*, 28. For the mandatory police registration and medical
examinations of prostitutes in Habsburg Galicia, see Stauter-Halsted, *The Devil's Chain*, 30–31.

49. Araten Warsaw file 2445; 2586–2587. Israel indicated that he invited professor Żuławski
to examine his daughter but failed to mention that he was a psychiatrist. His written account
about his daughter was read aloud by Julius Ofner in a public lecture taking place at the
Österrechisch-Israelitische Union, see "Kinderraub in Galizien," *Dr. Bloch's Oesterreichische
Wochenschrift*, November 2, 1900, 780–785, esp. 781.

50. Araten Warsaw file, 2441.

by Araten, Dr. Józef Szewczyk, also found Michalina healthy. When asked, she told him that she had her first monthly period three years beforehand.[51]

Michalina's bridegroom may have assumed that she caught a venereal disease because of her relationship with Müller. After all, soldiers at the time were known to catch such diseases from prostitutes' establishments that they frequented.[52] Perhaps he believed that a Hasidic daughter who wished to convert to Catholicism must suffer from a mental disorder.[53] Or perhaps he wished to use her "syphilitic condition" as grounds for terminating the betrothal, which would have been a grave action for a Hasidic Jew. By contrast, Araten claimed before her bridegroom that Michalina suffered from her heart, perhaps alleging that this was a result of her being held in the convent against her will. Still, it was Araten who had invited the psychiatrist Dr. Karol Żuławski to examine his daughter, presumably suspecting just like her bridegroom that she fled to the convent because of a mental disorder resulting from a venereal disease. Such a disorder would obviously require her to be taken out of the convent and institutionalized.

Michalina's Age

Since sending doctors to examine Michalina was not guaranteed to produce results, Israel Araten also set out to prove that his daughter had not reached the age of fourteen and hence could not convert to another religion. But how old was she really? When Araten and his family moved to Kraków in 1895, he submitted on July 31 the required notification of all new residents (*Meldung*), in which he indicated that Michalina was ten years old.[54] Gertha Rehefeld, the headmistress of the school that Michalina attended, told investigators that when the Araten couple had registered their daughter in the fourth grade, they told her that Michalina was born in Łódź on September 1, 1885. Despite the

51. Ibid., 2442.

52. Deák, *Beyond Nationalism*, 143.

53. The belief that insanity or mental instability was a factor in conversion to Christianity was apparently not uncommon among Hasidim. A well-known example is that of the conversion of Moshe, the son of R. Shneur Zalman of Lyady, the founder of the Ḥabad (Lubavitch) Hasidic dynasty, which was attributed to mental illness. See Assaf, *Untold Tales*, 92–93. Assaf cites Peretz Smolenskin's Hebrew poem, "The Madman": "He [Moshe] thought and he spoke, and implemented his plot / To desecrate his brother's [Dov Ber] name and that of the congregation he taught. / He chose a new faith and denied his own faith, / But the Hasidim exclaimed in unison: 'He has gone mad!'." Ibid., 53.

54. Araten Warsaw file, 2450.

discrepancy in dates, both pieces of evidence imply that Michalina was at least fourteen years old when she escaped from home. Araten himself informed the police on the day she disappeared from home that she was fifteen years old. To be sure, none of this would have mattered had Araten been able to produce Michalina's birth certificate. But her birth in Łódź had not been registered, and indeed, it was not uncommon for Jews in the Russian Empire to fail to register births in the Jewish metrical books as required. When needed to prove date of birth, parents sometimes brought witnesses years later to testify that they remembered the exact date of the birth. The protocol of such a testimony was then kept in the vital statistics' regional office for the appropriate religion.[55] The lack of a birth certificate provided an opportunity for Araten; all he needed to do was to find witnesses who would be able to indicate a date of birth that would make her a minor for the purposes of conversion.

And that is what he did. On January 19, Araten submitted to the police a copy of a Russian proof of birth document according to which Michalina was born on May 27, 1886 (May 15 in Russian old style), which would make her fourteen years old only on May 27, 1900.[56] If true, that would mean that Michalina's admittance to the convent was in violation of article 4 of the 1868 interconfessional law. According to the birth document, two tradespeople, Abraham Szlamowicz and Abraham Abrahamowicz, appeared before the civil registrar in Tuszyn, in the province of Łódź, in Piotrków Gubernia, and declared that they had known Michalina since her birth, and that they knew for certain that she was born in the settlement of Tuszyn on "May 15, 1886 [May 31 new style]" and "hence now she is thirteen years [old]." They stated that they were prepared to testify under oath.[57] The document was signed by the two Jewish witnesses and by the Tuszyn civil registrar.

The police commissioner presented the document to the Felician Sisters' convent as well as to the notary of the consistory, but on the next day he returned it to Araten. Since it was a copy of a document issued in Imperial Russia, it needed authentication (*Legalisierung*) by a Russian court of law to ensure it was not a forgery. The lengthy procedure, which was handled by the court and the Austrian consulate in Warsaw, took four months from the time Araten submitted the document until the time an official Polish translation of the Russian authentication document was accepted by the Kraków criminal

55. See Sliozberg, "A Boy's Gymnasium Life," 404.
56. Araten Warsaw file, 2436.
57. Araten court file, 180.

court.[58] The police suspected that the proof of birth document was forged not only because of Araten's earlier statement, but also because Michalina's external appearance suggested a more mature age.[59] There was another reason to question its veracity: Why did two witnesses from Tuszyn appear in the civil registrar's office on May 31, 1899, half a year before Michalina's entry to the convent, testifying that Michalina was born on May 27, 1886? There was no special significance to her being thirteen years old at that time.

Despite being authenticated by the court authorities in the Russian Empire, a recent search I conducted for the original Tuszyn proof of birth document revealed that it doesn't exist anywhere in the civil registries of the region. Instead, a different proof of birth document for Michalina, kept in the civil status office of the synagogue district of the town of Brzeziny, Łódź province, about 30 km north of Tuszyn, turned up. According to that document, two synagogue beadles of the city of Brzeziny, Aron Fridman and G. Goltsberg, claimed that on December 30, 1899 (January 11, 1900 new style), Israel Araten had presented before them a maiden, declaring that she had been born to his lawful wife, Dvoira-Tsivye, in the city of Brzeziny on May 3 (May 15 new style), 1886, and that she had been given the name Michalina while reciting a prayer. The belated declaration by the father was carried out due to his fault. This official declaration was read to the petitioner and the witnesses, and was then signed by those present, i.e., Fridman and Goltsberg, the mayor and the civil registar. Only the father, "who is illiterate," did not sign.[60]

How does one explain the existence of two different proof of birth documents? Corruption was widespread in Imperial Russia, and one could bribe state officials to produce all kinds of documents. Israel Araten desperately needed an official proof of birth document in which Michalina's year of birth would be 1886, thus making her younger than fourteen. He likely turned first to agents in Brzeziny, but that document proved worthless, since it stated that Araten appeared there personally with his daughter Michalina on January 11, when she was really in Kraków in the Felician Sisters' convent. [61] But that

58. Ibid., 49; 86; 120; Araten Warsaw file, 2453–2454.

59. Ibid., 2438; 2531–2532; 2620.

60. Files of civil status of the synagogue district of Brzeziny, act no. 277/1899, reference number 20.

61. One can surmise that Araten asked them to declare that thirteen years earlier; when he was temporarily residing in Brzeziny, he had brought a baby girl to the synagogue for her naming ceremony. According to Jewish custom, the name of a baby girl is announced in the prayer for

proof of birth document was already deposited in Brzeziny. Producing a second proof of birth document and keeping it in the civil registration office anywhere in the Łódź province was too much of a risk, and if discovered would totally discredit Araten. That is likely why the original of the forged Tuszyn proof of birth document doesn't exist in the appropriate registry.

Although the evidence—Araten's notification of residence when he moved to Kraków, his statement to Rehefeld upon enrolling Michalina, his statement to the police on December 31, 1899, Michalina's letter to Müller, and testimonies as to the girl's physical appearance—clearly showed that Michalina was at least fourteen and most likely fifteen when she entered the Felician Sisters' convent, Israel Araten nevertheless managed to produce a copy of a proof of birth document that implied she was thirteen. By the time the document was authenticated, Michalina had long disappeared from the convent. But her father could use it to bolster his claim in the court of public opinion that Michalina was underage when she entered the convent, and hence her admittance constituted an abduction.

Disappearance from the Convent

On Monday, January 29, at noon, two nuns from the Felician Sisters' convent came to the police station and informed commissioner Tomasik that Michalina had disappeared from the convent. They couldn't provide any additional information, so Sister Zagrabińska sent a note to the police indicating that Michalina had left the convent on the Sabbath, January 27, exactly four weeks after she entered it.[62] In trying to explain why they had no further information on her disappearance, the nuns explained that more than a hundred people lived in the convent, and there was considerable traffic throughout the day. Because the convent also contained a church, a sanctuary for poor children, and a daily lunch service for poor students, its doors had to remain open almost the entire day. The nuns assured the authorities that they did not know where Michalina went from the convent or where she was staying. Moreover, since girls from the catechumenate often left without notification, they were of no concern to the convent.[63]

---

the recovery of a woman who has given birth to a girl. The beadles, misunderstanding his instructions, declared that Michalina appeared before them with her father on January 11, 1900.

62. Araten Warsaw file, 2437; 2539.

63. Ibid., 2585–2586.

On the day before her disappearance, Michalina wrote two letters. The first was addressed to Kummer and Zagrabińska, whom she asked forgiveness for secretly leaving the convent, and thanked for their hospitality. She told them that she could not say where she was going because she still did not know it herself.[64] The second letter was for her father, and like the first, it was written in Polish; perhaps she had not been taught to write in Yiddish. When her father was informed that his daughter left a letter for him, he came to the convent to pick it up, but the convent agreed to give it to him only on the condition that he would read it aloud in the presence of a police representative, and that a copy would be kept at the police station. They feared that the father might claim that the letter contained allegations against the convent.[65] Araten rejected those conditions and left the convent empty handed. As a result, the investigative judge took the letter on February 20 and invited Araten to come to the court the next day and open it there.[66] The court intended to use the content of the letter for its investigation.[67] But Araten didn't show up in court on that day and instead sent his father, who informed the court that his son was not interested in the letter. Following this response, the court opened the letter and deposited it in its files.[68] Although one would expect the desperate father to be eager to read anything his daughter left, especially if addressed to him, he remained indifferent to it. Perhaps he suspected that the judge might find in the letter information that he preferred not to disclose.

The Search for Michalina

The highly publicized search for Michalina had the potential to reawaken the tensions between the Catholic and Jewish populations in Galicia that had only recently calmed down. Less than two years earlier, peasants had rioted against their Jewish neighbors in more than four hundred communities in Western Galicia. The restoration of peace and order by the Austrian authorities merely

64. Ibid., 2444.

65. Ibid., 2354; 2435; 2437.

66. Paragraph 10 of the fundamental laws prohibited the violation of the secrecy of letters and allowed the seizure of letters only by an order of a judge, see "Nr. 142. Staatsgrundgesetz vom 21. December 1867," *RGBl* (1867): 394–396, esp. §10, 395.

67. The National Archives in Kraków, C. K. Dyrekcja Policji w Krakowie (DPKr) 75, L. 128 pr./900, no pagination (henceforth: police file).

68. Araten Warsaw file, 2530–2531. The court also prepared a German translation of the letter for the Austrian authorities.

tamped down the tensions between the parties but did not extinguish them.[69] Michalina's disappearance and the subsequent official search instigated by her father was manipulated by different parties to advance their agendas, threatening the fragile interreligious peace.

The official investigation into Michalina's whereabouts was conducted under the authority of Stanisław Doliński, the Kraków public prosecutor (*Oberstaatsanwalt*). Its aim was to find out who was responsible for her disappearance and where she was being kept. Parallel to the official search, Araten conducted his own private investigation employing three approaches: offering monetary rewards to people who would provide him with information that might lead to finding his daughter, lobbying Austrian government ministers to pressure the Kraków authorities to complete their investigation, and mobilizing the Viennese liberal and socialist press to advocate for his cause. Araten chose to put his trust in the liberal and socialist camps and their organs, eschewing the traditional political alliance in Galicia between Orthodox Jews and Polish Catholic conservatives, an alliance that had held for more than two decades.[70] In Araten's struggle against the Felician Sisters' convent, his natural allies appeared to him to be the anti-clerical liberals and socialists rather than the conservatives. This choice made it clear to the local Polish authorities in Kraków that Araten lacked confidence in them.

The official investigation started on February 5, 1900, after Araten submitted a complaint to the office of the public prosecutor in Kraków. He also sent a similar complaint to the Viennese Justice Ministry. Araten related that after the convent superior (*Kloster-Oberin*, presumably Vicar General Marya Honorata Kummer) did not allow the parents to meet their daughter, he approached the police for help, whereupon commissioner Tomasik went to the convent to talk to Michalina, who informed him that she wanted to convert to the Catholic faith. Araten further alleged that Zagrabińska told Tomasik that she feared neither the court nor the public prosecutor and declared that she would drag out the matter until Michalina was fourteen years old and thus legally eligible to choose her religion. In the meantime, she would arrange for Michalina to disappear. According to Araten, Zagrabińska said this in the presence of his father Marcus Araten, Tomasik, and Rzeszódko.[71] Following this complaint

69. Unowsky, *The Plunder*, 180–185.

70. On the political alliance between the Orthodox and the conservative Poles see Manekin, "Orthodox Jewry in Kraków," 174–180.

71. Araten Warsaw file, 2435.

and the request of the Viennese Justice Ministry, Kraków's public prosecutor instructed the criminal court to open a preliminary investigation to clarify the facts. All relevant police files were subsequently transferred to the court to assist its investigation.[72]

It is important to note that unlike parents of other runaways who sued a third party for enticing their daughter to leave home and enter the convent, which would have been a violation of paragraph 96 of the Penal Code, Araten didn't sue the washerwoman or Dr. Müller. He preferred that the public prosecutor investigate the conduct of all the parties involved. The Austrian office of the public prosecutor was directly subordinate to the Austrian Minister of Justice and independent of the courts. Its major role was to investigate suspicions of criminal offenses that were brought to its knowledge and were of public interest. The public prosecutor first conducted a preliminary investigation to determine and clarify the facts of the case, namely, to find out who were the offenders and their accomplices and to gather evidence against them. The preliminary investigation would be carried out by an investigative judge who acted in the name of the criminal court with the assistance of the public prosecutor. If the preliminary investigation determined that there was enough evidence for indictment, the case would move on to a trial in court.[73] It seems that Araten preferred the option of the public prosecutor because of its direct link to the Viennese Justice Ministry, an office he believed would be more sympathetic to his case.

The Justice Minister took Araten's complaint seriously and asked the Kraków public prosecutor to send him weekly reports about the progress of the preliminary investigation. Soon after the beginning of the investigation, the public prosecutor wrote to his superiors in Vienna that abductions (*Entführungen*)[74] of Jewish girls from their homes and housing them in convents for the purpose of conversion occurred frequently in Galicia, but the authorities were unable to cope with this phenomenon.[75] The conversion of Jewish girls was a complex and complicated issue because it was interpreted differently by Christians and Jews. Every action taken by the authorities on behalf of the Jewish parents clashed with the religious belief of the local

---

72. Ibid., 2618.

73. "Nr. 119. Strafprocessordnung," *RGBl* (1873): 397–501, esp. §§29–37, 404–407.

74. The legal term "abduction" in such cases was understood as enticing a minor to leave her parental home.

75. Araten Warsaw file, 2614–2615.

Christian population that such an abduction, carried out with the consent of the abductee, granted salvation to the convert, and was therefore ethical rather than criminal. Since this conviction was shared by all classes of the Christian population, it undermined the energy of the local authorities when dealing with conversion cases. Furthermore, the local population believed that because the law permitted mature individuals to change their faith, and since a Jewish child who had converted to Christianity would not find any support in his or her parental home, either ethically or educationally, the father's legal custody over his minor child (defined as younger than twenty-four years) should be revoked. According to the public prosecutor, while this type of thinking existed for centuries, it had become even stronger with the rise of the anti-Semitic current in the Habsburg Empire. He then concluded: "I think I must say that I cannot promise much of a vigorous action, even if no doubt such an action must be initiated."[76] This admission of the complicating factors at the outset of the investigation shows that the Araten case was not viewed in official circles merely as a private issue concerning a Kraków Jewish family but rather as an example of a widespread phenomenon that involved deeply held religious beliefs at a particularly sensitive time, i.e., just a little more than a year after the 1898 anti-Jewish violent attacks.

This does not mean that the investigation was not conducted according to the rules. All procedures were followed as required, and more than 150 individuals were interrogated, including nuns of all ranks. Additionally, every allegation made by Araten in the press or in other venues was investigated by the court. What the investigation lacked was vigor and a sense of urgency, despite the repeated requests of the Justice Minister to conduct a speedy and robust investigation. Distrust of Araten's many allegations, especially those directed against local respected institutions or members of the Polish elite, was another factor affecting the attitude of the local authorities.

To aid in the search, Araten offered a reward of 1,000 crowns for information leading to finding his daughter, and he hired a Viennese detective.[77] Informants claimed that they saw Michalina in various locations: Wola Justowska, Stanisławów, Bieńczyce, Mariampol (district of Stanisławów), Kęty, the train station in Buczacz en route from Stanisławów to Jazłowiec, Niżniów,

---

76. Ibid., 2615–2616.

77. Ibid., 2457. This offer was mocked in a Kraków satirical journal which promised to share the reward with any reader who would report such leads to the journal, see *Bocian*, March 1, 1900, 10.

Łagiewniki, Staniątki, Morawica, Bieliny, Załośce, and on the train from Kraków to Rzeszów. According to Zygmunt Rosner, a relative of Araten who assisted him in his search, Araten received many letters informing him of locations where his daughter was allegedly being held. People claimed to have spotted her in different places at the same time, or in places that didn't exist on any map, always accompanied with a request for reward money.[78] Some places were in the Kraków area and others were farther away. Based on these tips, dozens of nuns and other witnesses—including the informants who were identified—were interrogated, but Michalina was not found in any of the convents named. Araten appeared to believe most of the informants, even those who kept bargaining with him about the sum of their rewards. In order to make sense of the information pointing to her being spotted in different locations, Araten created a narrative according to which his daughter was transferred from one convent to another every time her hiding place was found out. This narrative strengthened the public image of Michalina as an imprisoned victim held by church authorities in hiding until she was fourteen years old. A different narrative was constructed by Araten's private Viennese detective, Johann Müller, who received 1,000 crowns for his services.[79] According to his investigations, Michalina was picked up at the convent by Dr. Philipp Müller on the day of her disappearance. They drove in a carriage to the Hotel de Saxe (Hotel Saski) in Kraków and later boarded a train on their way to the Grand Hotel in Lwów. But the official interrogations of the carriage driver and the personnel of both hotels revealed that neither a young woman who looked like Michalina, nor a man who looked like Dr. Müller (who sported a "considerable big black moustache and a black wedge-shaped pointed full beard"), had been guests in either hotel.[80]

"The Secular Authority Ends at the Convent's Walls"

As part of his lobbying efforts, Araten traveled to Vienna with his Kraków relative, Sygmunt Rosner. Together with Alfred Stern (later the president of the Viennese Jewish community), on February 13 they met the newly appointed Austrian Prime Minister Ernest von Koerber, who also served as the Interior

---

78. Araten court file, 232. Testimony of Zygmunt Rosner from May 13, 1900.
79. Araten Warsaw file, 2458.
80. Ibid., 2387–2389; 2396; 2431; 2447–2448; 2517; 2534–2535; 2588–2589.

Minister.[81] The next day, this time accompanied by Josef Kareis, a Jewish Social Democrat and parliament member,[82] Araten and Rosner met the Justice
Minister Alois Spens von Booden. Both ministers seemed sympathetic to
Araten's plight and promised to look for clarity in the case. The two later also
met with Dr. Leonhard Piętak, professor of Roman law in Lwów, who had
recently been appointed Minister for Galician Affairs. According to reports
leaked to the press, Piętak remarked to Araten that he had no administrative
means at his disposal to solve his problem because "the secular authority ends
at the convent's walls."[83] The liberal *Neue Freie Presse* in its evening edition of
February 16 described Piętak's attitude as reserved and lacking any commitment to solve the problem.[84]

The remarks attributed by the press to Piętak had the potential to turn into
a political firestorm, and shortly after their publication, Benno Straucher, the
Jewish parliament member from Bukovina, submitted an interpellation with
Kareis and Ignacy Daszyński (one of the cofounders of the Polish Social
Democratic party in Galicia in 1892) to the Ministers of Justice and the Interior
concerning Michalina.[85] Straucher was not a Social Democrat, but in this case
he cooperated with the anti-clericals Kareis and Daszyński, who used the
whole affair to support their opposition to what they viewed as the privileged
power of the Catholic Church. The signatories on the interpellation requested
to know what the ministers intended to do on the matter and how they would
ensure that the law is not violated in the future.

While Straucher did not mention Piętak by name in his interpellation, another Jewish parliament member, Dr. Emil Byk, the pro-Polish president of
the Lwów Jewish community, prepared an interpellation which was first

81. TsDIAL, f. 146, o. 4, s. 2427, in microfilm copy in CAHJP, HM2/9171.1 (henceforth Araten
Gubernium file), 21.

82. On Kareis, see Singer and Ysaye, "Kareis, Josef."

83. "An den Pforten des Klosters," *Czernowitzer Presse*, February 15, 1900, 1–2. The paper
wrote: "We did not hear that Galician convents have special privileges in the state," and it is the
right and the obligation of the authorities to investigate whether there was something unlawful
going on behind the convent walls. See also "Die Krakauer Klostergeschichte," *Bukowinaer
Rundschau*, February 20, 1900, 3.

84. "Die Krakauer Klostergeschichte," *Neue Freie Presse, Abendblatt*, February 16, 1900, 1. See
also Buchen, *Antisemitismus in Galizien*, 305.

85. "Interpellation des Abgeordneten Dr. Straucher und Genossen an ihre Excellenzen die
k. k. Minister der Justiz und des Innern," *Stenographische Protokolle* (1900): 2133. See also "Eine
Rede des Abg. Dr. Straucher," *Die Neuzeit*, March 21, 1900, 120–121.

discussed in a meeting in the Polish Club where Minister Piętak was present.[86] Byk mentioned that Michalina was not yet fourteen, and repeated her father's claim that she was led to the Felician Sisters' convent by the family's washer-woman.[87] He asked Piętak whether he had made the statement attributed to him and if so, how it corresponded to existing Austrian laws. Piętak, in his response, denied the "absurd" statement attributed to him and asserted that the authorities were doing everything they could in the Araten case.[88] The Social Democrat *Arbeiter-Zeitung* was not impressed by Byk's intervention. It referred to him as a "patented Jewish representative" who had intervened in this case too late, namely, after supporting Piętak's candidacy in the recent parliamentary elections against that of the Social Democrat Daszyński, know-ing full well of Piętak's anti-Semitic affectations.[89] The *Neue Freie Presse* pub-lished a front-page article about what happened in the Polish Club, stating in the first sentence that "the shameful question of whether we live in a consti-tutional state, where the laws of Austria apply in Galicia, has often been raised in recent weeks." Turning the Araten story into a test case for the rule of law in Austria, the paper concluded: "If we want to become a cultured and a wel-fare state, we must above all be a constitutional state, and as long as a convent's superior is above the law, that is not what we are."[90]

In response to Piętak's denial of the statement attributed to him, Kareis sent a letter to the *Neue Freie Presse* insisting that the Minister for Galician Affairs did indeed make this statement; his rather belated disavowal did not change in the least the regrettable fact that viewpoints of this kind were nurtured and spoken by a minister in a constitutional state.[91] On the same day, February 26,

---

86. "Die Krakauer Klosteraffaire: Eine Interpellation im Polenclub (Original-Bericht des 'Neues Wiener Journal')," *Neues Wiener Journal*, February 25, 1900, 4–5. See also "Die Krakauer Klosteraffaire im Polen-Club," *Neue Freie Presse*, February 25, 1900, 4; "Die Krakauer Kloster-Affaire im Polen-Club," *Bukowinaer Rundschau*, February 27, 1900, 1.

87. Interestingly, in a public talk on the Araten case and other similar cases, Julius Ofner doubted the assertion of Israel Araten that the washerwoman led Michalina to the convent. It is difficult to believe, he said, that this poor woman had such an influence on a daughter of a rich family, see "Kinderraub in Galizien," *Dr. Bloch's Oesterreichische Wochenschrift*, November 2, 1900, 780–785, esp. 781.

88. For Byk's interpellation and Piętak's response see "Rechtsschutz in Galizien," *Genossen-schafts- und Vereins- Zeitung*, March 1, 1900, 2. This newspaper was published in Czernowitz.

89. "Die Krakauer Klostergeschichte," *Arbeiter-Zeitung*, February 25, 1900, 6.

90. "Wien, 24 Februar," *Neue Freie Presse*, February 25, 1900, 1–2.

91. "Die Krakauer Kloster Affaire," *Neue Freie Presse*, February 26, 1900, 4.

the *Abendpost* (the supplement of the independent *Wiener Zeitung* published in the state's printing house) published on its front page Piętak's explanation, repeating his declaration that he did not utter the statement that was repeatedly attributed to him: "[His] Excellency [Piętak] had only replied to a request to have the convent searched, a request made by the above-named state council deputy, that in consideration of the convent rules, the undertaking of a search in a convent of nuns would meet with considerable difficulties.[92] Unimpressed by this explanation, the *Neue Freie Presse* noted that a search could only be undertaken if there existed suspicion of a crime or delinquency, but that it was unaware that there were special provisions for convents in such a case.[93] Araten's cooperation with the socialist Kareis, and the press accounts favorable to his side of the story in the *Neue Freie Presse*, might have won sympathy for him among Viennese liberals, but the public denunciations of a highly respected Polish minister could not have garnered him much support in Kraków, where conservatives were particularly strong and influential. This was not the only time when Araten's efforts to garner support for his case had the effect of costing him what may have been important allies.

92. "Wien, 26 Februar," *Abendpost,* February 26, 1900, 1. The Catholic Viennese anti-Semitic newspapers defended Piętak as well as the Felician Sisters' convent, see "Der Polenclub gegen die Obstruction und über den Fall Araten," *Das Vaterland,* February 25, 1900, 3; "Die Klosteraffaire in Krakau," *Reichspost,* February 26, 1900, 9. Referring to what became known as white slavery, the paper mocked Jews for spending so much energy in helping one Jew and protesting against the abduction of one girl, while at the same time remaining silent about the hundreds of abductions of girls through Jewish dealers and pimps: "Of course, these robbed and disgracefully sold girls are just Christian girls. That explains everything." On the involvement of Jews in white slavery in Galicia, see Stauter-Halsted, *The Devil's Chain,* 122–136; Bristow, *Prostitution and Prejudice,* 67–75.

93. "Zur Krakaue Kloster Affaire," *Neue Freie Presse,* February 27, 1900, 5. Another Social Democrat parliament member, Eduard Zeller, referred to Piętak's infamous statement in an interpellation he submitted to the Justice Minister on another matter. Zeller rebuked Piętak, asserting that his statement was more appropriate for the Middle Ages rather than for the threshold of the twentieth century. See "Interpellation des Abgeordneten Zeller und Genossen an den Herrn Justizminister betreffend die Confiscationpraxis in Brüx," *Stenographische Protokolle* (1900): 2546–2548, esp. 2547–2548. Daszyński was one of the deputies signed on this interpellation. An interpellation on the Kareis-Piętak controversy was submitted to the parliament by Zeller and Josef Steiner, another Social Democrat deputy, demanding to determine which one of them spoke the truth, see ibid., 2561–2562. The motivation here seems to be protecting the Social Democrat Kareis.

Interpellation

des

Abgeordneten Dr. Straucher und Genossen an Ihre Excellenzen die Herren k. k. Minister der Justiz und des Innern.

„Die minderjährige Michalina Araten, mosaischer Confession, ist seit dem 30. December 1899 aus dem Hause ihres Vaters, Israel Araten in Krakau, verschwunden und hat ohne dessen Vorwissen und ohne dessen Zustimmung im Kloster der Felicianer-Nonnen in Krakau Aufnahme gefunden. Seither wird Michalina Araten gegen den Willen ihrer Eltern und gesetzlichen Vertreter, daher widerrechtlich, in diesem Kloster zurückgehalten und ihre Herausgabe dem sie wiederholt reclamirenden Vater gegen positives Gesetz und natürliches Recht verweigert.

Alle bisherigen Bemühungen des Vaters, mit Hilfe der Gerichte und Polizei die Herausgabe seines Kindes zu erwirken, sind erfolglos geblieben, ja selbst eine Zusammenkunft und Unterredung mit seiner Tochter ist dem Vater nicht gewährt worden.

Nun ist, Zeitungsberichten zufolge, Michalina Araten aus dem Felicianerinnen-Kloster verschwunden und wird ihr gegenwärtiger Aufenthaltsort geheim gehalten.

Angesichts dieses schreienden Willküractes und des unerklärlichen Umstandes, dass die berufenen staatlichen Behörden die in diesem Falle dringend gebotene Energie vermissen lassen, stellen die Unterzeichneten die dringende Anfrage:

„„1. Was gedenken die k. k. Minister der Justiz und des Innern zu veranlassen, dass dem verletzten Gesetze Sühne verschafft und die Herausgabe der Michalina Araten sowie ihre Rückübergabe an ihren Vater ermöglicht werde?

2. Gedenken die genannten k. k. Minister die Schuldtragenden zu eruiren und selbe der gesetzlichen Strafe zuzuführen?

3. Was gedenken die genannten k. k. Minister zu veranlassen, damit in Hinkunft solchen Willküracten und Gesetzesverletzungen begegnet werde?““

Daszyński.
Berner.
Schrammel.
Dr. Verkauf.
Hannich.
Zeller.
Resel.
Dr. Lecher.
Nowak.
Auspitz.

Dr. Straucher.
Kareis.
Dr. Groß.
Dr. Kopp.
Hybeš.
Dr. Menger.
Dr. Knoll.
Dr. Demel.
Herbst.
Röhling.
Dr. Nitsche."

FIGURE 2.3. Interpellation of the Austrian parliament member Benno Straucher regarding the disappearance of Michalina Araten. Courtesy of the Central Archives of Historical Records in Warsaw (AGAD), sygn. f. 305, s. 287.

"Forced Entry into the Convent"

The attacks on Piętak in the liberal press and the subsequent criticism in the liberal and socialist press of Galician convents as being beyond the reach of the law emboldened Israel Araten, who tried to circumvent the public prosecutor in his efforts to find his daughter. After being tipped off that Michalina was in the Capuchin convent in Kęty,[94] Araten sent his non–Hasidic looking relative Rosner to try to attain permission to search the convent. Rosner approached the district administrator of Biała on February 20 on behalf of Araten and told him that the latter received information that Michalina was being kept hidden in the Capuchin convent. The district administrator then communicated to the municipal council in Kęty that it should provide to Araten police assistance in his search after his daughter. This communication was apparently wrongly interpreted by the mayor of Kęty, who proceeded to instruct the police commissioner Stanisław Sowiński to conduct a search of the convent together with a local gendarme and Israel Araten. The search was carried out as instructed on February 21, with the gendarme waiting outside the convent gate.[95] Michalina was not found there.

The search wouldn't have attracted much attention had not the *Głos Narodu*, a Kraków Catholic anti-Semitic newspaper, brought it to the public's attention a week later under the provocative title: "The Jew's Forced Entry into the Convent." The report claimed that the "Jew," i.e., Araten, inspected the whole convent from top to bottom and demanded to open all doors and closets while uttering words desecrating Christianity. Only after he searched all the nuns' cells and all the rooms and bedrooms did he say that he believed that his daughter was not hiding there. The people of Kęty could not believe that such an event was possible in a Christian state following orders of officials who served a Christian ruler. The editors then called the Galician political representatives to demand clarification from the government and see to it that Sowiński and Araten were brought to justice.[96] A few days later, the Lwów

94. Kęty was a small town in the Biała district composed of 5,235 inhabitants, of which 4,873 were Roman Catholic, 365 Jews, and 7 Protestant, see *Szematyzm Królestwa Galicyi*, vol. 1, 366.

95. Araten Gubernium file, 38–38b.

96. "The Jew's Forced Entry into the Convent," *Głos Narodu*, February 26, 1900, 2 [Polish]. This newspaper continued to write about the case with harsh anti-Jewish rhetoric. The authorities censored parts of a lead article because of that, see "The Crime of Public Violence," *Głos Narodu*, March 5, 1900, 1 [Polish].

liberal *Dziennik Polski* reprinted the article, albeit with the slightly less provocative title: "The Forced Entry into the Convent."[97]

The conservative Kraków paper, *Czas*, followed suit and discussed the story in a lead article. It emphasized that the Austrian constitution guaranteed domicile protection (*Hausrecht*) against trespassing, and it allowed house searches only in cases where there was a well-grounded suspicion of a crime.[98] Since there was no real basis for suspicion in this case, the search constituted an illegal abuse of the convent, especially because, in addition to a police officer, an individual from another faith was allowed to roam within its walls. The paper added that the increasing anarchism, socialism, and anti-clericalism that found expression in all sorts of "convent stories" in the "radical newspapers in Vienna" was responsible for initiating a Kulturkampf in Galicia, which was nothing less than a surrender to the "red press." Although the paper emphasized that it was a fierce opponent of anti-Semitism, it felt that the Araten case had not been fairly reported in the Viennese press. Nobody had kidnapped Michalina and nobody locked her up; on the contrary, it was she who ran away from her parental home.[99]

The Viennese liberal and anti-clerical newspapers to which *Czas* referred were the *Neue Freie Presse* and the Socialist *Arbeiter-Zeitung*, which published reports about the Kraków convent that accused the enormously powerful Catholic Church in Galicia of disregarding state laws.[100] *Czas*'s earlier efforts to provide a different narrative based on local sources was disregarded by the liberal press and quoted only in the Viennese Catholic and anti-Semitic

---

97. "The Forced Entry into the Convent," *Dziennik Polski*, March 1, 1900, 2 [Polish]. Interestingly, this newspaper also commented that the authorities must bring to justice those involved in the search in order to calm the great anger of the Christian population and raised the hope that this would not be delayed.

98. The original law of the protection of domicile was first published in 1862 and then included in the fundamental laws of the Austrian 1867 constitution, see "Nr. 88. Gesetz vom 27. October 1862," *RGBl* (1862): 245–246; "Nr. 142. Staatsgrundgesetz vom 21. December 1867," *RGBl* (1867): 394–396, esp. §9, 395. See also "Strafprocessordnung," §139, 427.

99. "Kraków, March 5," *Czas*, March 6, 1900, 1 [Polish].

100. See for example "Die Krakauer Klostergeschichte," *Neue Freie Presse*, February 14, 1900, 5; "Wieder eine mysteriöse Klostergeschichte," *Neue Freie Presse*, Abendblatt, February 6, 1900, front page; "Die Krakauer Klosteraffaire im Polen-Club," " *Neue Freie Presse*, February 25, 1900, 4; "Die Krakauer Kloster Affaire," *Neue Freie Presse*, February 26, 1900, 4; "Zur Krakaue Kloster Affaire," *Neue Freie Presse*, February 27, 1900, 5; "Die Krakauer Klostergeschichte," *Arbeiter-Zeitung*, February 18, 1900, 7; "Die Krakauer Klostergeschichte," *Arbeiter-Zeitung*, February 25, 1900, 6.

press.[101] The Socialist *Arbeiter-Zeitung* even accused the *Czas* of representing the clerical camp and being too sympathetic toward the convent.[102]

The reports about Kęty in the Polish press were quickly manipulated by conservative Polish politicians, who rushed to submit interpellations in the parliament as part of their struggle against the anti-clerical liberal and socialist camps. The first interpellation was submitted in the upper house on March 6 by Count Stanisław Tarnowski and Dr. Zoll. Tarnowski, a moderate conservative, was a former rector of the Jagiellonian University and chairman of its literature department, as well as president of the Polish Academy of Sciences. The interpellation emphasized that the search in Kęty was carried out against the law and convent regulations, "especially the entry to the convent enclosure by an Israelite."[103] The second interpellation was submitted in the lower house by the deputy Andrzej Szponder, a member of the Galician Christian People's Party.[104] It used alarmist language, threatening that if these Jewish acts of violence went unpunished "one seriously has to fear that the Christian population will again turn to self-defense, through which law and order and the public peace will be badly endangered."[105] On March 28, the Polish members of the Galician Sejm submitted an interpellation to the Minister of the Interior demanding the investigation and punishment of the persons involved in the search, namely Sowiński and Araten. Almost all members of the Sejm signed it.[106]

101. See "About the Escape of Michalina Araten," *Czas*, February 16, 1900, 2 [Polish]; "Wieder einmal eine Klostergeschichte," *Das Vaterland*, February 17, 1900, 3; "Die Krakauer Klostergeschichte," *Reichspost*, February 18, 1900, 10.

102. "Die Krakauer Klostergeschichte," *Arbeiter-Zeitung*, February 18, 1900, 7. In response to the Czas, the paper wrote that even if Michalina were fourteen already, "it would be barbaric to leave a child, who demonstrated an affinity for a faith that differs from the parents, in the power of her religious fanaticism without any protection."

103. "Interpellation an Seine Excellenz den Herrn Ministerpräsidenten und an Seine Excellenz den Herrn Justizminister," 6. Sitzung der XVI. Session am 6. März 1900, *Stenographische Protokolle* (1900): 89.

104. Unowsky, *The Plunder*, 44.

105. "Interpellation des Abgeordneten Szponder und Genossen an Seine Excellenz den Herrn Minister des Innern, betreffend das Überfallen des Klosters der Schwestern Felicianerinnen in Kenty am 21. Februar l. J. seitens des hiesigen Polizeiinspectors Stanislaus Sowiński, eines Gendarmen, des Juden Israel Araten und des Staatsanwalt Dr. Rosner aus Krakau," 40. Sitzung der XVI. Session am 3. März 1900, *Stenographische Protokolle* (1899): 2619–2620. See also Buchen, *Antisemitismus in Galizien*, 306; 313–314.

106. *Haus-, Hof- und Staatsarchiv*, Vienna (HHStA), k. k. Ministerium des Innern, Nr. 1110, Präsidium, ad 1938–900. M. J; Nr. 1488, ZL. 3166/pr.

In an effort to calm tensions, the Minister of the Interior requested Leon Piniński, the governor of Galicia and a former professor of Roman Law, to conduct an investigation of the search in Kęty. As it turned out, the Polish press was wrong in its reports and Araten, according to the priest and deacon Maciej Warmuz, who discussed this with the convent, "behaved politely and decently, and even asked for forgiveness at the beginning of the search. He was very touched at the entrance to the conservatory and said that he believed all these women and did not want to continue the search."[107] Following the investigation Sowiński received a punishment of two days' imprisonment and a fine of 20 crowns, and the mayor of Kęty received a punishment of ten days' imprisonment.[108]

Emerging unblemished after the Kęty event, on April 26 Israel Araten was granted an audience with Emperor Francis Joseph to explain his situation and to ask for the emperor's assistance, a most unusual meeting for a Hasidic Jew. The emperor said that he was informed about Araten's daughter but not about the progress of the investigation. When the emperor asked whether the authorities were doing their job, Araten replied that the Minister of Justice had given detailed directives, but they had not yielded any result. The emperor also asked whether Araten himself had a theory about where Michalina may be, and the father responded that he believed that she was still in the country. He also added that his wife was very sick, and that an unfavorable answer about his daughter would be the cause of her death. When he fell at the emperor's feet begging for help, the emperor asked him to get up, saying: "I will give new directions to the authorities so that they should fulfill their duties and obligations."[109]

107. Araten Gubernium file, 50–51b, 79–80. Piniński's response was quoted in the Galician Sejm on April 4, but the exoneration of the district administrator, an Austrian appointment, was criticized, see *Stenograficzne sprawozdania z piątej sesyi siódmego peryodu Sejmu krajowego Królestwa Galicyi i Lodomeryi wraz z Wielkiem Księstwem Krakowskiem* (1900): 287. During the investigation, Israel Araten went to meet Piniński together with the Lwów rabbi, Isaac Schmelkes, probably to make sure he was not incriminated. Piniński assured him that he would not allow any illegal acts to take place, see "Die Entführungs-Affaire der Michalina Araten," *Neue freie Presse*, March 30, 1900, 5.

108. Araten Gubernium file, 70–71. See also "Zur affaire Araten," *Neue Freie Presse*, April 29, 1900, 10. This short notice was the only reference in the paper to what happened in Kęty.

109. "Audienz des Herrn Araten beim Kaiser," *Neue Freie Presse*, Abendblatt, April 26, 1900, front page.

Offending the Polish Nobility

Encouraged by the emperor's promise, Araten continued to push the limits of his actions, this time publicly accusing Róża Tarnowska (born countess Róża Maria Branicka), wife of Stanisław Tarnowski, of being involved in his daughter's disappearance.[110] Tarnowski submitted one of the interpellations concerning the search in Kęty just three months beforehand. On May 11, 1900, when the protests about Kęty finally died out, Araten asked the editor of *Słowo Polskie*, the organ of the Lwów democrats, to publish his letter detailing countess Tranowska's involvement. According to the letter, he was informed five weeks earlier by a certain individual that when he happened to be at the home of Tarnowska (the Tarnowskis lived in a palace on Szlak Street), he heard her asking two nuns present there what will happen with the unfortunate Michalina. The nuns answered that Michalina missed her parents and wanted to return home. Tarnowska then commented, "but she is in Wielowicz." In order to verify this, Araten sent a relative of his to check this out, and, indeed, she informed him that she saw his daughter there twice. He then traveled there with his wife and an assistant and approached the district administrator to get him involved, but the latter advised him to talk to the district judge Edmund Hartman. Araten met with Hartman, telling him that he was not requesting a search in the convent since he knew for certain that his daughter was there, but rather that his daughter be released. Hartman treated him harshly, refused to offer any help, and suggested that Araten approach the local public prosecutor and ask him to issue a decision on the matter. He added that they would delay any decision as they did in Kraków. After such an answer from a legal authority, said Araten, he had no choice but to return to Kraków.[111]

The man who gave Araten the information about the meeting at Tarnowska's house was Piotr Wiącek, a day laborer from Dzików, where another branch of the Tarnowski family owned the land.[112] When Wiącek was interrogated on July 5, he said that the Araten affair was well known to the public since it

110. On Róża Tarnowska, see Tarnowski, *The Last Mazurka*, 13–14.

111. "Just Araten. We Received the Following," *Słowo Polskie*, May 11, 1900, 4 [Polish]. See also the organ of the Galician Social Democrats, *Naprzód*, May 12, 1900, 5. About a week later, Araten wrote a letter to Emperor Francis Joseph in which he repeated the story about Tarnowska and Hartman. He added that according to new information he received, his daughter was already kidnapped from Wielowicz and transferred to a convent in Bieliny near Ulanów, see Araten Gubernium file, 110–111.

112. Tarnowski, *The Last Mazurka*, 82–85.

was written about in all newspapers and that many rumors were circulating about it. He denied informing Araten that he was present at Tarnowska's home or that he heard a conversation between her and two nuns and confessed that he did not know Tarnowska, never spoke to her, and never listened to any of her conversations. He added that Araten probably invented the story himself and admitted that he heard that Araten was paying money in exchange for information and so it was possible that when he met Araten, he told him that he had some information. He remembered that Araten gave him two złotys and asked him to sign a protocol that said something about a countess and Araten's daughter, and either he invented the story or Araten misunderstood him. Perhaps he was even a little drunk because of the few vodka glasses that Araten offered him. Araten also told him that he would travel with him to Vienna to meet a minister.[113]

Róża Tarnowska was interrogated on November 11, 1900; she was forty-six at the time. She claimed that she did not know Michalina, had never seen her, and knew nothing about her whereabouts. She also did not know Israel Araten or Piotr Wiącek, who apparently gave the information about her to Araten. The request that she should try to remember a meeting that had never happened upset her, and she asked to delete from the protocol some of the expressions she had used during her interrogation. She also asked to receive a copy of the protocol.[114] The information about Tarnowska's involvement was given to Araten, as he himself testified, when he happened to meet Wiącek on the street by chance.[115] This was clearly a non-credible source, since the likelihood of a poor manual laborer being present in a conversation between countess Tarnowska and the nuns was rather slim.

Araten's relative, the nineteen-year-old Anna Weinreb, who was sent by him to Wielowicz to check whether Michalina was in the convent there, testified that she had spotted Michalina on Sunday, May 6, when the latter accompanied other nuns on their way from the convent to the church. When she was confronted with other testimonies, including that of Israel Araten, Weinreb retracted some parts of her testimony.[116] Araten's allegations against Edmund Hartman didn't go well either; Hartman denied them. He also demanded that Israel Araten be punished for the lies he wrote about him to the Interior

113. Araten court file, 304.
114. Ibid., 360.
115. Ibid., 34.
116. Ibid., 227.

Minister and which damaged his professional reputation.[117] Interestingly, in his interrogation, Araten didn't repeat his allegation that Hartman told him that they would delay any decision on Michalina, but instead related that Hartman told him that he would not offer him any help, and he should go to the public prosecutor.[118] The many contradictions between the testimonies rendered the whole story problematic. Despite that, many nuns of the convent in Wielowicz were interrogated, including the Mother Superior, which led to the conclusion that Michalina was never there.[119]

Why did Araten choose to broadcast his allegations against a powerful Kraków figure like Róża Tarnowska in a popular Polish daily rather than just passing them to the public prosecutor or the police? While Araten distrusted the local authorities, his bold behavior seems like an act of desperation, a risky step that disregarded all possible repercussions. Perhaps he was inclined to believe informants' stories about his daughter being held in different convents, because it was less painful than believing that she chose to leave her family and convert to Roman Catholicism. Perhaps he was concerned for the reputation of his family. The Tarnowska story, unlike all the other ones, quoted Michalina as saying that she missed her family and wanted to return to Kraków. This powerful image contradicted those articles in the Hebrew press that viewed Michalina as a runaway who wished to convert, and even blamed the Araten family for that. *Ha-Magid* claimed already in early March 1900 that Michalina ran away from her home in order to convert and marry the military doctor with whom she had a "long-term" correspondence. It blamed the norms of female education common among Galician Jews as responsible for that and called upon Orthodox Jews to consider the Araten case as an example and a lesson of the results of such a flawed education.[120]

The Galician Jewish Orthodox newspaper *Maḥazikei Ha-Dat* responded to *Ha-Magid* in a special article published in the same month. The author of the article identified himself as a close friend of the Araten family who initially avoided saying a word about the affair because of the respect he had for the family. He didn't want to pour salt on their wounded hearts since they were already the talk of the town, and since their daughter ignored all their pleas, saying that her soul was attached to the Christian religion. Still, the writer

117. Ibid., 312.
118. Ibid., 34.
119. Ibid., 246; 247; 248; 249; 250; 251.
120. Lazar, "Precious Out of the Vile," *Ha-Magid,* March 1, 1900, 100–101 [Hebrew].

insisted that her parents had provided Michalina with a sufficient Jewish religious education at home, and so it was not for lack of religious knowledge that she decided to run away. The problem was that she had been overfed with sciences of the gentiles, and these led her to join bad company. In an effort to bring her back to the right path, her parents used beatings and lashes, as a result of which she ran away, leaving an affluent comfortable life in order to take revenge on them.[121] The shame associated with voluntary conversion had the potential of ruining a family, especially when it came to the marriage prospects of the siblings. Indeed, as late as December 1900, Araten admitted that the "crime of enticing his underage daughter [to convert] covered all his family with shame and disgrace and put him under the pillory, where he still stands."[122] So it was not just his daughter that he was trying to save, but also his own reputation and the reputation of his family.

Final Efforts

Ten days before Michalina's fourteenth birthday according to the Tuszyn proof of birth document, the Democratic parliament deputy Ferdinand Kronawetter submitted an interpellation in the lower house to the Ministers of Justice and the Interior requesting to solve the Araten case. Kronawetter was the only non-Jewish liberal deputy to speak out on this issue in the parliament, as the others avoided taking sides because they didn't want to be suspected of philo-semitism.[123] His interpellation, which clearly favored the kidnapping narrative, retold the story of what happened to Michalina since she left her home, mentioning that she was educated in a private German girls' school administered by "Rehfeld," a Protestant woman, and emphasizing that Michalina strictly observed all the Jewish rituals at home. The information about Michalina's school education, or the headmistress's name, was never mentioned in public before, and was probably meant to discredit allegations in the press that Michalina's education was responsible for her desire to convert to Catholicism. The interpellation alleged that Israel Araten heard his daughter sobbing in the convent and exclaiming that she wanted to return home; that on January 24, 1900, a police commissioner had recorded a protocol with Michalina in which

121. "The Tongue that Speaks Proud Things," *Maḥazikei Ha-Dat,* March 23, 1900, 2 [Hebrew].

122. Araten court file, 364.

123. Kolmer, *Parlament und Verfassung,* vol. 8, 51–53, esp. 52.

she had said that she required to see her father; that Anna Rosenblum, a young
Jewish woman who left the convent on the same day as Michalina had said that
Michalina looked miserable and constantly begged to be released; and that
after Michalina's disappearance from the convent, the police recorded a protocol according to which the Mother Superior declared that she wanted "to
vouch for the child."[124]

The Justice Minister forwarded the interpellation to the public prosecutor
in Kraków for his comments, who in his response said that Araten had never
alleged to the police that he heard his daughter crying in the convent and asking to return to her home.[125] On the contrary, Michalina declared in front of
Commissioner Tomasik and Rzeszódko that she refused to see her father and
it was Rzeszódko who tried to convince her to speak to him. As for the protocol from January 24, according to which she required to see her father, this was
not true either, and no evidence was provided to back this allegation. Additionally, the Mother Superior was never questioned by the police, so what the
interpellation said about her could not have been true.[126] As for the allegation
that Michalina was transferred from one convent to another, apart from very
vague rumors, no actual evidence was found to support that.[127]

124. "Interpellation des Abgeordneten Dr. Kronawetter und Genossen an die Herren Minister des Innern und der Justiz," *Stenographische Protokolle* (1900): 3458–3460. Among the signatories of the interpellation were Benno Straucher and the Socialist deputy Ignacy Daszyński.

125. Similar allegations were already reported in mid-February in the liberal press, for example that when Araten came to the convent on December 31 to inquire about his daughter, the
Superior told him that God called his daughter. When he asked to see his daughter, she went to
fetch her, at which point he heard her speaking with his daughter who was crying and sobbing
in the next room. The Superior came back alone and said that his daughter was too nervous and
he should come back in three days. The papers did say that Michalina met her grandfather twice.
See "Die Krakauer Klostergeschichte," *Neue Freie Presse,* February 14, 1900, 5; "Eine Rede des
Abg. Straucher (Fortsetzung)," ibid., March 21, 1900, 119–121, esp. 120–121; "Die Affaire Araten,"
ibid., 229–230.

126. For the minister's request see Araten Warsaw file, 2421–2425. For the response of the
public prosecutor see ibid., 2417–2419. For Anna Rosenblum's testimonies see ibid., 2418; 2608;
2437–2438; 2440–2441. Rosenblum never made the assertion attributed to her in the interpellation, but rather claimed that when she told Michalina that she should return home because
her family was rich, and in the convent she would need to work, Michalina burst into tears and
said: "I would go back to my parents, but I'm ashamed." According to the police, Rosenblum
had proven to be an untrustworthy witness, as she kept contradicting herself, and the police
suspected that she acted as an agent of the Aratens.

127. Araten Warsaw file, 2425; 2429–2430. The police director sent a detailed response to
Kronawetter's allegations to the Galician governor, emphasizing that the police protocols

When Michalina's birthday (according to the Tuszyn proof of birth document) passed, and Araten's disappointments kept mounting, he wrote the
emperor a four-page letter. He summarized all his allegations against the convent and the Kraków authorities, especially the refusal of the latter to allow a
search in the Felician Sisters' convent. Araten then mentioned that in the past
the emperor and his government supported a search in a convent, referring
specifically to the case of Barbara Ubryk. Ubryk was a nun who was discovered
in 1869 half-naked and in terrible physical condition in a cellar in the Carmelite
convent in the city, where she was kept locked for more than two decades. The
sensational story was broadly reported in Austria as well as in the world press
and fitted in with popular images of convents. According to a recent scholarly
article on Ubryk, "narratives of convent abuse flourished in the nineteenth
century across a range of nations [. . .] But whatever their form or focus, these
narratives of convent abuse shared a central message: that the convent was a
physical and spiritual prison in which young women were stripped not only
of their freedom, but of their feminine identity."[128] This was also how the Austrian liberal press viewed convents, and Araten may well have learned about
the Ubryk case from liberal circles. He ended his letter with a plea that the
emperor grant him a hearing.[129] This time he did not receive a response.

Araten was correct about the refusal to conduct a search in the Felician
Sisters' convent. Although there was a suspicion that the whereabouts of Michalina were not unknown to the Felician nuns,[130] the council chamber of the
court decided against a search in the convent.[131] Initially, the public prosecutor suggested conducting a search in the Kraków and a few other convents, but
this suggestion was first transferred to the diocese for its approval, claiming
that the latter had far too great an authority over all ecclesiastic institutions.
But the diocese didn't respond. For his part, the investigative judge had reser-
vations about the search, and so he transferred the issue to the council chamber of the court. The council thought that based on Michalina's letter to her
father (discussed below) it was clear that she was not being held in any

---

recorded Michalina's absolute refusal to see her father or to return home, a refusal she also communicated to her grandfather. After much convincing by Rzeszódko, Michalina agreed and the
date designated for that was January 30. (She left the convent three days beforehand.) See Police
File, p 5/6 1900 375/900.

128. See Verhoeven, "The Sad Tale of Sister Barbara Ubryk," 104.
129. HHStA, k. k. Ministerium des Innern, Nr. 2855, 3209/900.
130. Araten Warsaw file, 2601.
131. Ibid., 2429–2430.

Galician convent against her will, so a search would be pointless. And since there was no real evidence that Michalina was in one of the local convents, the legal requirements for violating the law about the protection of domicile did not exist in this case. Interestingly, the council added that apart from the legal reason, such a search would cause an uproar within the Catholic population and would thus require an enormous expenditure of time and security. Because a search required the consent of a judge, and in this case the investigative judge didn't give his consent, the public prosecutor accepted the decision of the council chamber of the court against such a search.[132]

The preferential treatment of the Felician Sisters' convent was also evident when the court accepted Vicar General Kummer's written complaint to the court in which she criticized the authorities' treatment of the convent, especially the requirement to submit the list of all the girls admitted to the catechumenate in the last three years. Kummer explained that the convent submitted the list of the girls who were in the convent when Michalina was admitted and alleged that the court was just trying to implicate the convent for not informing the authorities of her admittance. She said that while the court had given Israel Araten's testimony credibility, it treated the convent as a villain, and so she demanded that the request of the court be canceled. Not only did the court accept her request, but the convent was not rebuked or punished for its failure to inform the authorities of Michalina's admittance or registering her in its books.[133]

As the months wore on, and no trace of Michalina was discovered, Michalina's mother, Cywia, added her voice to that of her husband, but in a completely different tone. After being silent during the entire time of the search,[134] she published a personal letter in *Słowo Polskie*, the same newspaper Israel Araten used in the past to point to Tarnowska as an accomplice. Mentioning her failed hopes following her husband's meeting with the emperor in April, she revealed that she heard a rumor that her daughter was not alive:

> As a mother, my heart is pained hearing such rumors. Just like every other mother, I suffered raising the child, and at the end my child was to be torn away. Yes, I do not even know whether that unhappy one still lives! O, may

132. Ibid., 2533–2534; 2556–2562.
133. Araten court file, 192.
134. When she was called to give testimony in court on March 6, 1900, she was unable to answer any questions and cried the whole time, saying repeatedly, "Where is my daughter?" See Araten court file, 117.

my voice touch the hearts of all fathers and mothers. Maybe someone knows, or knows somebody who knows, to which fate my unhappy daughter had fallen into, then he may please inform me whether she lives. The hope to see her again, to be able to press her to the heart, gives me the strength to live on. And if—and I write this with trembling hands—if anyone has heard that she is no longer among the living, he should at least show me where the unhappy one was buried.[135]

Cywia's letter also yielded no result. The official investigation continued until mid-April 1901, when the Kraków public prosecutor reported to the Justice Ministry that it intended to set aside the criminal case of the abduction of Michalina Araten since the large-scale investigations into her whereabouts were all unsuccessful, and no evidence was presented that would justify bringing an indictment against a specific person. Israel Araten had been interrogated twice, on March 8 and April 1, 1901, but he did not provide any evidence for the new allegations he raised. The public prosecutor asserted that the investigation could be resumed at any time should new information important for the case be presented.[136] In May, the public prosecutor reported to the Justice Minister that the investigation was exhausted and "the riddle remains unresolved and must remain unresolved for the time being."[137] The case was then shelved with the knowledge that it might be opened again if new evidence arose.[138]

In the final analysis, Israel Araten did everything he could to locate and bring home his daughter, both via official and unofficial routes. He had the support of much of the Viennese liberal and socialist press. Through his efforts Michalina's case achieved worldwide notoriety, unlike those of the other girls who had run away to the Felician Sisters' convent. A worldly businessman, who shrewdly was able to use his considerable means to keep the case in the public eye, Araten did not fit the stereotype of the simple, pious, and backward Galician Hasid. But ultimately, his strategy of pursuing all leads and making public allegations against the convent was not successful. His many appeals to the imperial authorities in Vienna were misplaced, since they did not conduct

135. "On the Araten Case," *Słowo Polskie,* September 12, 1900, 4 [Polish]. See also the German translation, "Mädchenraub in Galizien," *Dr. Bloch's Oesterreichische Wochenschrift,* September 21, 1900, 682.

136. Araten Warsaw file, 2360–2362.

137. Ibid., 2358–2359.

138. The legal basis he quoted for that was "Strafprocessordnung," §90, 418.

the investigation. For example, in December 1900, a year after Michalina's escape from home, Araten wrote yet another letter to the Minister of Justice. This time he used a new argument: solving the case would improve the reputation of the Austrian legal system abroad, which had suffered because of the adverse publicity that the case had engendered.[139] But all the Austrian government could do was to lean on the Galician local authorities to pursue the case vigorously.

Even when the authorities appeared sympathetic, the investigation faced challenges. This can be seen from Governor Pininski's detailed report to the Austrian Minister of Justice written on May 23, 1900. Pininski explained that he sent a circular to all district administrations in Galicia asking them to inquire whether Michalina was in their district and immediately inform the courts of any information they received about her. He didn't think that there was anything else he could do, because according to the law, house searches in convents could be carried out only following specific orders issued by the judicial authorities. He doubted that any such search would reveal anything, because Michalina was probably in a convent outside the country. All the rumors about her being kept in Galician convents proved to be false. If Michalina would be discovered in Galicia, she would have to be taken to her parental home by physical force and constantly guarded there to make sure she wouldn't escape again. According to the governor, there was only one way to bring to light those rumors, namely, to conduct multiple searches on the same day in all Galician convents. The governor then discussed the possible implications of such an act:

> Although I am now aware of the indoctrination practiced by some convents with regard to underage Jewish girls, and I specifically disapproved of the nuns' action in this case, I nevertheless consider the use of such a drastic mean—even though I repeat, the only effective one—improper and unacceptable because of political and religious reasons. There is not the slightest doubt in my mind that such a measure would not fail to elicit the greatest resentment among the Christian population, which undoubtedly would result in serious disturbances of the peace and hostilities against the Jewish population.
>
> As for a possible intervention of the Church authorities in this matter, I find it absolutely impossible to obtain. A few weeks ago I have had the occasion to speak at length with the Kraków Bishop [Jan] Puzyna about this, and I was

139. Araten court file, 363.

convinced that he was ready to do anything except intervene in favor of the Araten family. There is no doubt that the other clergy also feel the same.

Finally, I find it necessary to emphasize that what complicates the investigation is that almost the entire non-Jewish population in the vicinity of Kraków is decidedly against the Araten family. The reason for that is that of those who have seen or known Michalina Araten, no one believes she had not yet reached the age of fourteen. Her appearance and physical development are such that they generally considered her to be at least seventeen or eighteen years old. Moreover, and I do not know if this is true, the general view is that the real reason that Araten left her parental home was because her father wanted to coerce her to marry a man she despised.

In the end, I repeat that I would like to do my utmost to bring about the desired result, but it is impossible to guarantee its success.[140]

Similar to the other Galician Poles, whether jurists, politicians, or journalists, the fear of agitating the Catholic population and public unrest, coupled with the distrust in Israel Araten's allegations, caused the Galician governor to be pessimistic about the chances of resolving the case. With such an attitude, the whole process was carried out pro forma, lacking efficacy and vigor. Araten's belief that the key to finding his daughter was in the hands of the Viennese authorities and the Viennese liberal press turned out to be wrong. Whether he would have been more successful had he adopted a quieter strategy that relied upon personal appeals to the convent and church hierarchy, without involving the Viennese press, is impossible to say. But the specifics of this case made it very difficult for the investigation to conclude in a manner satisfactory to him.

The discussion in the Austrian administration about Jewish runaways who found shelter in Galician convents continued even as the Galician authorities contemplated shelving the case. As late as November 1900, the Justice Minister asserted that since the conversion of Jewish girls was "considered by one side as a wrong and by the other side as a duty, each such case had the potential of exciting to a great extent the passions of the parties, which are in any event unfriendly toward each other, and are just waiting for the right opportunity for agitation within and outside the country." While emphasizing the need to follow the law, he also emphasized his commitment to the religious interests of the Catholics. He explained that he could not share the notion "that the case of an abduction of an Israelite girl is tantamount to a theft, arson, or another

140. Araten Gubernium file, 98–101.

crime,"[141] especially since in most cases there was a third party involved. While he suggested ensuring that conversions not be carried out in secret, and that investigations be conducted with energy and prudence,[142] the double language he used was hardly a formula for solving the Araten case.

The Riddle of the Disappearance Solved

About three decades after the flight and disappearance of Michalina, a volume about the history of the Felician Sisters' congregation, published by the congregation, revealed the convent's involvement in her escape and being smuggled out of the country. Written with a lack of awareness of (or concern for) the illegality of the convent's acts, the volume recorded and greatly embellished the details:

> Around the year 1898 [*sic*] an incident occurred that affected the entirety of what was then Galicia and even people abroad. A very young and pretty daughter of a very wealthy Jew, a man named Araten from Kraków, ran away from her parents' house, following the voice of God, and sought refuge in the care of our nuns in the catechumenate and asked to prepare her for baptism. The parents embarked on an intense search for her with the assistance of the police.
>
> Knowing that the catechumenate was located on Smoleńsk [street], they entered the convent with a whole mob of Jews, demanding the release of their daughter. It was on the eve of the Three Kings' Day [the Feast of the Epiphany] in the afternoon, during a procession with the priest at the solemn dedication of the convent. The priest sprinkled holy water on the walls, as well as on the Jews, who ran away screaming. However, they returned immediately, demanding to see their daughter. She told her parents through the nuns that she could not see them on that day and asked them to come back the next day at a given hour. Satisfied with this promise, they left.
>
> Meanwhile, in the evening, nuns transferred Miss Araten, who was disguised, to Krystynów[143] and hid her at the home of the nuns there, from

---

141. Enticing a minor to leave the parental home was considered kidnapping and listed under the crime of disturbing the public peace that included fourteen different crimes. The Justice Minister clearly did not consider all these crimes to be of the same weight.

142. See HHStA, Ktn. 1593, k. k. Justiz-Ministerium, No. 22.956/1791, November 1900, 8–10. The minister wrote it in response to Piętak's insistence to take religious concerns into consideration.

143. The pastoral center in Krystynów was founded in 1892 in Trzebinia by Andrzej Potocki (a deputy in the upper house of the Austrian parliament and the Galician Sejm, and governor

which she would not go out anywhere. It was carried out in such a secretive manner that apart from the nuns who transferred her, no one in the Kraków convent knew where she had gone, nor the gatekeeper, not even the Vicar General, who, when asked, could honestly reply that they didn't have any knowledge on the subject. At the given hour, the whole mob of Jews stormed into the convent building, expecting to take her away with the use of force. How surprised and furious they were with the news that she fled the convent the previous night! They didn't believe it and tried to reach the enclosure section to search for the fugitive. They were told that since nobody was allowed to enter the enclosure section, it wasn't possible for her to be hiding there. Desperately, they went to the police station and brought back the commissioner who interrogated all the nuns as well as the convent staff. After this futile search they searched for her in all the other convents in Kraków as well as outside the city, but to no avail.

Meanwhile, in Krystynów the talented young lady was preparing herself for the upcoming baptism and soon afterward she became a Christian. At that same time, two of our nuns were about to leave for America, so they took the neophyte with them on their trip, arranging for her to stay at a religious boarding school in Belgium to complete her education and consolidate her Catholic faith. After a few years she married a landed citizen in Poznań. As long as M. Honorata [Kummer, the Vicar General] lived, she directed her fate, and the two of them regularly corresponded with each other. In these letters the nuns read that her most cherished desire was for her son to become a priest.[144]

Even if one believes that Kummer did not know where Michalina had been taken, it is clear from this description that she knew that Michalina was removed by nuns of her convent. The nuns would not have carried out such a plan without the permission of their superior. Michalina and Kummer apparently had a close relationship, but the latter never disclosed any of this

---

of Galicia from 1903), with his mother and named after his wife, Krystyna Potocka. The center, which also included a convent, was under the care of Felician nuns. Its construction began in May 1892, and it was consecrated in 1895. See *Historja Zgromadzenia SS. Felicjanek*, vol. 3, 308–316. Potocki was one of the signatories on Tarnowski's interpellation as well as on the interpellation submitted to the Galician Sejm, so clearly he was familiar with the Araten case.

144. SS. Felicjanki, *Historja Zgromadzenia SS. Felicjanek*, vol. 2, 221–223. The language and tone of this chapter is derogatory toward Jews and joyful at successfully tricking the Araten family, who was looking for their daughter.

information to the court or the police who continued to investigate Michalina's disappearance for many months. Moreover, Michalina's temporary residence in Krystynów and her subsequent conversion there all took place in secret and was not reported to the appropriate authorities as the law required, clearly with the intention of avoiding being discovered. In short, multiple laws were violated by the convent and its accomplices, according to this account.

Still, such an elaborate plan couldn't have succeeded without Michalina's cooperation. Although she was young and probably given to the nuns' influence, there was another reason for her determination to leave the convent in secret. Michalina revealed this reason in the letter she left for her father that he refused to read. If in fact he was concerned about its content, his concern was not groundless. Michalina had been alarmed by the visit of the psychiatrist Dr. Żuławski in the convent because she was afraid that her father intended to commit her to a mental institution. She also was upset about his lying about her age. Therefore, and as a result of divine guidance, she decided to secretly flee "to America" and find shelter in a convent there.[145] She promised her father to inform him about her whereabouts in six to eight weeks, and assured him that the nuns did not know where she was going. She ended the letter by sending regards to her family and then wrote: "I am still your devoted daughter Michalina Araten. I commend you to the Lord God and wish for you, that the Lord Jesus watch over you and protect you."[146] Clearly, belief in Jesus was not something Michalina had heard about only during her four-week stay in the convent, but rather during her years in Rehefeld's school.

Epilogue

Michalina didn't fulfill her promise to inform her father where she was, perhaps because she knew about his efforts to find her and feared being returned home by force. After fleeing the country, she spent a few years in Belgium and then she was transferred to Goła in Poznań (part of Germany at the time), where she served as a governess for Count Potworowski's family. In the

145. The congregation of the Felician Sisters began establishing filial convents in America in 1877. In 1900 they were establishing their filial convent in Buffalo, New York. See ibid., vol. 3, 391–403.

146. Police file, L. 128 pr./900. For the full letter, see the appendix.

Trzebinia. Klasztor Krystynów.

FIGURE 2.4. The convent in Krystynów (circa 1910–1919). https://polona.pl/item/trzebinia
-klasztor-krystynow,NzE3MDIxODE/#info:metadata. Courtesy of the National Library of
Poland, Warsaw, and polona.pl.

beginning of 1904, she married the manager of the Potworowski's estate,
Wacław Rowiński (born in 1871), in England during a trip with her employer's
family. Her name on the marriage certificate is listed as Wilma de Weiss, age
twenty-one, daughter of the deceased Leo De Weiss. (Weiss was her mother's
maiden name.) This new identity was probably created for her when she left
Galicia, since the first name, Wilma, is German and not a characteristic Polish
name. Upon returning to Goła after her marriage she became active in the
Reading Room for Women, organizing in 1909 a successful exhibition of
women's needlework.[147] She was also a member of the Museum Society of
Poznań.[148] Having a son and a daughter, she adapted well to her new life as a
Polish Catholic woman, pursuing cultural and feminist interests. Her son,
Ksawery Rowiński, didn't become a priest but rather a well-known radiology

147. Czub, "The Reading Society for Women in Gostyń," 56; 60.
148. *Zapiski Muzealne* (1916): 43; (1917/18): 51. At that time she lived in Karczew.

professor and a member of the Polish Academy of Sciences. Michalina's first
husband died in 1926, and she remarried several years afterward with a
"Zielewicz."[149] After World War II and the death of her second husband,
she moved in with her son from the first marriage and his second wife in a
Warsaw flat.

Israel Araten and Michalina finally met in Breslau some time in 1905 or
1906. Michalina informed her father that she was married with a son, and
that she had chosen the life she wished to lead. He returned to Kraków, and
for his part, that was the end of their relationship. But in a surprising twist,
it was not the end of Michalina's relationship with her siblings. In subsequent years, Israel Araten and several of his children left Kraków and lived
in various places in Europe, before immigrating to Palestine. On a trip to a
professional conference in Amsterdam in 1958, his son Yehudah was approached by another attendee, Paolo Rowiński, who turned out to be Michalina's first husband's nephew. A correspondence was initiated between
Yehudah and Michalina which led to a meeting in Paolo's villa in Trieste in
1961, and subsequently brought Michalina to Israel in 1962. (Israel Araten
died in Jerusalem in 1959.)[150]

When Michalina's three-month tourist visa expired in 1962, she decided
to remain in Israel rather than to return to Warsaw. In order to become an
Israeli citizen under the Law of Return, she registered her nationality as a
Jew in 1962 and entered a senior housing facility in Haifa not far from her
brother Yehudah. Michalina did change her name in 1962 at the Israel Ministry of the Interior from Wilma Zielewicz to Wilma Michalina Araten.[151]
She died in 1969 and was buried in a Jewish cemetery in Haifa at the age of
"86," according to the date on her tombstone. Her age matches the age on
her marriage certificate, which probably matched the forged identity given

149. Interview with Dr. David Ashboren, Michalina's nephew, the son of her brother Yehudah Araten, on June 19, 2017. I was unable to find information on her second husband. Her last
address under the name of Rowiński was Szymańskiego St. in Poznań, an address she left in
1933. No information on her second marriage to a "Zielewicz" was found in a recent search
in Poznań archives, and thus his identity remains a mystery (email correspondence with a
researcher from Poznań, October 2018).

150. According to the diary of Paolo Rowiński, Michalina saw advertisements placed in
the papers by her father and contacted him. This led to their subsequent meeting in Breslau
(personal communication with Giorgio Rowinski, Paolo's son, on July 11, 2017).

151. See *Reshumot: Yalkut Ha-pirsumim* 1043, October 21, 1963, list 9/62.

to her after her conversion. The Israel chapter of Michalina's life, for which there is very little documentary evidence, is beyond the scope of the present book.[152]

————

Among the hundreds of cases of Jewish women runaways that are the subject of this book, Michalina Araten's is unique for its notoriety. Other young women had their names mentioned in the press, especially the Jewish press, and some were the subject of Austrian parliamentary interpellations. But Michalina's case became a cause célèbre not only for the reasons mentioned in the beginning of the chapter, but also due to the herculean efforts of her father, Israel, to restore her to the bosom of the family. His engagement of a prominent psychiatrist to enter the convent and evaluate Michalina's mental state may have been the final straw for the young girl, who feared being committed to an institution against her will. Clearly she was as strong-willed as her father. Only when Araten was confronted with his daughter as Catholic wife and mother did he give up the struggle and repudiate her. Whether he could have achieved his desired goal had he adopted other means is impossible to know; we will see below that a different approach by a different father seems to have brought his daughter back to her parents and into the Jewish fold.

If Israel Araten used means that were improper and even illegal to secure his goal, the nuns of the Felician Sisters' convent were no better. They may not have enticed Michalina to convert or conspired to abduct her from her home. But to save the young woman from an unhappy life in this world and perdition

152. This and the previous paragraphs are based on information I received from members of the Araten and Rowiński families, and from Rachel Sarna Araten's *Michalina, Daughter of Israel*. The book adopts wholeheartedly the father's kidnapping narrative, adding the unsubstantiated claim that Michalina was brainwashed in the convent in order to erase the memory of her life prior to her entry in the convent. There is no consensus in the Araten family today over the degree of Michalina's identification with Catholicism during her years in Israel. Her decision to declare herself a Jew for the purposes of obtaining Israeli citizenship under Israeli Law of Return should also be seen in light of the Israel Supreme Court's ruling concerning Oswald Rufeisen, which occurred the very same year. Rufeisen, known as Brother Daniel, was refused new immigrant status according to the Law of Return because he had converted to Catholicism and was a practicing Catholic. Sarna Araten does cite excerpts from letters written by Michalina to her brother Yehudah and refers to other correspondence that she saw; I was unable to locate any of this correspondence.

in the next, the nuns and their accomplices took the law into their own hands by abducting a minor who was still subject to parental custody, smuggling her out of the convent and the Habsburg Empire, and providing her with a new identity.

As for Michalina herself, although her separation from her family and city must have been heart-wrenching, she achieved what she had set out to do, which was to escape a marriage with a "wax doll" and a way of life she considered to be oppressive. Proudly Polish in culture and faith, she was unable to reconcile her values and aspirations with the life her parents had planned for her. Yet she never denied her family, even in her farewell letter to her father, which may be why she had no difficulty in reconnecting with her family a half century later, firm in her desire to remain true to the life she had adopted after her conversion. Although her case was an extreme one, her profile bears much in common with those of the other runaways.

3

Romantic Love

DEBORA LEWKOWICZ AND HER
FLIGHT FROM THE VILLAGE

ALTHOUGH THE CASE OF Michalina Araten publicized the plight of the
young Jewish runaways, it was in one respect atypical of the wider phenomenon, which may be why it captured the public's attention. As noted earlier,
most of the female Jewish converts to Catholicism in Kraków were young
women from the small towns and villages surrounding the city, and their background was lower middle class and middle class. Michalina, by contrast, was
the daughter of a wealthy and prominent Hasidic family. This was not the case
with young Jewish women living in villages, especially those with tiny Jewish
populations. They were as Polonized by their social contacts and education as
their urban Jewish counterparts, but they lacked a critical mass of Jewish
women that could reinforce their social identity as Jews.

We know very little about these village runaways besides their names and
in some cases the professions of their fathers, when recorded on their conversion protocols. Their families were not particularly wealthy, learned, or
well-connected, and their cases were not widely reported in the Jewish or non-
Jewish press. It is rare to find sources describing the actions, deliberations, feelings, and hopes of the young women from their perspective. Fortunately, there
is one person from a village outside Kraków whose story we can reconstruct
in considerable detail because her case, like that of Michalina, was pursued in
court and has left us with a large investigative file.[1] On the eve of her wedding

1. The National Archives in Kraków, Sąd Krajowy Karny w Krakowie (SKKKr) 416—Vr
632/01 (henceforth: Lewkowicz file). The file is unpaginated, so documents are identified here
by their date.

in early January 1901, at the age of eighteen, Debora Lewkowicz fled from her home in the village of Rzeszotary outside Kraków and spent several months in the Felician Sisters' convent before converting there in March 1901. The Lewkowicz file includes a substantial number of documents containing testimonies from the young woman, her family, and her circle of acquaintances. These enable us to reconstruct her story and to shed light thereby on the problems and challenges faced by a young Jewish woman living on the threshold of the twentieth century in the greater Kraków area. Her story, which ended quite differently from that of Michalina, is the subject of this chapter.[2]

The Education of Debora Lewkowicz

Debora was born on January 17, 1883, when her mother Ciwie was twenty-seven and her father Abraham, thirty-two. Three years later her sister Chaja was born, and two years after that, her brother Mendele. Debora's parents were tavernkeepers in Rzeszotary, which had a tiny Jewish population at the time, 21 Jews and 1,207 Catholics.[3] The Catholics belonged to the parish of the neighboring village Podstolice, whereas the Jews belonged to the Jewish community of Wieliczka, a district town that was fourteen kilometers from Kraków.[4] The village did not have ten adult Jewish males required for a prayer quorum; membership in the Wieliczka Jewish community enabled the Jews from the surrounding villages to participate in its synagogue on holidays and on special Sabbaths—on regular Sabbaths and during the week they would not always attend synagogue—and to benefit from religious services such as ritual slaughter. Life in a village with a small number of Jews rendered contact with the Polish surroundings necessary and natural.

At first Debora attended the one-room schoolhouse in Rzeszotary; later she studied at the public school for girls in Wieliczka, which was about eleven

---

2. What follows is a reconstruction of Debora's story based almost entirely on the testimonies contained in the file. Since there are no additional sources, the identity and possible motives of the one giving the testimony are highly relevant.

3. See Chlebowski et al., *Słownik geograficzny,* vol. 10, 150–151.

4. Surrounding the provincial town of Wieliczka were about a hundred small villages. The Jews of Wieliczka constituted about 15% of the population, and in 1900, 981 Jews lived there. See Meiri, ed., *Kehilat vilitchkah,* 16.

kilometers from her home.[5] At that time there were three public schools in Wieliczka: two for boys, the one with five grades and the other with three; and one for girls, with five grades.[6]

The number and variety of public schools in Wieliczka reflected the changes that had occurred in the last quarter of the nineteenth century with respect to the educational system in the Habsburg Empire in general, and in Galicia in particular. The primary school that Debora Lewkowicz attended in Wieliczka was considered at the time to be one of the more advanced public schools for girls in Galicia. The fact that her parents, traditional Jews from a small village, decided to send her to such a school testifies to their ambitions with respect to their daughter's education and their desire to give her the best schooling possible in their region. According to some contemporary observers, sending daughters to Polish public schools also carried with it risks, especially with regard to national and religious indoctrination promoted explicitly and implicitly by teachers.[7]

Debora belonged to the first generation of Jewish girls in Galicia who attended primary public schools for female students. Her mother could not attend such a school because they did not exist at that time. Clearly, she could not have undergone the same process of Polonization and acculturation that was an essential part of her daughter's education. The openness of Debora's parents to their daughter's education did not at all stand in opposition to their being traditional since, as we saw in the case of Michalina, there were no rabbinical rules or guidelines with respect to the education of daughters. In the absence of specific Jewish religious norms with regard to female education, Jewish families behaved like their Polish neighbors of the same socioeconomic class.

From the letters that Debora later wrote to her parents and to the convent which were attached to the court file, we learn that she was fluent in Polish but also knew how to write in Yiddish.[8] She wrote the Hebrew characters in a

---

5. Lewkowicz file, testimony of Ciwie Lewkowicz, March 18, 1901; testimony of Debora, March 14, 1901.

6. Chlebowski et al., *Słownik geograficzny*, vol. 13, 320.

7. Zvi Scharfstein, "From the Life of Our Brothers in Galicia: The Education of the Daughters," *Ha-'Olam*, September 29, 1910, 11–12 [Hebrew]. See similar complaints about the schools voiced by Ahron Marcus, "Peace Be on Israel and the Rabbis!" *Ha-Mizpeh*, June 28, 1912, 1–2 [Hebrew].

8. Apparently, girls, more than boys, were taught penmanship; see Parush, *Ha-ḥot'im bi-khtivah*, 80–85.

beautiful hand and with no spelling mistakes, with the exception of the word
Torah, which she mistakenly spelled with the Hebrew letter *tet* rather than with
a *tav*.[9] Her misspelling of such a basic word suggests that she was not familiar
with the written term, or perhaps that she had not been exposed to it for some
time. Jewish instruction for girls in Galicia during this period was generally
limited to teaching the blessings, and certain prayers from the prayer book,
and in some cases the ability to write in Yiddish, which is written in Hebrew
characters. That Debora was able to write Hebrew characters clearly and beau-
tifully is another testimony to her parents' efforts to give her what they considered to be the best possible Jewish education for a modern Galician Jewish
girl. It is not unlikely that they hired a tutor to instruct her in the rudiments of
Yiddish penmanship.[10]

By all accounts, Debora and her family led a peaceful life, in harmony with
their surroundings, right up until the hour of her escape. Their neighbors in
the village were Andrzej Gadocha, a thirty-three-year-old blacksmith, and his
wife Kunegunda, who was twenty-three. Although both were illiterate and had
resided in the village for a shorter duration than did the Lewkowiczes, the two
families enjoyed good relations. The Lewkowicz daughters visited Andrzej
Gadocha frequently at home and in his smithy, "out of friendship as well as to
request things, for example, to heat the clothes iron."[11] Debora also used to
record for Andrzej his shop's bills.

The Polish Lover and the Hastily Arranged Marriage

The ties between Debora and her Polish surroundings were not limited to her
immediate neighborhood. The school she attended in Wieliczka was a considerable distance from her home, and she made the journey either on foot or by
wagon. On one occasion she encountered a young Pole named Stanisław
Bakalarz, a resident of the neighboring village of Podstolice, who worked as
an administrator of an agricultural cooperative in Wieliczka. They would continue their conversations at the Gadocha's home when Bakalarz waited for his
horses to be shoed or his tools to be repaired; occasionally Bakalarz would

9. Lewkowicz file, Debora's letter to her parents, September 20, 1901. The word Torah is
underlined.

10. Stampfer, "Gender Differentiation."

11. Lewkowicz file, testimony of Andrzej Gadocha, March 18, 1901.

visit Lewkowicz's tavern, where Debora poured the beer and helped run the business.[12]

All knew Bakalarz to be a quiet and polite young man; Debora's mother told Andrzej more than once that "had they been gentiles, she would have willingly married off her daughter to Bakalarz, since she was fond of him, and he made a good impression on her."[13] Debora's younger sister Chaja considered Bakalarz to be "a respectable and bright young man, who behaved politely to all and to us."[14]

The friendship between Debora and Bakalarz grew into romantic love, which lasted more than three years. Those immediately surrounding the couple, apart from her parents, knew of it. The couple exchanged letters clandestinely, often through the intermediary of Kunegunda Gadocha. Debora burned the letters she received so that they would not be discovered by her parents.[15] Chaja, who knew about their romantic connection, was privileged to read some of Bakalarz's letters, and in her court testimony was able to cite some of the affectionate terms he had employed. It appears also that Bakalarz and Debora visited the market in Podstolice on one occasion, and there, while Bakalarz was intoxicated, they allowed themselves to utter terms of affection that others would also hear.[16] In his own testimony Bakalarz confessed his love for Debora and revealed that he had written her love letters. He added that he was unable to marry her since he was obliged to enlist in the military, but that he desired to marry her upon his release. Bakalarz was ambitious; although his present financial status was inconsiderable, he planned "to live in a respectable manner in the future."

When Debora's parents learned of the girl's romantic attachment to Bakalarz, they sought a Jewish bridegroom for her, choosing a young man from Kraków, Mechel Hirschprung. A meeting was hastily arranged between the two, and a

12. Lewkowicz file, testimony of Abraham Lewkowicz, March 6, 1901. On the rural tavern in Imperial Russia as a place of "interconfessional sociability" leading at times to conversion, see Schainker, *Confessions of the Shtetl*, 85–120. On assimilation and conversion among rural tavern-keepers in the Kingdom of Poland, see Dynner, *Yankel's Tavern*, 69–70. While the tavern was indeed a meeting place for Jews and Christians, it wouldn't have been safe for a prolonged intimate relationship as was the case of Debora and Bakalarz. In this case, the neighbor's private home provided a gathering space far from the watchful eyes of parents and other undesired observers.

13. Lewkowicz file, testimony of Andrzej Gadocha, March 18, 1901.

14. Lewkowicz file, testimony of Chaja Lewkowicz, March 18, 1901.

15. Lewkowicz file, testimony of Debora Lewkowicz, April 26, 1901. Bakalarz told investigators in his testimony of March 18, 1901, that he destroyed Debora's letters because his father was not on good terms with Abraham Lewkowicz, and he didn't want him to discover them.

16. Lewkowicz file, testimony of Jan Jania, July 2, 1901.

date was set for the wedding.[17] Upon hearing of her parents' plans, Debora made up her mind to escape. The idea to run away was something she had entertained for a long time, but she decided to go ahead with it when her parents intended to marry her against her will to somebody she met only once. Far from loving her intended bridegroom, she testified that "he aroused within me antipathy."[18]

But escape to where? And how was it to be managed? A friend of Bakalarz, Jan Śmieszkiewicz, made inquiries and informed Debora on the evening of December 29, 1900, three days before her scheduled wedding with Mechel, of the Felician Sisters' convent's willingness to receive her. Her mind made up, she asked Śmieszkiewicz to meet her the very next day, Sunday, near the bridge from Podgórze (a separate town until 1915, when it was integrated into greater Kraków) to Kraków. She and her mother would be traveling to Kraków to pick up dresses and to take care of some other business. According to her testimony, she did not inform Śmieszkiewicz of the purpose of the meeting.[19] As we shall see, she did not wish to implicate either Śmieszkiewicz or Bakalarz as accessories to her flight.

Escape to the Felician Sisters' Convent

Debora was no stranger to Kraków nor the city to her. She and her mother would travel there frequently for shopping, and in her testimony the young woman spoke of her extensive knowledge of the city and its streets. On Sunday, December 30, Debora traveled the fifteen kilometers from the village to Kraków with her mother. They rented a room in the well-appointed *Pod Czarnym Orłem* (Under the Black Eagle) hotel in Podgórze, where they changed out of their traveling clothes, and then crossed the bridge to Kraków to take care of their business.[20]

While still in the carriage, Debora spotted Śmieszkiewicz waiting for her on the bridge and signaled him to follow them. After changing at their hotel,

17. Lewkowicz file, the police inspector's report to the public prosecutor's office, March 3, 1901, and the report of the investigating judge, October 24, 1901. The local police chief described the chain of events leading up to the conversion in a response to a query by the public prosecutor.

18. Lewkowicz file, testimony of Debora Lewkowicz in the Felician Sisters' convent, March 14, 1901. This was her first testimony. On running away from home following a coerced marriage in Imperial Russia, see Freeze, "When Chava Left Home," 153–188; Freeze, *Jewish Marriage and Divorce*, 12–19, esp. 19.

19. Lewkowicz file, testimony of Anastasya Marya Lewkowicz, April 26, 1901.

20. Lewkowicz file, testimony of Abraham Lewkowicz, March 6, 1901.

Debora's mother left to see the notary. When she returned she discovered that her daughter had disappeared. She proceeded to search for her in the places in Kraków where they had intended to visit. After several hours of fruitless attempts to find her, she returned to her home. When Abraham learned from his wife of the disappearance of their daughter, he suspected immediately that she had run away from home, and that she was hiding in one of the Kraków convents.[21]

The father's reaction should not come as a surprise. The phenomenon of the runaway Jewish girls was widely reported in both the Jewish and non-Jewish press beginning in 1900. These stories were well-known also to young Jewish women, as Debora herself testified: "I knew from various stories that the Felician Sisters' convent in Kraków, on Smoleńsk, accepted catechumens. I knew where Smoleńsk was because I knew Kraków well, but I didn't know where exactly the convent was located."[22] Nor was this knowledge something that only she, as a potential convert, sought. Her sister Chaja had heard from Kunegunda that Debora read to her a letter that she had received from Bakalarz. In that letter Bakalarz explained that his friend had learned that the nuns at the convent at Staniątki, where he had made inquiries, were not interested in accepting new converts, "because they had a problem in the past when people were searching for Araten."[23] Clearly, the story of Michalina Araten was familiar to young Jewish women, even to a fifteen-year-old girl like Chaja Lewkowicz, as well as to the Polish neighbor who repeated this part of the letter. The Felician Sisters' convent was dubbed a decade later by a Jewish newspaper a *shmad fabrik* (apostasy factory).[24] Jewish girls stayed there mostly in the company of their coreligionists. The reputation of the convent as a place of conversion reached even Jewish women in Congress Poland, and

21. Ibid.

22. Lewkowicz file, testimony of Debora Lewkowicz in the Felician Sisters' convent, May 26, 1901.

23. Lewkowicz file, testimony of Chaja Lewkowicz, April 27, 1901.

24. "Baptized on the Death Bed," *Der Tog*, July 19, 1911, front page [Yiddish]. The paper claimed that people at first demonstrated great concern about the subject but then got used to it, and that stories of conversion of young Jewish women no longer caused a sensation. The newspaper added that at one time male or female apostasy was a stain that could not be cleansed, but "now the matter has become quite simple," like transferring one's membership in a social club. This was probably an exaggeration intended to emphasize the extent of the problem.

18 percent of the Kraków female converts arrived there from that part of Imperial Russia.[25]

Debora planned her flight to the convent in complete secrecy from her family. Those who shared her secret denied completely that her lover Bakalarz had a hand in it and insisted instead that she had thought of converting for a long time. Both Andrzej and Kunegunda Gadocha testified that Debora had made up her mind to convert long before, and that she occasionally read from Catholic prayer books in their home. According to Kunegunda, "[Debora] said that she did not want to know about Jews, nor marry one, since she couldn't abide him." She added that she had explained to Debora that the best thing was "to remain in her faith and in her situation, but Debora replied that she wished to be accepted into a convent."[26]

Even if these testimonies are credible, and Debora had decided to convert long before her marriage, there is no doubt that the impetus and timing of her flight were related to her impending marriage. For a young woman like Debora it was virtually impossible to escape from home. Where could she have gone if not to the convent? The flight to the convent may have been motivated partly by religious reasons, but the convent also provided a safe haven, far from her parents' house. The Felician Sisters' convent was the only convent in the area in which was located a catechumenate, and girls who wished to be accepted were provided with room and board for several months.[27] At the turn of the century there were Jewish girls in residence at almost any given time.[28]

25. Thon, *Die Juden in Oesterreich,* 78. When Jewish women from Congress Poland began to enroll at the Jagiellonian University, *Der Tog* issued a front-page warning to their parents under the title, "Apostates" (*meshumodim*), about the "*shmad fabric*" of the Felician Sisters' convent. See *Der Tog,* March 3, 1911 [Yiddish].

26. Lewkowicz file, testimonies of Andrzej and Kunegunda Gadocha, March 18 and April 24, 1901.

27. In response to the 1909 parliamentary interpellation by Benno Straucher on the issue of the conversion of young Galician Jewish women, the Austrian administration in Galicia explained on November 29, 1910, to the Austrian Minister of Interior: "As regards the conduct of the Felician Sisters' convent in Kraków mentioned in the interpellation, the chief thing to note is that of the female monastic orders in Kraków, only the said convent possesses a catechumenate school in which individuals who are to be accepted into the Christian Church are instructed in Christianity and prepared for baptism," TsDIAL f. 146, o. 4, s. 5067, in microfilm copy in CAHJP HM2/9440.7, 47.

28. Some examples reported by the press: In February 1900, sixty Jewish young women were in the Felician Sisters' convent, *Allgemeine Zeitung des Judenthums,* March 2, 1900, 163–164; thirty

For Debora, who studied in school with Polish Catholics, made friends with her Polish Catholic neighbors, and entered into a romantic liaison with a Catholic Pole, the non-Jewish environment was not viewed as threatening but as understanding and even friendly. She must have been familiar with Catholic processions from living in a Catholic village, and she must have had a knowledge of the Catholic religion and other rituals from attending a Polish school. There is no evidence that Debora had to overcome inhibitions or prejudice against Catholicism when she decided to convert.

The difficult part of the flight and subsequent conversion for Debora appears not to have been the abandonment of her faith but rather the separation from her family, and the guilt she felt for causing them pain. Her sister and her parents testified that she was gloomy on the eve of her flight, and that she was easily brought to tears.[29] On the other hand, it appears that during a short period of time—five months—she made such strong ties with the people connected with the convent, that she did not feel comfortable about returning to Judaism in Kraków, as we shall see below. From complaints made against the Felician Sisters' convent we learn that Polish noblewomen from Kraków visited the Jewish girls, bringing them flowers and candy, which instilled feelings of importance and belonging within their hearts.[30] And for the first time in her life, Debora was in an educational setting with a cohort of other young Jewish women like her.

The Court Case against the Polish Lover

While the Felician Sisters' convent was free to admit Debora and prepare her for baptism because she was over the age of fourteen and expressed her wish to convert, there was still a legal issue associated with her admittance.[31]

---

in May 1900, ibid., May 16, 1900, 126; fifty in March 1910, *Der Gemeindebote, Beilage zur Allgemeine Zeitung des Judenthums*, March 18, 1910, 4.

29. Lewkowicz file, testimony of Abraham Lewkowicz, March 6, 1901, and of Chaja Lewkowicz, April 27, 1901.

30. Julius Ofner, "Kinderraub in Galizien," *Dr. Bloch's Oesterreichische Wochenschrift*, November 2, 1900, 781. A Yiddish newspaper cited a report about the baptism of four Jewish girls where the enthusiastic baptism advisors were from the most important families of Kraków's nobility. "The Secrets of the Felician Convent in Kraków," *Der Tog*, June 12, 1912, 2 [Yiddish].

31. For the conversion protocol signed by Debora, see The National Archives in Kraków, Magistrat miasta Krakowa, Kr 54. For the notification about her intention to convert, see ibid., Pełnomocnik ds. metryk izraelickich przy Magistracie miasta Krakowa, PMI 56, 137.

Candidates for conversion had to commit to Catholicism of their own free will; aiding and abetting a minor to flee home, either by force or enticement, was considered kidnapping according to the Penal Code.[32] Indeed, the legal issue in the case of the conversion of young Jewish women in Galicia was not in most cases one of involuntary conversion, as we saw in chapter 1, but rather of enticing individuals younger than age twenty-four (the Austrian age of majority) to leave their parents' homes. The state institutions, the police and the courts, were supposed to ensure that the minor be returned to the parents' home, in this case to take Lewkowicz out of the convent and bring her home.[33]

Parents of young Jewish women who found shelter in convents were often provided legal advice by the Österreichisch-Israelitische Union, which employed the Kraków lawyer Dr. Rafael Landau especially for this purpose. Indeed, Abraham Lewkowicz approached the Union for assistance.[34] The legal strategy of the Union was to treat each case as a problem of non-enforcement of the law rather than as a religious conflict between Jews and the Church.

On February 1901, Abraham Lewkowicz submitted a complaint to the Austrian Interior Ministry claiming that Debora had been enticed and led to the convent by two young Polish men, her lover, Stanisław Bakalarz, and his friend, Jan Śmieszkiewicz.[35] His complaint was subsequently sent to the office of the public prosecutor in Kraków since Debora at that time had already been in the Kraków convent for more than a month. As a result, the state criminal court in Kraków was instructed to open an investigation of everyone involved in this affair: Debora, the convent representatives, Debora's mother, father, and sister, the Polish neighbors, Debora's Polish lover, his friend, and a few others. The authorities treated the case seriously and conducted a prompt investigation of all individuals connected to Debora's running away from home and entering the convent.

Debora's father, perhaps after receiving legal advice, also took pains to distinguish between his daughter's conversion and her leaving home. Blaming Bakalarz for the latter, he testified: "I, as her father, sense that an injustice has been done to me, regardless of whether my daughter Debora converted or not.

32. "Nr. 117. Kaiserliches Patent vom 27. Mai 1852," *RGBl* (1852): 493–591, esp. §§96; 97, 515.

33. Ellinger, *Handbuch des österreichischen allgemeinen Zivil-Rechtes*, §145, 76.

34. Lewkowicz file, testimony of Abraham Lewkowich, October 10, 1901. On the Österreichisch-Israelitische Union, see Toury, "Troubled Beginnings"; Wistrich, *The Jews of Vienna*, 309–343.

35. Lewkowicz file, report of the investigative judge, October 4, 1901.

I request that my daughter be returned to me, for despite religious differences, I have paternal feelings for her."[36]

To what extent did Bakalarz assist Debora in leaving her parents' home, and did that assistance constitute being an accessory to "abduction"? The various testimonies do not allow for a clear-cut accusation of Bakalarz or his friend Śmieszkiewicz in this crime. Apparently, Debora had initially thought to be admitted to the Benedictine Convent in Staniątki, not far from her village,[37] and as a result, Bakalarz sent his friend Jan Śmieszkiewicz to find out whether this plan would work. But Bakalarz said that he could not remember whether Debora had specifically requested that he find this out. Śmieszkiewicz testified that around a week before Debora's flight, he traveled to Staniątki at Bakalarz's request. "Of course, I went there and explained [Debora's] request to one of the nuns, mentioning that she wished to convert. But I received a negative response accompanied by an explanation that Debora should go to the Felician Sisters' convent in Kraków. I reported this to Bakalarz."[38] Debora's sister, Chaja, related in her testimony that according to what she heard from Kunegunda, Śmieszkiewicz traveled to the Felician Sisters' convent to see whether they had a place for her sister. Kunegunda also told her that on Saturday night, December 29, 1900, when he was at the Gadocha's home with Debora, Śmieszkiewicz transmitted to her the affirmative response of the Felician Sisters' convent.[39]

Later on in the investigation Śmieszkiewicz changed his previous testimony to say that he went to the Staniątki convent not merely because of Bakalarz's request but rather because of Debora's, "since she intended to convert, and she made that intention known to me when we met."[40] Bakalarz denied that he had tried to convince the young woman to convert, orally or in writing, adding that he was not the only Polish Catholic to receive letters from Debora.[41] It is quite clear that both men feared that they would be accused of enticing Debora to flee from her home and enter the Felician Sisters' convent, and

36. Lewkowicz file, testimony of Abraham Lewkowicz, April 22, 1901.

37. The Benedictine convent in Staniątki was well-known for its girls' school, which was considered to be one of the finest in Galicia. See Skąpska, "Galicia: Initiatives for Emancipation of Polish Women," 76.

38. Lewkowicz file, testimony of Jan Śmieszkiewicz, April 22, 1901.

39. Lewkowicz file, testimony of Chaja Lewkowicz, April 27, 1901.

40. Lewkowicz file, testimonies of Bakalarz, March 18 and April 24, 1901, and of Śmieszkiewicz, March 18, April 24, and May 31, 1901.

41. Lewkowicz file, testimony of Stanisław Bakalarz, March 18, 1901.

hence they disavowed all connection with it. Genowefa Łazowska, the Mother Superior of the convent in Staniątki, initially denied the entire story,[42] but later admitted that it was indeed brought to her attention that an unfamiliar person showed up at the convent and asked whether a Jewish young woman who wished to convert could be admitted there. He didn't reveal his name or the name of the Jewess, and so she was unsure how to handle his request. She claimed not to recall whether the young man had been referred to the Felician Sisters' convent.[43]

Debora's mother testified that she heard from the Bakalarz's domestic servant that Bakalarz used to bring articles of clothing to Debora when she was staying at the Felician Sisters' convent. The servant herself said that Bakalarz's mother visited Debora in the convent and even brought her a kerchief.[44] From all these testimonies it is clear that Bakalarz was very much aware of the plans for Debora's flight and the flight itself. Even if he was not its initiator or the instigator, he offered her all the help she needed, but this didn't constitute a crime.

Debora first testified on March 14, 1901, from inside the Felician Sisters' convent, and as part of the investigation into Abraham Lewkowicz's complaint against Bakalarz and Śmieszkiewicz. This was more than two months after she had entered the convent and a few days before her baptism. She testified that she had made up her mind to convert long before, but that she was waiting for the proper opportunity. That opportunity was her impending wedding, which had been thrust upon her. She emphasized that her flight and conversion were of her own free will and initiative, and that nobody had encouraged or enticed her in the matter. Displaying no hesitation or doubts, she was, at this point of time, utterly steadfast in her resolve to convert. And she took pains to sign her testimony, "Dorota Lewkowicz nie Debora" (Dorota Lewkowicz, not Debora), a conscious act of estrangement from her family and her Jewish past.

When she gave further testimony on April 26, which she signed with her new Christian name, Anastasya Marya, she denied the accusation that Bakalarz and Śmieszkiewicz were involved in finding a place for her in the convent at Staniątki, but she admitted that both of them visited her at the Felician Sisters' convent, along with "other people from Podstolice" whose names are

42. Lewkowicz file, testimony Genowefa Łazowska, April 24.

43. Lewkowicz file, testimony Genowefa Łazowska, June 11, 1901.

44. Lewkowicz file, testimony of Anna Michalec, the sixteen-year-old servant in the Bakalarz household, March 18, 1901.

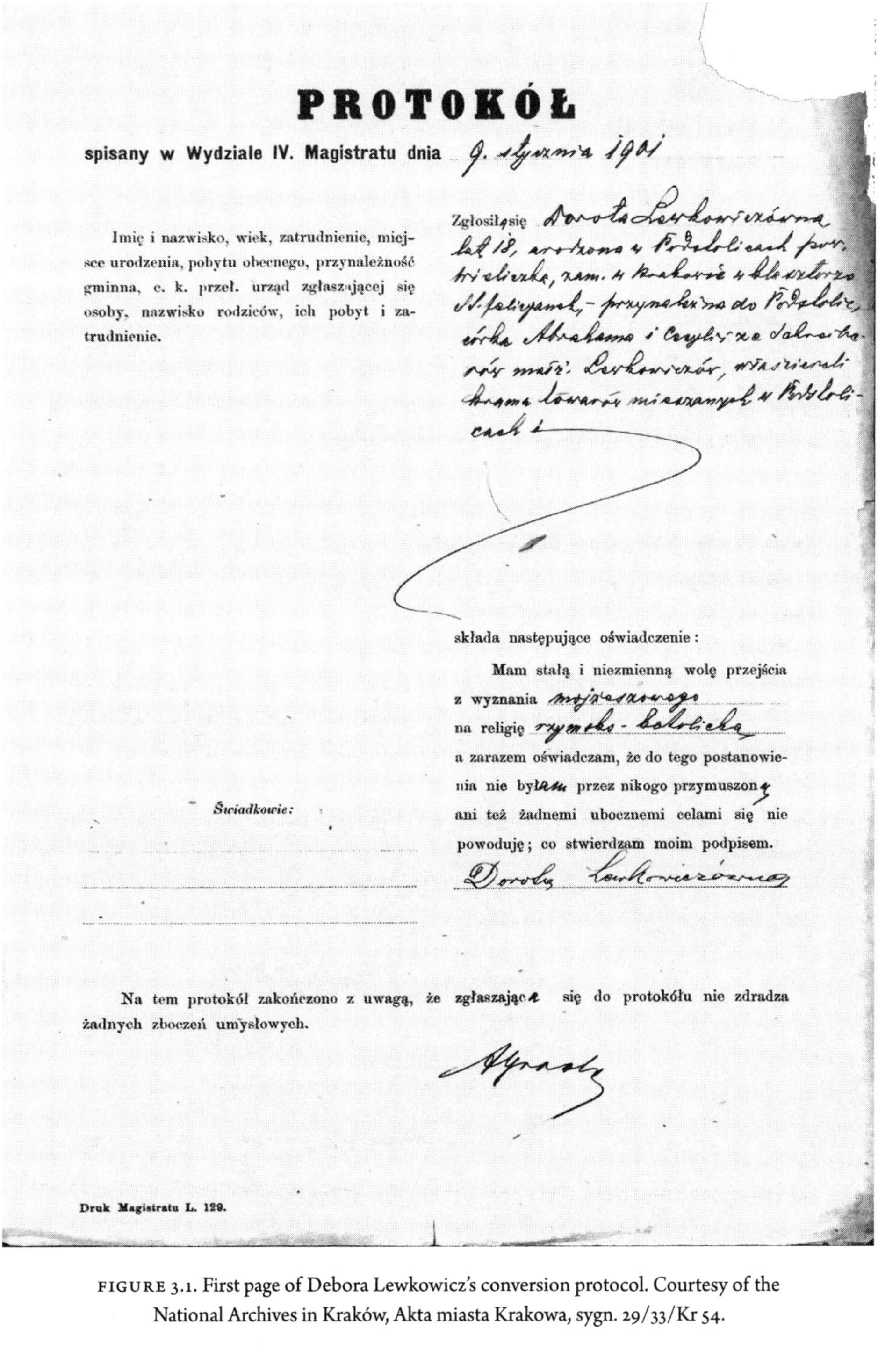

PROTOKÓŁ

spisany w Wydziale IV. Magistratu dnia *9. Stycznia 1901*

Imię i nazwisko, wiek, zatrudnienie, miejsce urodzenia, pobytu obecnego, przynależność gminna, c. k. przeł. urząd zgłaszającej się osoby, nazwisko rodziców, ich pobyt i zatrudnienie.

Zgłosiła się *Dorota Lewkowiczówna lat 18, urodzona w Podololicach pow. brzesko, zam. w Krakowie w Kleparze N. felicyami, — przynależna do Podololic, córka Abrahama i Cyryli ze Salresberów małż: Lewkowiczów, właścicieli kramu towarów mieszanych w Podololicach i*

składa następujące oświadczenie:

Mam stałą i niezmienną wolę przejścia z wyznania *mojżeszowego* na religię *rzymsko-katolicką*, a zarazem oświadczam, że do tego postanowienia nie były**am** przez nikogo przymuszon**ą** ani też żadnemi ubocznemi celami się nie powoduję; co stwierdzam moim podpisem.

Dorota Lewkowiczówna

Świadkowie:

Na tem protokół zakończono z uwagą, że zgłaszając**a** się do protokółu nie zdradza żadnych zboczeń umysłowych.

Druk Magistratu L. 129.

FIGURE 3.1. First page of Debora Lewkowicz's conversion protocol. Courtesy of the National Archives in Kraków, Akta miasta Krakowa, sygn. 29/33/Kr 54.

MAGISTRAT

stoł. król. miasta

K R A K O W A.

Kraków, dnia *9 stycznia* 1901r.

L. 85769/IV/00

Do Najprzewielebniejszego książęco biskupiego Konsystorza w Krakowie
W dniu 9 stycznia 1901r. . zgłosiła się w Wydziale
IV Magistratu Dorota Lewkowiczówna rodem z Podstolic powiatu wie-
lickiego, 18 lat licząca wyznania izraelickiego .

i oświadczyła protokolarnie, że ma zamiar zmienienia wyznania
izraelickiego .
na religię rzymsko-katolicką .
Magistrat przeto jako władza polityczna I instancji stosując się do
ustawy wyznaniowej z 25 maja 1868 L49 i rozp. min z 18 stycznia 1869
L13 dr u p. zawiadamia o tem Najprzewielebniejszy książęco biskupi
rzymsko-katolicki Konsystorz z oznajmieniem, że przeciw wyznaniu
Doroty Lewkowiczówny .
ze strony tutejszej władzy administracyjnej żadna nie zachodzi prze-
szkoda

L 85769/IV/00   *Udziela się*

Szanowny Rabinat

w Krakowie

do wiadomości.

Kraków dnia 9 stycznia 1901r

FIGURE 3.2. Copy of the notification about Debora Lewkowicz's declaration of her intention
to convert sent to the local rabbinate. Courtesy of the National Archives in Kraków,
Pełnomocnik ds. metryk izraelickich przy Magistracie miasta Krakowa, sygn. PMI 56, 137.

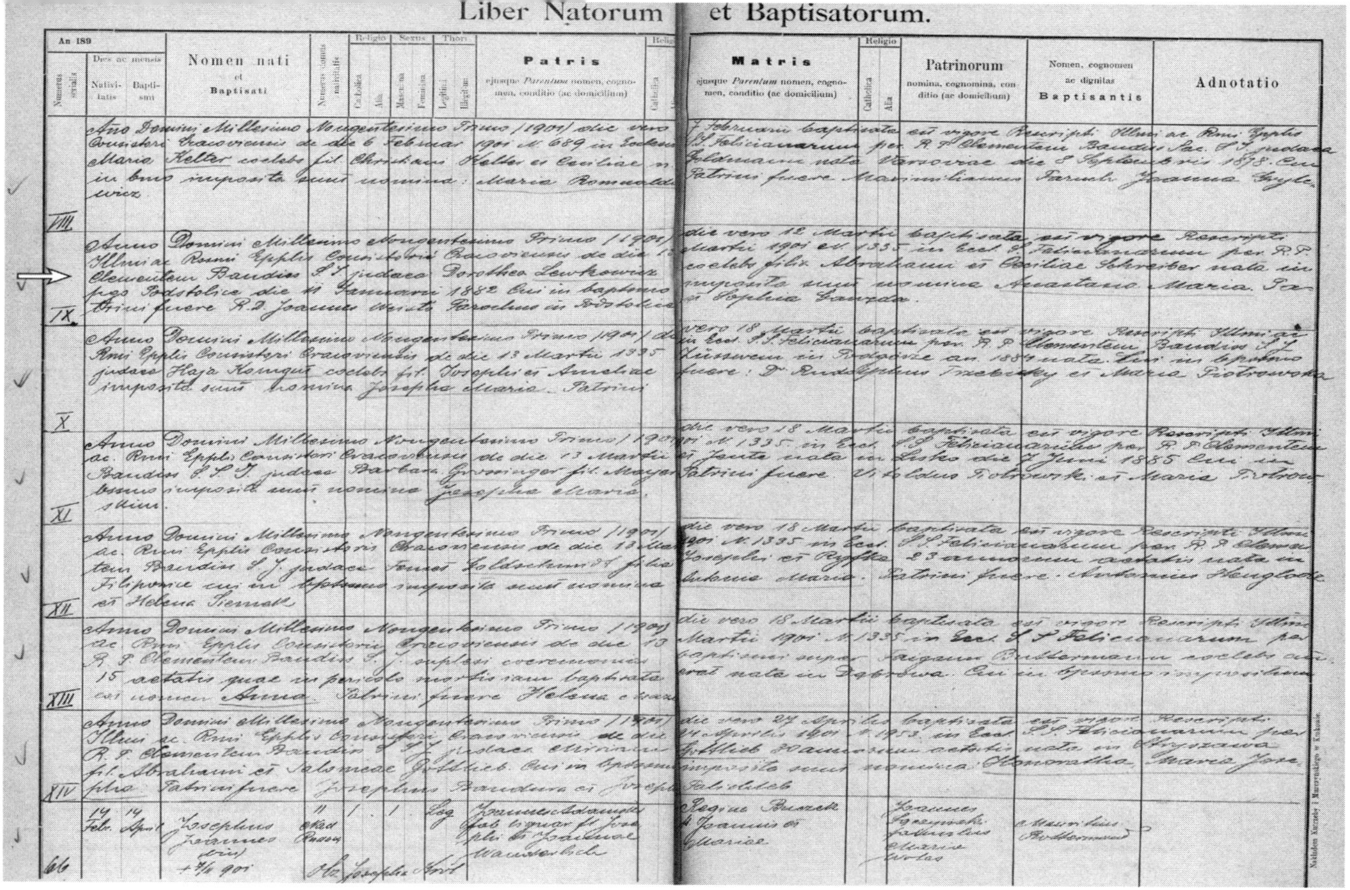

FIGURE 3.3: Baptism registration of Debora (Dorothea) Lewkowicz (IX, second row). Courtesy of the National Archives in Kraków, Akta stanu cywilnego Parafii Rzymskokatolickiej Wszystkich Świętych w Krakowie, sygn. 29/332/198, 30–31.

not mentioned.[45] On May 26 she gave further testimony, denying once again the involvement of the two men in her decision to convert.[46] Apparently, Debora did everything she could to protect them from an indictment. Interestingly, in one of her testimonies Chaja said that it was known that Bakalarz did not abduct her sister and did not accompany her to the convent, and anyway, he had no reason to do that.[47] Being close with Debora, Chaja also protected Bakalarz from being indicted.

Marya Honorata Kummer, the Vicar General of the Felician Sisters' convent, was also investigated. According to her account, Debora arrived at the convent out of breath, explaining that she had run away from her mother and had reached the convent of her own free will. Debora then said that she had a Catholic fiancé, that she wanted to become a Catholic, and that she had wanted this for a long time. The fear of her parents' reaction had made this impossible. Debora told her that had her parents known of her intention, "they almost certainly would have sold her and would have not enabled her to convert." It should be noted that in Debora's own testimony there is no mention of her intention to marry Bakalarz. According to the Vicar General's testimony, a few days after Debora's arrival her father came to the convent and met with her in the presence of a priest from the consistory of the Bishop of Kraków, and sister Rozalia Zagrabińska, who was in charge of the catechumenate.[48] The purpose of the father's visit was probably to persuade Debora to attend her wedding with Mechel. This was the only visit the father made during the entire time that Debora was at the convent.

Return to Judaism

Because the convent not only prepared the young women for conversion but also tried to provide living situations for them afterward, it was arranged for Debora to be employed as governess to the children of the administrator of the main post office in Kraków, Maryan Biliński. This ensured that she would continue to lead her life in a proper Polish Catholic atmosphere. The position also provided Debora with financial independence and the ability to survive

45. Lewkowicz file, testimony of Debora Lewkowicz, April 26, 1901.

46. Lewkowicz file, testimony of Debora Lewkowicz in the Felician Sisters' convent, May 26, 1901.

47. Lewkowicz file, testimony of Chaja Lewkowicz, March 18, 1901.

48. Lewkowicz file, testimony of the Vicar General Marya Honorata Kummer, March 14, 1901.

in the big city. A month after she began to work, the wife of her employer died, and propriety forced her to leave. A similar position was found for her in the house of a local clerk in Krosno (about 140 kilometers from Kraków),[49] but apparently Debora declined the position. Perhaps she wished to stay in the familiar vicinity of Kraków. The Krosno magistrate which was asked to inquire whether she was in that city found no traces of her.[50] When Debora remained without work her financial and emotional troubles increased, which finally led her father to renew contact with her.

This time he sent a young man named Józef Zoller, a commercial agent and business acquaintance, to speak to Debora. Zoller was a thirty-two-year-old married Jewish man who lived in 26 Starowiślna Street in Kraków, the same address as the Araten family. Perhaps Abraham Lewkowicz thought that a young urban Jew would find a better way to Debora's heart. Zoller pleaded with her to return to her father's home, and her father pleaded with her to return to Judaism. When she absolutely refused, her father asked her to return home, even as a Catholic.[51]

Debora left the home of Biliński on July 1, 1901, and went to the apartment of Julia Polek in Grzegórzki (a village on the Vistula River that was incorporated into Kraków in 1910). Polek was the midwife who had treated Biliński's wife, which is how she came to know Debora. Debora told her that she was looking for a new position and left a coffer with her. She returned two weeks later and told Polek that she had found a position in an office in Podgórze, and then took her belongings and left. According to Polek's testimony, Debora didn't share with her any of her plans and didn't tell her where she was in the days between July 1 and July 15.[52] It is unclear where Debora stayed at this time,

49. Lewkowicz file, letter to the office of the public prosecutor in Kraków, September 21. Maryan Biliński is listed in *Szematyzm Królestwa Galicyi,* vol. 1, 248. On the convent's efforts to make sure that the neophytes remain Catholic, see SS. Felicjanki, *Historja Zgromadzenia SS. Felicjanek,* vol. 2, 220–223. The profession of governess was one of the employment possibilities open to young women during this period. According to Skąpska, "they increased in number in the ranks of nursemaids and governesses, not only in the houses of gentry but also in those of well-to-do townsmen and higher orders of intelligentsia." Skąpska, "Galicia: Initiatives for Emancipation of Polish Women," 74–5.

50. Lewkowicz file, response of the Krosno magistrate, October 4, 1901.

51. Lewkowicz file, testimony of Debora Lewkowicz, November 12, 1901 (after her return to Judaism).

52. Lewkowicz file, testimony of Julia Polek, October 1, 1901.

although she, her father, and Zoller gave the impression to the investigators that she was still living with Polek.

Debora met frequently with Zoller and members of her family during this period. Although she did not initially intend to return to Judaism, her family kept pleading with her to do just that. "I was confused," she said to the investigator, "and I concluded that my situation was too much for me to bear." [53] She added that when she had entered the convent, she had not considered the various implications, and so she decided to correct "the step that had not been well-thought out" and to return to Judaism. Her decision does not appear to have resulted from a newfound acknowledgment of the truth of the Jewish religion, or any disappointment with Catholicism. Judaism was never an essential factor in Debora's life; she never mentioned it for good or for ill, at least not in her letters or testimonies that have been preserved.

Zoller related that he did not visit Debora in Grzegórzki where she was living, but rather that she would come to visit him in Kraków, where they would take long walks together. During this period Debora frequently also took walks with her parents and her sister, and the young businessman discerned the good relations among them. In those conversations the issue of her return to Judaism came up, and her main reason to discuss this issue was her desire to live with her family. Finally, she agreed to return to Judaism "out of her own free will and without any coercion."[54]

Zoller and Debora's father both related that after Debora expressed her willingness to return to the Jewish religion, she asked not to do so in Kraków, where she knew too many people, but rather in a city like Vienna. Zoller noted that Debora was careful not to tell her parents that Bakalarz was pursuing her in Kraków.[55]

Debora's father agreed to take her to Vienna, and he asked Zoller, who knew the city well, to accompany them. The formalities of Debora's return to Judaism were accomplished through the aid of the Österreichisch-Israelitische Union in Vienna, which was experienced in these matters. Both Zoller and Abraham Lewkowicz could only stay for a few days, so her father left her in the care of a "Mrs. Menkes," who, if one can judge from the name, was originally from Galicia.

53. Lewkowicz file, testimony of Debora Lewkowicz, November 12, 1901.

54. Lewkowicz file, testimony of Józef Zoller, October 1, 1901.

55. Ibid.

With the Union's assistance, Debora followed all the steps required for her return to Judaism. From the Jewish religious standpoint there was little for her to do, since a Jewish apostate is still considered legally a Jew. She apparently did not undergo the ritual immersion that some rabbis required for returning apostates.[56] But, since the Austrian 1868 interconfessional law regulated the civil aspects of religious conversion, Debora was considered a Catholic in the state vital records. For her to be considered a Jew by the state she needed to undergo the required civil procedures of conversion to Judaism. This entailed submitting appropriate forms to the civil authorities, who then transmitted them to the administrative or religious head of the abandoned church or religious association. The entry into the newly chosen church or religious association had to be declared in person in front of the relevant administrative or religious head, in this case the Viennese Kultusgemeinde (Jewish community council), since it was carried out in Vienna.[57]

Debora's letters to her parents shed light on the process of her return to Judaism. In a letter dated August 5, 1901, she wrote to her father that "Fleischer" went with her to the Viennese Kultusgemeinde,[58] where they were told that all she had to do was to go to City Hall and afterward to return to the Kultusgemeinde. She added that Fleischer told her that to spare her the unpleasantness, he would do it for her in writing. When the process was completed, she went to the Kultusgemeinde, where she was congratulated by everyone in a friendly manner. Debora noted that Fleischer accompanied her everywhere and behaved toward her with great warmth.

In that letter Debora thanked her father for the money he had sent her and asked her parents' forgiveness for all the trouble that she had caused them. "I am your daughter once more," she wrote, "who will try to bring sweetness and joy to your years." She sent kisses to her sister and brother and regards to all her relatives, signing the letter, "Your daughter, Debora." As in the previous

---

56. See the gloss of R. Moses Isserles to *Shulḥan Arukh, Y.D.* 269:12. For the medieval rabbinical debate over the necessity of ritual immersion for returning apostates, see Goldin, *Apostasy and Jewish Identity*, 54–60. Perhaps this practice was not observed in the Viennese Jewish community at the turn of the twentieth century.

57. " Nr. 48. Gesetz vom 25. Mai 1868," *RGBl* (1868): 99–102, esp. article 6, 100.

58. The reference is to Siegfried Fleischer, the secretary of the Österreichisch-Israelitische Union. Fleischer apparently was an expert in matters pertaining to Galicia; cf. his remarks at the Union's General Assembly in April 1905: "Eine Spezialität Galiziens ist bekanntlich die Entführung minderjähriger jüdischer Mädchen in katholische Klöster." See "Protokoll," *Monatschrift der Oesterreichisch-Israelitischen Union* 5 (mid-May 1905): 1–20, esp. 8.

stages in her journey, the name under which she chose to sign is revealing. At home she had been called not Debora but "Dorcia." But now, apparently, it was important for her to emphasize to her parents that she was once again a Jew.

Prominent in Debora's letters to her family are her repeated requests for forgiveness for the pain and sorrow she caused them. She was especially moved by a letter from her father in which he reminisced about their past, prompting her to write that "I will also during these high holidays swear once more that I will stay in my faith." She added that she committed one evil act—it is not clear whether she refers to her running away or to her conversion—but that she hoped that with God's help it will remain "the first and last case."[59]

Debora addresses all her letters to her father or to her parents, but never to her mother. In her letters she simply asks her father, the dominant figure in her life, to send her regards to her mother. It is her father who accompanies her to Vienna, and who later takes her to Hungary, even though she is visiting her mother's brother there. Of course, there may be many reasons for this. But one partial explanation is that Abraham Lewkowicz, a businessman who was in frequent contact with Poles, was better equipped than his wife to handle such matters, and to understand what was happening. An examination of Ciwie Lewkowicz's signature on the protocol of her court testimony reveals that the letters were formed with great difficulty; in another place she signed with a circle rather than with her name.[60] It is almost certain that she did not master reading and writing Polish, and perhaps not even Yiddish. Her daughter Debora belonged to a different generation, the generation of girls who attended Polish schools; the cultural gap between mother and daughter was even wider than that between father and daughter. Debora's mother, similar to Michalina Araten's mother, is mostly absent from the stories, highlighting another problem in the families of school-educated daughters.

Marriage Expectations at the Uncle's Home

The formal procedure for Debora's return to Judaism continued for about four weeks, at the end of which her father returned to Vienna to bring her home. During her stay in the Austrian capital the family had commenced

59. Lewkowicz file, Debora's undated letter to her parents.
60. Lewkowicz file, protocols of Ciwie Lewkowicz's testimony from March 18 and April 22, 1901.

preparations for moving their residence to Podgórze.[61] Apparently, many Jewish tavernkeepers in Western Galicia at this time were forced to leave their villages and move to nearby towns. Changes in the tavern leasing regulations led to a worsening of their financial situation.[62] Yet, according to Zoller, Debora was hesitant to live in Kraków or its vicinity as long as Bakalarz had not been called to military service, since he often visited Kraków.[63] When that testimony was read to her, she stated that she had not met with Bakalarz from the time she had returned from Vienna, adding that although she did not fear him, nor had she feared him in the past, "meeting him would cause me discomfort."[64] Her aversion to encountering her former lover and people she knew in Kraków after her return to Judaism and her reconciliation with her parents indicates her fragile and insecure emotional state. After she and her father spent three days in Kraków, they traveled together to Pilhov, Hungary (now Slovakia, about 30 kilometers from Nowy Sącz and more than 130 kilometers from Kraków), to the house of her maternal uncle, Moses Schreiber, also a tavernkeeper. She wished thereby "to breathe fresh air" and to rest from all the changes that she had undergone. Indeed, Pilhov, a hamlet close to the border with Poland, is located in a beautiful mountain region. Debora stayed in Hungary until the end of October of that year.

From a letter Debora wrote to her parents on September 25, we learn that they had moved to Podgórze, and that Debora's uncle had arranged a match between her and a young Hungarian Jew named Blaufeder. The uncle attached a few lines to Debora's letter in broken Hebrew announcing the match with the young man, whom he described as "attractive." Debora herself wrote:

> The wish, that you, most beloved father, expressed, that I may find a match in Hungary, might indeed perhaps be fulfilled. The young man with whom

61. Their new address was Kalwaryjska 14, Podgórze. This was an apartment building centrally located on a major street. For a photograph, see http://fotopolska.eu/Kalwaryjska_14_Krakow?f=655694-foto.

62. See Sapir, "Anti-Semitism in Western Galicia." The author also expresses what might have been a popular conception at the time: "Throughout Galicia we have all heard of the bad consequences of the education of girls in taverns. Almost all the Jewish girls that are forcibly being held in the convents in recent times who had been swayed by their lovers and had converted of their own will—almost all are daughters of tavernkeepers in those villages." Ibid., 151. (The contradiction in this description is noteworthy.) See also Unowsky, *The Plunder*, 14.

63. Lewkowicz file, testimony of Józef Zoller, October 1, 1901.

64. Lewkowicz file, testimony of Debora Lewkowicz, November 12, 1901 (after her return to Judaism).

the dear uncle already spoke, and of whom he also spoke to you, has already been here meanwhile a second time, and we liked one another very well, and God willing, I will become a Hungarian citizen. He is a young, very handsome man, intelligent, and can also learn Torah. He was born in Hungary and thus is a Hungarian citizen, which is of great value in Hungary. The matter is not entirely agreed upon yet, but I hope that, God willing, it will come about. I would feel very happy.[65]

According to the uncle, Blaufeder was supposed to go to the army for six weeks. He expressed his hope that a wedding between the two would be forthcoming, because they liked each other.

It seems that in the end Debora didn't marry Blaufeder (according to her December 11 testimony she returned to her home in Podgórze at the end of October), but we can learn from her letter to her father that she wanted a compatible husband, one she found handsome and intelligent. To please her father, presumably, she emphasized that the young man knows how to learn Torah, but, as we noted earlier, the word "Torah" is misspelled, and, indeed, it is the only misspelled word in the letter. The word is underscored, and if she was the one to emphasize it, then it is unlikely that she made a careless error; she probably simply did not know (or did not know well) the proper spelling of this basic term.

Indeed, aside from knowledge of the Hebrew alphabet which she used to write her Yiddish letters, her letters provide no evidence of any Jewish education or religious observance. Debora does write that she fasted [on Yom Kippur] but not that she recited prayers or attended synagogue services, about which events, had they occurred, she would have certainly told her father.

Love of Family and the Renewed Contact with the Convent

From what we have seen so far, Debora's embrace of Christianity seems to have been a temporary affair brought on by the hopelessness of her social situation rather than by religious considerations. Yet the picture that emerges from her private letters is more complex. While staying with her uncle in Hungary, she wrote a letter to Sister Rozalia Zagrabińska, the nun in charge of the catechumenate at the Felician Sisters' convent. Although the letter was undated and

---

65. Lewkowicz file, Debora's letter to her parents from Pilhov, September 25, 1901.

without a return address, it was mailed in "Mnisch" Hungary (today Mníšek nad Popradom, Slovakia) according to the postmark, and arrived in Kraków on September 5, 1901. In the letter, written in Polish, Debora presented herself as a faithful Catholic and accused "the Jews" of holding her against her will and of not allowing her to fulfill the precepts and obligations of the Church. She related that in Vienna the Jews compelled her to renounce her Catholicism and that she had pleaded to the court secretary for help. She added that she was forcibly taken to Hungary as well, from where she was sending this letter:

> For a month and a half, I have been without . . . Holy Mass and without confession. Oh, my Jesus, wherefore have I been so severely punished? Mother, I do not have so much time as to depict to Mother all my agonies; there is no quill which could describe my mortifications, but I gladly bear everything for Jesus. If only one time I could be at a Holy Mass where Jesus sacrifices himself for me. Oh God! Have mercy on me! The Jews don't harm me but maltreat me so that I become a Jewess again. But I only let them feel my disdain. I believe that shortly something will come from Kraków in order to free me from the Jews. I beg, Mother—for a prayer for me, for a prayer to Jesus that he have mercy on me and liberate me from the Jewish hands and that he may give me patience, so that in my despair I do not lay a hand on myself.

Debora ended her letter with a warning to the other Jewish girls in the convent:

> I also am asking the catechumen for prayer [that] Pepi shall not leave[66] . . . want to abduct [!]; Ela also—where is she?—must be careful. I kiss your hands, highly worthy one, my dearest Mother, I am asking sincerely for a prayer, for the mercy of the Holy Mother and her Holy Son. I kiss the hands and feet of the Sister, and in every prayer, I join and repeat the Our Father early in the morning and at night. I sing all litanies and everything outside of church, but I hope that Jesus will hear my prayers and will grant me return to the Mother, where I will tell everything in person.

Debora signed the letter, "Anastasya Marya who kisses the feet of the Sister."[67]

---

66. This is a reference to Peppi Singer, a fourteen-year-old girl from Drohobycz. For the December 1, 1901, notification of Peppi's intention to convert, see The National Archives in Kraków, Pełnomocnik ds. metryk izraelickich przy Magistracie miasta Krakowa, PMI 56, 139.

67. Lewkowicz file, Anastasya Marya's undated letter to Maria Rozalia, Felician Sisters' convent. The letter was written in Polish and translated into German for the authorities.

The first reaction of the convent upon receiving the letter was to complain to the police that Debora's religious liberty had been infringed upon, an act constituting an offense according to the Penal Code.[68] The Kraków police transferred a copy of the letter to the office of the public prosecutor so it could instruct the criminal court in the city to open an investigation. In the meantime, the criminal court in Kraków learned of Debora's whereabouts from the questioning of Zoller. Taking the matter seriously, the Kraków criminal court wrote to the regional court in Lubló, Hungary (today Stará Ľubovňa, Slovakia, 15 kilometers from Pilhov), explaining the situation and asking for a detailed interrogation of "Dorothe (Anastasya Marya) Lewkowicz who lives with Moses Schreiber in Pilhov," specifically about three questions: (1) when Debora left the convent, where she stayed, and whether all her actions since then were conducted out of her free will and without coercion; (2) whether and by whom was she persuaded, influenced, or coerced; (3) whether her letters to her parents and the convent [attached in a German translation] were written voluntarily, and how she explains the apparent contradiction between them. The result of the interrogation should then be compared with the attached testimonies of Zoller and Debora's father. The Kraków court requested that the Hungarian court send all the interrogation protocols to Kraków, so it can be determined whether this is a case of a criminal offense.[69]

The Lubló court cooperated and on November 8 issued a subpoena for Debora to appear at the court on November 19, at 8 o'clock.[70] Surprisingly, Debora was not in Pilhov at that time but rather back in Kraków, at least according to her upcoming testimony. It seems that after her hopes to marry Blaufeder did not materialize, she went to her parents' new home in Podgórze. Debora finally appeared in court in Kraków on November 12, where she had to explain the accusation of infringement of religious liberty specified in her letter to the convent. Debora admitted that her letter to the convent was not sincere, in contrast to her letters to her parents. She explained that she felt uncomfortable with the nuns since she had disappointed them, and that she didn't want them to know about her letters to her parents. She also added that she had regretted the trouble that she had caused, which is why she wrote to the convent.[71]

68. Nr. 117. Kaiserliches Patent vom 27. Mai 1852," *RGBl* (1852): 493–591, esp. §98, 515.

69. Lewkowicz file, letter of the Kraków criminal court to the regional court in Lubló ("alt Lublau"), October 28, 1901.

70. Lewkowicz file, subpoena for Debora, November 8, 1901.

71. Lewkowicz file, testimony of Debora, November 12, 1901.

Abraham Lewkowicz testified that he took Debora to Hungary "with her consent," allowing her to stay there as long as she would like. He emphasized that she was not being held against her will and her liberty was not infringed upon, and presented the court the last three letters she wrote as proof. Interestingly, he declared that he didn't withdraw his complaint against Bakalarz and Śmieszkiewicz.[72] Apparently, the investigation in this case ceased when the letter from Debora was received in the convent.

The court file doesn't say anything about the fate of the complaint against Bakalarz and Śmieszkiewicz, although the different court summaries leave the impression that it accepted the view that Debora's parents, when finding out about her relationship with Bakalarz, coerced her to marry a Jewish man, as a result of which she decided to flee from her home and convert. Debora then asked the help of Bakalarz and Śmieszkiewicz in carrying out her plan, rather than the other way around. It is also unclear what happened to the young woman after her final return to her parental home. One may assume with confidence that her parents, sensitive and loving as they were, did not try this time to coerce her to marry someone she was not interested in. But whether she ultimately remained a Jew is not known.

The overall impression Debora leaves in her letters to her father and to the convent is one of a deeply conflicted young woman, torn between rival loyalties, who is anxious to please everybody. Her letter to the convent may have been written out of her concern that her Catholic friends would feel angry or betrayed by her return to Judaism. Her personal confusion was perhaps exacerbated by religious confusion and feelings of guilt: shortly after she wrote to the convent about her recitation of the daily prayers, she wrote to her father about her observance of the Yom Kippur fast.

Although family ties prevailed, in the clash of loyalties between church and home Debora took care not to offend the Felician Sisters' convent or any of the Catholic Poles with whom she had been connected. She said nothing negative or derogatory about them in her testimonies. On the contrary, she felt guilty toward them, as if she had exploited their good will. She continued to insist that Bakalarz was not involved in her flight, even though she knew that her parents were pursuing a court case against him.

In a sense, Debora's ambivalence reflected her life on the boundary between the Polish-Catholic and Jewish worlds. Growing up in a small village, where there were very few Jews, and having friendly and open contacts with her

72. Lewkowicz file, testimony of Abraham Lewkowicz, October 10, 1901.

Polish neighbors, contributed in no small measure to her ambivalence. In the cities there were Jewish communities and a Jewish public space, of which one could feel a part. Moreover, in a city like Kraków many Jewish girls learned together in schools and thus could provide each other with a sense of social cohesiveness. By contrast, in a small village such as Rzeszotary, when Debora walked out of her house, she already was on the border between those worlds. With no Jewish community and Jewish indoctrination, and with significant Polish acculturation through the education system and through contacts with neighbors and other members of the public, it is small wonder that many Jewish women from villages around urban areas ran away from their homes and converted to Christianity, thereby becoming Polish.

Such young women were not provided the means by which they could pre-serve their Jewish identity in their confrontation with Polish society. The dis-sonance between home life and the outside world became greater as they grew older, with the conflicts becoming deeper and more pronounced. The climax would come when the parents expected them to marry a young man from the "old world," with whom they shared little in common. When such marriages were forced upon the young woman, the equilibrium between parents and daughter was knocked off kilter, and she fled to a refuge that not only sheltered others like her, but to which she had become acculturated in her schooling.

For young Jewish men, including those of the village, the Jewish world was fuller and more intense. Men bore the external signs of Judaism such as the skull cap and the *tallit katan* (a fringed undergarment), and their parents took care to send them to ḥeder rather than to public schools. They went with their fathers to the synagogue in the neighboring city, and a greater commitment to the ob-servance of the daily religious obligations was demanded of them. While urban Jewish women were, for the most part, able to live the double life of obedient Jewish wives and acculturated Polish women, the situation of educated women from the villages was completely different. But what ultimately attracted the at-tention of the Jewish public to the growing problem associated with young women was not what was happening with Jewish women from villages, but rather with those in the city, especially from Hasidic families in Kraków.

The "Daughters' Question"

More than a decade after the Araten affair and the Lewkowicz case, a writer observed in the religious Zionist *Ha-Mizpeh* that even the most Hasidic of the Hasidim is joyful when he discovers that his future daughter-in-law plays the piano, knows French and bookkeeping, and reads "scores of licentious books." He doesn't inquire whether she prays or whether she observes the Sabbath. The future father-in-law who will return the betrothal documents to the prospective groom if the latter is a member in a Zionist organization won't do the same if his future daughter-in-law desecrates the Sabbath, reads Catholic religious books, and accompanies her Catholic friends to church. The problem, according to the writer, was not that some Orthodox Jewish women were converting for lack of Jewish education, but that *all* of them were Jewish only by birth. Highly acculturated but Jewishly ignorant, these women were strangers to their parents, their people, and their society. The responsibility for the problem lay not with the government, or even the rabbis, but with Jewish society itself. "Everything is permitted for women, and nobody considers that these same women are the mothers of Jewish men, and even of Hasidim with sidelocks and silk clothes."[73]

The article in *Ha-Mizpeh* was the latest salvo in a debate conducted for several years in the Galician Jewish press, over the causes of, and responsibility for, the runaways crisis. While the Viennese liberal press continued to refer to Araten's and similar, less publicized cases as "abductions," the Galician Jewish press viewed them as the culmination of a problem that was long brewing and that resulted from the flawed education of young Jewish women. Since rabbis initially avoided speaking publicly about what became known as the "Daughters' Question," the Hebrew language press served as the main platform for discussions on the topic.[74] The moderate religious newspapers, generally Zionist in orientation, suggested establishing Jewish schools for girls in which they would be taught the Jewish religion, Hebrew language and literature, and Jewish history.[75] The Galician Orthodox press rejected this solution, insisting that there was no need to introduce innovations in the customary religious education of girls. Instead, it suggested limiting the secular education, teaching them only what was mandated by the state.

In 1902, the Orthodox organ *Kol Maḥazikei Ha-Dat* published a series of articles entitled: "But We Are Guilty on Account of Our Daughters." The

73. "The Education of Daughters: Response to Ahron Marcus," *Ha-Mizpeh*, August 2, 1912 [Hebrew].

74. "For the Betterment of the Daughters of Israel," *Ha-Magid*, June 19, 1902, 267–268 [Hebrew]. The author discusses conversions as well as the problem of white slavery, which involved young Galician, mostly poor, Jewish women.

75. Lazar, "Precious Out of the Vile," *Ha-Magid*, March 1, 1900, 100–101 [Hebrew].

author aimed his barbs not at village Jews but rather at the rich Hasidim, describing the way they educate their daughters as an "unforgivable sin." He too criticized the practice of providing daughters with more than basic primary schooling, especially the addition of private lessons in non-Jewish languages and literature. Such an education later leads to a gap between husband and wife, which is against the Torah commandment, "and they shall become of one flesh" (Genesis 2:24).[76]

In attempting to explain why the education of Jewish women had become a problem, the author described a time when Jews lived in seclusion from the outside world, surrounded by the walls built by foreigners as well as, voluntarily, by themselves. Literature taught to young men included only the Talmud and the works of the Jewish legal authorities; books for young women were the *Ze'ena u-Re'ena* and *Nofet Zufim*.[77] Jewish women found happiness in marrying a learned husband, and this created a life of true partnership. Since the fall of the ghetto walls, all daughters of Israel, including those of the very pious, have been attending schools and forming friendships with gentiles. The remedy the author suggested was more supervision and control by fathers in order to eliminate contacts with gentile men.[78]

In a subsequent article, the author claimed that the practice of giving girls an extensive secular education was particularly noticeable in Kraków. He quoted a friend who had told him: "Ten measures of external education (*haskalah hizonit*) descended upon the daughters of Israel in our country; the city of Kraków took nine of them."[79] The author rejected an acquaintance's suggestion to teach daughters Scripture, Hebrew, and the history of the Jewish people to the same extent that they were taught secular subjects and languages, arguing that this is but a minor remedy. The full remedy to the current problem is to limit the teaching of secular studies and foreign languages. Experience shows that men who had studied both religious and secular subjects abandoned religion. Torah and religion will not survive among daughters of Israel who are taught both. He

76. M. ben Yekeh [Mordekhai ben Yizhak ha-Levi me-Reisha], "But We Are Guilty on Account of Our Daughters," *Kol Mahazikei Ha-Dat,* January 31, 1902, 2–4 [Hebrew].

77. Also known as *Nahalat Zvi,* a popular eighteenth-century Yiddish compilation of ethical and narrative passages from the Zohar. See Baumgarten, "Yiddish Ethical Texts." The brief account of the history of Jewish education presented by the writer for *Kol Mahazikei Ha-Dat* reflects contemporary myths.

78. M. ben Yekeh, "But We Are Guilty on Account of Our Daughters," 3.

79. This is a play on the rabbinic dictum that ten measures of a certain quality descended to the world, and a particular city took nine of them. See B. T. *Kiddushin* 49a–b.

related a story of a friend who was present at the wedding of a daughter of a rich Hasid in Kraków. Watching her stepping down from a carriage, he thought that she looked and behaved like a true Polish young woman. After seeing her with the groom, a Hasid who looked like an "idler behind the stove" in a small town, he noticed the distance between them. On the Sabbath after the wedding he asked her about the quality of her marriage, to which she responded: "For matters of marital relations I am my husband's but nothing more."[80]

A few years later, the Orthodox weekly published another article on the subject, this time titled: "What Should Be Done with Our Sisters?." The author blamed the present crisis on a "breach" (*pirzah*) in the house of Israel, namely, the permission to study "*treifah pasul*" (ritually unfit food, i.e., secular subjects). It is this breach that caused fathers to allow their daughters to benefit from a higher education. Parents should ban their daughters from reading poisonous books and visiting the theater, providing for them instead the recently available books written in the spirit of Judaism (a reference to the books written by R. Samson Raphael Hirsch, the father of German Neo-Orthodoxy).[81] This author at least recognized the need for some Jewish education for women, albeit informal.

In 1904, a sixteen-year-old S. Y. Czaczkes (Shmuel Yosef Agnon, later the 1966 Nobel Prize laureate for literature), himself a religious Zionist, added his own interpretation to the question of education for Hasidic women. In a four-line poem titled "Out of Hate," published in *Ha-Mizpeh*, the young Agnon suggested a sarcastic parallel between the Hasidic families' practice of educating their daughters in Polish schools rather than establishing Jewish schools for them, and the Moabites' use of their daughters to entice the Israelites to the Baal worship in order to defeat them:

> The Moabites fought the Israelites with their deceitful tools
> By abandoning their daughters to beguile.
> The Hasidim send their daughters to [Polish] schools
> Since they hate the Haskalah vile.[82]

The Hebrew word *Haskalah* can mean education, but it was closely associated with enlightenment, which was a bête noire for the Hasidim. Part of the

---

80. M. ben Yekeh, "But We Are Guilty on Account of Our Daughters," 1 [Hebrew].

81. Shoham [Avraham Hayim Shenbakh], "What Should Be Done with Our Sisters?" *Kol Maḥazikei Ha-Dat*, February 21, 1907, 2–3 [Hebrew].

82. Sh. Y. Cz., "Out of Hate," *Ha-Mizpeh*, July 1, 1904, 6 [Hebrew].

rabbinic opposition to education for women may have stemmed from the fear that this education would employ the educational methods of the Maskilim, even the religious among them, something the Hasidim, who had battled with Maskilim since the dawn of Hasidism, would not tolerate.

Although the failure of the attempts of a few rabbis during the 1903 rabbinical assembly in Kraków to rethink the issue of female education put a quick end to the rabbinical involvement with this topic in Galicia, Jewish journalists kept raising it in the press. The solution of the Orthodox journalists was clear—restricting secular education for girls to what is necessary and mandatory—but as publicists, they lacked the authority to formulate clear religious norms in this area. The debate in the Orthodox press in the first decade of the twentieth century was not formulated in a systematic manner or carefully thought out, although it did alert the Orthodox public to a problem to which many preferred to turn a blind eye. Since it was carried out in the Hebrew press, it remained a debate within the boundaries of the Jewish community.

The question of female education finally became a pressing issue, not because of the many Jewish runaways from villages but only following a new scandal, the Kluger affair, which transcended the Jewish community and entered the Austrian legal and public spheres. This affair turned into a cause célèbre in Kraków and in Vienna, attracting much attention in the Galician and Austrian press, especially since it involved one of the most distinguished Hasidic families in the city, the Halberstam family.

4

Intellectual Passion

ANNA KLUGER AND HER STRUGGLE FOR HIGHER EDUCATION

IN CHOOSING TO run away from home and converting to Roman Catholicism, Michalina Araten and Debora Lewkowicz rebelled against their parents and the lives that had been planned for them. But they did not rebel against the traditional goal of youthful marriage; on the contrary, the crisis they experienced was precipitated by the prospect of marrying incompatible partners. Both came of age at a time when educational opportunities for women, while significant, were still limited. As more progress was made in this realm, especially in secondary and higher education, some Orthodox girls began to face different struggles. These were young, intellectually motivated women, who strove to take advantage of the new opportunities and continue their studies well beyond primary school. For women who depended upon the support of their parents to finance their secondary and even higher education, running away and converting was no answer.

Beginning in the early twentieth century, some affluent Orthodox Jewish parents, including Hasidim, allowed their daughters to attend secondary schools and even universities. Klara Gisela Baron, for example, the sister of the eminent historian Salo Wittmayer Baron, first enrolled in the philosophy faculty at the Jagiellonian University in Kraków for the academic year 1911/12 (a year before her brother). She left the university in 1914 in order to marry.[1] Klara Gisela Baron had grown up in Tarnów and had attended the local gymnasium. Her family was Orthodox and prayed in a Hasidic synagogue. Her

---

1. Gawron, "Salo W. Baron at Jagiellonian University," 74–75; Manekin, "Being Jewish in *Fin de Siècle* Galicia," 92–93.

father, Elias Baron, was a delegate in the founding conference of Agudat Yisrael party in Kattowitz in 1912.[2] Being affluent, the family could afford a university education for their children, and apparently did not resist their daughter's wish.

Other parents did resist. Wolf Kluger, a millionaire owner of a steam mill, buildings, and other assets, had a daughter, Anna (Chaja), who wanted nothing more than to pursue a university education.[3] Anna's mother was Simcha Halberstam, a great-granddaughter of R. Hayim Halberstam, the founder of the Hasidic Sandz dynasty. This Hasidic dynasty was known for its emphasis on Talmudic erudition and its "extreme conservatism in all aspects of education, dress, and everyday life and in its attitude toward modernism generally."[4] Anna Kluger's own rebellion revolved around her extraordinary efforts to continue her education, efforts that included running away from home with her younger sister, hiring a lawyer, and suing her parents not only to consent to their university study but to support them financially as students. Her story is the subject of this chapter.

The Education of Anna Kluger

Anna Kluger was born on June 24, 1890, in Podgórze. When she became of school age, her parents sent her first to an eight-year *Volks und Bürgerschüle* in Podgórze, where she studied for six years.[5] Anna was then sent for two years to the school of Ludmiła Tschapek, a private German *Töchterschule* in Kraków. Founded in 1881, the school taught students Polish, German, French, and English, as well as music and other subjects. The teachers were gymnasium

---

2. Agudat Yisrael, *Agudas Jisroel, Berichte und Materialien*, 33.

3. The Viennese *Neue Freie Presse* claimed that her father's fortune was worth two million crowns, see "Ein galizischer Familienstreit," *Neue Freie Presse*, June 7, 1910, 11. See also Rachel Manekin, "The Story of an Ultra-Orthodox Woman Who Fled Her Home Because of Her Desire for Education," *Haaretz*, Literary Supplement, July 29, 2016 [Hebrew]. After I wrote this chapter, I learned that an article about the Kluger affair had appeared in Poland; however, as its author explains in her English abstract: "The case of the Kluger sisters has been discussed here not so much in the context of women's struggle for the right to education, or traditions in a Hasidic family, but rather selected aspects of the model of paternal authority at that time against Galician civil and penal legislation." See Agata Barzycka-Paździor, "The Kraków Kluger affair."

4. David Assaf, "Sandz Hasidic Dynasty."

5. For the staff of the school, see *Szematyzm Królestwa Galicyi*, vol. 2, 564.

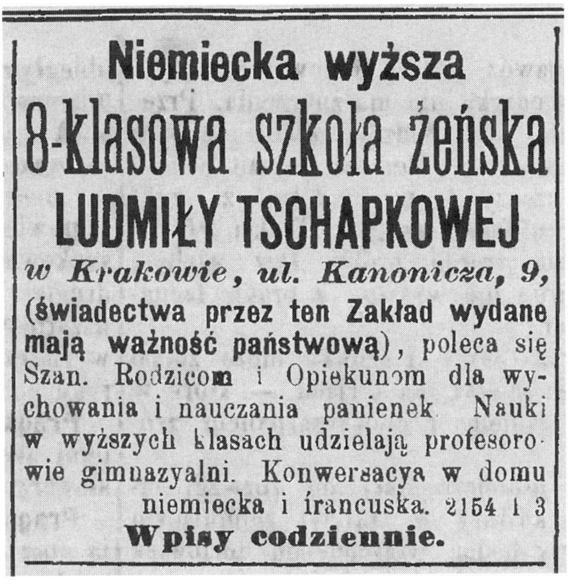

FIGURE 4.1. Advertisement for the Ludmiła Tschapek School.
Nowa Reforma, August 29, 1889, 4 (enlarged).

teachers.[6] Such a private *Töchterschule* was designed for daughters of upper-class Polish families and so was much finer than the school she had attended in her neighborhood.

Anna completed this part of her education in 1904.[7] Her parents also supplemented her formal education with private language lessons.[8] The highly publicized Araten affair, and the voices in the Orthodox press calling upon Hasidic parents to restrict their daughters' secular education to what was mandated by the government, did not deter the well-connected Klugers from providing Anna with the best general education, one that reflected their wealth and social status, as well as the intellectual gifts their daughter possessed.

6. On the school see *Krakowianin*, May 28, 1881, 5. The school diplomas were recognized by the state and enabled the graduating girls to continue their studies in the gymnasium, *Szematyzm Królestwa Galicyi*, vol. 2, 536–537, esp. 537. See an advertisement for the school in *Nowa Reforma*, August 29, 1889, 4 [Polish].

7. See the Curriculum Vitae written by Anna Kluger in her University of Vienna file, Vienna University Archives, PH RA 3892, Schachtel 58, 7.

8. "Ein galizischer Familienstreit," *Neue Freie Presse*, June 20, 1910, 10. This is a letter from the lawyer of the Halberstam family discussed below.

When Anna was fifteen, her parents arranged her betrothal with the fourteen-year-old Zacharias Arak (Arik), a nephew of the famous Galician Rabbi and Talmudic scholar Meir Arak, and grandson of the wealthy Mordecai Bergmann.[9] Up until that point Anna's life was not very different from other rich Hasidic daughters in Kraków who were well-known for their broad secular education. It was fully expected by her parents that Anna would follow the path of other Kraków Orthodox Jewish women, i.e., that she would marry and end her formal education.

Yet Anna was determined to continue her studies even after her betrothal. An Austrian law journal that reported on her subsequent court case described her as having a *"Wissensgier,"* a passion for learning.[10] She planned to prepare privately for the matriculation examinations and sit for them as an external student in one of the gymnasia in town. Unable to purchase the books for herself, Anna used the library of the Jagiellonian University, where she found the necessary materials. Upon discovering this, her parents appeared at the library with their lawyer, Dr. Jakob Aronsohn,[11] who demanded that the head of the library not provide books for their daughter. They could make this demand because, according to the Austrian Civil Code, children were considered minors and under the legal custody of their father until age twenty-four.[12] While the Civil Code recognized the duty of the family to educate their children, it was above all the duty of the father to do so. The mother's principal duty was to care for the children's physical needs and health. Since Anna had not reached the age of majority, her father's custody had to be respected. The parents' employment of a lawyer testifies to their absolute determination to stop their daughter's efforts at continuing her studies. What might have seemed to an outsider as a lack of consistency in the parents' attitude to their daughter's education was viewed by their social circle as quite normal. As one Orthodox man told his acquaintance: "When entering the marriage canopy, they will throw out all the nonsense (*shtutim*) and become pious women like their mothers,"[13] a prediction that, in this case, went unfulfilled.

---

9. "Eine Geschichte aus dem Ghetto," *Das Recht* 9:1 (1910): 5–9, esp. 6; "The Kluger Case," *Myśl Niepodległa*, June 1910, no. 138, 829–833, esp. 829 [Polish].

10. "Der Fall Kluger," *Das Recht* 7 (1910): 111–112, esp. 111. Two of her student friends described this as *"Wissendurst"* (thirst for knowledge), see Kluger, *Revisionsrekurs*, 10.

11. Aronsohn was a Podgórze lawyer, see *Verzeichnis der Advokaten und k. k. Notare in den im Reichsrathe vertretenen Königreichen und Ländern der österr.-ungar. Monarchie* 24 (1907): 58.

12. Ellinger, *Handbuch des österreichischen allgemeinen Zivil-Rechtes*, §21, 25.

13. "What Should Be Done with Our Sisters?" *Kol Maḥazikei Ha-Dat*, February 21, 1907, 2 [Hebrew].

Women's Higher Education in Its Habsburg Context

Although the behavior of Anna's parents toward their daughter's aspirations to continue her studies may seem today to be controlling and uncompromising, it should be noted that the general atmosphere in the Habsburg Empire, including that of the government authorities, was not particularly supportive of higher education for women at the same level as their male counterparts; women's organizations had to promote the establishment of private female gymnasia. This was also the case in Galicia.[14] Although elementary education for girls was already common in the late nineteenth century, albeit with an emphasis on skills viewed as necessary for females, Austria was slow in introducing secondary education for women. The first such school, a four-year secondary school, was opened in Vienna in 1871. In the next few years similar schools referred to as *Mädchenlyzeen* were established in the Habsburg Empire, including in several cities in Galicia. The aim of those schools was to teach girls languages and literature and a general education that was geared to women's domestic roles.[15]

In 1900 a new type of *Mädchenlyzeum*, a six-year school, became popular. These schools offered their students a graduation exam, but passing the exam did not qualify them to register as regular students in the university; rather, they were registered as special students who would train to become teachers in secondary schools.[16] Despite the pressure from female organizations, the Austrian authorities refrained from introducing public high schools for women that offered matriculation exams, especially since they viewed the female nature as unfit for academic studies.[17] As a result, only private gymnasia initially prepared their female students for the matriculation exams, like the first female gymnasium in Prague (1890) established by the *Minerva* society and the first one in Vienna (1892) established by the *Verein für erweiterte Frauenbildung*.[18] A private female gymnasium was established in Kraków in 1896; while it also prepared the students for the matriculation examinations,

14. Angelique Leszczawski-Schwerk, *Die umkämpften Tore*, 293.

15. Fischer-Kowalski and Seidl, *Von den Tugenden der Weiblichkeit*, 20–23.

16. Friedrich, *"Ein Paradies,"* 120–128; Engelbrecht, *Geschichte des österreichischen Bildungswesens*, vol. 4, 278–286.

17. Friedrich, *"Ein Paradies,"* 210–219.

18. When Anna and her sister studied at the University of Vienna, they became members in this society and paid four crowns for the annual fee, see *Jahresbericht des Vereines für erweiterte Frauenbildung in Wien* (Vienna, 1912), 21.

its main goal was more practical.[19] Students in these private gymnasia had to take their matriculation exams as external students in male gymnasia. The Austrian authorities did not wish to copy the male educational system for females, since schools for girls were viewed as institutions that should take into consideration the female "character" of its students.[20]

Given that higher education for women was opposed by many, the teaching profession for primary schools became a more accepted option for women, especially after 1870, when men still accounted for the majority of teachers. In 1871, female teachers' seminaries were established in Kraków, Lwów, and Przemyśl, many of whose graduates later enrolled at the universities.[21] Unlike men, most female teachers in the Habsburg Empire remained unmarried, partly because many of them were nuns.[22]

Galicia was quite advanced in the development of female secondary schools.[23] Of the 4,997 female secondary school students in the Habsburg Empire in 1912 (including the *Mädchenlyzeum* type), 3,606 were in Galicia, more than in any other Austrian crown land.[24] Three private gymnasia whose main aim was to prepare their students for the matriculation exams were established in Kraków; one was established in 1900 and the other two in 1906 and 1908. Between the years 1900 and 1918, 357 Jewish female students (including external students) received their matriculation certificates in two of the gymnasia, about 46 percent of the total number of students in those two schools. (There were no Jewish students in the third gymnasium.)[25] Anna, who planned to take her matriculation exams through the gymnasium established in 1900,[26] belonged to the first generation of young women in Kraków seeking a higher education.

19. Czajecka, "*Z domu w szeroki świat . . . ,*" 109–115.

20. Friedrich, "*Ein Paradies,*" 284.

21. Leszczawski-Schwerk, "*Die umkämpften Tore,*" 226. On the public discussions in Galicia on higher education for women see ibid., 225–256. See also Czajecka, "*Z domu w szeroki świat . . . ,*" 90–98.

22. Barth-Scalmani, "Geschlecht: weiblich, Stand: ledig, Beruf: Lehrerin," 374–376, 383–385.

23. Friedrich, "*Ein Paradies,*" 398.

24. Dutkowa, *Żeńskie gimnazja Krakowa,* 38. In 1914 their number rose to 3,921.

25. Ibid., 77. See also the names of the students, many of them distinctively Jewish. Ibid., 88–108.

26. Ibid., 96, where the name Chaja Kluger appears. The students had to take their matriculation examinations at the św. Anny male gymnasium in the city, see Czajecka, "*Z domu w szeroki świat . . . ,*" 123.

For more than a decade Kraków had been a hub of feminist activities.[27] While Anna's parents lived in a different social milieu, they were well aware of the recent educational opportunities that had opened up for women, and they may have been aware of prestigious primary girls' schools that were perceived as finishing schools, which did not contradict the future roles of women as wives and mothers. In contrast, the gymnasium and the university represented the modern world, specifically the recent new opportunities granted to women as a result of struggles waged by women's organizations demanding gender equality. Such opportunities threatened not only the lifestyle of the conservative Hasidic community, but also its ethos, which rested on clearly defined gender roles. Anna's determination to choose the path of higher education was thus viewed by her family as a rebellious act, and her family was determined to use all its power in order to keep their daughter from straying off the right path. As it turned out, Anna was just as determined to carry out her choice. A clash between family and daughter was inevitable.

The Passion for Study and the Unconsummated Marriage

Anna's intention to continue her studies did not alter her parents' plans for her. In August 1907, after a two-year betrothal period, she was married in a religious ceremony, avoiding the steps needed to make it a valid marriage according to Austrian law. (Such inaction was the norm among many Galician Jews.) [28] Her resistance to marry a man she barely knew was weakened when her mother promised her that after her marriage she would be freer to pursue her studies.[29] She initially refused to cut all her hair according to the Hasidic custom, consenting only after her mother had denied her food for two days.[30]

---

27. Kraków housed the third Galician women's conference in 1900 and another one in 1905, where issues connected to gender equality were discussed. The Kraków progressive biweekly for women, *Nowe Słowo* (1902–1907), published many articles discussing university education for women, as well as articles promoting feminist ideas written by Polish feminists such as Kazimiera Bujwidowa, Maria Dulębianka, Izabela Moszczeńska, and Gabriela Zapolska, see Leszczawski-Schwerk, *"Die umkämpften Tore,"* 242–244.

28. Such a marriage was considered by the state as invalid (*ungültig*), see Ellinger, *Handbuch des österreichischen allgemeinen Zivil-Rechtes*, §129, 69. For a history of the Habsburg Empire's legislation concerning Jewish marriage and divorce, see Manekin, "The Laws of Moses and the Laws of the Emperor: Austrian Marriage Laws and the Jews of Galicia," forthcoming.

29. "Aus dem dunkelsten Oesterreich," *Arbeiter-Zeitung*, June 6, 1910, 7.

30. *Das Recht* 9:1 (1910): 6.

Anna told her sixteen-year-old husband on the wedding night that she would not live with him "as a wife," to which he quietly acquiesced. As was the custom of young Jewish newlyweds, the couple first lived in her parents' home, and when her mother discovered half a year later that the marriage had not been consummated, the grandfather, Rabbi Moshe Halberstam of Chrzanów, as well as the young husband's grandfather, were called for a family consultation on the matter. R. Halberstam's advice was that if this continued, the young husband should consummate the marriage by force on a Tuesday, which according to Jewish tradition is a twice-blessed day.[31] His advice was not carried out since Zacharias Arak left that day for a family visit,[32] perhaps to avoid carrying out such an act. According to a Polish newspaper, Anna's husband was "a man of gentle virtues. He didn't claim his right as a husband; rather he allowed her to study, and even encouraged her to pursue her passion."[33] In spite of her mother's efforts to prevent her education, Anna managed to take her matriculation examinations. She received her matriculation certificate in 1908 and shortly thereafter clandestinely registered at the Jagiellonian University in Kraków.[34]

Realizing that she wouldn't be able to continue her studies under such difficult circumstances, Anna decided to flee from her home. She apparently planned her escape carefully, leaving on August 25, 1909, together with her younger sister, Leonore (Leja), who was studying at the time for her matriculation exams.[35] Leonore, who was not yet sixteen, was expected to become betrothed to a certain "Freilich" younger than she. According to her court

31. The arrangement and the expectations of the marriage, especially its consummation for the purpose of reproduction, seem to fit the customs of the Hasidic Sandz dynasty, see Granot, "Women's Status," 43–49; 52–53. The author emphasizes that R. Yekutiel Yehudah Halberstam reflects in his rulings the legal traditions of the Sandz Hasidic dynasty, ibid., 49.

32. "Ein galizischer Familienstreit," *Neue Freie Presse*, June 7, 1910, 11. This was repeated in many other newspapers. It should be noted that coercing a wife to have sexual relations is forbidden according to Jewish law, even in the case of a "rebellious wife" (*moredet*, a wife who refuses to have sex with her husband), see Rakover, "Coercive Marital Relations." See also Margalit, *The Jewish Family*, 10–39.

33. "Victims of Orthodox Jews," *Kurjer*, June 17, 1910, 1 [Polish].

34. See her name in the list of students, Kulczykowski, *Żydzi—studenci Uniwersytetu Jagiellońskiego*, 375. Kluger enrolled in the faculty of philosophy in the academic year 1908/09. In that year, 29 Jewish females and 28 Jewish males were enrolled in that faculty, ibid., 218. On women at the Jagiellonian University see Czajecka, "Z domu w szeroki świat...," 140–149.

35. See their names in a list of missing persons "Vermißt," *Volksblatt für Stadt und Land*, March 27, 1910, 8.

testimony she fell on her knees begging her mother not to compel her, but her mother pulled her up by her hair and hit her head on the wall. For undisclosed reasons the betrothal was canceled, and her parents betrothed her to a fifteen-year-old cousin "Halberstam" who was supposed to become the rabbi of Rzeszów.[36] The sisters took with them valuables worth 20,000 crowns and hid in a convent abroad, where they hoped they would not be discovered by their family.[37] Merely running away from home was not an option because, according to Austrian law, parents who were searching for their missing children who were minors were entitled to receive the help of the authorities in finding them.[38] The sisters hired a lawyer to represent them, Dr. Siegmund (Zygmunt) Marek, a known Social Democrat from Kraków (elected to the Austrian parliament in 1911) and one of the editors of *Naprzód*, the organ of the local Social Democratic party. There is no hint in any of the contemporary sources that Anna had ties with socialists prior to her escape, but since socialists in Galicia were among the supporters of granting women equal rights in education, the selection of Marek was reasonable.[39] Such a bold and unusual plan by a young woman is not only proof of Anna's absolute determination to leave the world of her parents and continue her studies, but also of her broken relationship with her parents.

The Court Case against the Parents

The relationship between children and parents was regulated in the Austrian Civil Code; so the only way for Anna and her sister to continue their studies despite their parents' opposition was to fight them in court.[40] Since Jewish

36. "Aus dem dunkelsten Oesterreich," *Arbeiter-Zeitung*, June 6, 1910, 7. Leonore Kluger's story merits a separate study.

37. The National Archives in Kraków, DPKr 75, 943/10 (henceforth: Police file). Apparently, those valuables—linen, clothing, precious objects, and cash that had been deposited in savings accounts—were given to them by their parents on different family occasions, see Kluger, *Revisionsrekurs*, 26.

38. Ellinger, *Handbuch des österreichischen allgemeinen Zivil-Rechtes*, §145, 76.

39. On the cooperation between Social Democrats and feminists in Galicia, see Dadej and Leszczawski-Schwerk, "Together and Apart."

40. Since I was unable to locate the relevant court files in the National Archives in Kraków, I have had to reconstruct the court proceedings based on newspaper reports and a copy of the printed twenty-seven-page appeal of the sisters to the Viennese Supreme Court which details the procedures in the local courts. See Kluger, *Revisionsrekurs*. It seems that parts of the appeal

religious marriages were not recognized as valid by Austrian law, Anna was not considered married but rather under the custody of her father.[41] But a father's custody was not absolute, and the Civil Code allowed the court to remove it under certain conditions, among them a proven accusation of abusive treatment at home.[42]

On October 30, 1909, about two month after the sisters' escape, and while they were still in hiding, their lawyer petitioned the district court in Podgórze to (1) recognize their freedom to study; (2) permit their residence outside their parents' home; (3) compel their father to provide appropriate living expenses; and (4) release them from his custody. In Anna's case, the petition was based on two claims: abuse at home and interference with her studies. The abuse claim rested on accusations of coercion to marry and the constant interference of the mother in the issue of the marital relations of Anna and her husband. This claim was essential for the request to remove the father's custody and thus had to be presented in detail. The district court recognized that there was a clash between parents and children and recommended appointing a guardian for the daughters. In response to the court's decision the parents submitted an appeal to the state court in Kraków, but on January 21, 1910, the appeals court determined that since it was established that Anna had already passed the matriculation exams and attended the university, and that the father had coerced her to get married in a religious ceremony and not according to state law, the parents' home was not a suitable place for the daughters. The daughters were estranged from their parents, and the conditions at home caused them anguish. Such circumstances could qualify as grounds for removing the father's custody according to the Civil Code. Satisfied with this decision, the sisters petitioned the court to appoint a guardian for them, let them live outside their home, study at the university, and receive financial support from their parents.[43]

The state court approached the district court on February 14, with a series of questions related to Anna's marriage. The latter court demanded that the sisters appear personally in court before it made any decision, something the

were sent by the sisters' lawyer to different newspapers, which then made use of them in their reports.

41. On the rights of parents and children see Ellinger, *Handbuch des österreichischen allgemeinen Zivil-Rechtes*, §§137–186; 72–92.

42. Ibid., §§174; 177, 87; 88.

43. Kluger, *Revisionsrekurs*, 6–7.

sisters refused to do. This was followed by another appeal by the sisters two weeks later, and when that didn't yield much result, they submitted another petition to the district court, this time requesting the testimony and interrogation of witnesses. Their request was granted and on March 15, 1910, the witnesses appeared in court, telling what they knew about the treatment Anna received at her home.[44]

Witnesses' Stories of Life in the Kluger Household

The first witness was Marie Kragen, a fifth-year medical student at the Jagiellonian University. Marie first met Anna in a biology colloquium in 1907 (Anna was probably an auditor at the time), and they became close friends. Anna told her that her parents had set the date for her marriage to Zacharias Arak, whom she barely knew, and who was a man with a worldview different from hers. While she was absolutely determined to continue her studies, something her parents had forbade her to do, Anna decided to marry Arak. She believed that her situation would become more tolerable, especially since her mother promised her that after the wedding she would no longer interfere in her affairs. Some time after the wedding, Anna told her that she was married in a religious ceremony and had informed her husband immediately afterward that since they don't know each other, she couldn't love him, had no sexual desire for him, and would not consent to marital intercourse with him. When they will get to know each other, perhaps she would love him and consent to it. Anna asked him not to attempt to make sexual advances, since any use of force on his part would create a lifelong chasm between them. She told Kragen that her husband consented and that they agreed to appear in front of the parents as if they were having marital relations with each other.[45]

Marie Kragen also told the court that Anna later visited her, appearing very tense, and told her that her parents refused to believe that Arak had marital intercourse with her, and that they asked him to consummate the marriage forcefully, as a result of which she felt compelled to leave her home. The witness told the court that she tried to convince Anna not to do that, describing in grim terms her future life as a runaway in a foreign place, and she received the impression that Anna was indeed convinced. A few days later Anna came

44. Ibid., 8–11.
45. Ibid., 8–9. Perhaps that had to do with the religious prohibitions connected to the status of *niddah* (a menstruant).

to her apartment telling her that she couldn't stay in her home any longer; after a family consultation, her parents decided to influence the juvenile Arak to have sexual relations with her on an agreed upon Tuesday. Marie tried again to convince Anna not to flee but rather to try and discuss this matter with her mother, who is after all a wife herself, and explain to her how indecent her approach was. Marie then went out of town for a while, and upon her return found out that Anna was still at her home, although determined to leave. She even wrote a farewell letter to her parents, but it was discovered by her mother who then promised not to intervene in her personal affairs. Meanwhile, Anna gave private German lessons in order to pay for her school fees and continued to prepare herself secretly at night for the matriculation exams. In response to a question by the judge, Marie said that she saw Anna after her marriage wearing a wig since all her hair was cut.[46] Marie added that Anna never complained about her father, and described him as a good, though not independent, man. Anna once told her that her father had asked her if she was indeed as cultured as people said, and whether she would be able to pass the matriculation exams. He expressed his wish, however, that she would not do that in Kraków but rather in a place like Vienna. When her mother found out about that conversation, she rebuked her husband and, since then, he too forbade Anna to study.[47]

Another witness, Helena Haeker, a third-year student at the Jagiellonian University, repeated similar conversations she had with Anna. She, too, said that Anna had consented to the marriage, thinking that it would free her from her parents' control. However, her mother had urged Arak to have marital intercourse with her as "a man," which he refused. Once, to deceive the parents, Anna even smeared the sheets with blood from her hand that she had wounded for that purpose. Haeker told the court that Anna's mother tried to put an end to their friendship and to that end sought her at her apartment. In response to the court's question, she said that Anna's mother suggested that she divorce Arak, but, fearing that she would be forced into another marriage, Anna refused, especially since Arak did not demand sexual relations. She too emphasized that Anna did not accuse the father in any wrongdoing, calling him a "henpecked husband" (*Pantoffelheld*) and a passive father.[48]

The last witness, Mrs. N. Rubinsten, a merchant's wife and a neighbor of the Kluger family, said that she heard that the Kluger sisters were well-educated and noticed that they were very decent girls. However, she did not notice any

---

46. Ibid., 9–10.
47. Ibid., 10.
48. Ibid., 8, 10–11.

conflicts between parents and children and did not hear that Anna was forced to marry Arak. She was busy with her own affairs and didn't care about the affairs of the Kluger family.[49]

Defeat in the Local Court

In their appeal to the local court the sisters attributed their parents' resistance to university studies to their Hasidic origin. They emphasized particularly their mother's origin, the Halberstam rabbinic dynasty, arguing that they believed that a Hasidic girl should acquire only elementary education and then, as soon as possible, get married and have children. Based on this principle, the parents absolutely opposed continuing their studies.[50]

During the court hearings in Podgórze on February 21, 1910, the parents declared openly: "We do not wish the continuing education of our daughter Anna, and in fact we oppose it resolutely and with full awareness." But then, on the same day, they recanted their declaration, claiming that they now permitted that education "resolutely and with full awareness." The daughters responded that they didn't believe this change of heart and would not return home. They viewed the parents' recent declaration as an act of hypocrisy designed to bring them back home.[51] Apparently, the parents had learned that according to the Civil Code, children past the age of fourteen who demand a different education than the one provided by the father, an education that is more suitable to their inclinations and abilities, and are refused, may submit their request to the court. The court would then make its decision based on consideration of the social class and wealth of the father, as well as the father's own arguments, and after an appropriate interrogation of the father and the request of the children.[52] As for the sisters' claim that their consent to marriage had been coerced, the parents responded that they were unaware of their daughters' opposition. They informed the court that they had already annulled the betrothal of the younger daughter, and they promised to bring about the

49. Ibid., 8, 11.

50. Ibid., 11.

51. Ibid., 12. The Viennese *Neue Freie Presse* cited the parents' declaration in court in which they said that they oppose with "complete determination and full awareness" the continued education of their daughter Anna, a declaration they reversed on the same day, see "Ein galizischer Familienstreit," *Neue Freie Presse*, June 7, 1910, 11.

52. Ellinger, *Handbuch des österreichischen allgemeinen Zivil-Rechtes*, §148, 407–408.

divorce of the older sister without any delay.[53] This declaration of the parents represented a concession to their daughters' principal demands and undermined the legal basis for removing the father's custody or any other request. The parents insisted that the sisters return home.

Although initially the court emphasized the coercion of the religious marriage as grounds for removing the father's custody, after hearing the testimonies and considering the parents' allegations, the court changed its mind, and on April 4, 1910, rejected the requests of the sisters. The court listed three reasons for its decision: (1) Anna Kluger consented to the marriage, thus misleading the parents. (2) Parents are not obliged to allow their daughters to attend the university. It is enough that they familiarize them with their future duties as wives and homemakers. (3) The sisters had ignored the religious practices at home and thus displayed a lack of deference toward their parents.[54]

Such a decision meant that the police were now required to help the parents find their missing daughters and bring them back home, even against their will.[55] Disappointed with the court's decision, the sisters' lawyer decided to appeal their case to the Supreme Court in Vienna. As a result, the Kraków court decision was stayed. According to the police file, the lawyer was trying in the meantime to gain sympathy for his clients in the daily press.[56] Indeed, the Viennese and the Polish Galician press continued to report on this sensational case, presenting it as a clash between benighted Jewish parents living in the "ghetto" of the periphery of the Habsburg Empire and their educated daughters, rather than in the context of the question of the rights of daughters to benefit from higher education versus the rights deriving from parental custody.

The Appeal to the Supreme Court in Vienna

In June 1910, the Kluger sisters appealed the Kraków court decision to the Viennese Supreme Court. [57] The appeal, signed by both sisters, is the only document we have in which the voice of Anna Kluger is recorded in the first

---

53. See *Das Recht* 9:1 (1910), 7. This article, which clearly sides with the daughters, cites the decisions and describes the events around the court case.

54. Kluger, *Revisionsrekurs*, 16. According to the Civil Code, children owed their parents respect and obedience, see Ellinger, *Handbuch des österreichischen allgemeinen Zivil-Rechtes*, §144, 76.

55. *Das Recht* 9:1 (1910), 7–8.

56. Police file, April 20, 1910.

57. Since the 1927 fire destroyed all civil archival documents of the Viennese Supreme Court, I had to reconstruct the event based on other sources. My thanks to the head of the library of the Supreme Court, Dr. Gerhard Schmaranzer, and its staff for their help.

person in a form of a personal statement.[58] While the appeal was carefully crafted with the help of her lawyer, the statement is still *her* story reflecting *her* experience at the time, thus making it an important and rare historical source. The main body of the appeal was designed to refute each of the points that the local court outlined as grounds for its decision. As for the consent to the marriage, Anna asserted that she was only fifteen years old when her parents betrothed her against her will to Arak, and in 1907, despite her begging and explaining that she refused to bind herself to a man who was completely unfamiliar to her, they had him marry her. The witnesses, who repeated what she had told them, explained that her tacit consent was the result of the torment she suffered at her parental home, and the belief that after the marriage she might attain a certain freedom and independence vis-à-vis the parents.[59] The Kraków state court didn't see or hear the testimony of the witness Haeker, which was given in the district court, who said clearly that Anna told her that she was forced to marry Arak. Anna emphasized that this witness did not say that she had pretended to live happily with her husband, but rather that she behaved as if she had marital relations with him. She did so to deflect the continuing stream of insulting and upsetting questions of the parents as to whether she was actually living with her husband as a wife.[60]

Anna explained that Haeker also testified that she disagreed with the proposed divorce, because she knew that her parents would force her into a new marriage. Anybody could sense the terrible situation in which she had found herself, so that she preferred the present evil to the uncertainty of a future in which she would perhaps suffer even more. On February 21, 1910, her lawyer stated clearly in court that she was prepared to divorce Arak at any moment, but in view of the search the parents have conducted for her "throughout Europe," it was not possible for her to receive the divorce. The most important aspect in this divorce was the actual delivery of the writ of divorce, an act that would have disclosed her whereabouts where she was safe from her parents' revenge.[61]

The local appeals court argued that, despite all this, "one can't say that the parents were trying to harm the children's well-being." This view of the court probably stemmed from the fact that the society to which the parents belonged held such views, namely, marrying their daughters even against their will. They

58. See appendix.

59. Kluger, *Revisionsrekurs*, 16.

60. Ibid., 17.

61. Ibid., 18.

assume that as young girls they are still ignorant and inexperienced, and their resistance is easily conquered; in time, however, things will get settled. Such views, Anna argued, do not correspond to the zeitgeist of the culture of the modern age and are reactionary and cruel to the highest degree. It is analogous to saying that parents have the right to awaken in the heart of their children the gentlest of human feelings with the use of a stick.[62]

Anna took issue also with the local court's opinion that no father is obliged to allow his daughters attend the university, and that it is enough that he familiarizes them with their future duties as wives and homemakers. She presented to the court colloquia and seminar grades from the first year of her university studies, emphasizing that during that time, because of the most terrible persecutions inflicted by her parents, she was only rarely able to attend lectures and was unable to study systematically. Despite that, she passed all lectures and colloquia examinations, receiving the grades of "excellent." She mentioned by name several of her professors, suggesting them as witnesses who "can confirm with what diligence, dutiful work, and interest, I devoted myself to scientific work."[63]

The sisters had to convince the Supreme Court that their parents' alleged change of heart was insincere. They did so by emphasizing that higher education was against their parents' *religious* beliefs:

> Our parents come from backward-Orthodox Jewish families; especially our mother, whose origin is from the rabbinical family Halberstam, which provides all Orthodox Jewish communities of Galicia with rabbis. In accordance with their origins and views, our parents are fundamentally against any higher education, for they uphold the view that a girl who comes from a Hasidic family is allowed to acquire only elementary knowledge, and she must get married and have children as soon as possible. [. . .] In the view of the Orthodox Jews it is altogether a sin if any of their children, especially

---

62. Ibid., 19–20.

63. Anna mentions Prof. Dr. Viktor Czermak (who taught world history), Prof. Dr. Wilhelm Michael Creizenach (grandson of the German-Jewish educator and theologian, Michael Creizenach, who taught German language and literature), Prof. Dr. Vinzenz Zakrzewski (a member of the Polish Academy of Science in Kraków who taught the history seminar), and lector Paul Ronieger (who taught French). See Kluger, *Revisionsrekurs*, 21. See also *Hof- und Staats-Handbuch der österreichisch-ungarischen Monarchie* 33 (1907): 812.

girls, strive for a higher education, and therefore our parents resisted our studies with all their might.[64]

The sisters further explained that the parents' lawyer initially declared that they believed that it is "a very severe sin" to study at the university.[65] They called the parents "fanatics" who insulted their "human rights and dignity" (*Menschen Rechte und Würde*) by forcing them to marry and expressed the hope that the Supreme Court will acknowledge their "absolute and unlimited right to personal freedom," and will not make them return to the parental home. They asserted that the physical and psychological anguish they suffered at home made it impossible to reawaken in their hearts the affection for their parents.[66]

The sisters concluded with a statement that the court's decision that they return to their parental home was tantamount to surrendering to the most shocking torments, "but it is also tantamount to a cruel disruption and destruction of our hitherto efforts and endeavors through which we can break down the barriers of a world full of superstition, a ghetto world, and step into the path of progress and of honest work."[67] The sisters claimed that after their escape from home, Orthodox rabbis ordered the recitation of a prayer for their death because they brought a disgrace upon their family.[68] The appeal, with its harsh words against the parents, was apparently formulated in order to satisfy the requirements of the sections in the Civil Code that would enable the Kluger sisters to be released from their father's legal custody, pursue their studies at the university, and live outside the parents' home. But for the average newspaper reader, the parts of the appeal quoted in the press entailed a lurid saga with sensationalist elements.

The sisters emphasized that the prescriptions in §148 of the Civil Code (inclinations and abilities not satisfied by the education given by the father) apply directly to their cause: The parents do not permit them to study at the university, whereas they themselves wish it. This issue is for them of the greatest importance and is essential for their spiritual-intellectual and moral development: "We do have abilities and are proving them with documents and witness statements; from this the conclusion follows that a consent from the

64. "Gettobilder aus dem Osten," *Deutsches Volksblatt*, June 9, 1910, 9; Kluger, *Revisionsrekurs*, 11.

65. Ibid., 12.

66. Ibid., 13.

67. "Gettobilder aus dem Osten," *Deutsches Volksblatt*, June 9, 1910, 9; Kluger, *Revisionsrekurs*, 14.

68. Kluger, *Revisionsrekurs*, 14. I did not come across any rabbinical source for such a prayer.

side of the court regarding permission of our further studies must supersede that of our parents, and that the parents are obligated to contribute some means to further our education."

The lower appellate court's view was that since the parents had provided them with an elementary education, and through their great wealth would also assure their future, the daughters should not demand anything further from them. To this the sisters reacted, saying:

Does the court really believe that only material wealth assures a human being a future, that is, happiness and satisfaction? [...] We have so far not discovered in us special abilities and assets for being good wives and housewives according to the recipes of the court. We are however of the opinion that it is far better to develop and further our already existing abilities and inclinations for scientific work, rather than to concern ourselves about guidance for a future role of good housewives, for which we do not show the slightest wish. [69]

The sisters also rejected the third point cited by the court, namely, the accusation of the lack of religious observance at the parental home, which apparently occupied a large part of the court's decision. The sisters claimed that the parents had never accused them of such and that they had no complaint in this regard. The two seemed surprised by the inclusion of this accusation in the court's decision, stating:

On the contrary, we behaved in perfect observance concerning the religious customs and mores in the house of our pious parents, and if in our original petition we emphasized that oftentimes such circumstances as for example the accidental extinguishing of a light on Saturday, or the carrying of a money purse on a Friday after the lighting of the candles—would provoke outpouring of rage, punishments, and curses in our parents, we only did this with the purpose of demonstrating and highlighting how fanatical our family is, but in no way was it our intention, to build up upon this any of the petitions presented to the court. Therefore, it was a pointless effort of the court to argue this, which neither the parents nor we ourselves disputed, and therefore we shall no longer concern ourselves with this issue.[70]

69. Ibid., 22.
70. Ibid., 23.

While the style of the counterarguments in the Supreme Court appeal conveyed passion, it seems that the point about the forced marriage indeed needed the additional nuanced explanation. The fact that Anna preferred to remain married to Arak didn't mean that her marriage was not coerced. On the other hand, she gave her consent to the marriage hoping that it would give her more freedom to study. The marriage question and the education question were tied to each other and clearly represented an abusive attitude at home, but separating the two questions, as the lower appellate court did, removed the grounds for Anna's claim about a forced marriage. The appeal insisted that the issue of university study was based on §148, although this paragraph talked about skills and inclinations in general. The sisters explained that this paragraph was written a hundred years beforehand and needed to be interpreted according to the spirit of the time. They used the terms "wives" and "housewives" as outdated concepts when applied to female education as the purpose of study. In that, they presented themselves as radical progressive women even according to the local feminist ideas of the time.[71] The issue of observing the religious commandments, which was apparently first used by the sisters when they tried to prove to the court how fanatical their parents were, shouldn't have been used against them. Citing specific transgressions, they told the court how they were abused by the family when they were caught committing them. Claiming that they were religiously observant at home, the sisters refused to even discuss this new allegation in their Supreme Court appeal.

The Debate of Narratives in the Press

Aware of their negative image in the press, which continued to cite parts from the Supreme Court appeal leaked by Zygmunt Marek, and its possible influence on the public opinion and the judges, the parents' lawyer requested of the Viennese *Neue Freie Presse* to publish their version of the events. That version was also tailored to correspond to what the Civil Code deemed to be their legal rights as parents. Because this is the only narrative of the parents' side available to me, it is reproduced here in its entirety:

> The parents of the sisters Anna and Leonore Kluger, though devout Israelites, nevertheless did not fail to provide an appropriate education for their

---

71. Polish feminism at this time didn't doubt the role of women as wives and housewives, see Leszczawski-Schwerk, "*Die umkämpften Tore*," 263–264.

daughters; not only did they not hinder their education but offered them opportunity to achieve an education appropriate for the bourgeois classes (*bürgerliche Stände*). Both daughters not only attended the *Bürgerschule* but after completing it, they enjoyed further lessons in a private school, and were especially able to learn foreign languages with private tutors.

Also, up until their escape in September of last year the two sisters never showed any indication that they were not in agreement with the education offered to them or with other customs in the parental home. To the greatest surprise of the parents now both sisters used the absence of their mother in September of last year to secretly leave the parental home, without having announced such an intention earlier or having attempted an escape. The dismayed parents, in spite of intensive investigations, have not been able to find out the location of their children, and to this day it is not known to them. Only through a petition handed to the regional court in Podgórze by the representative of the sisters did the parents find out to their greatest amazement that the sisters were not content with the conditions in the parental home. As reason for their discontent they stated that their wish to obtain university studies was supposedly not fulfilled, and the older sister, Anna, in particular, stated that she had been forced into a religious marriage by the parents. The latter statement by the older daughter however is entirely untrue, as the older daughter had of her own free will complied without resistance to the rites of the religious marriage customary in Galicia, and never mentioned to the parents her discontent about this marriage.

Only through the court reports of the sisters' attorney did the parents find out about the complaint that the sisters are concerned not only about permission for continuation of university studies, but that they are expressing a complete estrangement from their parents and are seeking permission to live away from the parental home and wish to withdraw from the parental custody. As the parents of course, more than anything, are concerned about the well-being of their children and would like to have the missing children return, the parents immediately and out of their own free will declared in court that they agree to the further education of their daughters and to provide the means for this. At the same time the parents, under great sacrifices, saw to it that the ritual marriage of the oldest daughter was ritually dissolved and obtained the proof that the divorce papers are filed at the appropriate rabbinate office. The only reason it cannot be sent to the daughter is that her current residence address is unknown. Although the parents thereby immediately, and of their own free will, complied fully with the daughters' complaints, and although the district court and the court of appeals upon the parents' agreement granted the sisters permission for university studies, the sisters have not returned to their hometown, are keeping themselves hidden, and are continuing their fight against the parents through the means of recourse to the Supreme Court; they want to push through their desire to live away from the parents' home and to be freed from the father's custody, although this petition has been denied by two lower court authorities. The reason given for this fight, which goes against all natural feelings of a child, is, that the sisters fear that the parents' promise, solemnly given in court, would later not be kept. As however the immediate agreement of the parents indicates that they only seek to obtain the return of the lost children, this fear appears to be unfounded. The entire affair, regarded from an emotional viewpoint, is such, that it should be solved not through the courts but through mutual accommodation and trust, and the parents have brought enough proof that they consider this path the right one and that they are always ready to offer their hand to forgive and forget.[72]

This version of the events denied in effect any abuse connected with the marriage, especially regarding the marital relations. It presented a picture of normality where the parents were totally unaware of any unhappiness of their daughters, and upon finding that out through the lawyer's petition, were willing to go all the way to fulfill their daughters' wishes. It seems that the most painful aspect of the whole affair from the point of view of the parents was the sisters' demand to be released of their father's custody and to live outside the parental home. That radical demand, more than things that pertained to religious customs, inflicted a public shame on the family and painted them as cruel parents.

Indeed, the parents, via their lawyer, expressed their arguments in a humble, gentle tone, probably with the hope of changing the narrative into a story of a family affair best resolved at home and not in court. The parents' lawyer sent a similar note to the democratic Kraków newspaper *Nowa Reforma* in an effort to influence Polish public opinion as well. Following this, the paper explained to its readers: "We received from the legal representative of the parents [of Anna and Leonore Kluger,] Dr. Aronsohn, a comprehensive letter depicting this sensitive matter in a completely different light than was presented in many journalistic reports." Unlike the Viennese paper, the Polish paper gave just a short summary of the lawyer's letter, emphasizing the agreement of the parents

72. "Ein galizischer Familienstreit," *Neue Freie Presse*, June 20, 1910, 10.

to let their daughters continue their studies, to terminate the marriage of Anna, and to give their daughters complete freedom in marriage decisions. Nevertheless, the parents insisted that their daughters return to their parental home.[73]

The somewhat sympathetic tone of this Polish newspaper did not remain without response. Just three days later it published selections from a long rejoinder mailed to the paper by Dr. Marek, the sisters' lawyer. The paper left it to the readers to make their own judgment:

> The widely disputed case of the Kluger sisters, which has been preoccupying the public opinion due to its background as well as its general significance, has recently entered the stage of a journalistic debate published in the press by the legal representatives of both sides of the conflict [. . .] A few days ago we published in this journal an "explanation" that Dr. Aronsohn provided us which presented the parents' approach toward their daughters. As a follow-up to this statement, we are now bringing the testimony written by Dr. Marek, a legal representative of both daughters, in which he drafts an opposite picture of the case, bringing several reasons substantial for the reader to come up with the conclusions about the essence of this dispute.[74]

Marek claimed that the arguments of the parents' lawyer were false. While criticizing the court's decision from April 4, especially its acceptance of the parents' statement which promised to allow Anna to study at the university, Marek revealed damaging new information about the parents:

> I do believe, however, that in its following ruling dated May 17, the Kraków court has substantially softened its previous strict ruling by stating that "the parents are admitting that they mishandled and behaved badly toward their daughters and the actions from the past shall be reversed as bad ones and shall be prevented in the future." Stating the above, the court has kept its negative ruling based on the above promise made by the parents, believing that "as for now we shall trust the father that he will fix the harm," and it wouldn't be until later, in case he did not keep his word, when the daughters would be allowed to seek again support in court.[75]

The court ruling of May 17 was not cited anywhere else. It was probably given after an appeal was filed against the April decision of the local court, and after

---

73. "On the Case of Anna and Leonore Kluger," *Nowa Reforma*, June 13, 1910, 2 [Polish].

74. "The Kluger Case," *Nowa Reforma*, June 17, 1910, 2 [Polish].

75. Ibid.

Marek drafted the appeal to the Supreme Court, and thus remained unknown to the public. As far as Marek was concerned, this was enough to discredit the parents' narrative.

Reports about the Kluger Supreme Court appeal also appeared in the Jewish press, although not in the Galician Orthodox Jewish press. Perhaps the involvement of one of the most important Hasidic families in Galicia made the story too sensitive for the latter to even mention.[76] The unaffiliated Lwów Yiddish newspaper *Togblat* printed the story with all its details, but tried to stay neutral by describing it as a "family opera."[77] The more ideological *Ha-Mizpeh* used the opportunity to mercilessly attack Hasidim in general and the Halberstam family in particular. In a tone dripping with sarcasm, it explained that the mother had forgotten that her daughters were also descendants of the great Rabbi Hayim and would not do anything against their convictions, an allusion to the zealotry associated with this Hasidic dynasty. The paper noted the public repercussions of the affair, especially that "private matters between a Jewish wife and her husband are bandied about by everybody in the taverns and published in all the newspapers. The Jewish name is desecrated, the anti-Semites have a field day; and the lives of modest Hasidim are the butt of scorn."[78] The cause for what happened, according to this paper, was the lack of Jewish primary schools wherein boys and girls could study both religious and secular subjects, thus eliminating the increasing gap between young men and women. Both papers failed to appreciate the passion women like the Kluger sisters had for higher education.

The Final Decision

Following the newspaper reports about Anna Kluger, the question whether fathers can be obligated to send their daughters to the university was raised in the budget committee of the Austrian Parliament by Herman Diamand, a

---

76. Apparently, after the sisters escaped from home in August 1909, the Gerer Hasidic prayer house in Kraków adopted regulations designed to avoid similar family tragedies, among them forbidding girls from attending more than a seven-grade public school, speaking Polish on the Sabbath, or visiting the theater, see *Ha-Mizpeh*, September 15, 1909, 4 [Hebrew].

77. "A Kraków Family Opera," *Togblat*, June 12, 4 [Yiddish].

78. "The Leech Has Two Daughters," *Ha-Mizpeh*, June 24, 1910, 2 [Hebrew]. See also the first report on the case, "Vengeance Against Parents and Teachers," *Ha-Mizpeh*, September 10, 1909, 3 [Hebrew].

member of the Social Democratic party from Lwów.[79] But the shift from a sensationalist Hasidic family drama to the story of a young woman's struggle for higher education occurred after the Viennese Supreme Court delivered its verdict on September 3, 1910. The Court canceled the decision of the Kraków court and called for appointing a guardian for the sisters to ensure the protection of their rights.[80] The Supreme Court refrained from making a final decision and instructed the Kraków court to conduct a detailed investigation, after which a final decision would be made.[81] The investigation, according to the Supreme Court, should determine whether the girls' books that the parents had torn and burned were textbooks or other books; whether the university lectures they attended had been accurately reviewed by the court, and whether the prohibition of the daughters to speak Polish at home was restricted to the days of the week or only to Jewish holidays. The Supreme Court also asked that the investigation determine whether the harsh treatment of the girls resulted from their opposition to the marriage arrangements or from their deliberate nonobservance of religious commandments, which would hurt the religious sentiments of the parents, or for other reasons.[82]

One of the Viennese law journals took issue with the type of questions detailed in the Supreme Court decision and voiced an open criticism:

> If posing these questions in this form is regarded as essential, then, depending on the different answers, a different decision on the case will likely be expected. Assuming that it was not school books that were torn up, but rather the works of a Friedrich Schiller or an Adam Mickiewicz, or even a volume by Zola—one does not even dare think of one of the great godless philosophers—will the brutal repression of the thirst for knowledge appear in a friendlier light? Or will the force used against the children for using a despised, seedy jargon instead of speaking with one another in the living language of their country be justified, when the people who are not allowed to use the name of God in vain, employed the required sanctification of God on Holidays as a pretext? And will the Supreme Court really take the position, as it implies it will, that the criminal misguidance of a girl, barely

79. "Ein galizischer Familienstreit," *Neue Freie Presse*, June 7, 1910, 11; "Aus dem dunkelsten Oesterreich," *Arbeiter-Zeitung*, June 6, 1910, 7.

80. Der Fall Kluger," *Das Recht* 7 (1910): 111–112, esp. 111.

81. Ibid., 112.

82. Ibid., 111.

of age, to commit to a legally-prohibited ritual "marriage" with a boy the same age—will the Court really say that such a "marriage" is an institution to be morally protected and approved, so that even abuses towards the resistant children should be excused?[83]

In any event, the Viennese Supreme Court's decision was sent by telegraph from Kraków, where it was first received, to the Viennese press, which published it in articles under such headings as: "The Struggle for Education,"[84] and "The Right for Education."[85]

The regional court in Kraków conducted additional investigations as instructed, and a succession of witnesses testified that the sisters were abused at home, and that Anna was required by her parents to have marital relations with her husband. Anna was also forced to promise in front of the Rabbi of Dąmbrowa (probably Rabbi Meir Unger, who was the leader of the Dąmbrowa Hasidim in Kraków) that she would not visit the theater. The sisters were strongly forbidden from speaking Polish in their parents' home and were punished when caught doing that. According to the witness Helena Haeker, the sisters were once beaten on the Jewish Day of Atonement when discovered speaking Polish with their friend. Interestingly, according to the testimonies, the parents allowed their daughters to read, but only novels. They were forbidden from reading scholarly books.[86] While reading of novels was generally frowned upon, it didn't pose the same threat as reading scholarly texts. Moreover, young women reading scholarly books was something new and associated with the higher education of women, which threatened the social norms, especially the roles assigned to women. Because of their modern outlook and thirst for study, they endured at their parents' home not only physical but also psychological anguish. Such treatment was enough to remove the father's custody over his children according to §177 of the Civil Code, and so the court appointed the lawyer, Dr. Salomon Oberländer of Podgórze, as guardian of the sisters. Oberländer then requested the court in the name of the sisters to allow them to live outside the parental home and attend the university, which the court granted soon afterward,

83. Ibid., 112.

84. "Das Kampf um die Bildung," *Grazer Tagblatt, Abend-Ausgabe*, September 6, 1910, 4; *Tages-Post*, September 6, 1910, 7; *Neue Freie Presse*, September 4, 1910, 15–16.

85. "Das Recht auf Bildung," *Neues Wiener Journal*, September 4, 1910, 15.

86. "The Kluger Case," *Nowa Reforma*, October 22, 1910, 4 [Polish].

based on §148 of the Civil Code. The sisters' request for financial support was also granted, based on §139, which among other things obligated fathers to provide for a decent livelihood for their children.[87] The court obliged the father, Wolf Kluger, to support each of the sisters with a monthly sum of 200 crowns, as they had requested.[88]

What made the Kraków court reverse its earlier negative decision and rule in favor of the girls? The atmosphere in the city had changed somewhat in the meantime. For instance, on June 6, several months before the Kraków court delivered its final decision, and after the first reports about the Kluger sisters' appeal to the Supreme Court had been published in the press, students at the Jagiellonian University assembled in the Copernicus auditorium to express their support for their fellow student, Anna Kluger, and to voice their anger at the Kraków court's earlier decision. A Polish press report hinted that the first court decision was a result of the influence of the economic power and wealth of the Kluger family. The students voted unanimously on a resolution supporting Anna and condemning the Kraków court's decision to accede to her parents' request to forbid her university studies.[89] The Zionist youth expressed their opinion that the older Jewish generation opposed higher education for the younger generation because experience proved that such education caused them to become indifferent to their people and traditions. As Zionists, they viewed the whole affair through a nationalist lens, giving less emphasis to the personal, individual issue. This explanation invoked some criticism among the participants, but at the end, the Zionists' resolution called for support of higher education and uprooting evil from within the community.[90] The increased publicity concerning the case, especially when the investigation proved that the sisters were abused at their home, may have been a factor in the court's reversal.

87. Ellinger, *Handbuch des österreichischen allgemeinen Zivil-Rechtes*, §139, 73.

88. "Der Kampf um die Bildung," *Neue Freie Presse*, October 30, 1910, 17; *Neues Wiener Tagblatt*, October 30, 1910, 15; *Arbeiter-Zeitung, Morgenblatt*, October 30, 1910, 13; "Children against Parents," *Togblat*, November 2, 1910, 1 [Yiddish].

89. "Victims of Orthodox Jews," *Kurjer*, June 17, 1910, 1–2 [Polish]. See also "Against Hasidic Clericalism," *Naprzód*, June 8, 1910, 2 [Polish]; "In den Fesseln des Ghettos," *Arbeiter-Zeitung, Morgenblatt*, June 9, 1910, 5.

90. "Victims of Orthodox Jews," *Kurjer*, June 17, 1910, 2 [Polish].

Doctoral Studies at the University of Vienna
and Professional Life

Anna Kluger left the Jagiellonian University on November 6, 1911.[91] She then
traveled to Vienna to begin her doctoral studies in the philosophy faculty of
the University of Vienna in the winter semester of 1911/12. She listed her residence place as "IX Wasagasse 20/18, Vienna," and her name as "Chaja alias
Anna Kluger." Her dissertation, "Die Jugend Mazzinis und seine erste Verschwörung 1833" ("Mazzini's Youth and His First Conspiracy in 1833") was
approved on May 25, 1914, less than four years after the Kraków court's final
decision. Anna's dissertation advisors, the historian Alfred Francis Přibram
and the constitutional expert Joseph Redlich, gave the work the grade "satisfactory" (*befriedigend*), but added: "When assessing the work, it should be
pointed out explicitly that by its scholarly quality, the treatise in question sur-
passes the standard of the ordinary, and it demonstrates the aptitude for independent research in an exceptionally excellent manner." After her two-hour
thesis defense on November 26, 1914, Přibram gave her the grade "distinguished" (*ausgezeichnet*) and Redlich, "sufficient" (*genügend*).[92] Kluger was
granted her doctoral degree on December 22, 1914.

In 1922, at the Kraków Temple, Anna married the attorney Dr. Jakub Bross
(1883–1942), a Galician social democratic politician and later a member of the
Jewish Social Democratic Party (ŻPPSD) and the Bund.[93] I do not know
when she collected her writ of divorce from Zacharias Arak, which had been
deposited at the office of the Kraków rabbinate. Following Jewish law, Arak
had already received permission from a hundred rabbis to marry another wife
before the writ of divorce was received by Anna.[94] As was the case with many
women with university degrees at the time, Anna became a gymnasium
teacher; in her case, she taught history and geography at the coeducational
Hebrew Gymnasium in Kraków, where initially she was the only female
teacher with a PhD. She also worked in her spare time as a professional

91. For her university file, see The Archives of the Jagiellonian University in Kraków, Katalog
główny studentów, S Il 205 b, 1908/09 Filozofia; SII 206B 1908/09 Filozofia; SII 218 1909/10
Filozofia.

92. "Rigorosenakt No. 3892," Vienna University Archives, PH RA 3892, Schachtel 58, 6, and
unpaginated pages.

93. See http://www.jhi.pl/psj/Bross_Jakub.

94. Cohen, ed., *Sefer Butshash*, 207.

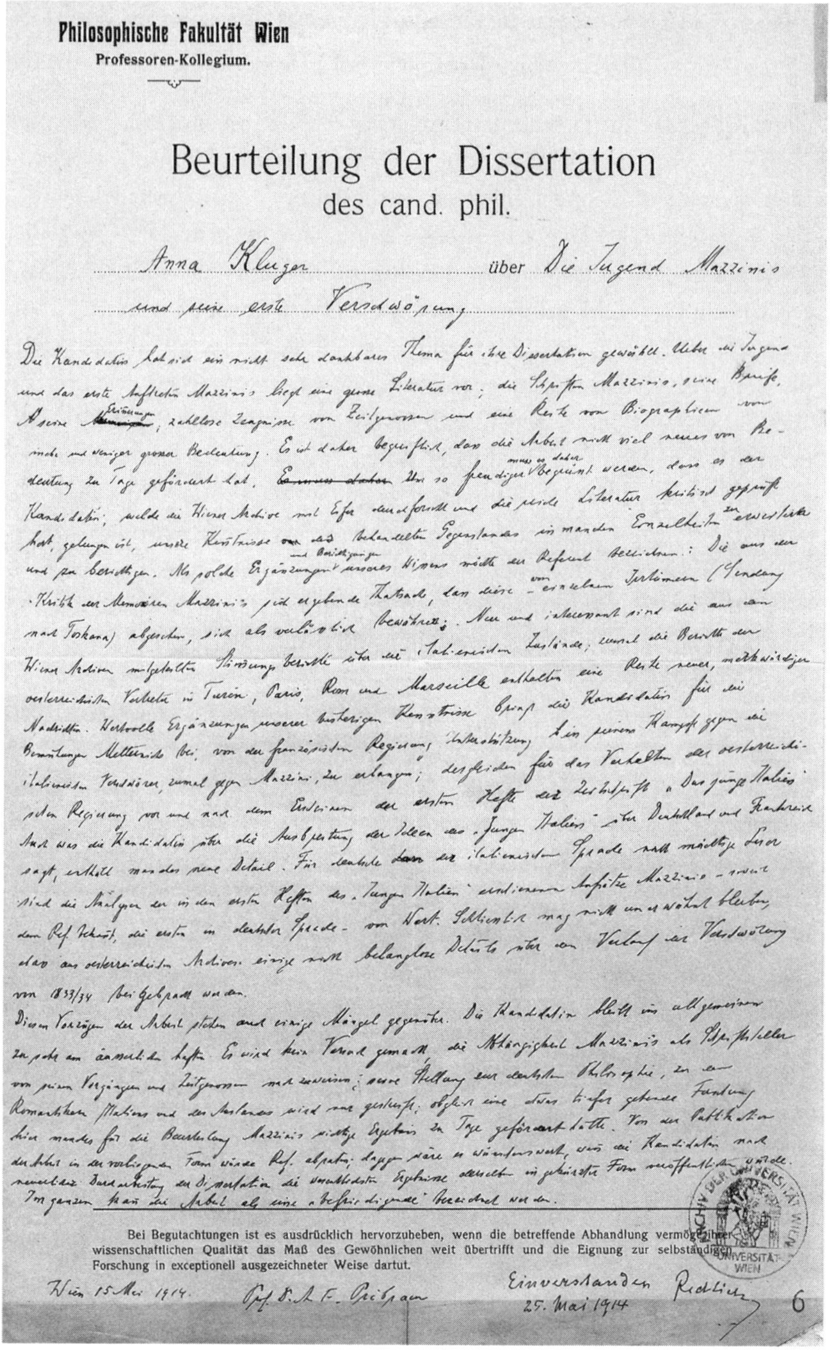

Philosophische Fakultät Wien
Professoren-Kollegium.

Beurteilung der Dissertation
des cand. phil.

Anna Kluger über Die Jugend Mazzinis und seine erste Verschwörung

Bei Begutachtungen ist es ausdrücklich hervorzuheben, wenn die betreffende Abhandlung vermöge ihrer wissenschaftlichen Qualität das Maß des Gewöhnlichen weit übertrifft und die Eignung zur selbständigen Forschung in exceptionell ausgezeichneter Weise dartut.

Wien 15 Mai 1914.

Einverstanden
25. Mai 1914

6

FIGURE 4.2. Evaluation of Anna Kluger's dissertation. Courtesy of Vienna University Archives, PH RA 3892.

translator, advertising her knowledge of French, German, Italian, Hebrew, and Yiddish in addition to Polish.[95] During this period she continued to publish her research under the name Anna Bross, first in historical and later in pedagogical journals.[96] In 1939 she published her book, which was based on her dissertation.[97] Her remarkable life was cut short when she was murdered with her husband by the Germans in Kremenets (Krzemeniec) in 1942.[98]

To appreciate Anna Kluger's extraordinary achievements, it should be noted that women were first admitted as regular students to universities in the Habsburg Empire in 1897, and then only to the philosophy faculties.[99] (In 1900 they were admitted to faculties of medicine and in 1919 to law faculties.) Their admittance met with much resistance, especially because of fear of future economic competition with males.[100] When Anna started her studies in Vienna, there were only a few hundred female students in the philosophy faculty. Most of the women studied pedagogy and about a third studied history. The number of PhDs granted to women in the philosophy faculty in the year 1913/14 was twenty-nine (altogether 51 females between the years 1903/4 and 1911/12).[101] Interestingly, Galician women made up 14.2 percent of the female students in 1913/14, more than any other Austrian province except Vienna. In that year 2.7 percent of the female students in the philosophy faculty listed Yiddish as their mother tongue.[102] Among the Galician female students in Vienna, Jewish students were the largest group.[103] Clearly, Anna Kluger belonged to the pioneer generation of the female doctoral students in the Habsburg Empire. Her career signified the potential that the new educational opportunities held for

95. *Dziennik urzędowy Ministerstwa Sprawiedliwości* 1 (1936): 13.

96. Her articles include: "Quelques rapports à Metternich sur Charles-Albert de Savoie" (cited in Paul W. Schroeder, "Metternich Studies Since 1925," *Journal of Modern History* 33.3 (1961): 250); "Die pädagogischen Ideen Berthold Ottos"; and "Pestalozzi und der polnische Freiheitsheld Kosciuszko." She also published numerous articles in the Polish journals *Przegląd Pedagogiczny* and *Filomata*.

97. Anna Bross, *Józef Mazzini*.

98. Manuel Rympel, "A Word about Kraków Jews in the Interwar Period 1918–1939," 555–588, esp. 564. Her life after receiving her PhD deserves additional research.

99. For the 1897 law allowing women to be admitted to the philosophy faculties in Austrian universities, see Beck and Kelle, *Die österreichischen Universitätsgesetze*, 567–569.

100. Heindl, "Zur Entwicklung des Frauenstudium in Österreich," 18–20; Tichy, "Facetten des Widerstands," 27–29.

101. Tuma, "Studienwahl—Fächerwahl—Studienabschlüsse," 84; 87; 90.

102. Heindl, "Regionale und nationale Herkunft," 114; 116.

103. Waltraud Heindl, "Die konfessionellen Verhältnisse," 140.

FIGURE 4.3. The teachers of the Hebrew Gymnasium in Kraków (Anna Kluger-Bross is fourth from the left on the first row). Courtesy of the Association of Cracovians in Israel.

capable young Jewish women who thirsted for intellectual development. Such thirst was viewed as dangerous by the society that raised her, and it now needed strategies for containing and channeling that passion.

Moving the issue of the education of Jewish girls from the Jewish public sphere into the civil court houses and the non-Jewish media was a turning point in the decade-long debate over the "Daughters' Question" that no one could have predicted. The complete lack of control of Orthodox Jewish society in this case was a painful reminder of its ultimate helplessness when confronting determined young women ready to fight for their aspirations. The silence of the Orthodox press reflected the community's shock in the face of the public shame inflicted on the Halberstam family. This was arguably the moment when gymnasium and university education for women became a red flag for the Orthodox leadership. The traditional permission to teach daughters secular subjects needed clearer parameters. Such subjects could still be considered an adornment or a useful preparation for the job market, but nothing leading to an academic path. As we shall see in chapter 6, the eventual Orthodox response to the "Daughters' Question" was to establish, when possible, educational institutions for women that included secular subjects, but in a controlled fashion that limited their dissemination and belittled their independent value.

5

Rebellious Daughters and the Literary Imagination

FROM JACOB WASSERMANN TO S. Y. AGNON

PRESS REPORTS about Jewish women runaways in Galicia left their trace on works of contemporary authors, playwrights, and even filmmakers, a point that has hitherto gone entirely unnoticed by literary critics and historians. In 1913, the silent film *Der Shylock von Krakau* (now lost) was released with a script by the Austrian author and critic Felix Salten, the author of *Bambi*, and its protagonist portrayed by the Austrian actor, Rudolph Schildkraut. The film tells the story of Isaak Levi, a money lender and God-fearing Kraków Jew, whose daughter runs away to Berlin with her lover, a Polish count and a client of her father. Abandoned there by her lover, the daughter had become a beggar to support herself. After many years she returns to Kraków, only to find her father cold, bitter, and old. The father rejects the lost daughter, but finally forgives her on his death bed.[1] As a Viennese Jew, Salten would have been very familiar with the Galician runaway stories, which made Kraków a logical setting for an Eastern European version of the Venetian Shylock.

In 1902, the noted German Jewish author Jakob Wassermann (1873–1934) published a story titled *Der Moloch*.[2] The book tells the story of Arnold Ansorge, who while living in the Moravian village of Podolin meets Samuel Elasser, a poor Jewish peddler, and learns from him that his thirteen-year-old

---

1. Warnke and Shandler, "Yiddish Shylocks in Theater and Literature," 99; "Der Shylock von Krakau," *Neue Freie Presse*, November 28, 1913, 15; "Der Shylock von Krakau," *Kinematographische Rundschau*, October 19, 1913, 108, 110.

2. Wassermann, *Der Moloch*.

daughter Jutta was kidnapped by Felician nuns and held in a convent against her will. Upon hearing this, Ansorge decides to help Elasser to get his daughter back, especially since the law alone had failed to achieve the justice he deserved. Ansorge's friend, Maxim Specht, is convinced to join the mission, and in order to pressure the authorities he keeps sending articles to the Viennese press about this disturbing convent story (*Klostergeschichte*). Ansorge later travels to Vienna for the same purpose, but while in the big city—the modern-day Moloch—he is lured by the worldly pleasures it offers and forgets his original commitment to seek justice for Elasser. Afflicted with guilt after his life takes a turn for the worse, Ansorge compensates Elasser with a significant sum of money and subsequently commits suicide.

Samuel Elasser's story was based on that of Israel Araten. Wassermann copied details of Araten's repeated failures to obtain his daughter from the Viennese liberal press, especially the *Neue Freie Presse*, without acknowledgment, and placed them in the story after changing the names of the main characters. These details include all of Israel Araten's allegations against the convent and the authorities, his lobbying efforts at government ministries, and his meeting with the emperor. They even include the search in Kęnty and the infamous sentence attributed to the minister for Galician affairs: "The secular authority ends at the convent's walls."[3]

---

3. Ibid., 40. Other details include the intention of the convent to drag the case out until the daughter reaches the age of fourteen, the father's allegation that he heard his daughter crying and sobbing in the other room, the nun's assertion that the daughter was sick and unable to see her father, the father's request that his daughter be allowed to see her ailing mother and the response of the Mother Superior that she will see her in heaven, the medical examinations of the court doctor and the university professor who both found her perfectly healthy. When Elasser came to the convent after seven days as suggested by the convent superior, he was told that his daughter disappeared from the convent two days earlier. Wassermann writes that early on, Elasser discovered that his daughter was taken to Galicia and transferred by two nuns to Łagiewniki by Podgórze, and subsequently to other convents, including in Kęnty, Wola Jus-towska, Bieńczyce (spelled here Binczice), Morawica, and Wielowicz. See Wassermann, *Der Moloch*, 21–28; 39–40. All those details are copied from the *Neue Freie Presse* articles on the Araten affair published in 1900 on February 6, 14, 15, 16, 18, 24, 25; March 6, 30, 31; April 6, 12, 13, 26, 29; May 6, 19; July 7, 8; October 17; 21. For example, Wassermann, *Der Moloch*, 23: "[D]ie Mutter des Kindes liege schwer darnieder und wünsche die Tochter vor ihrem Tode noch einmal zu sehen. Durch diese List gedachte er das Herz der Oberin zu rühren. 'Sie wird sie im Himmel wiedersehen,' antworte die Oberin mit feierlich erhobener Hand und mit langsamer, zu peinvollem Laüschen zwingender Stimme." *Neue Freie Presse*, February 14, 1900, 5: "Mit tränen in den Augen stehte der alte Mann das Kind an, es möge zu seiner Mutter zurückkehren,

Scholars have noted Wassermann's habit of borrowing from others without proper acknowledgment.[4] In this case, the Galician-born publicist and historian Simon Bernfeld (1860–1940), reviewing *Der Moloch* in the Hebrew press, wrote, "The case of Israel Araten is woven into our story in all its simplicity, without any poetical shading, as if Wassermann took the details of the case from some newspaper and affixed them here."[5] According to Bernfeld, the Moloch is not a metaphor for the city and its false attractions, as other critics had interpreted it, but rather for the failed promise of liberalism to solve social injustices, specifically those directed against Jews. A supporter of Jewish nationalism, Bernfeld was disappointed by contemporary liberalism, which was unable to stop the tide of anti-Semitism. Neither Wassermann nor Bernfeld writes anything about the girl, they focus instead on the failed search for her and the injustices committed by the church and the state authorities. Like Israel Araten, they blame factors outside the Jewish community for her unfortunate fate.

A different approach to the Araten affair was taken by Shmuel Yosef Agnon (1887–1970) who was born and raised in Buczacz, Galicia. Agnon was likely familiar with the Araten case as it unfolded, since in 1904 he published a short poem on the problem of female education as we saw in chapter 3. Moreover, at one point a rumor spread that Michalina was in the train station in Buczacz, and later in the convent in the neighboring town of Jazłowiec. Like the contemporary Hebrew newspapers, Agnon looked for the root of the problem of the rebellious daughters within Jewish society.

In his 1950 novella "Tehilla," Agnon tells the story of an elderly, pious Jewish woman, Tehilla, living in the Old City of Jerusalem in the early twentieth century. Before she dies, Tehilla asks a young writer to compose in Hebrew her life story, which she proceeds to recount in Yiddish.[6] The purpose of this request is to ask the forgiveness of her former fiancé, Shraga, who died many

---

die krank daniederliege und sich noch dem Anblicke der Tochter sehne. Da bemerkte eine der Nonnen mit sanfter Stimme und in milden Tone: 'Das Kind wird ja seine Mutter im Himmel wiedersehen.'"

4. Cf. John C. Blankenagel, "More Unacknowledged Borrowing by Jakob Wassermann."

5. Simon Bernfeld, "From the Literature (A Literary View)," *Ha-Zeman*, June 4, 1903, 7–9, esp. 7 [Hebrew].

6. Interestingly, Tehilla tells the writer: "I shall tell you in Yiddish and you will write it in the Holy Tongue. I have heard that they teach the girls how to speak and write in the Holy Tongue. So you see, my son, the Blessed Holy One in his loving-kindness conducts His world better in each succeeding generation." See S. Y. Agnon, "Tehilla," 31.

years ago; she plans to have the written account buried with her, presumably so that Shraga can read it in the world to come. Her father had broken off their arranged engagement after he discovered that Shraga was a Hasid. Because Tehilla's father had not asked Shraga for forgiveness for the shame he had caused him, she attributed a succession of tragedies that befell her to Shraga's curse. Those tragedies included the death of her husband and her two sons, and an unclear incident involving her daughter. Tehilla doesn't specify what happened to her daughter, only that "an evil spirit" entered her, and she went crazy.[7] A careful reading of the story reveals that the daughter's fate is one of the major themes of the novella, if not the major one.

The character of Tehilla appears to be based in part on Israel Araten, who settled in Jerusalem in the early twentieth century and died at a ripe old age. Agnon scatters hints to the historical origins of the story in several places, especially in the words of the other characters in the story. One of them is the grumpy rebbetzin (rabbi's wife), whose father had been engaged to Tehilla's daughter. The writer, who is also the narrator of the story, is curious about Tehilla and keeps begging the rebbetzin to tell him more about her:

> And if I do tell, she answered, will it make things easier for me or for her? I don't like all this tale telling [. . .] But one thing I shall tell you, the Blessed Holy One took pity on that saint [the rebbetzin's father and Tehilla's prospective son-in-law], and so he put an evil spirit into that apostate, may her name be blotted out.

She then tells him what happened to her righteous father, whom she describes as a "real" rabbi:

> [S]o the matchmakers in the country were all eager to match him off. There was a certain rich widow. When I say rich, I mean she was very rich. She had only one daughter, and if only she hadn't had her! She took a barrel of gold coins and told them, those matchmakers, if you match him to my daughter, then he gets this barrel, and if it's not enough I'll add to it. The daughter was not worthy of that righteous saint, because he was a saint, and she, may she be damned, was an apostate, just as her end proved about her beginning, because she ran away and entered some nunnery and changed her religion. And when did she run away?—when they were leading her to the bridal canopy. Her mother wasted half her wealth on her in order to get

---

7. Ibid., 42.

her out of there. She got as far as the Emperor, the wretched mother did, and even he couldn't help her at all, because anybody who once enters a nunnery never comes out of there any more. Do you know who that apostate is? The daughter of—hush, she's coming.

Tillie [i.e., Tehilla] came in with a pot of food in her hand.[8]

The rebbetzin was the only person who had personal knowledge of what happened to Tehilla, but the distraction caused by the latter's entrance leaves the readers to draw their own conclusions. The parallel to the Araten affair in this paragraph is quite obvious: Araten's riches, his daughter's engagement, his monetary spending in an effort to find her, and especially the meeting with the emperor, which no other parent of a runaway merited. Unlike Wassermann, Agnon uses the Araten affair in an artistic fashion and builds around it an elaborate literary structure, in which Tehilla's shameful secret—the religious conversion of her daughter—is the cloud that cast its shadow over all of it.

Another character in the story, the sage, is a son of a mother who knew Tehilla abroad, and Agnon puts in his mouth another hint. Realizing the writer's curiosity about Tehilla, the sage says:

What she was outside the Land of Israel I do not know apart from what everybody does: that she was very rich indeed and conducted big affairs, but finally her sons died, and her husband died and she went and abandoned all her affairs and came up to Jerusalem. My mother, may she rest in peace, used to say, "When I see Tehilla I see that there are things even worse than widowhood and loss of children." But mother never told me what these things were, so I do not know and now we never shall know; for all those who knew Tehilla abroad are already dead, and Tehilla never has much to say.[9]

The sage doesn't mention a daughter, so it is clear what he meant when saying "there are things even worse than widowhood and loss of children." But not mentioning the daughter explicitly helps Agnon to keep the secret that Tehilla was so careful not to tell anybody.

As the story progresses, Tehilla, unlike the rebbetzin and the sage, adds context to the story of her daughter:

---

8. Ibid., 23–24.
9. Ibid., 28.

Business was good and we conducted our household decently. We took good teachers for our sons and a gentile governess for our daughter, for in those days God-fearing people kept the Jewish teachers—except those who taught Hebrew—at their distance, because they were held to be atheists.[10]

Tehilla continues to describe the effect her sons' "good teachers" had on the household: "Since they were alone in the world, they used to eat at our table on the Sabbath. My husband, too occupied with business to study regularly, enjoyed having such guests who spoke to him Torah." Agnon then puts the cards on the table and lets Tehilla tell the last part of her life story to the writer, exposing her paradoxical and unrealistic expectations and their results:

> While my husband lived I had already been helping him in his affairs, and now that he was dead I threw myself entirely into business [. . .] I thought to myself, all my toil I am toiling for my daughter, so the more wealth I acquire the more I shall benefit her. The affairs increased so that I had no time for my home apart from Sabbaths and Festivals, and even then half the day was spent in synagogue and half in receiving guests. To all appearances my daughter did not need me, since I had taken teachers for her and she was busy with her studies and I received many praises about her. And even the Gentiles who mock at us for speaking an outlandish tongue used to praise my daughter, and said that she spoke their tongue with the best of them. And above all, the Gentile teachers made much of her and invited her to their homes. I called the matchmakers and they found me a bridegroom renowned for his knowledge of Torah and an ordained rabbi.
>
> But I never had the privilege of leading them to the canopy, for an evil spirit entered into my daughter and she became crazy.
>
> And now this is what I ask you, my son, write to Shraga that I have forgiven him for all the troubles which have come upon me on his account; and write to him that he too has to forgive me, since I have already been stricken enough.[11]

Agnon magnifies here the blindness of Tehilla, demonstrating the complete misunderstanding of cause and effect with regard to the issue of female

10. Ibid., 38.

11. Ibid., 43. See also Rachel Manekin, "Tehilla's Daughter and Michalina Araten," *Haaretz*, Literary Supplement, June 27, 2003 [Hebrew].

education, even after so many decades. His depiction of Tehilla throughout the story as a God-fearing innocent woman turns out to be written with not a little irony, as Tehilla's exaggerated piety and superstitious beliefs come at the expense of a sober and realistic view of the effects of the education she gave to her daughter.

Other contemporary literary works focused on the plight of Galician village girls like Debora Lewkowiecz. In 1907, a Yiddish melodrama was published in Kraków called *Tate mames tsures: Lebnsbild in 4 akten* ("Father's and Mother's Sorrows: A Life Picture in 4 Acts").[12] The popular play by Max Gebel was based on the true story of a young Jewish woman, the daughter of a tavern-keeper in a small Galician village, who fled from her parents' home on the first night of Passover, then converted to Christianity and married her Polish lover in 1889. In the theatrical version the Jewish woman elopes with her lover after her mother reveals to her the identity of her groom-to-be, a Jewish yeshiva student, and the date of her impending marriage. Unlike the story on which it was based, the play ends happily for the Jewish audience, with the young woman returning to her family and her faith.[13]

A similar story is related by Agnon in the chapter "Solomon Jacob's Bed" of his novel *Hakhnasat kalah* (translated into English as *The Bridal Canopy*).[14] The narrator tells the tale of a village tavernkeeper who quickly arranged a match between his daughter and a yeshiva student after he and his wife learned of their daughter's romance with a Pole. The story is told from the viewpoint of the naïve yeshiva student, who knows nothing of the background to the engagement. The parents invite him to their house for the Passover Seder. After being affectionately greeted outside by the bride's father, the shy young man meets the girl for the first time:

12. Gebel, *Tate mames tsures*.

13. The Galician publicist Gershom Bader relates in his memoirs that he was personally acquainted with the young woman on whom the play's heroine was based. He emphasizes that "whole books" could have been written about Jewish girls who fell in love with gentiles and married them, a natural outcome of the education they received in their homes. Girls lived a double life; at home with "fanatic and uneducated" fathers and brothers, and outside in a free and intelligent atmosphere. Their stories ended in tragedy, with the girls escaping to convents or causing other problems. In either case "they were lost to the Jewish people." See Bader, *Mayne zikhroynes*, 333.

14. S. Y. Agnon, *The Bridal Canopy*, 68–79.

While he stood so, his betrothed came out of the kitchen and stood before him pink and pretty, her plaits in her right hand and a smile on her lips. Shifting her plaits to her left hand she greeted him, and as her plump hand gripped his, a quiver passed through him so that his tongue shriveled up, and he lost his power of speech. He bowed his shoulders even more, bent his hand and gripped the back of the Gemara [Talmud] firmly with his fingers. Said his betrothed, Put away your Bible and sit down; and she took it out of his hands gently and set it on the table.

In came his mother-in-law-to-be, in festive array, veiled and adorned like a dowager, with felt shoes on her feet which had grown swollen during the winter while she stood out in the open to prevent her daughter meeting that gentile.[15]

The contrast between the Talmud student and the daughter can't be greater, and things get even more awkward later in the evening:

And Solomon Jacob read out of the same Hagada as his betrothed, holding his breath so that she shouldn't feel his presence, while she, far from being frightened by him, was actually touching him.

After the meal the parents get ready to go to sleep, but the two young people start reading the Song of Songs as is customary on Passover night. Agnon uses the verses of the Song of Songs to drop hints about the girl's relationship with her Polish lover:

The candles began guttering. There was a whistle outside. The wench started but immediately went on reading in a sweet and happy voice, "'Tis the voice of my love; behold he cometh." And Solomon Jacob, keeping his finger on the place, went on interpreting in accordance with Rashi, "The poet returns to the beginning like a man who stops short and returns saying, I never told you the beginning. Behold he standeth behind our wall, peering through the window, peeping through the lattice chinks." And so they read until they finished the book.[16]

When in his bed, Solomon Jacob, who was used to sleep on a bench in the house of study, admires the many pillows and crisp sheets, while whispering verses from the Song of Songs:

15. Ibid., 74.
16. Ibid., 75.

"Behold thou art fair, my love, and our couch is likewise fresh; the voice of my love that knocketh, open to me; they have taken my veil from me, I did not know my mind." [...] But ere he entered the bed he heard the housewife weeping. Had the evil eye gained sway, God forbid, over his betrothed? Solomon Jacob turned his face toward the window and saw the housewife standing with arms outstretched, howling and wailing and weeping, while his father-in-law-to-be ran half naked after a coach which was dashing off as though driven by furies. Suddenly the crack of a whip rent the air. His father-in-law-to-be came stumbling back, his hand over his cheek, crying, There's no daughter, no daughter. Solomon Jacob's betrothed had fled with her gentile lover.[17]

Agnon describes the helpless parents and their pain, but while their daughter was the source of that pain, neither the play by Gebel nor the novel by Agnon depicts the young women in a negative light. On the contrary, the authors reveal to their audience the unbridgeable gap between the reality in which the heroines live and the future lives that their parents have arranged for them. The village woman in *Tate mames tsures* is a free spirit who reads philosophy and believes in a love that transcends religious and national differences, a love that symbolizes the "spirit of the new times." She knows that her mother belongs to a generation that is incapable of understanding this. Nevertheless, she loves her mother deeply and torments herself with the knowledge that her choice will break her mother's heart. After her mother reveals the identity of her intended bridegroom, she breaks down in tears:

Mameniu! What are you talking about?! That yeshiva student, that idler? [...] No, no, mamele? What are you saying? How can you even imagine a thing like that, that I, so young . . . You did not ask me, with the son of Zalman Peseles? . . . No, this cannot be. I am so miserable.[18]

In Agnon's story the daughter is a sensuous, determined young woman with a strong physical presence, in sharp contrast to the wretched appearance and shy demeanor of the Talmud student. She attempts to create some sort of bond with him after the Passover Seder has concluded, but it is clear to the reader that the bond cannot hold. The responsibility for the failed engagement,

17. Ibid., 75–76.
18. Gebel, *Tate mames tsures*, 5.

implies Agnon, lies not with the young woman but with the Talmud student. In commenting upon the unhappy ending, the narrator asks:

> Solomon Jacob, who studied the Bible a great deal and the Talmud a great deal and spent his life in the House of Study, and derived not even as much as his little finger was worth of pleasure out of the world—why was he punished so much? Because he never learnt anything except Torah. My sons, it is a man's duty to know writing and other tongues, and anyone who does not know writing and other tongues is called contemptible; as our sages of blessed memory remark in the Talmud about the verse in Obadiah, "Thou art extremely contemptible," because they know neither writing nor other languages. And they also say elsewhere in the Talmud that a disciple of the wise has to know to write.[19]

Both authors portray the young village women as modern women who know what they want and who are not willing to lead the sort of life their mothers led. They understood, as did the reviewer of Bertha Pappenheim's tract mentioned in chapter 1, that Galician Jewish women did not convert because they were uneducated women who had become physically attracted and emotionally attached to Polish peasants among whom they lived. In Gebel's play, the heroine elopes with a tax superintendent; in Agnon's story, the daughter's father is a well-to-do tax collector and tavernkeeper. Such women did not dream of tending livestock or of working the soil alongside their peasant husbands in order to escape from their parents' Jewish homes. They expected a husband who could appreciate what they appreciated. Like their urban counterparts, they had emotionally and spiritually left Judaism long before they converted; the prospect of living a life chained to what they considered to be a boorish idler ultimately pushed them out of their home.

A writer who understood well the dissonance in the life of Jewish educated village women was Poland's national playwright, Stanisław Wyspiański (1869–1907). His play, *Wesele* ("The Wedding"), first performed in 1901, describes the wedding of the Kraków poet, Lucjan Rydel, with a young Polish woman from the village of Bronowice, near Kraków.[20] Marriage to village women became fashionable at the turn of the century among Kraków literati, who

---

19. Agnon, *The Bridal Canopy*, 76–77. Especially since Agnon says in the beginning (p. 71): "But the Holy and Blest One does not withhold the reward of any youth," and then ends it with what appears to be a terrible divine injustice, something that demands an explanation.

20. Wyspiański, *The Wedding*.

romanticized about a return to nature and authentic Polish roots. (Wyspiański himself married a village woman.) In the play, the characters of the wedding guests are all based on real people from contemporary or historical Kraków, and the same is true of the play's Jews. The character of the tavernkeeper, "The Jew," is based on Hirsch Singer, a bearded Orthodox Jewish tavernkeeper in Bronowice. The character of the Jew's daughter Rachel is based on Singer's own daughter Pepa (Józefa Perel) Singer.[21]

Pepa Singer, who was born in 1881, lacked a formal secondary education. Like Debora Lewkowicz she too studied first in the school of the peasants' children in the village, and afterward in a public primary school in Kraków.[22] We know that she loved modern Polish literature, and in the library of the Academy of Sciences in Kraków there is a copy of the Kraków literary annual *Życie* with the signature "Józefa Singerówna 1898," i.e., a few years before the play was produced.[23] Pepa Singer considered conversion to Christianity as a young woman, but her mother asked her not to do so as long as her father was alive. She finally converted in 1919.[24] In *Wesele* the Jewish tavernkeeper boasts of his daughter Rachel to the poet bridegroom:

As soon as books come, she reads them,
But still she rolls out dough herself.
At Vienna she's been to the Opera,
But at home she still plucks chickens,
She knows all of Przybyszewski
And wears her hair in braided loops,
Like angels in those Italian paintings.[25]

Wyspiański's Rachel knows that although her desires conflict with her father's faith and way of life, he appreciates her achievements and adopts an

21. On the characters in the play, including the Jews, see: Żeleński (Boy), "Plauderei über Wyspiańskis 'Hochzeit' (Auszüge)." See also Plach, "Botticelli Woman."

22. The daughter of the poet Lucjan Rydel, upon whom the play's hero is based, writes that "the Polish school and the Polish village transformed Józefa Singer into a Pole in heart and in spirit, if not in blood." See Brandstaetter, *Ja Jestem Żyd z "Wesela,"* 57.

23. Ibid., 37. Żeleński notes that there were many girls in Kraków like Rachel. They could be found in the reading clubs, the libraries, the theater, and the concert hall. See Żeleński (Boy), "Plauderei über Wyspiańskis 'Hochzeit' (Auszüge)," 278.

24. Brandstaetter, *Ja Jestem Żyd z "Wesela,"* 25.

25. Wyspiański, *The Wedding*, 50.

attitude of forgiveness toward her. She in turn appreciates his liberality and is not ashamed of him:

> He allows me everything
> And even boasts about me.
> It's interesting—isn't it?
> Exploitation, business, I and he?[26]

Rachel's problem does not lie in any discord or bad relations with her father, but rather in the conflict between the way of life she has chosen for herself and her father's traditional ways.

The father's inability to influence his daughter Rachel's way of life was typical of an entire generation of Jewish parents in the villages around Kraków whose daughters attended Polish public schools.

Interestingly, the Polish-born Israeli author, publicist, and literary critic Yoram Bronowski (1948–2001) viewed Wyspiański's Rachel as a ridiculous figure, a traitor to her people who tried to assimilate into a foreign culture and play there the role of "a female Pope more than the Pope." Of the two Jewish characters in the play, Rachel's father is the admirable one since he remains loyal to the religion and traditions of his ancestors and looks with aversion on the gentile world.[27] Bronowski, a secular Jew, wanted the Jewish character in a Polish play to be proud of her tradition; he even considers the representation of Rachel to possess a certain streak of anti-Semitism. One may speculate that Agnon, an observant Jew from Galicia who knew what Orthodox women faced during that period, would have disagreed.

The Kluger affair is the basis of a 1913 novel by the Jewish feminist writer, Aniela Kallas (pen name of Aniela Korngut, 1868–1942), the only female author who wrote about the runaways during this period. Born in Galicia, Kallas wrote about the "local realities and problems, remaining within the regional horizons [...] both in big cities such as Lwów and Kraków as well as anonymous towns in the province."[28] Kallas named her novel *Córki marnotrawne* ("Prodigal Daughters"),[29] an allusion to the parable of the prodigal son in Luke 15: 11–32. The novel is about the travails of a young Jewish woman, Malcia

26. Ibid., 77.

27. Bronowski, "Poets, Peasants, and Jews in *The Wedding*," 15.

28. Prokop-Janiec, *Pogranicze polsko-żydowskie*, 142.

29. Kallas, *Córki marnotrawne*. On Kallas, see Prokop-Janiec, "A Woman Assimilationist and the Great War." On women and university education in Polish Jewish literary works written by

Klinger, who is torn between her family and her yearning for academic inquiry, which her family, especially her mother, opposes. Kallas bases Malcia Klinger largely on Anna Kluger and preserves in the novel almost all the elements of the Kluger affair as reported in the press. Even the character of Malcia's best friend, the medical student Regina Karmel, is based on Marie Kragen, Anna's friend and a witness for the prosecution, who was herself a fifth-year medical student. Contemporary readers who had followed the Kluger case in the press would immediately recognize its affinities with the novel.

The novel also describes Malcia's student-friends and their discussions on literature, philosophy, and current ideological movements, using these scenes to introduce different types of young Jewish women, who aspire for a university education, and their parents, who react in different ways to these aspirations. In her efforts to stop her daughter's friendship with the progressive Regina, Malcia's mother tells Regina:

> My daughters are different. Your parents could not raise you as our fathers did. Although your father is a "Polish Jew" [polski żyd] with a long coat [żupan], he is quite progressive and does not care about the rabbis or what people might say about him [. . .] Nu, he's a very respectable man! But my husband is something else. My husband belongs to the "Hasidim" and he is a rabbi. My ancestors were like that, and I want to go this way too and my children must be like that.[30]

Malcia is unswerving in her desire to study and complete her matriculation examinations, despite her mother's insistence that she cease her studies and become a wife and a mother.

In contrast to Malcia's gentle father, Kallas portrays her mother as mean, vulgar, and physically abusive. This differs from the aforementioned literary works in which the mothers of the runaways play little or no role; the voices we hear are those of the fathers.[31] In many runaway cases the heartbroken mothers lacked the knowledge or ability to deal with the situation in the

---

women, see Kołodziejska-Smagała, "'Nature Has Created a Woman to Be a Wife and Mother,'" 175–184.

30. Kallas, *Córki marnotrawne*, 4.

31. Citing *Córki marnotrawne*, Prokop-Janiec notes the conflicts between females in Kallas's works, specifically between the generation of the uneducated mothers and educated daughters, explaining that "[i]t is the Jewish mothers that are usually presented by the writer as the most dangerous and the most ardent guardians of the traditional patriarchical order and its norms. [. . .] Young women usually communicated better with their fathers and brothers—Hasidim or

outside world, and they relied on their husbands to carry on the fight for the return of the daughters. Anna Kluger's case is different in that regard. As a direct descendant of the founder of the Sandz Hasidic dynasty, Anna's mother was raised in privilege and with a feeling of entitlement. As we have seen, she took an active role in the conflict with her daughter, insisting that she stop her education, enter into an arranged marriage, and after she did that, perform her marital duties as a Hasidic wife. That plays to her disadvantage in Kallas's novel.

A significant part of the novel concerns Malcia's marriage to the man her parents have chosen for her, and her consent to that marriage in order to continue her studies. Hania, Malcia's younger and more rebellious sister, urges Malcia to run away from home and promises to follow her, "I will not allow such misery, and I will not be bullied! Let them only start with me and I will escape to the convent," she says to her older sister.[32] But Malcia tells her: "Girls like you do not go there."[33] This may be a reference to the fact that most female converts came from small towns and villages around Kraków and not from cities like Kraków, where a young woman like Malcia could find her place amidst a group of like-minded progressive Jewish students.

Several scenes in the story describe Malcia's efforts to explain to her father her passion for study and her determination to take the matriculation exams instead of getting married, and his inability to understand it. He replies that he can understand the wish to train in a profession that will provide her with a better job and livelihood, but not a wish to study for no practical purpose. Ultimately, he agrees to convince her mother to allow her to study for the matriculation exams after her marriage, but only on the condition that she promise to remain Jewish and respect the Jewish tradition. He makes her swear on a prayer book that she will remain a Jewish daughter and marry her fiancé, which she does.[34] Malcia finally understands that the gap between her and her father is unbridgeable, but her love for him makes her submit to his will.

Orthodox Jews." Prokop-Janiec, *Pogranicze polsko-żydowskie*, 147–148. Historically, this is true for the Kluger case but not necessarily for other cases, such as Araten and Lewkowicz.

32. Kallas, *Córki marnotrawne*, 12–13. In another place, one of the story's female characters, Freiówna, who later runs away from her parental home, says: "The old people still think that the Goyim want to kidnap their daughters to the convent," ibid., 44.

33. Ibid., 16. Malcia tried to discover who put that idea in her sister's head, feeling certain there was a Christian man involved. It turned out to be the editor of a literary magazine.

34. Ibid., 62–68. When Malcia says that she doesn't know the fiancé, her father says: "I saw your mother once at the engagement, and then after the wedding I just saw how she looked [...] Believe me my child, a woman should marry because nature created her to give birth to children.

If the father fears that Malcia's continuing education will lead her to abandon the Jewish religion, the mother fears that it will lead her to neglect her duties as wife and mother. Kallas takes Anna Kluger's claim that her mother interfered in her most intimate marital relations with her husband and paints a salacious scene in which the mother enters Malcia's bedroom after her daughter has gone to bed and urges the young woman to perform her wifely duties, while Malcia's husband stands near the door.[35] This humiliation ultimately leads Malcia to rebel and run away, arranging to meet up with her sister Hania, whom she instructs to take with her wedding jewelry and money.

Shortly after the appearance of the book, Kazimiera Bujwidowa, the noted feminist and one of the founders of the Reading Room for Women in Kraków, reviewed it for the Kraków Jewish weekly *Tygodnik*. Declaring that she will not comment on the literary merits of the book, Bujwidowa focused instead on the phenomenon of the runaway daughters described by Kallas. It is not clear, she writes, what these girls want and for what purpose they sacrifice themselves while causing pain to their families, even lying and stealing, especially since none of them achieves freedom. Malcia, the heroine of the story, gives up everything in order to get her matriculation certificate, but for what purpose? She is willing to cheat and marry so she can escape the ghetto, but lying begets lying. If girls like Malcia are really unhappy there is only one thing that they should do—cut their ties with their families, especially their financial dependence on them, and find a job to support themselves. Bujwidowa emphasizes that she is writing as a mother, and indeed she is specifically critical about the relationship of these girls with their parents. Since she can't imagine mothers who do not wish happiness for their children, she expects that children will find a way to the heart of their parents or simply leave, find a job, and become independent. Relying on legal provisions on the obligations of parents, she says, and coercing them to comply with these obligations by way of legal proceedings and coercion is something so shameful that it is difficult to speak about it without abhorrence; lying and other measures are not only ugly but meaningless and ineffective in their consequences.[36]

One who is lonely can never be happy and no science and no book can replace the joy that a woman has when she is fulfilled by her destiny."

35. Ibid., 201.

36. K[azimiera] Bujwidowa, "Prodigal Daughters?" *Tygodnik*, September 19, 1913, 2–3 [Polish]. See also Kołodziejska-Smagała, "'Nature Has Created a Woman to Be a Wife and Mother'," 164–166.

This last point shows that Bujwidowa was not talking so much about *Prodigal Daughters* as about the events that inspired it. Kallas had omitted from the novel all mention of the Kluger sisters' lawsuit, perhaps because the final verdict had not been rendered yet when she wrote the book, or because she thought that it detracted from the broader phenomenon that the novel describes. By the time Bujwidowa wrote her review, the court's verdict was already known, and Bujwidowa took the opportunity to express her dissatisfaction with the price the Kluger sisters were willing to pay in exchange for their freedom to study.

Kallas wrote a response a few weeks later. She states that she took it upon herself to be the voice of the prodigal daughters, of whom there are many. She describes the difficult conditions under which they live, their striving for knowledge, and their dreams about a different life. She received many letters from them, she writes, and they are crying for help. She cites a short part from a letter of a girl who dreamed about studying and taking professional courses, only to give it all up because of the tears of her mother, who objected to her plans. Kallas accuses Bujwidowa of not reading the book with adequate attention and rebukes her for the impractical suggestions she offered. These daughters love their parents, and some of them get tired of the constant fight and so ultimately they yield. They receive no help and no support from anybody. They don't cut themselves off from their parents because not everyone possesses the courage to take such a step. Alluding to the title of the novel, she writes that even the prodigal son in the biblical story returned home. It is not easy for a young woman to leave her home and survive as a respectable woman in the big city, even for those who find a job, as they are frequently exploited and even go hungry. The solution recommended by Bujwidowa grants neither freedom nor independence, according to Kallas, who concludes: "I had a different intention when writing my novel about the prodigal daughters. So far, no one has taken up this problem. I am waiting."[37]

The editorial staff of the weekly also responded to Bujwidowa's suggestions, alluding that as an outsider she was unable to appreciate the importance of the struggle of the young generation. The suspicion held by pious Jews that education leads to the loss of religious faith is particular to Jews and not common among Christians. But the editorial expresses the view that in time all that will change. For one thing, "if the surging wave of conversion that we are witnessing

---

37. Kallas, "Prodigal Daughters," *Tygodnik*, October 31, 1913, 2; November 7, 1913, 2 [Polish]. See also Kołodziejska-Smagała, "'Nature Has Created a Woman to Be a Wife and Mother,'" 164–165.

would stop," then social evolution would lead Jews, similar to Christians, to agree to a certain compromise between religious faith and education. They would stop fearing that education will lead to the abandonment of religion.[38]

While Bujwidowa, the non-Jewish feminist, suggested that Jewish girls try to convince their parents to accept their wish for higher education or leave their families and become independent financially in the city, Kallas wanted to arouse the public attention to the growing problem of prodigal Jewish daughters because nobody did anything about it. The Kluger case served as a model for her novel because it included dramatic elements that appeared to be torn from the pages of fiction. For its part, the Jewish weekly adopted a progressive attitude, suggesting that if the tide of conversion would stop, suspicion would give way to a social evolution that would weaken the Orthodox resistance to higher education of their daughters.

What none of these writers anticipated was the change in the educational ideology within the Orthodox camp that aimed at controlling the drive for higher education among their daughters and channeling it to other areas. This change was first conceived by Sarah Schenirer, who was well aware of the problem of the prodigal daughters and personally experienced the double life of being attracted to lectures in the Reading Room for Women on the one hand, and love for her Hasidic parents and their religious values, on the other hand. She also experienced the pain of an arranged marriage that she accepted in deference to her parents, and the decision to free herself of the chains of this marriage. Schenirer was a pious woman, and her solution to the rebellion of the daughters was to strengthen their religious identity and weaken the attraction of secular education. Her innovative approach was later developed by Agudat Yisrael into a formal and well-developed educational system that turned the passion for intellectual creativity and freedom into a passion for religion and commitment to Orthodox ideology and practice.

38. Kallas, "Prodigal Daughters," *Tygodnik*, September 26, 2 [Polish].

6

Bringing the Daughters Back

A NEW MODEL OF FEMALE ORTHODOX JEWISH EDUCATION

THE REBELLION OF THE DAUGHTERS in Habsburg Galicia continued until World War I. True, the interwar period in Poland saw many young men and women from Orthodox Jewish homes abandon the ways of their parents. But the specific phenomenon of Galician young Jewish females running away and seeking refuge in the Felician Sisters' convent, with many subsequently converting, stopped. The First World War changed the map of the Habsburg Empire, making Galicia in 1918 part of the newly created Second Polish Republic. In fact, the laws in the new state eliminated the legal conditions that facilitated the runaway phenomenon. Although the new state didn't initially cancel some of the nineteenth-century civil codes, as a result of which different Polish regions were governed by different legal systems, the age of majority in the former Galician territory was changed from twenty-four to twenty-one.[1] But, the Polish state did not have a clearly defined civil procedure for religious conversion, and it seems that conversions were carried out according to the 1917 Canon Law, which also defined twenty-one as the age of majority.[2] The only provision in the 1917 Canon Law for a baptism of a minor without parental consent was for an infant whose life was in danger.[3] Baptism of minors who

---

1. "Ustawa z dnia 21 października 1919 r. o wieku pełnoletności w b. zaborze austrjackim," https://www.prawo.pl/akty/dz-u-1919-87-472,16873771.html. See also Markowski, "State Policies Concerning Jewish Conversions," 31–32; Żyndul, "Conversion of Jews in Łódz in the Interwar Period," 218.

2. See Peters, ed. and trans., *The 1917 Or Pio-Benedictine Code of Canon Law*, Canon 88, §1, 53.

3. Ibid., Canon 750, §1, 277.

have reached the age of reason (thus treated like adults) had to be deferred to the local bishop.[4] With that, the free path to baptism of underage girls who could just enter a convent and declare their wish to convert came in effect to an end. Running away from home ceased being an easily accessible option.

Parallel to the upheaval in the political situation during the First World War, formal religious education for Orthodox Jewish girls was introduced in Galicia for the first time. We saw in chapter 1 how R. Tuvia Horowitz of Rzeszów, writing in 1925, had blamed himself and other rabbis for not attempting to save the "lost generation" of Jewish women. But after rebuking the religious leadership for their past inaction, he went on to praise them for finally agreeing that the situation must change: "It is therefore a historic turning point in the history of Judaism that the great sages of our generation and the truly God-fearing began to realize that this neglect cannot continue and that real practical steps must be taken for the organization of an educational system."[5]

When and how did this historical turning point occur? Who were the "great sages" and the "truly God-fearing" who took the first steps to change the situation? Before describing the change that finally occurred in Jewish female education in Kraków, it is essential to first discuss the broader context of Orthodox female education, specifically the changes that took place in Frankfurt am Main and Berlin, and the influence they had on several regions in Eastern Europe. These changes were part of a dynamic process that was accelerated by the First World War and ultimately also affected Kraków, making it the center of formal Jewish education for Orthodox young women.

The Hirschian School Model

The first Orthodox Jewish school that accepted girls was established in Frankfurt am Main in 1853 by R. Samson Raphael Hirsch, the rabbi of the separatist Orthodox community there. Considered the father of what became known as Neo-Orthodoxy, Hirsch transformed the rabbinic phrase *Torah 'im derekh erez* ("Torah with the way of the land") into an ideology that combined a strict Orthodox way of life with openness to European culture. Hirsch's institution was a secondary school, the first of its kind in Germany. Until then there were only Jewish primary schools in the German lands. Since Hirsch considered the education of the youth of primary importance, he planned the secondary

4. Ibid., Canon 744, 276.
5. Horowitz, "What Do Jewish Daughters Lack?" 75.

school even before his synagogue was built. When the school opened, fifty-five boys and twenty-nine girls were enrolled in four classes, and Hirsch served as its director. Because of lack of space, the lower three grades were initially co-educational. Once space was available the school was restructured to include two wings, a *Realschule* for boys and a lyceum for girls, each composed of seven grades and practically oriented. The school, which implemented modern pedagogical theories, taught secular subjects alongside Jewish ones and was supervised by the state authorities. Boys were also offered intensive non-mandatory classes in business, and girls were offered classes in housekeeping, English, Italian, hygiene, and pedagogy for those who wanted to become kindergarten teachers.

The most innovative element in the school was the formal teaching of religion to girls. Their curriculum included classes in the Pentateuch and several biblical books, as well as in religious observances relevant to women. Unlike the boys, girls were not taught the Talmud or other works of the Oral Law (legal codes, commentaries, etc.). By the time of the outbreak of the First World War, the school's status had been upgraded and its graduates qualified to be admitted to universities without an entrance exam. Following the success of Hirsch's school, similar secondary schools were established in several German cities.[6]

While the introduction of formal religious education for young Jewish women was an innovation embraced in reaction to the sweeping social and cultural changes taking place in German cities, as well as to the rise of the Reform Movement, the rhetoric justifying it emphasized its intrinsic religious value, specifically the preservation of tradition and maintaining a religious home. According to the historian of German Neo-Orthodoxy, Mordechai Breuer, "One would not be going too far in saying that restructuring the education and position of women among Orthodox Jewry was one of the most significant divergences [of Hirschian Neo-Orthodoxy] from old Judaism."[7] Ultimately, this innovation proved successful in raising generations of Orthodox educated women who were strict in their religious observance.[8] Still, there was

6. Ellenson, "German Orthodox Rabbinical Writings"; Breuer, *Modernity within Tradition*; Elias, "The Educational Work of Rabbi S. R. Hirsch"; Fürst, "Die jüdischen Realschulen Deutschlands."

7. Breuer, *Modernity within Tradition*, 122.

8. In practice, religious studies for girls were rather limited and basic, as evident from what Judith Rosenbaum (later Grunfeld) described: "All things considered, one might expect such

no Neo-Orthodox teachers' seminary for women until 1906, and formal female religious education deliberately remained in the hands of men.[9]

The secondary school was not the only school model developed by the Neo-Orthodox. In 1869 Azriel Hildesheimer, the rabbi of the Orthodox congregation in Berlin, established a religious school there that offered extensive religion classes for boys and girls, two-thirds of whom attended non-Jewish secondary schools. In 1898 500 students were already enrolled, a third of them girls. Many of the teachers studied at Hildesheimer's rabbinical seminary, and a large number of them had academic degrees. The girls' program in Hildesheimer's religious school included the Pentateuch, selected chapters from the Bible in translation, *Pirkei Avot* ("Chapters of the Fathers," a tractate of the Mishnah), basic Hebrew, Jewish history, and religious instructions. According to R. Hildesheimer, the purpose of the school was "to bestow upon the youth an in-depth knowledge of the Bible, promote religious practices, and instill traditional Jewish consciousness."[10]

Hildesheimer not only believed that teaching girls the Bible was "permitted both by the Talmud and the codices," but as he wrote in 1888 in a letter to a former student living in Hungary, it was "recommended from a religious as well as from an educational point of view":

> In former times the parents could always be trusted to set an example of religious life, but unfortunately—as is well known—times have changed. Even educationally a knowledge of the original text of the Bible is most desirable. The education of a boy, and naturally, of a girl, too, rests in the first place on an ethical consciousness and on promoting a sense of morality, which, however, can only be achieved by a knowledge of the original text of the many passages not included in the prayer book. One must add to the first point that it is a disgrace and humiliation of our holy faith if

---

a school to have an intensive Jewish curriculum. But we had only one class of Jewish studies each day. This was because we did not have the partition between Jewish and secular studies that exists today. The way we learned our secular subjects obliterated the line between secular and Jewish studies. Therefore, one period of strictly Jewish learning a day meant more than it means today. In that one session we did not cover a lot, but what we learned was remembered. [...] In our Hebrew classes we learned Chumash, *Pirkei Avos* and sometimes a little *Tehillim*. We did not learn the primary commentaries such as Rashi or Ramban, but rather concentrated thoroughly on R. Hirsch's commentary." See Grunfeld, "Growing Up in Frankfort," 120–121.

9. Breuer, *Modernity within Tradition,* 277–281.

10. Cited in Hildesheimer, "Religious Education in Response to Changing Times," 118.

girls—and this does not only happen in the so-called upper classes—are taught Hungarian in German districts and German in Hungarian districts, as well as French and often English, as well as dancing and music, but are not given the slightest idea of the sources of their own religion.[11]

Several decades would pass before rabbinical authorities in Eastern Europe reached a similar conclusion. Anna Kluger would not have had to fight her family to allow her to study for her matriculation exams had she been raised in Berlin, and Michalina Araten could have studied in Hirsch's school after graduating primary school had she lived in Frankfurt. The involvement of the most respected Orthodox rabbis as administrators and teachers in those institutions granted them the seal of approval, at least within the Neo-Orthodox community.[12]

West Meets East: Jewish Schools for Orthodox Young Women in Eastern Europe

Some ideas of Hirsch's *Torah 'im derekh erez* ideology spread to Eastern Europe via individuals who spent time in Germany in the late nineteenth and early twentieth centuries, but these did not include the Neo-Orthodox education system, especially its education of women. Matters in Poland began to change only during World War I, after the German army occupied Warsaw in early August 1915. The civil branch of the occupying army soon created a Jewish department administered by the Jewish Reichstag member, Ludwig Haas, who was put in charge of Jewish affairs. In an effort to help their Eastern European Jewish brethren, two German Jewish organizations approached Haas and other German authorities with the request to be involved in matters concerning the Jewish population: the Committee for the East, a Jewish organization established at the beginning of the War composed of German Jewish leaders of different political and ideological stripes, and the Free Association for the Interests of Orthodox Judaism, established in 1885. After many petitions by the latter organization and a visit of its special delegation in Warsaw, the Germans

11. Cited in Isi Jacob Eisner, "Reminiscences of the Berlin Rabbinical Seminary," 39–40.

12. One of the sharpest opponents of Hirsch's ideology was R. Seligmann Baer Bamberger, the Rabbi of Würzburg, who remained loyal to traditional practices. Bamberger was not against teaching secular subjects to boys, but he opposed the integration of the two when the time allocated to secular studies came at the expense of the traditional Jewish disciplines.

agreed, to the chagrin of the Committee for the East, that a few Orthodox delegates should stay in Warsaw as informal advisors for Jewish affairs. The two delegates sent there were R. Dr. Pinchas Kohn (1867–1941), the rabbi of Ansbach, and R. Dr. Emanuel Carlebach (1874–1927), the rabbi of the Orthodox community in Cologne and director of the Jewish male teachers' seminary there. Both were graduates of Hildesheimer's rabbinical seminary in Berlin. The two arrived in Warsaw in early January 1916, and since they lacked official status, their expenses were covered by several rich German Orthodox Jews.[13] Haas told Kohn privately that he saw as his "highest and most historic task to turn these half-wild tribes with their side-locks and long kaftans [i.e., Polish Hasidic Jews] into cultured people. Most of all, he wanted to abolish the ḥeders and establish good German Jewish compulsory schools for Jewish children."[14]

Since Carlebach's main task, as defined by the German civil administration, was to reform the ḥeder system, he had to come up with a plan that would be acceptable also to Warsaw's Hasidic leadership. But shortly after his arrival, he wrote to his wife that he lamented the local state of Orthodox girls' education.[15] Later in the summer he wrote her that a delegation of women and older girls asked him to deliver religious talks to them at least once a week, as they had never heard any. He would not refuse them because of his endeavor to help guide women in their "unquestionable prevailing spiritual misery."[16] In fact, Carlebach already had given several talks to other women; in early March he wrote his wife that he received endless applause for a talk he gave to a women's group;[17] and in another letter he wrote that he had received loud applause from more than 500 women who came to hear his talk entitled: "The Merit, Dignity, Status, and Position of the Jewish Woman." Carlebach's sensitivity to the status of women is also apparent in his description of a Friday night meal that he attended at the home of a Hasidic leader: "During the Kiddush [the blessing on the wine] I quickly noticed the

13. Breuer, "Rabbis-Doctors in Poland-Lithuania"; Kohn, "Eine würdige Jubiläumserinnerung."

14. Rosenheim, *Erinnerungen 1870–1920*, 145.

15. Grill, *Der Westen im Osten*, 275; Carlebach, "A German Rabbi Goes East," 77. Letter dated February 3, 1916.

16. Carlebach, "A German Rabbi Goes East," 99. Letter dated July 13, 1916.

17. Grill, *Der Westen im Osten*, 276; Carlebach, "A German Rabbi Goes East," 88. Letter dated March 4, 1916, 88.

female members of the household sneaking a look behind a Spanish wall [folding screen]."[18]

Jewish women in Warsaw displayed a greater intellectual thirst for Jewish knowledge than those in Kraków, but the administrative situation in the two communities was very different. Carlebach was working for the German administration in Warsaw, and that position enabled him to cultivate a close relationship with Hasidic leaders, especially the leader of the very powerful Ger Hasidic dynasty, R. Abraham Mordechai Alter; having won the support of the latter, he was looked upon with great respect. There were no comparable figures in Kraków, and hence no change in the tradition of excluding women from public Orthodox religious talks.

Not satisfied with giving talks, Carlebach planned for the establishment of a gymnasium for Orthodox girls, writing his wife in early November 1916 that this was one of his main tasks. He approached different people in Germany in an effort to find an appropriate curriculum for a girls' gymnasium, and while he envisioned a school in which the secular subjects would be taught in Polish, he preferred to import pedagogical ideas from Germany for Jewish subjects. The expenses were to be paid by wealthy Orthodox German Jews. Carlebach chose as director R. Dr. Moses Auerbach, a graduate of Hildesheimer's rabbinical seminary, who taught in different schools in Palestine for several years.[19] The seven-grade gymnasium named "Ḥavaẓelet" (Hebrew: "lily"; cf. Song of Songs 2: 1–2) opened in October 1917. According to an item in the German Neo-Orthodox newspaper *Der Israelit*, permission was granted to open adjacent to it a seminary for secondary school teachers.[20] From the item's language it is clear that the seminary was intended for *male* teachers, which accords with the Neo-Orthodox policy not to employ women as teachers.[21] A winter lecture series for young Jewish women under the leadership of Kohn and Carlebach was also announced.[22] No attempt was made by

18. Carlebach, "A German Rabbi Goes East," 72. Letter dated "The Kaiser's Birthday," 1916.

19. Grill, *Der Westen im Osten,* 277–278.

20. "Polen: Orthodoxe Mädchenschule," *Der Israelit: Ein Centralorgan für das orthodoxe Judentum,* October 12, 1917, 4. Auerbach arrived in the school in early November 1917, see Breuer, "Rabbis-Doctors in Poland-Lithuania," 132. In early December 1917, Carlebach wrote to his wife that the belated official opening ceremony would take place on the following Sunday, the last night of the holiday of Hanukkah. See "A German Rabbi Goes East," 111. Letter dated December 4, 1917.

21. Breuer, *Modernity within Tradition,* 277–278.

22. Kohn, "Eine würdige Jubiläumserinnerung," 157.

Carlebach or Kohn to open primary schools for girls in Warsaw. But Auerbach left for Germany in 1918, and Emanuel Carlebach had to take his place.[23] In 1919, a Polish Jew who had studied in Hildesheimer's rabbinical seminary in Berlin was appointed as director, and he continued the policies of his predecessors.[24]

There is no evidence suggesting that the Neo-Orthodox model of girls' education implemented by Carlebach in Warsaw was opposed by local Hasidic leaders. At this time, because of the efforts of Kohn and Carlebach, the Orthodox in the former Congress Poland were already organized politically in Agudat Yisrael, which received formal approval in the summer of 1916, and the Gerer Hasidim provided many of its leaders and members.[25] A 1918 article in *Dos Yidishe Vort,* the daily Orthodox newspaper of Agudat Yisrael, blamed Polish Orthodoxy for the ignorance of their daughters in the Jewish religion and declared that, particularly at such a time, "a Jewish daughter must get a thorough knowledge in Torah, Prophets, Writings, and in religious laws and customs. Only such knowledge would allow them to relate critically to empty theories and non-Jewish conduct. Only this would allow them to conduct themselves independently in such important Jewish life issues as observing the Sabbath."[26] The author did not bother to justify or to defend Torah instruction for women with religious legal sources, but simply wrote that Torah *must* be taught to girls. This suggests that at least at this time and place, the idea of reforming the practice of female education, especially teaching girls Torah, was considered legitimate enough to be published in the organ of the Orthodox party.

Such a deviation from past norms was not imposed on male education. The reform of the ḥeder system implemented by Carlebach was mostly cosmetic and lasted until the end of the German occupation due to the local resistance to this project. The Hasidic leadership in Warsaw viewed the preservation of the ḥeder system as their main achievement, especially in light of the efforts

23. Grill, *Der Westen im Osten,* 275–279.

24. Grill, *Der Westen im Osten,* 282. In later years the principal was Dr. Levi Niemcewicz and the director of the religious studies was Mordechai Baumberg (Boymberg), see Frydman et al., "The Religious-Educational Movement 'Beit Yaakov,'" 358–359; "Krakau," *Der Israelit: Ein Centralorgan für das orthodoxe Judentum, Blätter,* September 16, 1928, 4. Boymberg authored many textbooks (in Yiddish) for Beit Yaakov schools.

25. Bacon, *The Politics of Tradition,* 43. Agudat Yisrael was founded at a conference at Kattowitz (Katowice) in 1912, but the organization did not get off the ground for several years.

26. "Where Is Our Shame! . . . ," *Dos Yidishe Vort,* 117 (1918), 2 [Yiddish].

of the German occupying powers to transform it into something more modern.[27] Unlike Hasidic male youth, many Hasidic girls were already attending schools, including gymnasia, and their alienation from religion was a fact recognized by all.[28] In this sense, Carlebach's girls' gymnasium was viewed as a corrective measure to a grave situation. Indeed, Keren Ha-Torah, Agudat Yisrael's Torah education fund that was established in 1923, later became the body in charge of the pedagogical aspects of Ḥavaẓelet.[29]

The encounter between German Neo-Orthodox rabbis and Eastern European Jews during the war years was not limited to Warsaw, as Orthodox German Jews also served in the German military occupying Lithuania. Among them were two prominent individuals: R. Dr. Leopold Rosenak, a brother-in-law of Emanuel Carlebach, who served as a Jewish chaplain, and R. Dr. Joseph Carlebach, the brother of Emanuel Carlebach, who was ordained in Hildesheimer's rabbinical seminary. Prior to his military service he taught in Hidesheimer's religious school in Berlin, as well as in the Lämel School in Jerusalem. Joseph Carlebach volunteered to serve in the German army and was sent to the military censorship office in Kovno (Kaunas). Unlike Warsaw, Lithuania didn't have a significant Hasidic population, and its rabbinical leadership was known for its Talmudic erudition. Lithuania was famous for its yeshivas in which young males studied the Talmud in a highly charged intellectual atmosphere. The male rank and file, including yeshiva students, were mostly clean-shaven and dressed in modern European garb.

Starting in November 1915, Rosenak served as an advisor for Jewish religious and educational matters in Kovno. In December 1915, following joint efforts by Rosenak and Carlebach, a Jewish gymnasium for boys and girls (*Realgymnasium,* a secondary school that focused on teaching sciences and modern languages) was opened in Kovno. Carlebach was released from his service to become its director. In order to ensure that it had enough students, Rosenak and Carlebach went from house to house dressed in their military uniforms and with yarmulkes on their heads and convinced Jewish parents to send their children to the new school. The visual image of the two made a great impression on Jews and contributed to the success of their efforts. Local rabbis agreed to teach the religious subjects and German officers, Jewish and non-Jewish, taught the secular ones. The school had separate classes for boys and girls, and

27. Breuer, "Rabbis-Doctors in Poland-Lithuania," 150–151.
28. Ibid., 132.
29. Grill, *Der Westen im Osten,* 282.

with the quick rise in the number of students, it was subsequently divided into two separate wings, one for boys and one for girls. The gymnasium, which numbered 500 male and female students in 1918, operated according to the Hirschian *Torah 'im derekh erez* model and taught secular subjects in the German language.[30]

One of the teachers in the school was R. Dr. Leo Deutschländer, who would later help establish and administer the Beit Yaakov teachers' seminary in Kraków. Deutschländer was ordained as rabbi in Hildesheimer's rabbinical seminary and was drafted into the German military when the war broke out. Excelling as a pedagogue, in 1918 Deutschländer published a German literature reader, *Westöstliche Dichterklänge*, for teaching German to Jewish students that was composed of selections from classical German literature, as well as some modern Jewish works, all pertaining to biblical and Jewish themes. The passages in the textbook were chosen not to reflect the best of German literature but rather to project a positive image of Jewish history and tradition by German Jewish and non-Jewish writers, and create a harmonious curriculum in the gymnasium.[31] Both Carlebach and Deutschländer stayed in Lithuania after the war ended, with Carlebach leaving in March 1919 and Deutschländer staying a little longer as the head of the Jewish education section in the Lithuanian Religion and Education Ministry.[32]

In order to further develop Jewish education in Lithuania local rabbis together with Deutschländer and Nachman Schlesinger, the director of the Jewish gymnasium in Kovno after Carlebach, established Yavneh, an organization for promoting Jewish education. Yavneh opened many Jewish Orthodox primary schools for girls (and for boys) in Lithuania, where they were taught the Pentateuch with the commentary of the eleventh century commentator, Rashi, a clear deviation from the local practice of female education in the past.[33] There is no evidence to my knowledge of any Lithuanian rabbinical opposition to this innovation. The crown of Yavneh's educational activities for girls was the establishment of gymnasia in Telz (Telšiai) (1921), Kovno (1925), and Ponevezh (Panevėžys) (1928). Some of the teachers in those schools were yeshiva students and some, at least in the beginning, were imported from

30. Grill, *Der Westen im Osten,* 301–305.

31. Deutschländer, ed., *Westöstliche Dichterklänge.*

32. Grill, *Der Westen im Osten,* 308–313; Breuer, "Rabbis-Doctors in Poland-Lithuania," 134–147.

33. Grill, *Der Westen im Osten,* 319.

Germany.[34] By 1937, the number of female students in those gymnasia reached 400.[35] As in Warsaw, the schools received the support of the local rabbinical leadership.[36]

Kraków was not occupied during the war by the German military, and so no German rabbis filled administrative positions of authority. In Kraków there was no meeting of east and west. But with many Galician Jews seeking refuge from the war in Vienna, a different sort of encounter between east and west made its mark on one of those refugees, the Kraków woman whom we encountered in chapter 1, Sarah Schenirer. It was her experience in Vienna that helped her to discover her life's mission, which was the establishment of a girls' religious school in Kraków that would not only keep young Jewish women in the traditional Jewish fold but would make them into enthusiastic and committed Jews.

Sarah Schenirer: From Kraków to Vienna

Sarah Schenirer was of the generation of the rebellious daughters in Kraków. Born in 1883, Schenirer was seven years older than Anna Kluger and almost two years older than Michalina Araten. She lived in the same apartment building as Anna Klimas, the washerwoman in the Araten home who was accused by Israel Araten of enticing his daughter to enter the convent.[37] Klimas was questioned several times by the police, something that was no secret in Kraków. With even village girls like Debora Lewkowicz and her sister being aware of the Araten affair and the Felician Sisters' convent in Kraków as a place of refuge for young Jewish women, Schenirer was surely acquainted with the stories of the young Jewish runaways that appeared in the local press.

Still, Schenirer never mentions in her writings the hundreds of conversions in Kraków. This painful and embarrassing phenomenon was totally suppressed also in the internal historiography of female Orthodox education in the

34. Ibid., 320.

35. Keren Hathora-Zentrale, *Programm und Leistung*, 65, 266.

36. According to Mordecai Gifter (whose grandfather-in-law, Rabbi Yosef Yehuda Leib Bloch, the head of the Telz yeshiva, founded the girls' gymnasium), there was some initial rabbinical uneasiness with the project, but ultimately that dissipated. See Gifter, "The Telz Yeshiva," 169.

37. Both lived on 5/80 Krakówska Street. See Klimas's address in the Kraków census for the year 1900, *Spis ludności miasta Krakowa z r. 1900*, vol. 15, entry 1381, 278–279, and Schenirer's address in the same volume, entry 1372, 276–277.

interwar period, which preferred to frame its story as an Orthodox reaction to secularization and cultural assimilation of young women from Orthodox families. Schenirer herself used vague language to describe the situation, writing that "each Jewish father must be sad today watching how [...] his own child is walking around with alien ideals, poking fun at him, the fanatic. No less, though, is it the fault of the mothers";[38] or in a similar vein: "Many times already, in writing and in speaking, I reminded our brothers and sisters about their holy obligation to their children, and mostly their daughters, who are being educated in ways distant from the spirit and the culture of the Torah. This abnormal phenomenon damages and breaks the Jewish home and the Jewish family life. The children become the enemies of their parents, as well as the enemies of the entire nation and what it holds sacred."[39]

However, Schenirer does seem to allude to the Kluger affair about a year after Kluger won her court case. Writing in her Polish diary after hearing a lecture by the Jewish literary critic Wilhelm Feldman (1868–1919), Schenirer says:

> If I would only have the courage, I would have gotten up and read from the *siddur* [prayer-book], I would have said that secular science is incapable of quenching the thirst of the Jewish soul, a thirst that only Torah study is able to satisfy. [...] Only books, books of our Torah can do this, because only the Creator, who chose us from all the nations of the earth, can know what can nourish our soul! I wonder if one student [*studentka,* the Polish term for a female university student] is as happy as I am when I read on the Sabbath the Ḥok [*le-yisrael*] sea [of knowledge].[40]

Attending lectures, like that of Feldman's, did not shake Schenirer's religious commitment. On the contrary, she was convinced that a "Jewish soul" would be able to be satisfied only by Jewish religious texts. Comparing her own happiness when reading on the Sabbath Ḥok le-yisrael with the happiness of "one student," Schenirer asked herself who was happier. This is the only reference to a "student" in her handwritten Polish diary, and clearly she was not

38. Schenirer, *Gezamelte shriftn,* 23.

39. Ibid., 24.

40. Dekiert and Lisek, eds., "*Żydówką być to rzecz niemała,*" entry for December 6, [1910]. This entry was translated into Hebrew and published in an edition of Schenirer's writings, however the reference to Feldman was omitted. See Schenirer, *Em be-yisra'el,* vol. 1, 39–40. Feldman grew up in a Hasidic family but left that world at age 18, see Opalski, "Feldman, Wilhem."

referring here to one of her friends. Kluger represented the new class of young
Jewish women from Hasidic homes, namely, students at the university. By emphasizing the superiority of the Jewish religious texts Schenirer could point to
something she herself experienced which Kluger, or someone like her, did not.

During the years before the war Schenirer attended public lectures delivered by academics and literary figures on different subjects, a common activity
for young women of her circle. From her diary it appears that some of these
lectures served not to broaden her intellectual horizons but rather to confirm
her religious identity. After attending a lecture on the concept of God according to philosophers like Spinoza and Leibniz, she writes that she had to re-
strain herself from jumping on the podium and screaming:

> Fools! What are you searching for? Don't you see the wonders of our Cre-
> ator at every step? Doesn't the smallest grass in the field tell you that if it
> were not for the Creator up there, if he did not give rain, the grass wouldn't
> grow there? [...] Ah! Fools! How long. How long will you look for what
> you see at every step? [...] Our science is the holy Torah which will never,
> never, be changed, because it is the true word of the Creator who revealed
> it in fire in front of millions of people [...].[41]

These are the words of a woman deeply secure in her faith, not of one searching for answers.

But the life in Kraków to which Schenirer had become accustomed soon
came to an end. With the outbreak of the First World War, she fled to Vienna,
where she began attending the synagogue of R. Moses David Flesch (1879–
1944). Flesch was born in Pressburg, Hungary (now Bratislava, Slovakia) and
studied in the famous yeshiva there, but in 1906 he traveled to Frankfurt to
study for several years at the yeshiva of R. Solomon Zalman Breuer, the
Hungarian-born son-in-law of R. Samson Raphael Hirsch. While some of the
students in that yeshiva also studied at the university, there is no evidence that
Flesh pursued academic studies. But the exposure to the Hirschian ideology
of *Torah 'im derekh erez* influenced Flesch, who subsequently became an ad-
mirer of the works of R. Hirsch. As a synagogue rabbi, Flesch was known also
as a gifted orator and his sermons attracted many listeners.[42] Although R.
Flesch's synagogue was not strictly speaking a Neo-Orthodox synagogue, it

41. Dekiert and Lisek, eds., "*Żydówką być to rzecz niemała*," entry for April 20 [1913].
42. See Leventahl, "A Biography of R. Moshe David Flesch."

was very different from a Galician Hasidic prayer house. Flesch delivered his sermons in the German language, and gave classes on the Bible, which were viewed by some congregants as a religious innovation. The prayers were recited according to the Ashkenazi rite, which differed from the rite common in Kraków Hasidic prayer houses.

In her Yiddish memoir, Schenirer claimed that Flesch's synagogue was "the cradle of the nowadays popular Beit Yaakov movement."[43] When she visited there for the first time she was surprised to see the *Rabbiner* (German-style rabbi) stepping on the *bimah* (the raised platform in the synagogue) before the commencement of the Torah service. When she asked the woman seated next to her for an explanation, she was informed that the *Rabbiner* was about to deliver a sermon on the occasion of the holiday of Hanukkah. Schenirer's initial surprise reflects her experience in Hasidic houses of worship where such events did not take place. A Hasidic rabbi delivered sermons not during the main service but rather at Sabbath-meal gatherings from which women were excluded. Those sermons were delivered in Yiddish and were often replete with Hasidic themes that were unintelligible to women. Flesch spoke about the Jewish heroine, Judith, and called upon Jewish women and their daughters to emulate female models from Jewish history. Deeply moved, Schenirer began to attend his synagogue regularly for prayers and classes on the Pentateuch, Psalms, and *Pirkei Avot*.

Schenirer recalls wishing that all the girls and women of Kraków could have heard the sermon and discovered the heroism of their female ancestors. Schenirer then discloses what might have been the real motivation behind her subsequent educational initiative. While in Vienna she heard a "secret voice" calling on her, "You must implement the idea of establishing a religious girls' school in order to save the generation of women for the sake of the legacy of the Jewish people (*Israel Sava*)."[44] She was convinced that she was entrusted with a mission to mold the religious character of Kraków women through educational activities that would imbue them with a deep sense of Jewish identity and religious enthusiasm. Indeed, Schenirer is best described as a religious enthusiast, rather than as a student, much less scholar, of Torah. In her published writings she used Yiddish words like "enthusiasm" (*hislahavus, bagaysterung*) and "feelings" dozens of times, and was viewed by her admirers as a

43. Schenirer, *Gezamelte shriftn*, 8.
44. Ibid., 8–10.

charismatic figure.[45] After her sojourn in Vienna, her earlier interests in theater and lectures on culture diminished, and she devoted herself exclusively to her educational mission.

Schenirer's religious inspiration evoked by a Viennese Germanized synagogue stood in sharp contrast to the feelings of religious inspiration experienced by German Jewish males when visiting Polish Jewish communities. For example, in a letter from May 28, 1918, the philosopher Franz Rosenzweig described his impressions as a German soldier in Warsaw during the First World War:

> On Saturday I chanced into a Hasidic *steebel* [prayer room]: on Sunday I went into several bookstores and two *heders* [...] There were two classes in one of them, one for the older children and one for the younger. The contrast with the Mohammedan school in Usküb was very pronounced. First because there were only boys there. Also, among the Hasidim the purely masculine character was striking; all the more so because the meal came between *minhah* [afternoon prayer] and *maariv* [evening prayer], at dusk, the so-called *sholeshsudes,* "the third meal." The "first" comes Friday evening, and Sabbath lunch is the "second." It was only a token meal, whether because of the war or by custom I don't know; the singing was the main thing; I have never heard anything like it. These people don't need an organ, with their surging enthusiasm, the voice of children and old men blended [...]. Nor have I ever heard such praying.[46]

Interestingly, he also wrote: "One of the [ḥeder] teachers had a course with Carlebach, the German Orthodox rabbi who went to Poland last year to guard the interests of Orthodoxy from the looming emancipation of the *Ostjuden.*" Two days later he added: "One hears again and again about Dr. Carlebach, the Orthodox rabbi from Cologne who has come here; I'd like to participate in one of his lectures and see how he starts it; he seems to communicate in a compromise between High German and Yiddish."[47] Clearly, Carlebach's presence in Warsaw was also noticed by non-Orthodox German Jews.

Such impressions about the enthusiasm of Eastern European Hasidic Jews were not unique to Rosenzweig but were also shared by German

---

45. In the New York edition of her writings, the different forms of *bagaysterung* appear 40 times and *hislahavus*, 13 times.

46. Cited in Glatzer, ed., *Franz Rosenzweig,* 75.

47. Rosenzweig, *Briefe,* 321, 323. In his English translation of the first letter Glatzer omitted the reference to Carlebach.

Neo-Orthodox rabbis who traveled to Eastern Europe. The Hamburg-born R. Dr. Wolf S. Jacobson, an Agudat Yisrael activist, travelled to Kraków for the first time in 1924 with a group of Orthodox political activists and published his impression in the Orthodox German newspaper *Der Israelit*. He emphasized the warmth and enthusiastic prayers in the Hasidic prayer houses and lamented: "Woe to us people of the west who are so removed from this atmosphere, so distant from the Hasidic influence. If we would only be smart enough to transfer even a little of the warmth of this place to our place and to influence the coldness in and around us, then we would have been happy."[48]

Rosenzweig was well aware of the "purely masculine character" of Hasidic enthusiasm, recognizing it as an exclusively *male* experience. Jacobson too described the male experience in Hasidic prayer houses in Kraków. It appears that Sara Schenirer had to take a journey in the opposite direction in order to be emotionally touched in a synagogue prayer service. Here was a rabbi delivering a sermon about women to men *and women*. In Kraków things were different, as Schenirer observed when she returned home:

> Nowadays Jewish children, especially Jewish daughters, have stopped praying altogether, and when they already come to the synagogue, prayer is for them nothing more than a routine lacking heart and soul . . . our daughters do not know their history, know nothing about the greatness of their nation, and do not understand the depth of the passionate prayers. Can it continue to remain like this?[49]

Schenirer didn't comment on the synagogue service she attended in Kraków, which was probably Hasidic. Instead, she attributed the indifference of Kraków girls to their ignorance of Jewish history and prayers.

The Return from Vienna to Kraków

Upon her return to Kraków Schenirer did not take steps to start a school, at least not at first. Rather, she established an association for young Orthodox women and a lending library in which she included books "from Frankfurt" written by R. Hirsch and Marcus Lehmann.[50] It will be recalled that books by these German Neo-Orthodox figures had been recommended for Galician

---

48. Cited in Ya'akobzon, *Zikhronot*, 206.
49. Schenirer, *Gezamelte shriftn*, 12.
50. Ibid., 14.

women during the 1903 rabbinical assembly in Kraków. In fact, those books were among the few written by Orthodox authors for Jews with a modern education. Whether she discovered them in R. Flesch's synagogue in Vienna, or learned about them from the Jewish press, Schenirer used the German Neo-Orthodox writings to inspire the girls in her association. She also gave them lectures on various topics. Yet she noticed that although some of them were affected when hearing a beautiful talk or were touched by a biblical poetic verse, they continued to be lax in their religious observance. That is when, according to her own account, Schenirer decided to establish a religious school for young girls, with the hope that elementary-age students would be more receptive to her efforts.[51] Lacking the required educational qualifications to administer or even teach in a primary school, as well as the necessary financial means to operate such a school, Schenirer's vision was limited to establishing a religious school that would supplement the secular and religion classes taught in primary schools. Unlike in private primary schools, the curriculum in private supplementary religious schools was not supervised by school councils and did not require their formal approval. However, it is likely that her school required some sort of approval by the Jewish community council with respect to its sanitary and safety conditions, as was the case with ḥeders that taught only religious subjects.

Those were still the war years, and although Kraków was not then directly under attack, the loss and destruction suffered in other Galician regions caused a massive influx of Jews, including major Galician Hasidic leaders, to Vienna. Determined to open her school, Schenirer wrote her brother, whom she respected as a Torah-learned Jew, asking for his advice. There was no need to consult with him about starting a girls' association, but the idea of a school had been debated in the press for almost two decades with the Orthodox expressing opposition to it. Indeed, her brother, apparently aware that this had become a contentious issue, responded, "What will you benefit from battling with factions (*partayen*)?" When she made clear to him that she was resolute in her decision, he wrote to her that she should come to Marienbad (Mariánské Lázně), the spa town where the leader of the Galician Belz Hasidic dynasty, Yissachar Dov Rokeach (1854–1926), was staying at the time, and "we will hear whether the sage of the generation would grant his approval for this."

---

51. It is thus somewhat unclear why, if Schenirer felt in Vienna that her calling was to establish a religious girls' school, she only took steps in this direction after her women's association did not produce the desired results.

Schenirer wrote in her memoir that this response filled her with endless joy.[52]
Clearly, she hoped to receive rabbinic sanction for her school project.

Approaching Rokeach was a good strategic move, as the newspaper of the
Maḥazikei Ha-Dat association, which was under the influence of the Belz Hasidic leader, had rejected before the war any innovation on the issue of female
religious education. Schenirer's brother, a follower of the Belzer rebbe, may
have realized that nothing would materialize without the rebbe's blessing; his
advice echoed that of R. Schwadron, who told Meir Jung two decades earlier
that founding an association of the Orthodox would require the blessing of the
Belzer rebbe.[53] Schenirer traveled with her brother to Marienbad in 1917, and,
according to her memoir, her brother wrote to the rebbe a *kvitl* (note submitted to a Hasidic leader) which said, "She wants to guide Jewish girls in the
Jewish path." This vague formulation, which avoided the use of the loaded
term "school," turned out to be a smart one, as Rokeach responded with the
words, "blessing and success!"[54]

The Hasidic leader's response filled Schenirer with the hope that her dream
would be realized. In October 1917 (the Hebrew month of Ḥeshvan, after the
high holidays), the same month and year when the Ḥavaẓelet gymnasium
opened its doors to female Orthodox students in Warsaw, Schenirer opened
her supplementary religious school with twenty-five primary school students.
Shortly thereafter that number grew to forty. The room, as she described, was
small, the benches were old, and there was no blackboard, but Schenirer was
joyful: "The girls came to school eagerly, where they heard fresh things every
day. They knew already that the purpose of life was not limited to eating and
drinking, and that one could lead a happy life only when he serves the Creator
with a true enthusiasm."[55]

According to Schenirer, when a Hasidic father came to enroll his daughter,
he asked her what she actually wished to accomplish. Schenirer answered that
her principal goal was to teach girls "to be enthusiastic about Jewishness."[56]
The father, Mordechai Luksenberg, who would soon become one of the
founders of the local branch of the Orthodox Agudat Yisrael party, was so

52. Ibid., 15.

53. R. Schwadron came to this conclusion after the newpaper *Kol Maḥazikei Ha-Dat* successfully thwarted the formation of Agudat Yeshurun. See chapter 1.

54. Schenirer, *Gezamelte shriftn*, 15; Manekin, "'Something Completely New'," 80–81.

55. Schenirer, *Gezamelte shriftn*, 16.

56. "Ich mayn der ikar zay tsu bagaystern far yidishkayt," ibid., 51.

pleased with the answer that he became the first to offer assistance to her. When the number of her students kept growing, she selected her two most diligent students to help her, girls who were barely thirteen years old, but "who could understand the great responsibility entrusted on their shoulders."[57]

It is important to note that there is no evidence of any contemporary opposition, rabbinic or otherwise, to Schenirer's supplementary religious school. In addition to Luksenberg, Schenirer was assisted by the "young *rebbetzin* [a rabbi's wife] Halberstam a granddaughter of the *Divrei Hayim,* may the memory of the righteous be for a blessing, of Sandz," who with an unusual zeal recruited girls, convinced parents, and dedicated every free moment to the school project.[58] Schenirer is referring here to Chaya Fradel, a granddaughter of the founder of the Sandz Hasidic dynasty R. Hayim Halberstam, who married her cousin R. Ben-Zion Halberstam, also a grandson of R. Hayim Halberstam and leader of the Bobov Hasidic dynasty. The latter was innovative in the religious education of the male youth, establishing several yeshivas in Western Galicia for them. He spent the war years in Vienna and then stayed for a while in Marienbad. In 1919 he opened a yeshiva in Kraków and stayed there for several years. Both husband and wife were relatives of Anna Kluger (whose mother was a Halberstam) and surely experienced the shame and pain brought upon the Halberstam family during the Kluger affair. The involvement of the wife of such an influential Hasidic leader in Schenirer's school project is testimony to the readiness of the Orthodox in Kraków for change in the practice of female education. This was also a result of the war, especially the move of many Jews outside Galicia in search of a place of refuge, which weakened the authority and control of parents and religious leaders and opened the door for creative initiatives.

Schenirer tells us little of what she actually taught in those years, but a handwritten report card, preserved by one of her earliest students, provides a clue. The card's heading, "Report Card for Birenbaum Devorah. A Student in the Fifth Course of the First Strict Orthodox Girls' School," is written in Yiddish

---

57. Ibid.

58. Ibid., 17. While she writes that her brother and father were followers of the Belz dynasty, Schenirer had connections also to the Sandz Hasidic dynasty. Writing about her family, she notes that her father was among the first Sandz Hasidim, and her parental grandmother supported the Zaddik of Sandz, ibid., 5. Schenirer also used to attend the Simḥat Torah celebration (*hakafot*) in the prayer house in Kraków of R. Isaac Isaiah Halberstam, a son of R. Hayim Halberstam and a leader of the Hasidic Czechów dynasty. See Schenirer, *Em be-yisra'el*, vol. 2, 39.

and it lists grades in the following areas: Ethics, Diligence, Religion, Blessings, Prayer, Translating [from Hebrew to Yiddish], Composition, Assignments, Yiddish readings, German readings, and Jewish history.[59] The readings in German were likely selections from the stories of Marcus Lehmann. The report card does not include "Pentateuch" or any other texts as subjects. Indeed, none of the subjects listed was religiously controversial, but the mere fact that they were taught to Orthodox girls in a formal setting was an innovation that demanded creativity and dedication. The constant growth of the school and its popularity among Hasidim sent a clear message that there was a thirst and a need for formal religious education for girls.

Schenirer's supplementary religious school was not the first or only Jewish religious school in Kraków. There were several initiatives by the preachers of the progressive Kraków Temple to provide religious classes for boys and girls starting in 1868. In 1894, Samuel Landau established a private religious school for boys and girls in his apartment. Girls were taught to read in Hebrew, write in Yiddish, and translate the prayers. They were also taught the Bible.[60] In 1908, an elementary school for boys named "The Hebrew School" was opened in the city, and three years later it added four weekly hours for girls in cooperation with the Ruth Zionist women's association; the girls learned Hebrew, Pentateuch, and Jewish history.[61] In 1918, when Kraków was already a city in the recently created Second Polish Republic, the school developed into a coeducational elementary school with a gymnasium called "The Hebrew Gymnasium." It was housed in a new three-story building with fifteen boys and girls in its first gymnasium class. The orientation of the school was not Orthodox, although the Jewish curriculum included Bible, Hebrew, and Jewish History, and many of the students came from traditional homes. In 1926 the Hebrew Gymnasium conducted its first matriculation exams. The school possessed excellent teachers, many of them with an academic education, including Anna Kluger, whose last name was now Bross. The level of the teaching was high and its ideology Zionist.[62]

59. Benisch, *Carry Me in Your Heart*, 36.

60. Maślak-Maciejewska, *Modlili się w Templu*, 278–279; 357. It is unclear how long the school existed, and which families enrolled their children there.

61. See advertisements for the girls' courses in *Ha-Mizpeh*, September 1, 1911, 1; September 11, 1912, 1; January 31, 1913, 1 [Hebrew].

62. Samsonowska, "The Hebrew Secondary School and the Jewish Educational System in Kraków," 13–38. Lazar, *Beit ha-sefer ha-'ivri bi-krakov 1908–1936*.

This development, especially the early inclusion of formal religious education for girls, made the lack of educational initiatives among the Orthodox religious leadership in Kraków appear even worse than before. No wonder that when the recently established local branch of the Agudat Yisrael Orthodox party learned about the success of Schenirer's supplementary religious school, it considered in 1919 placing the school under its auspices in order to enable its growth. An educational committee composed of three of its members suggested to Schenirer to place the school under the management of the local Agudat Yisrael, which would take care of all the school's expenses. Schenirer consulted with the aforementioned R. Ben-Zion Halberstam, known as an opponent of Agudat Yisrael, and he gave his approval.[63] Clearly, she did not want to lose his support or have her school at the center of a controversy. Practical as she was from the beginning, she knew the value of receiving consent from a religious authority for each step she took. The local Agudat Yisrael's adoption of the school, now named Beit Yaakov, proved beneficial, and in 1923 the school moved to a newly built third floor on top of an existing building with eight large and furnished rooms.[64]

Following the adoption of the school by the local Agudat Yisrael, matters moved quickly. According to Leo Deutschländer's account:

> The example of the Kraków School served as a guide. After the rabbinical council of Agudat Yisrael [Council of Torah Sages] had expressed itself in principle in favor of the spreading of the Beit Yaakov idea, requests were made by many provincial cities to Kraków to assist them in the establishment of such schools. [. . .] The school in Kraków itself experienced a rapid expansion [. . .] Until the autumn of 1924, in addition to the Kraków institution, there were 19 [similar] schools in Poland with about 2,000 students.[65]

Deutschländer also mentioned the approval given by the rabbinical council of Agudat Yisrael to the establishment of additional schools on the model of the Kraków Beit Yaakov school in his talk in the second assembly of Agudat Yisrael in Vienna (1929).[66] Although he doesn't provide details about this approval, it is clear from his description that what contributed to the spread

63. Weissman, "Bais *Ya'akov*," 56; Schenirer, *Gezamelte shriftn*, 52.

64. Ibid.; Deutschländer, ed., *Beth Jakob: 1928, 1929*, 7.

65. Ibid., 7.

66. Scheinfeld, ed. *Ha-Knesiyah ha-gedolah*, 44–50, esp. 45.

of the schools at this early stage was *inter alia* rabbinical endorsement.[67] One may speculate that the Kraków branch of Agudat Yisrael approached the party's rabbinical council before adopting the local school, and the content of its response spread quickly.

Compared to the innovation in Orthodox women education in Warsaw, the Kraków model was more conservative and represented much less of a break with past norms. This is especially true of its curriculum: a German Orthodox newspaper reported in 1920 that the expanded Kraków school taught Hebrew and Jewish religion and offered classes in women's handiwork and different cottage industries. The school also organized historical lectures and special events. Clearly, at this time the school did not offer classes devoted to studying the Pentateuch or other parts of the Bible. The staff included eight teachers in addition to Schenirer and gained great popularity among large segments of the Kraków Jewish population. When the number of students reached more than 500, lack of space limited its future growth.[68]

Shortly after the local Agudat Yisrael took the school under its auspices, Sarah Schenirer was invited to participate in a Shabbat Hanukkah event at the Ḥavaẓelet gymnasium in Warsaw. She traveled with seven of her students, and on Saturday evening, December 11, 1920, the students presented talks on religious themes that were crowned "a great success." On the next evening, Ḥavaẓelet students cooperated with Schenirer's students in a special Hanukkah celebration for young women and children that took place in the school.[69] Schenirer does not record this meeting in her writings, and while we don't know what she thought about Ḥavaẓelet as a possible model for female Orthodox education in Kraków, such a model was not implemented in Kraków or in any other Polish city.

The Warsaw visit was beneficial for Schenirer, as immediately thereafter an advertisement for the Yiddish play she wrote, *Yehudis* ("Judith"), appeared almost every day on the front page of *Der Yud*, the Warsaw Yiddish daily of Agudat Yisrael. Under the heading "The Most Beautiful Present for Children" (later changed to "The Most Beautiful Present for Girls"), the play was described in the advertisement as "a historical scene in five acts" written by

67. On Agudat Yisrael's Council of Torah Sages see Bacon, "Enduring Prestige, Eroded Authority," 359; Bacon, *The Politics of Tradition*, 85–91.

68. "Briefe aus Krakau," *Jüdische Presse: Organ für die Interessen des orthodoxen Judentums*, December 17, 1920, 3.

69. "Frauen-Chanuka-Abend in Warschau," ibid., December 24, 1920, 4.

"Sarah Schenirer, the head of the Orthodox girls' school Beit Yaakov, Kraków."
Since it was rather unusual to have a contemporary literary work written by a
woman advertised in this Orthodox newspaper, one can speculate that Schenirer's name and her school were noticed by the Warsaw Orthodox readers.[70]
Apparently, Schenirer consulted with the Belzer rebbe about staging plays in
her school, as she revealed in a letter she wrote in 1923 to Chaim Israel Eiss, a
Galician-born Swiss Jew and one of the central figures of Agudat Israel. Schenirer sent her *Yehudis* to Eiss but told him that the Belzer rebbe "forbade me
to stage plays because this is *ḥukat ha-goy* [a gentile practice], and I promised
him that [I would obey]." She expressed to Eiss her hope that nevertheless she
could stage the play as a "declamation."[71] In subsequent years Beit Yaakov
schools staged plays without encountering the opposition of the rabbinical
council of Agudat Yisrael; however, that body was not under the influence of
the Belz Hasidic dynasty. This anecdote suggests that from the beginning the
educational practices of Beit Yaakov were subject to rabbinical approval, and
that the school's initial rabbinical authority was the Belzer rebbe.

In mid-September 1924, the central council of Agudat Yisrael met in
Kraków and discussed among other things the question of the religious education of girls, a discussion that turned out to be of crucial importance. Just one
year beforehand, in August 1923, the first great assembly of Agudat Yisrael took
place in Vienna, and although the question of female education was briefly
mentioned there by a few speakers, it was not formally debated and no practical solutions were suggested.[72] Keren Ha-Torah, the education fund established during this assembly, was entrusted only with supporting the Torah
education of male institutions, especially ḥeders and yeshivas. Things were
different in the 1924 meeting in Kraków. The most prominent speaker raising
the issue of female education was Nathan Birnbaum, the well-known Viennese
publicist who reembraced Orthodoxy during World War I and served for some
time as the general secretary of Agudat Yisrael. Birnbaum suggested establishing a committee to discuss the "important question" of the attitude of Jewish
women to their Judaism, and expressed sorrow that there were those who
oppose even raising this issue. "We need teachers steeped in the knowledge of
Torah and Judaism. We must lay the cornerstone for this work during this

70. *Der Yud*, December 11, 1920, and subsequent days.
71. Yiddish written letter of Sarah Schenirer to Chaim Israel Eiss, November 11, 1923. I thank
Eluzer Mermelstein for sharing a copy of this letter with me.
72. "Small Notices on Large Issues," *Do'ar Hayom*, October 25, 1923, 2 [Hebrew].

meeting and accept resolutions on this matter; [we need] to establish a committee and gather all our strength to solve this problem," he said.[73] Levi Niemcewicz spoke about the need for religious female education in Poland, pointing to the danger posed to Orthodox Judaism by the growing number of secular Yiddishist schools. He called for the establishment of local committees that would function according to pedagogical instructions composed by a central organization.[74] Alexander Zysha Frydman, an Agudat Yisrael activist, cited statistics on the development of the Beit Yaakov schools and added: "There are 30 more towns who are interested in having such schools. In order to allow the diligent director [Sarah Schenirer] to train capable teachers there is a need for a sum of $3,000 to build an appropriate institution in Kraków with dorms for the students."[75] Evidently, the 1924 gathering was looking for practical solutions, especially in training able female teachers for Orthodox girls' schools.

What prompted this change in attitude toward female education was the visit of several of the participants in the 1924 meeting to Schenirer's apartment to see how she trained teachers.[76] According to Deutschländer this visit demonstrated both "the promising kernel that lay dormant within [the pedagogical program]" and the necessity of it being run by Keren Ha-Torah. After the Gerer rebbe and other rabbinical authorities gave their consent, the meeting accepted a decision in that spirit. Deutschländer, the director of Keren Ha-Torah who had proven experience as an educator in Lithuania, was entrusted

73. Scheinfeld, Ḥoveret shel Keren Ha-Torah, 32–40, esp. 37.

74. Ibid., 36–37.

75. Ibid., 38.

76. For a detailed impression of that visit see [Wolf S. Jacobson], "In Krakau," Der Israelit, Blätter, October 9, 1924, 3. Jacobson, who participated in the Kraków meeting together with Pinchas Kohn and Leo Deutschländer, wrote about Schenirer:

Without any financial help, only moral support from outside, she created a group of like-minded co-workers, whom she trained in her home in Kraków and then sent them out as pioneers in this holy cause to 25 to 30 Polish towns in order to function as she did [. . .] She has no textbook by which she teaches: that which she wants to teach her students she herself has compiled from the aforementioned writings [Hirsch and Lehmann], and her helpers are writing it down; that's how primitively everything is constructed, and yet the success and the impression of her striving is tremendous [. . .] Whoever was present in this Central Meeting knows that the Jewish problem of the East is that of the education of daughters, [and] will have an idea what an enormous deed this woman has done and what gratitude all Jewry owes her.—To stand by her in support with all possible means seems to me as one of the holiest duties of the Jewesses of the West.

with the responsibility of developing a pedagogical plan for a Beit Yaakov school network for girls.[77] The details were to be discussed in a special meeting in Warsaw in February 1925.

This rapid development was enabled by geopolitical changes resulting from the end of the First World War and the creation of the Polish Second Republic, in which Western Galicia became one of its regions. Warsaw, the capital city, was the large metropolis where significant changes within the Orthodox society had taken place already during the war years. Having Agudat Yisrael with its Keren Ha-Torah in charge of using the Kraków school as a springboard for developing a large network of schools promised much progress and a chance to solve the problem of Orthodox women's education in a sustainable way. But this takeover came with a price, as Schenirer, while remaining involved in the project as an educator, inspirational figure, and a public speaker to promote attendance in the new schools, was no longer independent.[78] Deutschländer credited the great popularity among all sectors of Orthodox society of Schenirer's first school, "which she established on her own initiative," to the decision of the local Agudat Yisrael to take it under its patronage, but he claimed that girls' Orthodox education in Eastern Europe owed its upsurge, both educationally and economically, to Agudat Yisraels' Keren Ha-Torah.[79]

However, the new patronage of the central council of Agudat Yisrael was frowned upon by two of the major Galician Hasidic dynasties, Belz and Sandz, who were among Schenirer's first supporters. After Agudah's takeover, they viewed the Beit Yaakov schools as a strong weapon in the hands of Agudat Yisrael and the Ger Hasidic dynasty,[80] and as a result, according to one report, "they started harassing [Schenirer], and she suffered not a little from them."[81]

<hr/>

77. Deutschländer, ed., *Bajs Jakob: Sein Wesen und Werden*, 32. See also Deutschländer, ed., *Beth Jakob: 1928, 1929*, 8; Scheinfeld, ed., *Ha-Knesiyah ha-gedolah*, 45–46.

78. See Oleszak, "The Beit Ya'akov School in Kraków."

79. Deutschländer, ed., *Beth Jakob: 1928, 1929*, 7.

80. On the negative attitude of Galician Hasidic dynasties, especially Belz, to the Agudat Yisrael political party, see Bacon, *The Politics of Tradition*, 91–95. The Hasidic dynasties of Czortków (Czortkiv), Bojan, Husiatyn (Husyatyn), Otynia, Sadagóra (Sadahora), and some others, supported Agudat Yisrael and its educational institutions.

81. Moshe Blatt, "The life Journey of Sarah Schenirer of Blessed Memory," *Unzer exspress*, March 13, 1933, 5 [Yiddish]. Blatt, a Kraków correspondent, describes Schenirer's first school as an afternoon "ḥeder" for girls who studied in the morning in public schools. More than thirty years later, the Israeli journal of the Beit Yaakov movement published a Hebrew translation of Blatt's article, but omitted the part about the opposition of the Sandz and Belz Hasidim,

Indeed, different rabbis associated with the Sandz Hasidic dynasty, all from the Halberstam family, as well as Yissachar Dov Rokeach, the leader of the Belz Hasidic dynasty, expressed their opposition to Agudat Yisrael and their educational institutions.[82] As it turned out, the early warning Schenirer had received from her brother of avoiding factional politics was not an empty one. This newfound opposition to Beit Yaakov was motivated more by politics, specifically by the Galician Hasidic dynasties' suspicion of Agudat Yisrael, than by religious arguments against women's education (although these were occasionally utilized by the opponents).

Yehudah Leib Orlean, the Gerer Hasid from Warsaw who would become the sole director of the teachers' seminary in late 1932, mentioned this politically motivated opposition years later in his tribute to Schenirer:

> As much as we'd like to see in [Schenirer's] project a result of the traditional spirit that was very strong in the Jewish street in Poland; the continuity of generations, it can't be denied that her project carried in its wings something completely new. A tremendous project was born out of nothing, a wide network of schools, a very powerful movement [. . .] Only after she raised the curtain, Orthodox society began to understand her, the great Torah scholars fathomed her intentions, and the people and its leaders began to trust her. But even after she acquired a stable status in the life of the Jewish public in Poland, she was not released from the small-minded party-operatives and communal functionaries who tried to constrain her moves and limit her vision and horizons. At times, as she was guarding the Beit Yaakov movement which she created and fostered with dutiful hands,

---

probably to preserve the positive reputation of Schenirer. See Blatt, "In Kraków—At the Time of the Passing of Sarah Schenirer Peace Be Upon Her," *Beit Yaakov* 125 (1970), 22. [Hebrew]

82. See the undated letters written to R. Hayim Elazar Shapira of Munkács (Mukačevo, now Mukachevo, Ukraine), for example, the letter by R. Chone Halberstam of Koloshits (Kołaczyce) in which he cites the opposition of the leader of the Belz Hasidic dynasty (Yissachar Dov Rokeach) to Agudat Yisrael female institutions, Havaẓelet, Yeshurun, and vocational [Beit Yaakov] schools, calling them despicable. Goldshtein, ed., *Tikun 'olam*, letter 45, 57–58. According to Halberstam, Rokeach asked him to cite his opposition in response to Agudat Yisrael's use of his name to the contrary (presumably his 1917 blessing to Schenirer). See also the letter by R. Menachem Mendel Halberstam of Fristik (Frysztak) in which he criticizes Agudat Yisrael in Poland, "which was established by two German rabbis, Doctor Carlebach of Köln and Doctor Kohn," as well as Havaẓelet and Beit Yaakov. Ibid., letter 55, 68–69. He also states there that the education of Agudat Yisrael for males and females is built on a ramshackle foundation.

she had to adopt a male attitude in order to push away the opposition of parents and short sighted operatives for the benefit of the daring idea of Beit Yaakov."[83]

Of course, as a Beit Yaakov leader it was in Orlean's interest to portray opposition to the movement as the work of "party operatives and communal functionaries" and not to mention the contemporary opposition of the Belz and Sandz rabbis.

Between Warsaw and Kraków

In 1925, several months after the principled decision of Agudat Yisrael to have Keren Ha-Torah develop a pedagogical plan for a Beit Yaakov school network, a meeting to discuss this plan took place in the Havazelet gymnasium in Warsaw. The participants included Deutschländer and the administration of Keren Ha-Torah, the Kraków education committee, as well as Sarah Schenirer and female teachers in the supplementary Beit Yaakov schools that were already established in different locations.[84] Such a mixed-gender group of people discussing female education would have been inconceivable in the years prior to the opening of Schenirer's religious school, especially in Kraków. But although the meeting took place in Warsaw, the decisions accepted signaled a deviation from the model of female education implemented there. Among the decisions was a plan to develop Schenirer's enthusiastic if unprofessional training of teachers into a serious pedagogical program, as well as to organize annual two-month continuing education courses for currently employed teachers. It was also decided to build in Kraków a teachers' seminary and house within it the headquarters of the pedagogic and administrative work of the Beit Yaakov school network. To begin implementing this ambitious plan, Keren Ha-Torah recruited three qualified young Jewish women from abroad to run the teachers' training program. Those young women came from Frankfurt, Breslau (Wrocław), and Zürich.[85] As for Warsaw, it was decided to

83. See Orlean, "Sarah Schenirer—Image and Program," 4, 30. See also Manekin, "'Something Completely New'," 85.

84. For the participants, see "Aus der polnischen Agudas Jisroel: Beth Jakob Konferenz in Warschau," *Der Israelit: Ein Centralorgan für das orthodoxe Judentum, Blätter*, March 12, 1925, 3. Seidman, *Sarah Schenirer*, 83–84.

85. Schenirer, *Gezamelte Schriften*, 53; Deutschländer, ed., *Bajs Jakob: Sein Wesen und Werden*, 33–34; Deutschländer, ed., *Beth Jakob: 1928, 1929*, 7–9.

establish teaching courses (those generally lasted three months) there for graduates of Ḥavaẓelet. The educational plan for the Beit Yaakov school system which was prepared in the subsequent months was sent to the Gerer rebbe and approved by him on March 14, 1926.[86] The right to establish Beit Yaakov religious supplementary schools was recognized by the Polish education ministry in 1926 and 1927 and remained the valid legal basis in subsequent years. Representatives of Agudat Yisrael succeeded in having these institutions defined as "religious courses" rather than "schools" in order to exempt them from the strict regulations that applied to schools. But they were not successful in convincing the education ministry to exempt the girls in these schools from attending the religion classes in public schools.[87]

The decision to make Kraków, not Warsaw, the headquarters of Orthodox female education signaled the new direction in female religious education. Ḥavaẓelet would continue to function and even house conferences for Beit Yaakov teachers, but its curriculum would not be adopted by any Beit Yaakov school in Poland. In the years following the 1925 meeting, the teachers' seminary in Kraków, not the gymnasium in Warsaw, would become the flagship of the Beit Yaakov educational system. The Lithuanian Yavneh would still manage to establish a gymnasium in Ponevezh in 1928, but no Orthodox gymnasium was established in Poland under the patronage of Beit Yaakov.[88] Each of

---

86. Deutschländer, ed., *Das Erziehungswerk der Gesetzestreuen Judenheit,* 27.

87. Seidman, ed., *Żydowskie szkolnictwo religijne,* 24–33 in the Yiddish section. According to the statute signed by teachers, classtime was limited to seven hours per week (three hours for prayer, two hours for Bible, Prophets, and Psalms, and one hour each for Jewish history and religious laws). In practice, teachers also led cultural and educational activities for their students. See Frydman et al., "The Religious-Educational Movement 'Beit Yaakov,'" 319.

88. The name "Ḥavaẓelet" was adopted by several primary girls' schools in the interwar period, none of them connected to the Warsaw gymnasium or Agudat Yisrael. The Yavneh organization in Poland which, unlike in Lithuania, was associated with the religious Zionist Mizrachi party, opened in Kalisz a primary school for girls named Ḥavaẓelet; see Beit-Ha-Levi, *Toldot Yehudei Kalish,* 378. Girls from the Kalisz school, as well as from public schools in the city, participated in the activities of Bnot Agudat Yisrael, the girls' youth movement of the Orthodox party, see Karmeli et al., eds., *Sefer Kalish,* vol. 2, 96. See also a letter about the school, "The Orthodox Girls' Schools, Orthodox Women's Associations; Kalisz," *Bajs Yaakov ortodoksisher zhurnal* 1 (1923), 11 [Yiddish]. According to the letter, the school was established three years earlier. In 1931, the director of the Beit Yaakov schools in Łódź, Yoel Naphtali Kamenets, opened a prestigious private religious primary school for Orthodox girls with an intensive general studies program and named it Ḥavaẓelet; see Religyose techter shul Khavatseles, *Khavatseles oysgabe.*

the three girls' gymnasia in Lithuania was called "Yavneh Girls' Gymnasium" and none of them was incorporated into the Polish Beit Yaakov school network.[89] The curriculum in the Lithuanian Yavneh schools was rigorous and the language of instruction was Hebrew. The teachers in the Yavneh schools, including in girls' gymnasia, had their own conferences as well as their own summer courses.[90] Moreover, after the establishment of the Polish young women's association Bnot Agudat Yisrael, the Lithuanian Orthodox called upon establishing their own young women's association composed of Yavneh school graduates and teachers.[91] The Lithhuanian women's association established later was called "Beit Yaakov" and its center was in Kovno.[92] Although Yavneh belonged politically to Agudat Yisrael, and was supported by Keren Ha-Torah, its educational philosophy remained more moderate than the one of Agudat Yisrael's Polish educational institutions, all of which operated under the influence of a

89. For a report on the tenth anniversary of the Telz Yavneh Girls' Gymnasium, see "Celebration of Girls' Education in Lithuania," *Ha-Ne'eman*, Shevat-Adar [February] 1931, 14 [Hebrew]. The author refers to the gymnasia in Kovno and Ponevezh as the younger sisters of the Telz gymnasium, calling all of them "Yavneh Girls' Gymnasia." See also Eżyon, "The 'Yavneh' Educational System in Lithuania"; Keren Hathora-Zentrale, *Programm und Leistung*, 64–67, esp. 65. Eżyon was the director of the Telz Yavneh Girls' Gymnasium for ten years. Curiously, in a work dedicated to the history of Beit Yaakov schools, Deutschländer refers to the Ponevezh girls' gymnasium by the name "Beit Yaakov," and he includes a photograph of the school building. However, as can be seen in the inscription on the photograph, the school is a "Talmud Torah Beit Yaakov" [=boys' religious school] named after Yaakov Luria, the philanthropist who financed the building. See Deutschländer, ed., *Beth Jakob: 1928, 1929*, 16, 20. The Ponevezh girls' gymnasium was later housed in that building. Deutschländer did not include any of the girls' gymnasia in Lithuania in the lists of the Beit Yaakov schools he published in his works, see ibid., 45–47 (although the Lithuanian cities were marked on the map).

90. See "The Conference of the Yavneh Teachers in Kovno," *Ha-Ne'eman*, Tevet [January] 1929, 13–14 [Hebrew]; "The Teachers' Courses in Palanga," ibid., Tishrei [September] 1930, 13–14 [Hebrew].

91. See "In Our World: The Conference of 'Bnot Agudat Yisrael'," *Ha-Ne'eman*, Sivan [May] 1931, 13 [Hebrew].

92. The association published a Yiddish journal titled *Beys Yaakov: Gevidmet di interesn fun der froyen bavegung "Beys Yaakov" in Lietuva*. A report in the section dedicated to news from the branches of the association detailed the activities of a study group in Telz. The young women met twice a week, studying Bible on Tuesdays and Torah with the commentary of Rashi, as well as Halakhah and Agaddah, on Sabbaths, in which 120 women participated. The women organized a "*Siyum*" celebration, with talks, songs, and violin music, when they completed studying the book of Exodus. See *Beys Yaakov: Gevidmet di interesn fun der froyen bavegung "Beys Yaakov" in Lietuva*, 1938, 16.

more insular Hasidic worldview. This was particularly true for Yavneh's girls' gymnasia.[93] The takeover of the Orthodox female education system in Poland by Agudat Yisrael marked the end of the educational path that was charted during the war years in Warsaw and Lithuania under the influence of Neo-Orthodox and Lithuanian rabbis. Kraków, which had been plagued for more than a generation by the scandal of runaways, conversions, and Jewesses "in name only," would become the center for producing pious female teachers for Orthodox daughters.

Preparations for a Teachers' Seminary

The plan to establish a teacher training program moved quickly. A two-month continuing education course for Beit Yaakov teachers took place in the Galician countryside in the summer following the meeting in Ḥavaẓelet. It was the first of five similar summer courses taking place between the years 1925 and 1929. The instructors in those courses included, in addition to Sarah Schenirer and local teachers, several female teachers brought from German-speaking countries, all followers of the Hirschian *Torah 'im derekh ereẓ* ideology, as well as several male teachers.[94] The most influential of these was Judith Rosenbaum (later Grunfeld) who had been raised in the Neo-Orthodox community in Frankfurt and was recruited to help set up the teaching program after attending a gymnasium and a teachers' seminary at home. Schenirer wrote that she doubted at the time whether the foreign teachers would be at all suitable for the "Polish Hasidic ways," but when she heard their classes and became aware of their truly Jewish enthusiasm and dedication, she was filled with contentment and hope.[95] The summer courses included the study of prayers, Pentateuch, selections from the Prophets, Psalms, *Pirkei Avot*, religious obligations, and history, as well as pedagogy and psychology.[96] Years later Rosenbaum described her experience in the first summer course:

> I was fortunate; *Hakadosh Baruch hu* ["The Holy One, Blessed Be He"] helped me to give over that which I did know. I was able to present concepts, ideas, things I had already learned and make them meaningful to

93. "A Daughter of Israel Then and Now," *Ha-Ne'eman*, Iyar [May] 1928, 12–13 [Hebrew]; Zalkin, "'Let It Be Entirely Hebraic,'" 125–129.

94. For the list of teachers, see Scheinfeld, ed., *Ha-Knesiyah ha-gedolah*, 47.

95. Schenirer, *Gezamelte shriftn*, 53–54.

96. Deutschländer, ed., *Bajs Jakob: Sein Wesen und Werden*, 13–19, esp. 14, 17.

these girls. I drew knowledge and inspiration from the commentary of R. Shamshon Rafael Hirsch. Of other commentaries I did not know much, but perhaps it was better that way. Everything was taught along the same lines, each lesson adding to the other, forming a complete building. [...]

The *chassidim* educated their boys in *yeshivos*, but kept their daughters ignorant, while we [in Germany] educated both the boys and the girls. While the boys learned *Gemara* and *mishnayos*, we girls were taught *Chumash*. When the boys went to *shul* on Shabbos, we girls also went. This is why Sarah Schenirer needed educators from Germany. We had something to give over to these girls.

I did not know much, but what I knew I could present with warmth, feeling and enjoyment.[97]

From this description it seems that the level of the studies at the summer course was rudimentary and rested on sections of the Pentateuch being taught through the commentary and teaching of R. Hirsch. Much emphasis was placed on presenting a positive view of Judaism and creating an appealing social atmosphere. Several delegations and rabbis visited those courses, but none of them voiced opposition against teaching the Pentateuch in this manner to the participants. Not only was the Pentateuch already taught to women in Warsaw starting in 1917, but given Rosenbaum's own limitations, the study of the Pentateuch could not have been rigorous or textually based, and certainly could not be aimed at duplicating the intense way it was taught to boys in high-level ḥeders.

But Torah study was not the only goal of the summer course. As Rosenbaum writes,

We did not just lecture, we made the school days lively with a song, game or joke. We translated *deracheha darchei noam* ["Its ways are ways of pleasantness" (Prov. 3,17)] through actions showing that G-d's ways are pleasant, righteous and enjoyable. We can also be happy, we can also dance, we can also be young and we can see the beauty of Torah in everything. [...]

When Friday night came, I showed them that it was time to dress a little nicer, brush one's hair a little fancier and that this, in honor of Shabbos, was not only allowed but preferable. They needed to know that the desire to look nice and feel good can be acceptable within the sphere of Torah.

---

97. Grunfeld, "Growing up in Frankfort," 128–129. The spelling "Shamshon" reflects how the name was pronounced in the vernacular.

So I was in Robov [Robów, where the first summer course took place] for six weeks, teaching on the meadow, sitting on the grass, learning in a pleasant, country atmosphere. Morning calisthenics, *davening* [praying], eating, learning were all done together in a unique *heimishe* [homey] environment. We went for walks together, sang together and played together. There was a friendship and comradeship for girls who had never had such harmonious camaraderie before.[98]

The purpose of the summer courses was not to provide Jewish girls with an intensive study experience, but to make them into proud, happy, and religiously enthusiastic Orthodox women, through socialization with like-minded individuals and activities like study, singing, and taking walks. This foreshadowed to a large degree the goal of the Beit Yaakov schools, including its seminary.

The only rabbi who directly addressed the issue of teaching Torah to girls in the summer courses was R. Jacob Rosenheim (1870–1965), a student of R. Hirsch, one of the Neo-Orthodox founders of Agudat Yisrael, and its president for many years. Rosenheim visited the summer course in Jordanów in the summer of 1927 and delivered a talk to the female students there. Citing the verse from the Torah portion of the week: "A woman shall not wear that which pertains to a man (Deuteronomy 22:5)," he explained that this prohibition applied not only to external garb but also to the general boundaries between men and women. He delineated three areas of the human soul that were influenced by God's laws: intellect, emotions, and will. The first area was intended exclusively for males, while the last two pertained also to women. Hence the study of the Oral Law (Talmud) belonged to males (intellect), the study of the Written Law (Bible) and the Midrash belonged also to women (emotions), as did the study of religious conduct (will). The boundaries between the duties of men and women, he warned, should not be crossed.

Rosenheim offered a "scientific" explanation for the boundaries. According to Rosenheim, contemporary science confirmed what the sages of Israel had always known, namely, that if women cultivate intellectual abilities in the same way as men, it might lead to the extinction of the male line. Since Jewish males had been following the commandment, "Thou shalt meditate therein day and night" (Joshua 1:8), they must be supplemented by females possessing the virtues of a woman of valor, and not by intellectually driven women. That is why "If nowadays our women should wish, God forbid, to leap with false

98. Ibid., 129–130.

ambition over the boundaries that the law has drawn for them [. . .] they would sin not only against the law but also against life and the future."[99] Whatever scientific studies Rosenheim had in mind,[100] he didn't rely on the oft-cited prohibition against the study of the Oral Law by women. His warning seems to have been intended to restrict not only the permissible texts but also the goals and methods of their study.

From the time Agudat Yisrael took the Beit Yaakov school system under its wings, the study of the Pentateuch became a part of the curriculum, and selections of it were taught in the teachers' seminary with the commentaries of Rashi and R. Hirsch.[101] However, as we shall see below, the commentaries were taught in Yiddish translation by the female teachers, whose own textual background was limited.

The educational ideology of Beit Yaakov that began with the first summer course remained consistent throughout the years: Torah was to be studied not for its own sake (*Torah li-shemah*) but in order to forge women's mental and emotional commitment to Orthodox Judaism. This was a central plank in Sarah Schenirer's ideology, one she repeated time and again. Thus, in a letter to the members of the female youth organization of Agudat Yisrael, Schenirer emphasized that Torah was not only for them to study or to understand its contents, but the main thing was to fulfill what it teaches and commands them to do. Each word in the Torah should penetrate deep into their heart until it becomes a part of it.[102] Elsewhere, she called upon girls to learn Torah, Prophets, the wisdom of the Jewish sages, religious obligations, prayers, and Jewish history, so that the Jewish spirit would rise within them and excite them to become the biblical Hannah. Schenirer suggested that they take the example of the women of previous generations and the enthusiasm with which they fulfilled their Jewish duties. They drew this enthusiasm from books such as the *Ze'enah u-re'enah, Menorat ha-ma'or, Kav ha-yashar, Lev tov,* and the *Kizur*

99. Deutschländer, ed., *Bajs Jakob: Sein Wesen und Werden,* 25–30, esp. 29. Cf. Oleszak, "The Beit Ya'akov School," 278–279; Seidman, *Sarah Schenirer,* 136.

100. The claim that increased female intellectual activity led to infertility or the inability to breast-feed was already made by Herbert Spencer in the *Principles of Biology* in 1871, but it gained steam with the entry of women into colleges and universities. See Burstyn, "Education and Sex."

101. According to one of the seminary students: "She [Rosenbaum] taught us *Chumash* [Pentateuch], *Navi* [Prophets], *Hashkafa* [religious views], and a Torah perspective of psychology; see Bender, "The Life of a Beit Yaakov Girl," 179.

102. Schenirer, *Gezamelte shriftn,* 31.

Shulḥan Arukh.[103] She emphasized that they should remember that she does not call upon them merely to learn Torah, but to fulfill their Jewish obligations and not be ashamed of them.[104] And six months before she died, Schenirer wrote in a letter to parents of prospective pupils in Jerusalem, "Know that the Beit Yaakov school does not strive to provide a lot of knowledge, but rather a lot of spirit, a great amount of enthusiasm in fulfilling the commandments, a great amount of good character traits."[105]

Schenirer's own knowledge of Jewish teachings, stories, and midrashim was based on the Yiddish paraphrases and commentaries of the works she mentioned to her students, as well as on works such as *Ḥok le-yisrael* (translated into Yiddish) and those of Hirsch. She did not teach the Pentateuch at the seminary, as is evident from the reminiscences of a student:

> Sarah Schenirer was our teacher as well as our principal. However, aside from what we learned in her classes—the wonderful lessons on *Pirkei Avos, Tefillah* [prayer], and *Hashkafa*—we learned much more just from being in her presence. Even in a casual conversation one of her unique *vertlach* [pithy homilies on Biblical and rabbinic subjects] always surfaced. Not only were they insightful pieces of *divrei Torah* [words of Torah], they were spiced with her special sense of humor and sharp wit.[106]

There is no evidence that Schenirer was able to read the Hebrew text of the Pentateuch with Rashi's commentary without the help of a Yiddish translation, and it is most unlikely that she could read and comprehend the Talmud in the original, much of which was written in Aramaic. Her references to these

---

103. *Menorat ha-ma'or, Kav ha-yashar,* and *Lev tov* are popular ethical works; the first two were translated into Yiddish from the Hebrew, and the third was written originally in Yiddish. The *Kiẓur Shulḥan Arukh* is a popular digest of Jewish customs and laws. These books were written for laymen (*ba'alei batim*) and not for Torah scholars; they would not be in the curricula of ḥeders, much less a yeshiva.

104. Schenirer, *Gezamelte shriftn,* 66–67.

105. The letter was requested by Hillel Lieberman, the principal of the Jerusalem Beit Yaakov school. See Lieberman, "A Letter from Sarah Schenirer, Peace Be Upon Her, to the Land of Israel." Cf. Atkin, *The Beth Jacob Movement in Poland,* 25. Schenirer's letter appeared years later also in Hebrew translation, see Schenirer, "A Letter to the Land of Israel," 5.

106. Bender, "The Life of a Beit Yaakov Girl," 179–180. Indeed, Schenirer taught prayer, religion (Jewish worldview), and *Pirkei Avot,* but not the Pentatuech or the Prophets. See the two curricula in *Ginzach Kiddush Hashem,* "Judith Rosenbaum's Protocols of Teachers' Meetings in the Seminary, 1931–1932," 7, 29. This suggests that Schenirer didn't have the appropriate textual skills to teach these subjects.

works in her *divrei Torah* were gleaned from secondary literature and adapted Yiddish translations. Moreover, there is no indication that she was interested in advancing the Hebrew textual skills of her students beyond the basic level.

From the start, the traditional values of Orthodox Jewish male education—learning Torah for its own sake, understanding Torah in its deepest sense, becoming a *talmid ḥakham,* a Torah scholar—were alien to the educational philosophy of Beit Yaakov and its Hirschian underpinnings, which distinguished between the intellectual and emotional needs and capabilities of men and women. The educational achievements of Beit Yaakov students would be lavishly praised by the movement's teachers and educators, especially in comparison with their mothers' generation, but only relative to the aforementioned goals of female education. Female intellectual achievement was not otherwise valued, and the development of female intellect virtually ignored.[107] Indeed, the founders of Beit Yaakov could be said to have prized female students' emotional attachment to *yiddishkeit* over intellectual achievment; we shall see presently that they opposed the higher education of Orthodox women, and they attempted to convince Orthodox parents not to send their daughters to university preparatory schools like gymnasia.

The Beit Yaakov Teachers' Seminary in Kraków

Money was raised in Poland and especially abroad for a permanent seminary building that would replace the two rooms in Schenirer's apartment used for teacher training. The cornerstone for the seminary building was laid down in September 1927 in a festive ceremony in the presence of rabbinical authorities as well as Jewish and non-Jewish dignitaries. The ceremony included addresses given by several board members of the seminary and songs performed by the

---

107. Cf. Judith Rosenbaum's description of the public final oral exams in the seminary, Deutschländer, ed., *Bajs Jakob: Sein Wesen und Werden,* 20–22. Rosenbaum expressed her amazement at how girls who had come to the seminary only a year and a half earlier ignorant in Jewish matters had been enriched in their thinking and feelings through an "intensive Jewish education of the intellect" (*intensiv jüdische Ausbildung des Intellekt*). It seems that for Rosenbaum, the goal of a Beit Yaakov education was not expanding or developing the horizons of the female intellect but educating it *Jewishly* in order to root it firmly on Jewish soil. One searches in vain in Schenirer's writings for comments on women's intellectual capacities or appreciation of their intellectual achievement per se. Her emphasis on religious enthusiasm may be derived in part from her Hasidic background and in part from her growing up in the deeply religious atmosphere of Kraków.

choir of the old Kraków synagogue. The last speaker was R. Jacob Rosenheim, symbolizing the firm connection of Agudat Yisrael to the new institution.[108] While the speakers included only males, the cornerstone document of the building included the names of different dignitaries, rabbis, committee members, and of Sarah Schenirer, the only female with her name on this official record.

Around this time some opposition was raised against the Beit Yaakov schools. Indeed, in a work published in 1929, Deutschländer asserted that "even today, opponents from the right against the Beit Yaakov schools still invoke the old argument that the Talmud forbids teaching Jewish subjects (*Disziplinen*) to women under all circumstances." Deutschländer's response to these opponents was that "this objection was met by the ruling made by Israel Meir Ha-Kohen (Ḥafeẓ Ḥayim), probably the greatest Halakhic authority of our day, decades ago in his work *Likutei Halakhot*, Sota 21,[109] and that provided Keren Ha-Torah's Beit Yaakov work with the most valid sanction."[110] Similarly, in his talk in the second assembly of Agudat Yisrael in Vienna (1929)

108. Deutschländer, ed., *Bajs Jakob: Sein Wesen und Werden,* 35–38. During the same month, the head of the Ḥakhmei Lublin Yeshiva returned from America after he raised enough money to complete its construction. An article on the two festive occasions by the editor of *Diglenu,* the Hebrew journal of the young male association of Agudat Yisrael, emphasized the connection between the two projects, explaining that just as it used to be in the old days, the seminary education will help raise women for whom marrying a yeshiva student will not only be considered a disadvantage—"as it is now"—but rather women whose views and ways of conducting a home would fit that of a yeshiva-educated man, and who will help him in his duty, in raising their sons, and in his work for the benefit of the public. See A[lexander] Z[ysha] Frydman, "The Completion in Lublin and the Beginning in Kraków." For Frydman, who was active in Agudat Yisrael and later served as a the supervisor for Beit Yaakov schools, the goal of the seminary was to produce women who would be helpmates to their yeshiva-educated husbands because, unlike these women's own mothers, they would understand the importance of Torah learning. That this goal was already articulated by a prominent Agudat Yisrael activist at the time of the founding of the seminary is striking.

109. The publication date for *Likutei Halakhot* on *Sotah* is given in the literature as 1911 or as 1918, but both dates are incorrect. An article on the subject of the correct publication date, 1921/22, and its significance, is currently in preparation.

110. Deutschländer, ed., *Beth Jakob: 1928, 1929,* 7. Deutschländer mentions a 1913 conference in Czernowitz (Chernivtsi) in which Eastern European rabbis discussed the issue of female education. I haven't come across any report about such a conference. However, during the founding conference of the Agudat Yisrael in 1912 in Kattowitz, R. Abraham Schnur of Tarnów raised the issue of female education as a question that demands attention, Agudat Yisrael, *Agudas Jisroel, Berichte und Materialien,* 71–72.

FIGURE 6.1. Cornerstone document of the Beit Yaakov Teachers' Seminary in Kraków (1927). Courtesy of the National Archives in Kraków, sygn. 29/576/480.

בעזרת השם יתברך.

נעשתה זאת בפ"ק קראקא ששה עשר לחדש אלול שנת חמשת אלפים ושש מאות ושמנים
ושבע לבריאת עולם בשנה התשיעית לתחית ממלכת פולין.

בעת אשר נשיא המדינה הוא איגנאצי מאשצישקי ראש הממשלה המביא יוסף
פילסודסקי, סגנו קאזימערז בארטעל ומיניסטער לדי"הות והשכלה גוסטאוו דאב־
רוצקי. בעת אשר נשיא בית המחוקקים הוא מאציעי ראטאי ושו"ט הסינט וואיצעך
טראמפצינסקי.

וסגנין: יוסף סארע, וויטאלד דאראווסקי, ראש העי"ר מיכל ראלליע
לודוויג שניידער ופאטר וועלגוס. לעדת ישראל בפ"ק קראקא הוא הרב ר' יוסף נחמי קארניטצער שליט"א
ומתיראה הוא העוד ד"ר רפאל לאנדא. בעת אשר נשיא ועד הפועל של ההסתדרות העולמית אגודת ישראל הוא הרה"ג
ר' פנחס כהן א"ו ר' יעקב ראזענהיים ונשיא המועצה במדינת העולמית של אגד בהנהלות הוא הרב ד"ר אהרין
לעווין ס' אב"ד ריישא ציר הסיים.

בעת אשר נשיא ההסתדרות הארצית של אגדת ישראל הוא הרה"ב ר'
מאיר שפירא ס' אבד"ק פיעטרקוב וציר הסיים וסגנו: הרב"ד ר' יצחק מאיר
לעוון ס' וחרב ר' טוב' הארשאווסקי.

בעת אשר היו"ל של הפרקצ' האורטודוקסית בסיים הפולני הוא ציר לסיים ר'
אלי' קירשברוין ס'.

בעת אשר הנהלת הבבושה המקומית של ההסתדרות אגודת ישראל הוא ר' מאיר הכהן ראפאפארט ס' וסגנו: ר' אלטר דוד
קורצמאן ס'. בעת אשר היו"ל של החוע המרכזי למוסדות "בית יעקב"
הוא ר' אשר הכהן שפירא ס' וסגנו: הסינטור ר' משה דייטשער ור' משה
ליפער ס' והמנהלת דא מרת שרה שעניער תחי'

נוסד ונבנה בית לבנין בית סמינריון לחינוך מורות חדריות בעד בתי ספר ר' יעקב
אשר אליו נכנסו חברי אגדת ישראל באירופא ונעבד לים ואשר בראשם עמדו הרב
ר' אלי' יונ מנד"ז ווׂרק, ד"ר שמיל דייטשלענדער מונה, הסינטור ר' יצחק
בוימינגער ס', הד"ר לסיים ר' פייניש סטעמעל ס', ר' אשר הכהן שפירא ס' אשר
חיים פרײזלי"ג ס' מקראקא. והעצר היה לקח על עצמו התורה לאסוף נדבות לדי הוצאת
הבנין הנכבד הזה.

והודרת להתקיימות שנגיע מאתינו המתנדבים גם במדינתנו וחוצה לה ובתקותינו כי אחינו
אלה עוד יוסיפו להראות לנו חסדם ולתמוך אותנו נדיבה יבריח יכלו בעזר הצור
לגשת היום אל בין הבית הנהדר הזה אשר נמסר בידי המנהדרי המרי
אלעזר דוק בקראקא.

והיום בהתאסף על מקום הבנין הבני המנהלי ההסתדרות אגדת ישראל
מארצות שונות ממזרח וממערב, באי כח קרן התורה' בוינה ובוארשא
בצירוף חבוי ועד הבנין הנה מנחים בהמן הזגג ובתרועה שמחה
אבן הפנה תחת בנין הבית אשר ממנו יצאו קרני אור והאמונה
הטהורה היראת השם בשלוה על פני חוצות חבר מורות ישריות
נאמנת כידרונו היריוושה, אשר מלאנה תפקדין במדי"ה גדושה
בהתאם לדיי תורתנו הקדושה משאת יפשטו ורוח אפנו!

ה' הטוב יהי' עמנו ויפרוש סכת שלכיו עלינו ועל כל עמו בית
ישראל יברך את הבנין ואת הבונים ואת כל המתנדבים
ומעשה ידינו יכונן, וכאשר זכינו להתחיל היום את המלאכה
שנזכה להדרהיב דעת ד' בארץ ולראות את הבית כשתוה
ויהי נועם ד' אלקינו עלינו אמן כן יהי רצון.

he said: "True, even today there are still those Orthodox Jews who oppose the establishment of schools for girls, claiming that anyone who teaches his daughter Torah it is as if he is teaching her *tiflut*. We in our work on behalf of Beit Yaakov walked in the light of the ruling of the righteous *ga'on* the Ḥafeẓ Ḥayim, which is mentioned in his book *Likutei Halakhot* on *Sotah*."[111] Deutschländer may have been referring to an article published in 1928 by R. Seckel Bamberger (1863–1934), the rabbi of Bad Kissingen in Germany, whose grandfather, R. Seligmann Baer Bamberger, had been an opponent of Samson Raphael Hirsch.[112] Seckel Bamberger claimed that because the commentary of Rashi and popular legal digests like the *Ḥayyei Adam* and the *Kiẓur Shulḥan Arukh* contained material from the Oral Law, women should not be taught anything from them that was not pertinent to practical observance of commandments—and he cited the same passage by the Ḥafeẓ Ḥayim to which Deutschländer referred in order to support his view![113] The Ḥafeẓ Ḥayim had written that

> For those girls who have accustomed themselves to study the writing and the language of the nations it is certainly a great mitzvah to teach them the Pentateuch, Prophets, Writings, and rabbinic ethical works such as *Pirkei Avot, Menorat ha-Ma'or* and the like, so that our holy faith be verified for them, for otherwise they are liable to stray entirely from the way of the Lord and will transgress all the foundations of religion, God forbid!"[114]

Bamberger understood him to recommend *only* the text of the Pentateuch without Rashi's commentary, whereas Deutschländer understood him to mean, "Jewish subjects." Bamberger's appeal to contemporary rabbinical authorities to weigh in on the issue met with a tepid response,[115] another indication that rabbis had no inclination to follow his lead in the matter.

111. Scheinfeld, ed., *Ha-Knesiyah ha-gedolah*, 44–45.

112. Deutschländer was probably not referring here to the opposition of the Galician Hasidic dynasties of Belz and Sandz, which was directed against Agudat Yisrael and *all* of its educational institutions rather than only to Beit Yaakov.

113. See Bamberger, "Torah Study for Women." Bamberger was an outlier on this issue, and I am not aware of other Neo-Orthodox rabbis adopting his position. Cf. Fuchs, *Jewish Women's Torah Study*, 49–50.

114. *Likutei Halakhot* on Tractate *Sotah*, 21–22 (according to the pagination of Tractate *Sotah*).

115. Two rabbis answered him in *Oẓar ha-ḥayim*, 5 (1929): 14–18 [Hebrew].

The seminary moved to its new home on June 10, 1931, with the inauguration ceremony taking place on January 23, 1932. The internal administration of the seminary, including curriculum, teachers, and learning plan, was directed by Deutschländer, but he was careful not to impose his western religious values on the Galician religious atmosphere of the place. This attitude neutralized the fears of the locals concerning the penetration of western ideas into the institution. Deutschländer introduced professionalism in the teachers' training program and order into the administration, while Schenirer inspired piety and religious enthusiasm among the students.[116] Despite the fact that the religious subjects were taught according to the Hirschian model of religious female education, the Kraków seminary was *not* conducted according to *Torah 'im derekh erez* principles.[117] German Neo-Orthodox like Deutschländer and the female foreign teachers had studied at German universities and embraced many aspects of western culture. But at the seminary, where western culture was viewed as inferior at best and dangerous at worst, its positive aspects, if any, were ignored.

This respect for the traditional values of Galician Jewry is best demonstrated in a story attributed to Judith Rosenbaum. One of her students wrote the following about her:

> Years later, when she [Rosenbaum] recalled her experience during her first days in Robov she spoke with excitement about the girls who attended the course [...]
>
> "It was hard work," she continued, "but it was a pleasure to teach these intelligent, open minded girls. They loved literature and admired the world classics."
>
> She withdrew from a chest a miniature leather-bound copy of Goethe's *Faust*. "This is a gift from my favorite and most beloved student," she explained, eyes moist with nostalgia. "This girl was a recalcitrant student and lover of *Faust* and other secular literature. Eventually, however, she became

---

116. Keren Hathora-Zentrale, *Programm und Leistung*, 244–249.

117. There were several other Beit Yaakov teachers' seminaries in the 1930s, all much smaller and less prestigious than the one in Kraków. Each of them had its own philosophy. The seminary in Vienna adopted the German *Torah 'im derekh erez* principles, the program in Bratislava adapted itself to the Hungarian-Orthodox characteristics, and the seminary in Czernowitz, Bukovina, had no consistent philosophy because of the lack of a uniform religious worldview in the Jewish population in the area, ibid., 245–246.

both a lover of Torah and a pillar of Beit Yaakov movement and seminary."

At that time, the girls were still inspired by Western literature and were influenced by its loud proclamation of humanitarian ideas. This sophisticated young woman [Rosenbaum], raised in Western culture, applied her personality and persuasive powers to dispel the girls' admiration of "great" Western civilization. "Girls," she would say, "the world's great writings are full of nonsense. If you find a meaningful thought and a decent moral concept in world literature, you should know that it was stolen from the rich treasure-house of Jewish knowledge."[118]

Rosenbaum, who attended a non-Jewish teachers' seminary at her home in Frankfurt, later continued her studies at the Frankfurt University and received a doctorate in the natural sciences in 1929. Such an option was unavailable for Beit Yaakov seminary alumnae in Kraków because they lacked the prerequisite study and certificate to enroll at a university.

Beit Yaakov also attempted to "de-Polonize" the students by emphasizing the importance of mastering Yiddish. Schenirer called at a Beit Yaakov conference for the embrace of the Yiddish language and suggested that the delegates speak for three months with their friends only in Yiddish. Schenirer discussed the value of Yiddish, describing it as a holy language, and called upon Beit Yaakov girls to speak Yiddish at all times, whether at home, in the street, or at the school.[119] This was supposed to counteract the attraction to Polish language and culture which was promoted in Polish schools. Such distancing from the language of the country was contrary to the spirit of the Hirschian *Torah 'im derekh erez* ideology of the German Neo-Orthodox.

The Beit Yaakov Kraków Model

Why was the Warsaw female gymnasium model abandoned after the establishment of Beit Yaakov seminary in Kraków? After all, Ḥavaẓelet was established with the approval of the leader of the Ger Hasidic dynasty and was well

118. Benisch, *Carry Me in Your Heart*, 61–62.

119. Schenirer, *Gezamelte shriftn*, 45–49. Cf. Lisek, "Orthodox Yiddishism." Interestingly, unlike the Beit Yaakov journal which was published in Yiddish (in the first few years with a Polish supplement), *Diglenu*, the journal of the young male association of Agudat Yisrael, was published in Hebrew with an emphasis on high-level literary articles and poetry. On Yiddish newspapers for Jewish children in Poland, see Bar-El, *Bein ha-'ezim ha-yerakrakin*, 25–46.

received by the local Orthodox elite, including rabbis. One example of such an approval is an address delivered by Menachem Mendel Landau, the rabbi of Zawiercie (1862–1935),[120] and published in Warsaw's official daily of Agudat Yisrael in early 1918. Landau was the rabbi who had spoken at the 1903 rabbinical assembly in Kraków in favor of teaching girls Torah, but his motion was never brought up for a vote. In his published address Landau criticized the practice of Orthodox Jewish female education and contended that the only hope for improvement was in teaching girls in a new type of school that would be compatible with the Jewish religious spirit. He called for the establishment in every city of a school modeled after the recently opened Ḥavaẓelet school in Warsaw, and thanked Carlebach, the founder of the Warsaw school, for his initiative.[121]

The major advantage of the gymnasium was the option of matriculation exams that enabled interested graduates to continue their studies at the university. Although few Ḥavaẓelet students chose this option, the classes in secular subjects were on a high level and thus satisfied the needs of intellectually motivated girls. One of the students in the school in the early 1930s was the granddaughter of R. Abraham Mordechai Alter, the leader of the Ger Hasidic dynasty, and according to the memoirs of a graduate of the school: "She needed intellectual stimulation—she couldn't live without it. But although her father allowed her to attend, it was on condition that she would not take the *matura* examinations, because having the *matura* would have enabled her to go to the university."[122] Clearly, Anna Kluger was not the only young woman from a Hasidic family who thirsted for higher education. According to the Orthodox daily in Warsaw, many Hasidic daughters attended private Jewish secular gymnasia in Warsaw. In 1918, several of those girls caused a scandal when they took the written matriculation exam on the Sabbath. Only one girl, a daughter of a rabbi, protested and refused to take the exam.[123] Ḥavaẓelet was intended to provide a comparable high-level Orthodox school alternative.

120. Landau took the rabbinical position in Zawiercie in 1904, after serving as the rabbi of Nowy Dwór. On Landau see "Rabbi Mendel Chaim Landau," *Degel Israel*, March 28, 1928, 9, 14 [Hebrew].

121. "The Address of the Zawiercier Rabbi Mendel about the Education of Children (end)," *Dos Yidishe Vort*, Nr. 6 (date illegible) (1918), 6 [Yiddish].

122. Sternbuch and Kranzler, *Gutta: Memories of a Vanished World*, 21.

123. "Where Is Our Shame! . . . ," *Dos Yidishe Vort*, Nr. 115–117 (1918) [Yiddish].

In Kraków things were different. The trauma of the runaway phenomenon, especially the Kluger case, was still fresh in peoples' mind, and the wounds were still open. The Beit Yaakov seminary would serve as a bastion against the possibility of future Anna Klugers. It accepted girls who had completed seven grades of primary school and were at least sixteen years old.[124] The two years of seminary study (which also included several weeks of practical training) provided significantly less schooling than a gymnasium education. Even the adoption of secular subjects in the Beit Yaakov seminary curriculum was an Orthodox response to the problems in Kraków prior to the First World War. Those subjects were designed in such a way as to thwart any plans for higher education. Out of a total of thirty-six hours in the first year (thirty-nine hours in the second year), four weekly hours were dedicated to pedagogy and psychology (five in the second year), four weekly hours to Polish literature, history, and geography (six in the second year), two weekly hours to German (two also in the second year), and two weekly hours to handiwork (two also in the second year). The Polish program was dictated by the state requirements of teachers' seminaries, and the two weekly hours in German were divided between reading Hirsch's works and passages of German authors such as Goethe, Lessing, and Zweig, most of them from Deutschländer's textbook, *Westöstliche Dichterklänge.* As noted above, these passages were not selected for their literary value but because they contained positive views of the Bible, Jews, and Judaism by well-known authors, and so validated the student's Jewish identity.

Indeed, in trying to explain the role of the secular subjects in the Kraków seminary, Beila Gross, a teacher with an academic education (she signed her article with the title "Magister Phil.") who taught the state obligatory subjects, gave two reasons for their inclusion. The first was to enable the girls to go out into the world not in order to get recognition there, as some of the youth think, but rather "to win it [the world] for our view" and show the worth of Judaism. The outside world would not let people in unless they can speak its language and understand its ways. The second reason was to be able to communicate to the world "what is essential for our work [displaying] the benefit of Judaism." According to Gross, the need to study general subjects is the product of assimilation and neglect of girls' education. Jewish males who studied in

124. On the entrance requirements for the seminary, see Weissman, *"Bais Ya'akov,"* 62–63; cf. "The Upcoming New Course of Beit Yaakov in Kraków," *Bajs Yaakov ortodoksisher familien-zhurnal* 44 (1929), 19 [Yiddish].

yeshivas have no need for secular studies because assimilation didn't penetrate there and so there is nothing to save via the use of foreign means. "Perhaps in the future," Gross concludes, "also among us, among Jewish girls, the question would be solved."[125] This explanation by the general studies teacher, no less, was intended to devalue such education in the eyes of readers of the Beit Yaakov journal. With regard to extracurricular activities, such as those conducted at Bnot Agudat Yisrael, while they also included libraries that contained secular books, each book had to get the approval of a special local three-man commission of the party—a "*mener rat*" (male council).[126]

The Kraków seminary presented itself not only as the highest educational institution for Orthodox Jewish women, but also as providing their ultimate educational goal. From its outset the seminary marked additional higher education as forbidden. This was stated explicitly by R. Jacob Rosenheim in 1930 in a conference dedicated to the Beit Yaakov school system. Rosenheim asserted that Jewish women should be women of valor and should not be sent to universities because their spirit would be corrupted there, and they would not find suitable husbands.[127] Such an attitude toward higher education could be considered an innovation, since, as we saw in the first chapter, there is no explicit religious prohibition for girls to study secular subjects.

In 1932, after Judith Rosenbaum, who had been running the day-to-day curricular activities at the Kraków seminary, returned to Germany to marry, Yehudah Leib Orlean was appointed the sole director of the seminary, as well as the director of the Beit Yaakov headquarters ("Tsentrale"), which oversaw the network of schools. Orlean was introduced in the headquarters' first newsletter as "a man who was aquainted with the specific conditions and needs of Polish Jewry, from whom the seminary students originate and whom they later educate," one who could harmonize the "tested methods of our

125. Gross, "The Role of Secular Studies in the Beit Yaakov Seminary."

126. Tsentral Sekretaryat, *Di organizirung fun Bnos Agudas Yisroel*, 33–34. See also Frydman, *Beys Yaakov*, 19–20. Frydman presents an elaborate plan for establishing local organizations for Orthodox girls called "Beit Yaakov" aimed at making them true religious women and daughters. He suggests, among other things, establishing a library in each branch that would include also "general books," but that would not have a corrupting influence on the religious and moral spirit of the readers. The organization would be administered by ten women who would seek advice and answers to questions from a permanent commission composed of Orthodox men—a "*beratungs-mener*" (male advisory), ibid., 20.

127. "Convention of the Orthodox Beit Yaakov Girls' School," *Haynt*, February 18, 1930, 6 [Yiddish].

Western-European brothers with the core content of the Polish-Jewish center."[128] Unlike Deutschländer or Rosenbaum, he was a Hasid and not a product of a Neo-Orthodox education. Orlean emphasized the importance of sheltering the Beit Yaakov students from the pernicious effects of the Polish environment. Before he became the principal of the teachers' seminary he had introduced a new subject, *Yahadus* (yiddishkeit, Jewish worldview), in the Beit Yaakov primary schools, "since the influence of the secular teachings in the upper grades doesn't offer any extra good for our religious educational work." Classes in *Yahadus* were intended "to weaken the damaging influence of the secular teachings."[129]

While the primary school received proper attention in the new female Orthodox school system, no special consideration had been given to the question of post–primary school education other than the teachers' seminary, a solution obviously intended for a small number of young women. This was apparently not a coincidence. In an editorial discussion of the Beit Yaakov journal on the occasion of the Beit Yaakov conference in Warsaw in 1930, Leo Deutschländer admitted that the question of post–primary school education is an important one, especially for girls who attended a Beit Yaakov school which also offered secular studies. He believed that the best solution was to establish secondary trade schools in large urban areas that would also offer a continuing religious education. He revealed that the advisory board in Łódź was ready to act in this direction and expressed his hope that it would be the beginning. Deutschländer explained that he considered giving a gymnasium education to Beit Yaakov primary school graduates as wrong and pointless, and described such an education as essentially just a fad. Thousands of young academics in Europe, whether in Berlin, Vienna or London, couldn't find appropriate jobs, and it is clear that an academic education has no use for making a living. "We need to instill the idea," he said, "that we shouldn't pursue a higher education just for its own sake." The major factor in educating the youth is the question of purpose (*tachles*).[130] Clearly, Deutschländer believed that a gymnasium education led to academic studies. Being an academic himself,

---

128. See *Ginzach Kiddush Hashem*, Beys Yaakov Tsentrale, *Byuletin* 1 (1933): 2. This was a monthly Yiddish newsletter sent to teachers as well as to the press. It contained news about the Beit Yaakov schools, statistics, and congratulations to teachers who got engaged or married.

129. Orlean, *Program funem Yahadus limud*, 3.

130. "What Did the Conference in Warsaw Contribute?" *Bajs Yaakov ortodoksisher familien-zhurnal* 52 (1930): 5 [Yiddish].

he didn't offer ideological reasons for rejecting a gymnasium education but rather practical ones. Still, his comments indicate that aspirations for higher learning did exist among the school's target population.

Ultimately, a safe alternative to the classical gymnasium did materialize with the establishment of a trade gymnasium in Warsaw. The school trained its students in bookkeeping and other trade-related skills in addition to providing classes in religion. The school received an official recognition by the state as a trade gymnasium in 1936 (with no preparation for matriculation exams).[131] In 1937, Beit Yaakov established in Łódź (through its young women's association) a secondary school that offered vocational courses for graduates of primary schools in addition to religion classes.[132]

In contrast to Deutschländer, Orlean's opposition to gymnasium education was ideological in nature. In his 1933 article, "The Gymnasium-Idol," Orlean harshly rebukes Orthodox parents who contemplate sending their fourteen-year-old daughters to a gymnasium. According to Orlean, parents think that gymnasium study "leads to the hall of science, creates a cultured person, prepares for a humanistic profession, guarantees a respected status in European society, and opens the way for a top carrier." Orlean was not talking about parents who were lax in their commitments to the Orthodox way of life, as he further explained:

> It is remarkable that even the most extremely devout and zealous Jews would not lose a single hair by doubting the benefit of a gymnasium education or a matriculation certificate for their daughters. If one of the devout parents should trouble themselves about the gymnasium, it is only because of the anti-Jewish tendencies that prevail there. But they are not against gymnasium study [itself]. If only it would be possible to attach mezuzahs on the gymnasium's doors, provide the female students with prayer-books, and inject in the curriculum a few drops of [Jewish] history, then they would consider everything to be perfectly kosher. The educational ideal would be achieved: a religious gymnasium for the most meticulous Jews! For God and for humanity! Torah and Bildung! [...]
>
> As long as the gymnasium mania grips Hasidic homes, it is not important whether all graduates of primary schools attend the gymnasium or only a small number of them. It is sufficient that the reverence for the

131. Kazdan, *Di geschichte fun yidishe shulvesen*, 491–492.
132. Ibid., 492–494. Seidman, *Sarah Schenirer*, 132–133.

gymnasium is held by all [...] The desire for a matriculation path among those who were unable to receive a gymnasium education is stronger than that by the fortunate ones. They create in our home the atmosphere for a gymnasium education. *All the mothers who remained mired in the path of their youthful ideal are the first to arouse in their children the appetite for it.*[133]

Orlean placed the blame for the desire to send daughters to the gymnasium on the mothers, those of the "lost generation" who were unable, or not allowed, to study in a gymnasium. In an effort to stop this trend he appealed to his readers, "Run away from the Gymnasia!"

Orlean relates that from hundreds of conversations that he had conducted with devout Jews he learned that it was not because of economic reasons that parents wished to send their daughters to a gymnasium, but rather because of their belief that one needs to be educated in secular subjects, "for without that, one is not a mentsh! That's what lies behind it. Therein lies the whole tragedy." For Orlean, on the other hand, the gymnasium is "the modern idol, whom one worships with boundless fanaticism," and so he concludes his article calling for a rescue mission whose slogan should be: "Now therefore put away the strange gods that are among you (Joshua 24:23)." His call is intended for the Orthodox: "Our Agudat Yisrael circles must internalize with complete perspicacity the lack of purpose, harm, and inferiority of a gymnasium education. They must prepare an appeal to Jewish homes for a true Jewish education, for a true Jewish Bildung!"[134]

Orlean would not have had to publish such a rebuke had he not viewed the attraction of higher education as a real threat. But other than a rebuke and an effort to paint the gymnasium education in negative colors, he offered no alternative. Moreover, he refrained from even mentioning the existence of Ḥavaẓelet religious gymnasium. He was against gymnasium education in principle because its curriculum would inevitably include a broad program of general studies in an unfiltered manner to satisfy state requirements and would open the way for higher education, with all its threat to Orthodox Jewry.

Orlean envisioned the Beit Yaakov seminary as producing a new kind of teacher, one who would instill within her students the love of *yiddishkeit* that Orthodox Jewish girls had traditionally received, he claimed, at home. He

---

133. Orlean, "The Gymnasium-Idol," 5–6. Emphasis added. Kazdan, *Di geschichte fun yidishe shulvesen,* 490–491.

134. Ibid., 6.

rejected the notion that the religious education of girls had been neglected prior to World War I or that the religious leaders of past generations should be held responsible for failing to establish schools for Jewish girls.[135] On the contrary, the education they received at home was *superior* to learning in school. Although a girl did not study Torah or engage herself in Talmudic questions, she observed her father and brothers arguing vigorously about a difficult Talmudic passage, and that left a profound impression on her:

> One needs to consider that a girl's sense is more developed to receive the impressions of that scene; it absorbs them more quickly and digests them more thoroughly. Her intellect doesn't grasp that much energy, nor does it absorb all her attention. How many such moments did a girl experience in her home? [...] And why was it necessary to replace a devoted father and a good and merciful mother with a professional teacher?[136]

The answer was that times had changed. Jewish parents were not what they were previously; the "patriarchical splendor" had disappeared; the home was desiccated and gray; observance of the commandments was mechanical; the customs were foreign. What a Jewish school lacks is "not a lesson plan, nor grades, *for knowledge is not the main thing.*" On the contrary, since the Jewish home is not what it used to be, nor the school what it should be, the mission of the Kraków seminary is to replace today's Jewish father and mother with a teacher-father-mother.[137] Orlean's underlying assumption is that Jewish women's educational needs must be geared to their "sense" and not to their intellect.

Even intellectually minded students fell under the spell of Orlean's charisma. Gutta Sternbuch (née Eisenzweig) was the daughter of a Warsaw Hasidic family, who reluctantly allowed her to attend the Ḥavaẓelet gymnasium provided that upon graduation she enroll in the Beit Yaakov seminary. The transition from Ḥavaẓelet to the Kraków seminary was not easy:

> When I arrived at Bais Yaakov the term had already begun, and at first my negative expectations seemed almost entirely warranted. Everything seemed to rub me the wrong way. Some of the girls spoke only Yiddish,

135. Orlean, "Beit Yaakov: Bnot Agudat Yisrael," 65. Orlean first published a version of this article in Yiddish in 1933, see *Ginzach Kiddush Hashem*, Beys Yaakov Tsentrale, *Byuletin* 5 (1933): 1–2; *Byuletin* 6 (1933): 1–3.

136. Orlean, "Beit Yaakov: Bnot Agudat Yisrael," 66–67.

137. Ibid., 67. Emphasis added. Cf. Atkin, *The Beth Jacob Movement in Poland*, 84–85.

which I associated with narrow-mindedness and outdated ideas [...] And friends from Chavatzelet wrote me letters asking, "When are you going to leave that medieval cloister?"

Although the seminary had a secular studies program which included history, math, Polish and German (the last so that students could study the works of R. Samson Raphael Hirsch in the original), my mastery of these subjects was so far advanced that I was excused from most of these classes [...] I longed to return to my enlightened hometown, to the meetings I had secretly attended, to the youth burning with dreams of a new world.[138]

But after a difficult time at the beginning, Sternbuch's attitude toward the seminary changed, a change she describes as a "rebirth." It was the class lecture delivered by the charismatic figure of R. Orlean that was responsible for that:

After the lecture, I remained frozen in my place. Rabbi Orlean's words had affected me profoundly and I felt that I had been touched by the light of truth. That was the beginning of my rebirth [...] Although Sarah Schenirer was also a pioneer, the extraordinary and dedicated visionary who founded the basis of Jewish girls' education, Rabbi Orlean was a much more profound thinker. Those Bais Yaakov students who would have reacted against a Sarah Schenirer type due to the modern influences of pre-War Poland respected Rabbi Orlean and his message.[139]

Her description of his classes emphasized the emotional and religious feelings he inspired in the students:

Bais Yaakov brought about a revolution in our minds and hearts, greater than any social or political upheaval. It was a revolution of our entire being. It wasn't only a question of *frumkeit* [strict religious observance] or *davening* [praying]. Bais Yaakov changed our personalities. We thought differently, we saw reality from an entirely new perspective.[140]

That a religious school could assume a familial role was not unususal in a religious city such as Kraków, nor was it perhaps coincidental that Sternbuch's friends in Warsaw called the Kraków seminary a "medieval cloister." Schenirer was referred to by her students as "mother," while she referred to her students,

138. Sternbuch and Kranzler, *Gutta: Memories of a Vanished World*, 36–37.
139. Ibid., 42, 44.
140. Ibid., 45.

and in general to Beit Yaakov students and members of the different associations for young Orthodox females, as "sisters" (*shvester*). Similarly, seminary
students referred to each other as sisters.[141] Such a vocabulary fit the model
of female religious education familiar to all in Kraków, albeit in Catholic convents rather than in a Jewish setting. It also was in keeping with the view of
Beit Yaakov as a surrogate Jewish family.

The Kraków context may help explain why Schenirer composed a Yiddish
catechism in order to teach the girls in her first school about Judaism.[142] Catechisms were originally used to teach young Catholic children the Christian
religion, but this form was adopted early on by Jewish authors.[143] Most of
these were written in German, but in the second half of the nineteenth century
they were also composed in the Polish language and even in Yiddish.[144] Presumably, Schenirer used a Polish catechism in her Jewish religion classes when
she attended public school. She also may have seen at home the immensely
popular *Sha'arei Yizhak* by Yizhak Zaler (first published in 1875 and in many
subsequent editions), an Orthodox primer for heder boys written in Yiddish
as a dialogue between a rabbi and student, a popular catechismal form. As we
shall see, *Sha'arei Yizhak* was used in the Beit Yaakov teachers' seminary.[145]

The gymnasium and the university were vastly different types of institutions from the Beit Yaakov teachers' seminary. From the early twentieth
century, they presented a path for young women where they could satisfy their
intellectual aspirations and prepare themselves for better career options. Beit
Yaakov deliberately blocked that path for Orthodox women by providing not
only an alternative educational path, but an alternative model of female

141. Already in 1931, a Hebrew newspaper noted the reference to Schenirer as "mother," see
"Behind the Partition," *Ha-Zefirah*, April 29, 1931, 3 [Hebrew]. Schenirer was called "faithful
spiritual mother" and "caring mother" in a 1937 publication, see Keren Hathora-Zentrale, *Programm und Leistung*, 240, 242. See also Benisch, *Carry Me in Your Heart*, 39–41. Several Hebrew
volumes that included many of Schenirer's writings were titled *Em be-yisra'el* (Mother in Israel).
"Sisters" was used by Schenirer numerous times; see Schenirer, *Gezamelte shriftn*.

142. Benisch, *Carry Me in Your Heart*, 34–35.

143. See Kaufman Kohler and E. Schreiber, "Catechisms," *The Jewish Encyclopedia*, http://
www.jewishencyclopedia.com/articles/4149-catechisms.

144. Maślak-Maciejewska, *Modlili się w Templu*, 351–352. See for example the late Jewish
catechism composed by Taubeles, *Podręcznik do nauki religii żydowskiej*. This work was published in five editions between 1900 and 1917.

145. The book received approbations by several rabbis including Abraham Mordechai Alter,
the leader of the Ger Hasidic dynasty, and was later adapted into Hebrew and English.

fulfillment, one that steered women away from advanced intellectual achievement, even in the study of traditional texts.

To be fair, the Kraków teachers' seminary could not have aspired to excellence in the study of Jewish texts even if it had set that as a goal. The minimal entrance requirements, the need for the two-year curriculum to devote significant time to subjects such as pedagogy, Jewish history, Jewish worldview (*Yahadus*), Polish language and literature, etc., the requirement for students to begin supervised teaching after a year and a half as part of their training, were enough to ensure that their achievements in Jewish studies would be modest. In the second year, for example, the students spent the same amount of class time—six weekly hours—on Polish literature, history, and geography, as on the study of the Pentateuch, whose commentaries were limited to that of Rashi and Hirsch. Four weekly hours were devoted to the study of Prophets and other biblical books.[146] That the published curriculum did not always represent what was actually taught is clear from Rosenbaum's handwritten protocols of the teachers' meetings between 1931 and 1932.[147] Because of the lack of qualified teachers and absences of teachers who were sent for fundraising and recruiting missions, teaching was often improvised. Rosenbaum suggested to send some of the local younger teachers who taught Jewish subjects to Vienna, where they could take courses in pedagogy and psychology and continue their Jewish education.[148] According to one of the protocols Rosenbaum explained: "We have already said that we have to reduce the number of literature lessons in the upper grades. I would like to consult with Miss Gross about this. I am very sorry, but I see no other way out. Finally, we must not forget that our girls become teachers of religion. I really don't know where to reduce."[149] To make up for the reduction of literature, Rosenbaum suggested that Gross organize a "home evening" dedicated to reading literature with the girls, but the latter rejected this suggestion.[150]

146. For the curriculum of the seminary see Deutschländer, ed., *Bajs Jakob: Sein Wesen und Werden*, 39–43. For a more detailed curriculum see *Der Israelit: Ein Centralorgan für das orthodoxe Judentum, Blätter*, November 15, 1928, 3–4.

147. *Ginzach Kiddush Hashem*, "Judith Rosenbaum's Protocols of Teachers' Meetings in the Seminary, 1931–1932."

148. Ibid., 6.

149. Ibid., 61.

150. A letter written by Dora Zupnick in January 10, 1939, to her friend Fritta Diller in Frankfurt, details the curriculum in the seminary at that time. There were six morning classes with two short breaks and one longer break. The subjects included the Pentateuch, prayer, halakhah

The instruction of sacred texts at the seminary were almost entirely based on Yiddish translations and commentaries intended for laymen. The list of books that the seminary students were required to bring with them included the *Beit Yehudah ḥumash* (Pentateuch),[151] which contained a Yiddish translation and explanation of Rashi, as well as Yiddish adaptations of midrashim and other commentaries; the *Kitvei kodesh 'esrim ve-arba'* (Prophets and Writings), which contained a Yiddish commentary; the practical halahkic guide, *Kiẓur Shulḥan Arukh* in Yiddish; *'Amudei ha-golah,* a German textbook for teaching religion composed by Ludwig Stern, the Orthodox director of the Jewish school in Würzburg;[152] and *Sha'arei Yizḥak,* the above-mentioned Yiddish textbook composed for ḥeder boys. The Yiddish curriculum explains why Yiddish reading and writing were among the required skills for girls wishing to study in the Kraków teachers' seminary.[153]

By contrast, the seminary students' Hebrew skills after completing the two-year program were limited; for their final examination they had to answer questions on twenty-five Hebrew verses from Deuteronomy, for which they prepared in advance.[154] According to a newspaper report from 1928, the girls showed a lack of knowledge of the Hebrew language during the exam, and it is unlikely that they could read unvocalized Hebrew.[155] Although in internal

---

("dinim"), Prophets, *Pirkei Avot*, Hebrew, Jewish history, and hygiene. In the second year, students were also taught Psalms, Jewish *hashkafah* ("worldview"), and pedagogy. The curriculum also included Polish literature and geography, from which she was exempt. In the afternoon girls took a walk and later spent one or two hours preparing for the next day's translations of Hebrew words provided to them by second-year students. The rest of the time was spent on homework, laundry, mending socks, etc. They later recited the evening and night prayers. See *Ginzach Kiddush Hashem*, "Letter of Dora Zupnick." Dora, who studied with Fritta in Frankfurt, was expelled from Germany with her family before World War II and was accepted by the seminary in Kraków. Dora was killed in the Holocaust.

151. Interestingly, Ita Kalish, who broke away from her Hasidic home in 1923, writes in her memoirs that her father bought this Pentateuch for his daughters. See Kalish, *A rebishe heym*, 77.

152. This was later adapted for Beit Yaakov students in Poland and translated into Yiddish under a new title as advised by the rabbis, see Ludwig Stern *Amudei ha-yahadus*.

153. "The Upcoming New Course of Beit Yaakov in Kraków," *Bajs Yaakov ortodoksisher familien-zhurnal* 44 (1929): 19 [Yiddish].

154. Deutschländer, ed., *Bajs Jakob: Sein Wesen und Werden*, 44.

155. "From the Last Meeting of the Beit Yaakov Administration," *Der Israelit: Ein Centralorgan für das orthodoxe Judentum, Blätter*, October 18, 1928, 2. In the section about new books, *Diglenu* commended the benefit of the Beit Yaakov journal for the Beit Yaakov movement, as well as the Bnot Agudat Yisrael, but expressed its lack of understanding of the inclusion of an

Beit Yaakov literature the intellectual achievements of the seminary students were lavishly praised,[156] Gutta Sternbuch realized how little she knew compared to her fellow male students when she briefly attended the Warsaw Institute for Jewish Studies: "When I saw how much they knew, I felt humbled. I was like a child next to them."[157] Yet her lack of knowledge and Hebrew skills compared with her male classmates at the Institute did not sour her on her Beit Yaakov experience. On the contrary, while Sternbuch enjoyed her time at the Institute (which she decided to leave), she writes that its impact on her could not be compared to that of the Beit Yaakov seminary.[158]

Even in the official curriculum of the Kraków seminary drawn up by Deutschländer, the study, much less mastery, of sacred texts was not listed as a goal. Rather, the goal was to produce graduates who possessed "comprehensive familiarity in areas of Jewish knowledge, and the ability to continue to work independently in these,"[159] in other words, to produce competent and motivated teachers who could continue to read religious literature, albeit in Yiddish translation. As a result of their education, the young women possessed a greater familiarity with, and a much deeper commitment to, Torah-true Judaism, to use the Hirschian phrase, than did their mothers, the rebellious daughters of the "lost generation." Unlike them, the new generation of Beit Yaakov young women were educated to embrace with pride their roles as faithful Orthodox Jewish women.

To sum up: in its efforts to reduce the chasm between Orthodox husband and wife, between parents and daughter, the Beit Yaakov educational movement set as its goal not just religious observance but religious enthusiasm and fervor, using songs, dances, plays, and nature trips as vehicles by which this enthusiasm was inculcated. The scope of the religious studies program introduced in the Kraków Beit Yaakov teachers' seminary, while itself an innovation, was limited and on a level far below what the traditional educational system offered to young Jewish males. The balance between the intellectual life and the religious life in the Kraków seminary, the flagship of the Beit

---

unvocalized poem written by Zysha Frydman in the Beit Yaakov journal: "Which of the Beit Yaakov readers would be able to understand such a poem, which is also unvocalized?" *Diglenu* 7:2 (1927), 17.

156. See the description of the final exam by Judith Rosenbaum in Deutschländer, ed., *Bajs Jakob: Sein Wesen und Werden*, 20–22.

157. Sternbuch and Kranzler, *Gutta: Memories of a Vanished World*, 56.

158. Ibid., 59.

159. Deutschländer, ed., *Bajs Jakob: Sein Wesen und Werden*, 39.

Yaakov school system, was clearly meant to tilt toward the latter, making religious piety and ideological commitment the mission and highest achievement for Orthodox Jewish women and extinguishing any desire they may have for higher education. The seminary, under the guidance of its male leadership, set out to produce a religiously learned, albeit non-scholarly, cadre of female teachers who were imbued with the Beit Yaakov Orthodox ideology. Judging by the movements' growth in interwar Poland, it appears to have succeeded. But of course, it was only one of several ideological options (e.g., Socialism, secular and religious Zionism, etc.) available to the daughters of the rebellious daughters.

Conclusion

FOR A CENTURY after the partition of Poland, the Jews of Habsburg Galicia generally had autonomy over how and whether to educate their children. Sporadic attempts to control or to influence that education from above were shortlived and were rebuffed by the rabbinic and communal leadership. Jewish law and tradition obligated fathers to educate their sons, or to arrange for their education, in the classical Jewish texts, but it exempted women from the commandment to learn Torah and hence their fathers from teaching them. A wellknown rabbinic statement actually prohibited teaching Torah to women, and so girls were taught their religious duties in the privacy of the home by their parents or by tutors and by observing their mothers' practices. Girls were generally taught the Hebrew alphabet, which enabled them to read prayers, and some were taught the meaning of the prayers, Yiddish adaptions of the Pentateuch, and ethical works. While Orthodox Jews in Eastern Europe often frowned upon or forbade teaching secular subjects to their sons, they had no such strictures with respect to their daughters. On the contrary, girls with knowledge of European languages, or who could help their fathers with their business accounts, were highly esteemed, even in the most Hasidic households.

So when, in 1873, the Galician version of the 1869 Austrian compulsory law mandated primary education for all children, Orthodox Jews saw no harm in complying with the law and sending their daughters to public and private Polish schools. The Orthodox leadership was more concerned with the effects of the law on their sons. Through political alliances with conservative Poles, who were happy to keep an influx of Jewish boys out of the public schools, they continued to send them to traditional ḥeders. Some of the rich Orthodox provided their sons with private lessons in school subjects, an option available to them by law; others were ready to pay fines and not send their sons to school. Before the promulgation of the compulsory education law, daughters had been taught European languages and the refinements of European culture at home by hired tutors, when that was financially feasible. What difference would it make if their education was at home or in a school?

As it turned out, the difference was considerable. Contracting out the education of Orthodox Jewish girls to institutions outside Jewish society brought about a fundamental transformation of past norms and a revolution of sorts. The girls were schooled according to a state-mandated curriculum and underwent an unavoidable process of socialization with Polish classmates and engagement with Polish culture. At a time of growing Polish nationalism, they were taught Polish language, history, and culture in institutions that valued these subjects. Although they studied Judaism in their religion classes in school, they were not taught to value the subjects learned by their brothers or the ḥeders in which they were taught. Still, Orthodox parents from all classes, even the most pious Hasidim, sent their daughters willingly to these schools and took pride in their accomplishments and knowledge. Hasidic families who could afford it, like the Aratens and the Klugers, enrolled their daughters in private prestigious girls' schools in Kraków, which brought them into contact with daughters of rich Polish Christian families. A village tavernkeeper like Abraham Lewkowicz sent his daughter to the advanced girls' school in a neighboring city after she completed the first few grades at the school in her village. Sarah Schenirer convinced her parents to allow her to complete the seventh grade, but family circumstances forced her to abandon her dream of a high school education. Such parents clearly valued the education and betterment of their daughters, but because they had not attended school themselves, they could not know of the effects of Polish acculturation.

Nor did this acculturation end with graduation. Cities, notably, Kraków, offered young women cultural activities inspired by the new feminist ideas. Public lectures on a range of topics designed for women and delivered by university professors, authors, and public figures attracted even pious Hasidic women like Sarah Schenirer. These young women also visited the theater, a popular pastime, which exposed them to the latest cultural currents, and many were avid readers of Polish literature. Unlike most of their brothers, who did not share those experiences (unless clandestinely), young Orthodox women mastered the Polish language, which opened the door to the world around them.

The result was that young Galician Jewish women from Orthodox homes lived a bifurcated existence, experiencing a chasm between their world and that of their parents and brothers. Friction within the family reached a crisis when a marriage arrangement was imposed by parents on daughters who aspired for a match with men who shared their values and cultural world. In such cases, a significant number of young women saw no other way but to rebel and run away from home. Such girls already found out that the catechumenate in the Felician Sisters' convent in Kraków provided Jewish runaways not only with room and board while preparing them for baptism, but in many cases arranged for them employment that would enable them to be independent after leaving the convent. The nuns instructed them in a religion with which they were already familiar, having attended Polish schools, and which held out the promise of a rewarding life in this world and salvation in the next. In some cases, girls converted out of conviction, not convenience, for after all, what bound such young women to Judaism besides the ties of filial obligation?

But not all Jewish women who sought the temporary refuge of a convent wished to abandon their religion. Anna Kluger stayed briefly in a convent so that she could pursue her desire for higher education free of parental interference. She wished to take advantage of the educational opportunities for Kraków women that had expanded considerably in the first decades of the twentieth century. Private female gymnasia were established in Galicia starting in 1896, offering their students preparation for the matriculation exams; universities opened their doors to women as regular students in 1897 (first to philosophy faculties and in 1900 also to faculties of medicine). If in the 1870s the only post-primary option for young females in Galicia was the teachers' seminary, in early 1900 institutions of higher learning offered intellectually motivated young women career pathways that they had never had before. As in the first stage of the transformation affecting young Jewish women following the compulsory education law, the second stage found the Orthodox Jewish society unprepared for this new challenge.

Since it may seem odd to some that university studies would be attracting Galician Hasidic women so early in the twentieth century, it is worthwhile to cite at length the testimony of an Orthodox journalist from early 1902:

> The rich commit a sin in the education of their daughters that we would not be able to forgive. In their arrogance and pride they don't seek to educate their daughters in the spirit of the Jewish tradition, but rather send them to local schools [. . .] and after they complete primary school they send them to middle schools, and after the middle schools, although they already have sufficient education, sufficient language and reading skills necessary for a housewife, in the big cities they send them to high schools, whereas in small

ones they provide them with teachers and tutors to instruct them in disciplines and languages in addition to what they were taught in school, creating a situation where all the rich Jewish daughters are learned and educated in every language and book, but not in a Jewish book. [...] In Kraków all (?) the daughters of the pious Hasidim attend the university and hear the sermons and the lectures of Tarnowski [a reference to Stanisław Tarnowski who was at that time the rector of the Jagiellonian University]. Along the way their faces rejoice at the young students in this high institution, they greet the academics, and their love of foreign disciplines and languages builds a nest in their hearts. When a marriage arrangement to religiously devout Jews, which they hate, is imposed on them, some women graduates of such schools confess, according to what I heard from honest and true people, that "they each belong to their spouse only in their body, but not in their spirit and soul."[1]

Even if we take into account that the author of this article exaggerates for effect, it is unlikely, given his readership, that he would have made up completely the fact that Hasidic young women attended the university. The education of Hasidic women from comfortable backgrounds is terra incognita for most historians of Hasidism, even those who focus on Hasidic education, partly because of a dearth of sources, but partly because of the tendency to view Hasidism from the perspective of Hasidic men. Yet even if one focuses on how Hasidic men interpreted the experience of the women in their lives, the results will be surprising.

A striking testimony of pride in the achievements of one Hasidic woman is provided in the memoir of Israel Dov Halberstam, a descendant of the family branch of the Sandz Hasidic dynasty, who moved to Bardejov (now Slovakia), where many followers of Sandz Hasidic dynasty lived. Halberstam writes that Jewish daughters in Slovakia, just like those in Galicia, were required by law to attend school (neglecting to mention that this requirement applied to Jewish sons as well) where they spent the greater part of the day learning arithmetic and languages. His mother (born in 1913) was known to all as a pious woman and as a very learned individual.

[I]n short, she was perfect in everything, an example of a Jewish daughter and a Jewish mother, and on top of everything she also had a good head

1. M. Ben Yeke, "But We Are Guilty on Account of Our Daughters," *Kol Maḥazikei Ha-Dat*, January 31, 1902, 2–4, esp. 4 [Hebrew].

and always received the best grades in the Bardejov school. She was out-standing in arithmetic and knew several languages such as Slovak, Hungar-ian, Rumanian, German, all the spoken languages in the countries where she lived. There was only one language she did not know, and that was the holy tongue [Hebrew]. She was also not allowed to learn the holy tongue.[2]

As Halberstam takes pride in his mother's knowledge of languages and arithmetic, so he takes pride in her ignorance of Hebrew and Jewish texts. He praises the way she recited the Kol Nidrei prayer on Yom Kippur with tears in her eyes and a broken heart, although she did not understand a word of it. Similarly, she would recite the same chapter of Psalms when praying for a good livelihood or recovery of one of her children from an illness, because she didn't understand the meaning of the words she was saying. For Halberstam, his mother's ignorance was a mark of her religious piety, which he found superior to prayers of women who understand the meaning of the words.[3] Halbers-tam opposed formal religious education for women, and his family opposed the establishment of a Beit Yaakov supplementary school in their town.[4] But can it be said of him that he opposed modernity in all its forms? Or that he advocated keeping Jewish women away entirely from secular culture?

Halberstam may not have been aware of the Galician runaway phenome-non or even the Araten case. The aforementioned article about Hasidic women attending the university was written while the Araten affair was fresh in the minds of Kraków Jews. Mass media, money, and politics turned it into a sen-sational saga that went beyond the confined boundaries of the Jewish com-munity. It gave rise for the first time to a debate in the Jewish press on the practice of female Jewish education. But the debate didn't cause any changes on the ground, and each side continued to hold steadfastly to its own posi-tions. If anything, the immediate effect of the Araten affair spread the word about the Felician Sisters' convent to places outside Kraków, reaching Jewish village girls like Debora Lewkowicz. Knowledge that there was a place of ref-uge that would welcome them with open arms facilitated their decision to run away from home. They lived in the convent with other Jewish young women in a safe and gender-segregated environment.

2. Halberstam, *Sefer mi-beit avotai*, 107–108.
3. Ibid., 109–110.
4. A Beit Yaakov school was opened in Bardejov (Bartfeld) only in 1934, see Keren Hathora-Zentrale, *Programm und Leistung*, 255. See also Benisch, *Carry Me in Your Heart*, 116.

Orthodox Jewish society in Western Galicia knew about the conversions of young women, and some presumably knew that the conversions were voluntary, though this is something they could not admit. The voluntary conversion of a young woman was a family disgrace that could destroy marital opportunities for the siblings. But Orthodox Jews clung firmly to accepted norms, and the norm of Galician Jews since the 1870s was to send the daughters to Polish schools and not to provide them with anything more than a rudimentary Jewish education at home. The fact that religiously progressive Jews started educating their daughters in the Jewish religion in a formal setting was another reason why Orthodox Jews would not wish to adopt similar practices. Even if the majority of Orthodox young women didn't take the drastic step of fleeing home, their alienation from Jewish religious life as a result of their new educational opportunities became known as the "Daughters' Question."

It is difficult to draw broad conclusions about dynamics between daughter and parents from the cases we have studied. According to the archival documents in both Michalina's and Debora's cases, the dominant parental figures in their lives, before and after runing away, were the fathers. The mothers, barely capable of signing their names on the court testimony protocols, are generally absent from the police and court files. Lacking a school education, or business contacts, they could not serve as role models for their daughters. But mothers did play dominant roles in other cases, as the story of Anna Kluger demonstrates. Anna's mother, Simcha Halberstam, was a direct descendant of R. Hayim Halberstam, the founder of the Hasidic Sandz dynasty, and with that lineage she was the parent who made the decisions that impacted Anna's life. Her strong will seems to have been inherited by Anna and her sister, who sought not only to escape the mother's control but to make her parents pay for their university education.

University studies had the potential of turning into an even greater threat to the Orthodox society, robbing it of the best and the brightest and affecting the most distinguished rabbinic families and Hasidic dynasties. Just like the disgrace associated with the conversion of a daughter, the well-publicized court case of Anna Kluger against her parents inflicted pain and shame on her family. After completing her doctorate at the University of Vienna, Anna returned to her hometown, got married at the Kraków Temple to a prominent Jewish socialist, and led a life alien to her family and Hasidic lineage. In genealogies of the Sandz Hasidic dynasty she is nowhere to be found.

Like Michalina Araten, Debora Lewkowicz, and Anna Kluger, Sara Schenirer belonged to the "lost generation" of Galician Jewish women who, unlike their mothers, attended Polish schools. But Schenirer's response to her personal crisis was different. Mostly self-taught in Jewish religious subjects, and empowered by a sense of religious mission, Schenirer chose to suppress a curiosity for secular culture that had led her to attend lectures and visit the theater, and to create a vision of a Jewish religious life for women free from constant conflicts and contradictions, a choice that later developed into an ideology. With the help of the Agudat Yisrael organization, rabbinic support, and a Neo-Orthodox administrator and teachers from Germany, Schenirer's modest religious supplementary school in Kraków developed into the Beit Yaakov educational movement and network.

Lacking adequate financial means, most of the network's institutions were supplementary religious schools whose students attended public Polish school and thus were exposed to Polish language, literature, and culture. For such girls the youth organizations Batyah and Bnot Agudat Yisrael provided extracurricular activities whose goal was to instill in them Jewish pride and a sense of belonging to a female Orthodox Jewish world, something that was not available to their mothers.

The Beit Yaakov teachers' seminary in Kraków, the flagship of the school network, was designed to produce a female Orthodox cadre of teachers to staff the growing network of supplementary schools. But, unlike the Neo-Orthodox female teachers who were brought to the seminary from German-speaking countries, all of them graduates of gymnasia or universities, the alumnae of the Beit Yaakov Kraków seminary were not able to enroll at universities, since they lacked the requisite qualifications. The seminary was a two-year post–primary school that trained its students to become primary school teachers. Beit Yaakov not only did not establish classical gymnasia, but by not offering an option for matriculation exams it blocked the path to higher institutions of learning. This decision aimed at insuring that Orthodox young women would not turn into women like Anna Kluger and wander beyond the boundaries of the Polish Orthodox Jewish society.

By not providing advanced general studies, something not explicitly forbidden for women by Jewish law, graduates of the Kraków Beit Yaakov seminary were unable to enter high-status professions or from becoming university-trained gymnasium teachers, like Anna Kluger, options that were available to non- or moderately Orthodox women. The institution of the teachers' seminary, the highest available educational option for young women in the Habsburg Empire in the last quarter of the nineteenth century, was embraced as the highest and most prestigious learning institution for

Orthodox young women in the interwar period in Poland. Kraków, for decades the eye of the storm of the scandal of female runaways, became the center for producing an elite class of pious and religiously committed women, enthusiastic believers in the Beit Yaakov ideology, but limited in their intellectual aspirations.

Unlike the male Orthodox elite, the new Orthodox female elite were not prepared to pursue advanced Torah studies. True, the religious knowledge of Beit Yaakov graduates was vastly superior to that of their unschooled mothers; however, the knowledge and especially the textual skills that they received were lacking in breadth and depth. In the end, the Beit Yaakov movement, while a revolution in Orthodox Jewish education, was a counter-revolution in women's education, a reaction designed to limit women's exposure to outside society and culture, especially in the sphere of higher education, and to promote piety and pride in being an Orthodox Jewish woman.

In Their Own Words

Michalina Araten

1. Letter to Dr. Philipp Müller

Kraków, December 10, 1899[1]

Highly honored Sir,

I ask your forgiveness for not having sent any news of myself for such a long time, but it was almost impossible for me, as I was constantly exposed to the lurking eyes of my mother. And you must be able to imagine for yourself whether I could feel happy in such a situation. Last week when I went with my aunt to a [female] teacher who was to teach music to me, my mother noticed that you were at the window, and merely because of that she did not let me go out to the street for the entire week. In this way the days and the weeks are passing, and I do not see any help for my sufferings, which increase daily. So many times I have thought to myself: "If only you wished to jump down through the window, then you would soon be released from your sufferings," and I was already about to carry out this thought, but the Almighty, who does not leave His children when they are in danger, watched over me too. I have already spoken enough of my suffering, although these are not a one-thousandth part of all that I suffer. Yet I must come to the main purpose of my writing, which is [as follows]: A few hours

---

1. Araten Warsaw file, 2457–2458.

ago my father came into my room and spoke in a solemn voice:
"Michaline, you know that on the twentieth of the month you
will have completed your fifteenth year; you also know that all
your cousins of your age are already engaged to be married,
although they are not the oldest ones, and after all, you are my
oldest child, so you shall know that I have already chosen a
bridegroom for you, and in two weeks the engagement will take
place." When I heard these words I began to weep deeply, and to
beg that he might give me time to think it over, but his decision
remained immovable. I went to my confidante, a thirty-four-
year-old woman, and asked her for advice. But she replied,
"Write amenably to Mr. Mueller; for he is so much older and
more experienced than you, and he will straightway give you
good advice." I followed her [advice] and am turning to you with
folded hands and with tears in my eyes, to please help me a little.
I must leave the paternal home at any price, for I cannot possibly
become betrothed to this wax doll that my father has presented
as the bridegroom to whom I am to become betrothed.

In the pleasant hope that you might reply right away, and that
with your esteemed writing you will send me good advice,
which I will surely follow. Yours, constantly thinking of you,
Michaline A.

Please write to me at this address by mail————*Starowiślna* 26.[2]

[On face of envelope] To Dr. Müller Kraków, *Starowiślna* Nr. 27
(Postal stamp: Kraków 11. XII. 1899)

2. Letter to Her Father Israel Araten

Kraków, January 26, 1900[3]

Dear Father,

With a desperate heart and tears in my eyes I am writing to you,
my Father, for my heart bursts when I hear the rumors being

2. Letters were picked up at the post office.
3. The National Archives in Kraków, DPKr 75, L. 128 pr./900.

spread in the city—that Mr. Znawski,[4] or rather Warjacki
[Polish for lunatic], supposedly had me brought to him by the
police, and you, dear father, supposedly were able to watch your
daughter being dragged to the insane asylum by the police. Oh,
Father! My head bursts when I think that all the tender words
with which you bestow upon me in your letter are nothing but
a lie.

However, I forgive you, even the false oath that you intend to
swear about my not having yet completed my fourteenth year.
And do you know why I forgive you?—for the simple reason
that the Lord Jesus had said: "Forgive those who hate you and
pray for those who persecute you." But I will no longer speak of
it, my father, I pray for you daily that the dear God may convert
you, as He converted me, and when you are worthy of His grace,
maybe He will hear my plea. But I must come to the most
important part of my letter. For when I found out that the
physician who had visited me, was Mr. Znawski, I began to ask
what he wished; the Sisters said that this gentleman, who had
come from the insane asylum, asked if I was not afflicted with
the raving madness, and when I heard the rumors being spread
about me in the city I understood the whole matter and turned
to the Mother General or Vicar with the question whether she
could take me under her protection. The Mother replied that
she cared little about this and, moreover, if she were to take me
under her protection, she had no right to it. So I decided to flee
across the ocean, and as I heard that there are also Sisters in
America, I left all the Sisters unaware about this and prepared for
the journey across the ocean. The dear God Himself gave me
that advice in saying: "Over there nothing bad will happen to
you, and I will guide you to the purpose of your journey."

Dear Father, when you will receive this letter, I will no longer
be in the convent, but where you will not be able to reach me.

As far as the Sisters are concerned, I assure you that they will
never hear from me where I went; you alone I will notify after
6–8 weeks of what is happening with me, and how I am faring. I
send my regards to the entire family, the mother, the father, the

4. She is referring to the psychiatrist, Dr. Karol Żuławski.

grandfather, the grandmother, the uncles and all aunts, cousins, and the entire family altogether.

> I am still your devoted
> daughter,
> Michalina Araten

I commend you to the Lord God and wish for you, that the Lord Jesus watch over you and protect you.

Address: I am asking the Sisters to hand this letter to Mr. Israel Araten in person and am asking them also not to open it, for the owner alone is entitled to open this letter.

> Respectfully,
> Michalina Araten

To Mr. Israel Araten
Here.

Debora Lewkowicz

1. Letters to Her Family

Vienna, August 5, 1901[5]

Dearest Father!

I received your letter and money; I was glad that I was already finishing and travelling home, but it is impossible for I have to stay a few more days in Vienna. Today we were at Fleischer's, and he came with me to the *Kultusgemeinde* [Jewish community council], where I was told that one needs only to register at the magistrate that I am Jewish, and then at the rabbinate. Mr. Fleischer however, who is a fine man, wanted to spare me the unpleasantness and will do that by himself in writing. He told me that he would write to me when I will be able to travel, so I won't have to run around. Now I am done with running around and am very pleased that the matter is going through so

---

5. Lewkowicz file.

well. In the *Kultusgemeinde* everyone congratulated me in a
very friendly manner; they are very fine people, especially
Mr. Fleischer; he walked with us in the heat etc.; I thanked him
very politely, also in your name, and left. Perhaps I will already
be able to leave before Saturday, at any rate, I will write to you; I
am well and thank God also pleased, that I will already be done;
write to me how you are over there; I kiss your hands, dearest
parents, forgive me for the bad things I have done so far, that I
aggrieved you so; I am your daughter once more who will try to
bring sweetness and joy to your years; kiss the dear siblings
Cheiche and Mendele, give regards to all acquaintances,

> Farewell,
> Your daughter,
> Debora

————

[No place name, No date]

Most precious, dearest parents!

I received the things you sent as well as the beautiful letter for
which I thank you very much. Your reminiscences, dear father,
are very pleasant for me; I will try to accommodate your wishes.
Will ask earnestly the Almighty and beg forgiveness for my
heavy sins, as I will also during these high holidays swear once
more that I will stay in my faith, that I will strive all my days to
pray for you and to ask the dear God forgiveness for my very bad
behavior. But, dear Parents! You too I ask for forgiveness!
Forgive your child who was bad only once and who swears at the
beginning of these high holidays, God willing, that this was the
first and last case. Oh! Forgive; and at that time the merciful
God will surely forgive because of my heartfelt efforts! Also you,
dearest Parents! May the Almighty grant your dear life dearest
ones all the best and happiest, and all that might aggrieve you
may yet belong to this terrible year, in which you had so many
misfortunes, that the dear God should always preserve your life
in the best of health, that all your prayers and wishes may be

heard and fulfilled in the full meaning of the word by God; may God grant that the business in Podgórze goes well, that I may be with you, dearest Parents. I also wish all the best for Cheiche and Mendele, am praying for all the best for you, all as you wish it,

> Your true and good
> daughter,
> Debora

———

Philo September 25, 1901

My dearest and most precious parents!

I received your dear letter and your postscript in Zoller's letter. I am very glad that all of you are healthy and that you already are living in Podgórze. May God grant that things go well for you there and that all worries will belong to the previous year. I fasted very well,[6] and in the evening we recuperated ourselves very well. And you, dear Parents, did you recuperate yourselves well? The wish, that you, most beloved father, expressed, that I may find a match in Hungary, might indeed perhaps be fulfilled. The young man with whom the dear uncle already spoke, and of whom he also spoke to you, has already been here meanwhile a second time, and we liked one another very well, and God willing, I will become a Hungarian citizen. He is a young, very handsome man, intelligent, and can also learn Torah. He was born in Hungary and thus is a Hungarian citizen, which is of great value in Hungary. The matter is not entirely agreed upon yet, but I hope that, God willing, it will come about. I would feel very happy. Let it remain so, most precious parents! May the Almighty always bless us that all that we do will be for His praise and glory. I and everyone is doing very well. Kiss Mendele affectionately for me and also Cheiche. Please, write to me how

6. The Yom Kippur fast began on the evening of September 22, 1901, and lasted until the evening of September 23.

everyone is doing. I wrote Zoller a postcard, but I told him nothing, since I have not found out yet. I just took it to the post office when I met Mr. Blaufeder. You all stay healthy, may God grant that our wishes will be fulfilled; am wishing you cheerful holidays.

Your good child,
Debora Lewkowa

———

2. Letter to Sister Rozalia Zagrabińska, Felician Sisters' Convent

[No place name, No date] [7]

Most worthy Sister Marie Rozalie, Felician Convent
Kraków, Smoleńsk Nr. 2

Jesus be praised! Most worthy, most precious Mother. I take the opportunity given to me in order to sum up the situation in which I am in to the most precious Mother. So, a month ago I was seized by the Jews who first led me away to Vienna in order to state legally that I am a Jewess. I went to the court there and fell to the feet of the secretary in order to beg for assistance; he had no authority however to free me from the Jews, drove them out and wrote immediately to Kraków to the court, that the court may free me from the Jews; meanwhile I was seized again and put down in Hungary where I currently am. For 1½ months I have been without . . . without Holy Mass and without confession. Oh, my Jesus, wherefore have I been so severely punished? Mother, I do not have so much time as to depict to Mother all my agonies; there is no quill which could describe my mortifications, but I gladly bear everything for Jesus. If only one time I could be at a Holy Mass where Jesus sacrifices himself for me. Oh God! Have mercy on me! The Jews don't harm me but

7. Lewkowicz file.

maltreat me so that I become a Jewess again. But I only let them feel my disdain. I believe that shortly something will come from Kraków in order to free me from the Jews. I beg, Mother—for a prayer for me, for a prayer to Jesus that he have mercy on me and liberate me from the Jewish hands and that he may give me patience, so that in my despair I do not lay a hand on myself. This week I am to see the local priest; perhaps he will give me good advice. I ask, Mother, that you write to my godfather, priest Waisło to his own address: Podsdolice Region Wielieczka, describe to him my current situation and ask him to address a prayer to Jesus for me, because I cannot write to him directly. Oh, most precious Mother: I ask once more for a prayer that Jesus have mercy on me, for I have enough of the torture. Priest Rothermund has handed my baptism certificate to the Jews; everybody has conspired against me. I ask Mother once more to write to my godfather. I also am asking the catechumen for prayer [that] Pepi shall not leave . . . want to abduct [!]; Ela also—where is she?—[she] must be careful. I kiss your hands, highly worthy one, my dearest Mother, I am asking sincerely for a prayer, for the mercy of the Holy Mother and her Holy Son. I kiss the hands and feet of the Sisters, and in every prayer, I join and repeat the Our Father early in the morning and at night. I sing all litanies and everything outside of church, but I hope that Jesus will hear my prayers and will grant me return to the Mother, where I will tell everything in person.

> Anastaya Marya kisses the
> feet of the Sister

Anna Kluger

1. Personal Statement in Her Supreme Court Appeal

June, 1910[8]

I was born on June 24, 1890. I attended primary school from the year 1896 to 1902. After this I enjoyed schooling in the boarding school of Mrs. Tschapek,

---

8. Kluger, *Revisionsrekurs*, 2–5.

where I completed the four-grade *Bürgerschule* in 1904. After that I received private lessons from Mrs. Clossmann; but after one month I had to give these up upon my mother's behest, because Mrs. Clossmann was a Catholic. With that the provisions of the parental care for my education came to an end.

Since that time I studied exclusively on my own without any help by eagerly visiting the Jagiellonian Library, where I used the rich treasure of books and by being in contact with my former colleagues who loaned me school books.

When I was 15 years old my parents decided to have me betrothed; thus on December or November of the year 1905, I was betrothed against my will to a younger, barely 14 year old Hasidic boy, Zacharias Arak. At that time I was still an ignorant child, however I instinctively resisted this; but the parents soon knew how to break this childish resistance and to assert their will through my betrothal.

From this moment the parents began to pay active attention to my way of living, taking the position that a Hasidic girl who soon would get married, should not be allowed to occupy herself with any kind of scientific work, but must prepare herself exclusively for her future role as mother. From this time on I was constantly exposed to persecution because I wanted to study. I had to hide my school books at my girlfriends', because my parents, if they found any at home, destroyed and burned them. For this reason I studied in secret, either during the night at home, or in the reading room of the Jagiellonian Library, in order to avoid the continuous scenes at home, which ended with blows and curses, whenever the parents surprised me with a book they found.

I lived two years under such circumstances, when the parents decided to have me married to Zacharias Arak in August of 1907. As I was older by that time—I was already 17 years old—I stood up for myself with all my might; I begged and pleaded, and tried to explain to the parents that I was not a machine, that they should not disrespect my will and not tie me for my entire life to a man who was a complete stranger to me and on top of that had a severe lung disease. All my pleas remained unsuccessful and found no hearing with my parents, to whom I had to submit and had to get married to a total stranger to me, an unprogressive person. I had no means for flight; my studies had not reached a proper end, for I was not sufficiently prepared for the matriculations examinations; thus, I had to give up my resistance to this connection, help-lessly and under duress, in thinking I would be able to obtain a greater freedom if I got married, as my mother always promised me.

After the Jewish religious marriage, my way of life did not change; I worked as before on my education by secretly studying, away from my parents, who, in spite of their promise to let me have complete freedom after the wedding, kept forbidding me to study as before, destroying any school books they found at home, even cursing and beating me for it.

I lived with my husband for a year and a half in my parents' home, but not as a wedded wife.

Soon after the wedding the parents began to monitor my relationship with my husband and discovered with "horror" that I did not live with my husband in a conjugal relationship. For, when my husband demanded of me right after the wedding the fulfillment of the marital relations I explained to him that he was a complete stranger to me, that I did not know him and was unable to agree to become his wife, and that any act of violence on his part would forever create a chasm between us that could not ever be bridged by anything. My husband, a decent lad, accepted my position and no longer assailed me with demands. My parents however decided, when they found out about our agreement, that I absolutely must give myself to my husband, and for this purpose, my grandfather, the rabbi from Chrzanów Moses Halberstam, as well as Bergmann, the grandfather of my husband, arrived to Podgórze, and together they began to harass me and literally torture me psychologically, but when I declared outright, that I would never agree to marital relations with my husband, they decided, that my husband should empower himself and take me by force, and they even determined the day, a Tuesday, for this purpose.

During this time I suffered terrible agonies, for as a human being and as a woman I was subjected to being the object of such deliberations and cajolery and assignments, which were aimed against my human dignity; my parents however regarded this as triviality or even as disobedience of a child toward the parental authority!

During these few weeks before the designated deadline, on which my husband was supposed to violate me, I had to protect myself from various assaults of my parents in acting towards them in such a way as if I actually lived in conjugal relationship with my husband; for I wanted to escape from the horrible psychological torments I was subjected to, as at any moment I had to be prepared to answer a question from my parents if I had already given myself to Arak.

Out of a whole series of such embarrassing scenes I remember a particular event. A certain time after the wedding I ran into my mother during the night in the corridor, and she began to ask me about our conjugal relation; when I remained silent she began to pull at me and push me towards the railing and threatened to throw me down from the hallway.

During this time I decided to flee from home and the disgrace which my parents planned for me, but the attempts were discovered and foiled prematurely by my mother.

Now my mother along with my father began to calm me down and to assure me that they would let me have complete freedom, not to meddle in my marital matters, as well as not to disturb me in my scientific studies.

However, this promise was never kept, for the domestic conditions remained, and things were completely unchanged as far as my studies were concerned. My parents disturbed me as before when I tried to study, heaped beatings and curses on me whenever they saw me with a book, spied to see if there was still a light on in my room after 10 o'clock at night, and when all this did not help they took away the electric light, so that I was forced to study at night by candlelight; and in that way I prepared for the matriculation examinations. My parents went so far as to intervene through the advocate Dr. Aronsohn with the director of the Jagiellonian Library, so that I would be forbidden to read books there or to borrow any: in particular my mother, together with Dr. Aronsohn, went to the director of the library.

As I was studying at home alone for the matriculation examinations without any help, for which I needed information regarding curriculum as well as the pertinent school books, I would need to give private lessons in the German language, in order to acquire the means which I would be able to earn the money and buy the books.

Regarding the meddling of the parents in my marital relations, the situation changed only when my husband travelled for some time to visit his family, so that the opportunity was not there for that question to be asked.

These circumstances brought me to the conclusion that any further stay in my parents' home was impossible, and so I decided to leave the house without fail, but beforehand to prepare myself for my life ahead by completing the matriculation examinations, in order to have something solid.

The flight itself was now just a matter of time, and so it was indeed made reality in August of 1909.

I could not remain in the parental home any longer, for everything that occurred there was foreign to me and hostile, and I can assert with a clear conscience, that in our house I have never experienced what one calls love for a child.

Besides what was mentioned above, as well as the facts given in the court documents, the following incident may depict my situation during this time more clearly: Because I did not let my hair cut—and with the Hasidim every married woman has to have her hair shaved to the scalp—my mother did not wish to give me anything to eat for two days; and when I finally found an opportunity to escape from the house to buy something to eat, my mother wanted to take everything away from me. Only when I agreed to have my hair trimmed to the scalp did she let me buy something to eat and give me some herself later.

In the autumn of the year 1908, after completing my matriculation examinations, I enrolled in the philosophy faculty at the Jagiellonian University. Although I was dedicated to my studies with full diligence, as I was able to study only secretly and covertly, I soon realized that I would be unable to fulfill my duties, and these circumstances became the deciding factor for my escape.

I hereby declare that the facts stated here as well as all facts recorded in the court files are true and that I am prepared to confirm them by oath at any time; however I have been so far unable to appear in court for questioning, for I fear the fanatical revenge of my parents, and the court will not permit me to be heard in a different Austrian court, for instance, in Vienna.

BIBLIOGRAPHY

Archival Sources

Archives of the Jagiellonian University in Kraków
Central Archives for the History of the Jewish People, Jerusalem (CAHJP)
Central Archives of Historical Records in Warsaw (AGAD)
Central State Historical Archives of Ukraine, Lviv (TsDIAL)
Ginzach Kiddush Hashem, Bnei Brak
Haus-, Hof- und Staatsarchiv, Vienna (HHStA)
The National Archives in Kraków
Vienna University Archives

Newspapers and Periodicals

Abendpost
Allgemeine Zeitung des Judenthums
American Jewish Yearbook
Arbeiter-Zeitung
Bible Echo
Bukowinaer Rundschau
Czas
Das Recht: volkstümliche Zeitschrift für österreichisches Rechtsleben
Das Vaterland
Degel Israel
Der Israelit: Ein Centralorgan für das orthodoxe Judentum
Der Tog
Der Yud
Deutsches Volksblatt
Die Neuzeit
Do'ar Hayom
Dos Yidishe Vort
Dr. Bloch's Oesterreichische Wochenschrift
Dziennik Polski
Gazeta Narodowa
Gazeta Lwowska

Genossenschafts- und Vereins-Zeitung

Głos Narodu

Grazer Tagblatt

Ha-Magid

Ha-Mizpeh

Ha-Ne'eman

Ha-'Olam

Ha-Ẓefirah

Ha-Zeman

Haynt

Hof- und Staats-Handbuch der österreichisch-ungarischen Monarchie

Izraelita (Polish supplement of *Der Israelit*)

Jahresbericht des Vereines für erweiterte Frauenbildung in Wien

Jüdische Presse: Organ für die Interessen des orthodoxen Judentums

Kalendarz Krakowski

Kinematographische Rundschau

Kol Maḥazikei Ha-Dat

Krakowianin

Kurjer

Kurjer Lwowski

Landes-Gesetz- und Verordnungsblatt für das Königreich Galizien und Lodomerien sammt dem Grossherzogthume Krakau

Maḥazikei Ha-Dat

Monatschrift der Oesterreichisch-Israelitischen Union

Myśl Niepodległa

Naprzód

Neue Freie Presse

Neues Wiener Journal

Nowa Reforma

Public Opinion: A Comprehensive Summary of the Press Throughout the World

Reichs-Gesetz-Blatt für das Kaiserthum Oesterreich (RGBl)

Reichspost

Reshumot: Yalkut Ha-pirsumim

Sammlung von Civilrechtlichen Entscheidungen des k. k. obersten Gerichtshofes

Schematismus für das kaiserliche und königliche Heer und für die kaiserliche und königliche Kriegsmarine

Słowo Polskie

Stenograficzne sprawozdania z piątej sesyi siódmego peryodu Sejmu krajowego Królestwa Galicyi i Lodomeryi z Wielkiem Księstwem Krakowskiem

Stenographische Protokolle über die Sitzungen des Hauses der Abgeordneten des österreichischen Reichsrathes

Spectator

Spis ludności miasta Krakowa

Szematyzm Królestwa Galicyi i Lodomeryi z Wielkim Księstwem Krakowskiem

The Times

Togblat

Unzer exspress

Verzeichnis der Advokaten und k. k. Notare in den im Reichsrathe vertretenen Königreichen und Ländern der österr.-ungar. Monarchie

Volksblatt für Stadt und Land

Zapiski Muzealne (Poznań)

Zgoda

Primary Sources

Agudat Yisrael. *Agudas Jisroel, Berichte und Materialien*. Frankfurt a.M.: Büro der Agudas Jisroel, [1913?].

Austria. *Politische Verfassung der deutschen Volksschulen für die k. k. österreichischen Provinzen*. Vienna: k.k. Schulbücher-Verschleiss-Administration, 1847.

Beck, Leo von Mannagetta and Carl von Kelle. *Die österreichischen Universitätsgesetze: Sammlung der für die österreichischen Universitäten gültigen Gesetze, Verordnungen, Erlässe, Studien- und Prüfungsordnungen usw*. Vienna: Manz, 1906.

Chlebowski, Bronisław et al. *Słownik geograficzny Królestwa Polskiego i innych krajów słowiańskich*. Vol. 10. Warsaw: Druk Wieku, 1889.

————. *Słownik geograficzny Królestwa Polskiego i innych krajów słowiańskich*. Vol. 13. Warsaw: Druk Wieku, 1893.

Deutschländer, Leo, ed. *Westöstliche Dichterklänge: Jüdische Lesebuch*. Breslau: Pribatch, 1918.

————, ed. *Bajs Jakob: Sein Wesen und Werden*. Vienna: Keren Hathora-Zentrale, 1928.

————, ed. *Beth Jakob: 1928, 1929*. Frankfurt a.M.: Hermon, 1929.

————, ed. *Das Erziehungswerk der Gesetzestreuen Judenheit*. Frankfurt a.M.: Hermon, 1929.

Ellinger, Joseph. *Handbuch des österreichischen allgemeinen Zivil-Rechtes: Enthaltend den Text des allgemeinen bürgerlichen Gesetzbuches vom Jahre 1811 mit kurzen Erläuterungen desselben*. Vienna: Braumüller, 1853.

Felbiger, Johann Ignaz von. *Allgemeine Schulordnung für die deutschen Normal- Haupt- und Trivialschulen in sämmtlichen Kaiserl. Königl. Erbländern*. Vienna: Johann Thomas Edlen von Trattnern, 1774.

Frydman, A[lexander] Z[ysha]. *Beys Yaakov: A ruf tsu di yudishe froyen un techter*. Warsaw, 1922.

————. "The Completion in Lublin and the Beginning in Kraków." *Diglenu* 7,10 (1927): 1–2. [Hebrew]

Frydman, B. et al. "The Religious-Educational Movement 'Beit Yaakov.'" *Almanach Szkolnictwa żydowskiego w Polsce* 1 (1938): 316–362. [Polish]

Gebel, L. (Max). *Tate mames tsures: Lebnsbild mit gezang in 4 akten*. Podgórze: Amkraut & Freund, 1907.

Goldshtein, Moshe, ed. *Tikun 'olam*. Mukačevo: Guttman, 1936.

Gross, Beila Tz. "The Role of Secular Studies in the Beit Yaakov Seminary." *Bajs Yaakov ortodoksisher familien-zhurnal* 100 (1933): 56–57. [Yiddish]

Hirsch, Samson R. *Horeb: Versuche ueber Jissroels Pflichten in der Zerstreuung, zunaechst fuer Jissroels denkende Juenglinge und Jungfrauen*. Altona: Johann Friedrich Hammerich, 1837.

Horowitz, Tuvia. "What Do Jewish Daughters Lack?." *Bajs Yaakov: Ortodoksisher familien-zhurnal* 16 (1925): 75–76. [Yiddish]

Kagan, Israel Meir Ha-Kohen. *Likutei Halakhot* on *Sotah*. Piotrków: H. H. Polman, 1921/2.

Kallas [Korngut], Aniela. *Córki marnotrawne.* Lwów: Wydawnictwo Kultura i Sztuka, 1913.

Keren Hathora-Zentrale. *Programm und Leistung: Keren Hathora und Beth Jakob, 1929–1937: Bericht an die dritte Kenessio Gedaulo.* London: Keren Hathora-Zentrale, 1937.

Kluger, Anna and Eleonore. *Revisionsrekurs der Anna und Eleonore Kluger.* 1910.

Kolmer, Gustav. *Parlament und Verfassung in Oesterreich.* Vol. 1, 1848–1869. Vienna: C. Fromme, 1902.

———. *Parlament und Verfassung in Oesterreich.* Vol. 2, 1869–1879. Vienna: C. Fromme, 1903.

———. *Parlament und Verfassung in Oesterreich.* Vol. 4, 1885–1891. Vienna: C. Fromme, 1907.

———. *Parlament und Verfassung in Oesterreich.* Vol. 8, 1900–1904. Vienna: C. Fromme, 1914.

Landau, Menachem Mendel Chaim. *Mekiz nirdamim*, edited by J. G. Halevy. Piotrków: Cederbaum, 1904.

Lieberman, Hillel. "A Letter from Sarah Schenirer, Peace be Upon Her, to the Land of Israel." *Bajs Yaakov ortodoksisher familien-zhurnal* 130 (1936): 39–40. [Yiddish]

Orlean, Yehudah Leib. *Program funem Yahadus limud far di beys yaakov shulen in Poyln.* Warsaw: Bajs Yaakov-Zentrale, 1931.

———. "The Gymnasium-Idol." *Bajs Yaakov ortodoksisher familien-zhurnal* 94–96 (1933): 5–6. [Yiddish]

———. "Beit Yaakov: Bnot Agudat Yisrael." *Darkenu* 50 (1935): 65–67. [Hebrew]

———. "Sarah Schenirer—Image and Program." *Beit Ya'akov* 10 (1960), 4, 30. [Hebrew]

Pappenheim, Bertha. *Zur Judenfrage in Galizien.* Frankfurt a.M.: Knauer, 1900.

Peters, Edward N., ed. and trans. *The 1917 Or Pio-Benedictine Code of Canon Law: In English Translation with Extensive Scholarly Apparatus.* San Francisco: Ignatius Press, 2001.

Rosenzweig, Franz. *Briefe,* edited by Ernst Simon and Edith Rosenzweig. Berlin: Schocken, 1935.

Scheinfeld, Shabtai, ed. *Ḥoveret shel Keren Ha-Torah.* Vienna: Keren Ha-Torah, 1925.

———. *Ha-Knesiyah ha-gedolah ha-sheniyah shel Agudat Yisrael.* Vienna: Agudat Yisrael, 1929.

Schenirer, Sarah. *Gezamelte shriftn.* Brooklyn, NY: Beth Jacob Teachers Seminary of America, 1955.

———. *Em be-yisra'el: Kitvei Sarah Schenirer,* edited by Henia Alter Schiff et al. 2 vols. Tel-Aviv: Neẓaḥ, 1955.

———. "A Letter to the Land of Israel, From Sarah Schenirer Peace Be Upon Her." *Beit Ya'akov* 10 (1960): 5. [Hebrew]

SS. Felicjanki. *Historja Zgromadzenia SS. Felicjanek na podstawie rękopisów.* 3 vols. Kraków: Nakładem Zgromadzenia SS. Felicjanek, 1929.

Stern, Ludwig. *Amudei ha-yahadus: Lehrbukh fun religie far hoyz un shul,* translated and edited by Simḥah Moshe Prager. Będzin: Levin-Alter, 1926.

Taubeles, Samuel Aron. *Podręcznik do nauki religii żydowskiej.* Lwów: Zakład Narodowy imienia Ossolińskich, 1917.

Tsentral Sekretaryat. *Di organizirung fun Bnos Agudas Yisroel.* Łódź: Beit Yaakov Zhurnal, 1930.

Wyspiański, Stanisław. *The Wedding: A Drama in Three Acts,* translated by Noel Clark. London: Oberton Books, 2010.

Zaler, Yiẓḥak. *Sha'arei Yiẓḥak.* Warsaw, 1875.

Secondary Sources

Adler, Eliyana. *In Her Hands: The Education of Jewish Girls in Tsarist Russia*. Detroit, MI: Wayne State University Press, 2011.

Agnon, S. Y. "Tehilla." In *Tehilla and Other Israeli Tales*, translated by I. M. Lask. London: Abelard-Schuman, 1956, 11–46.

———. *The Bridal Canopy*, translated by I. M. Lask. New York: Schocken Books, 1967.

Araten, Israel Yaakov, et al. *Ha-Shevet li-Yehudah*. Bnei Brak: 'Et Sofer, 1967.

Assaf, David. "Sandz Hasidic Dynasty." *The YIVO Encyclopedia of Jews in Eastern Europe*. Online edition http://www.yivoencyclopedia.org/article.aspx/Sandz_Hasidic_Dynasty, 2010.

———. *Untold Tales of the Hasidim: Crisis & Discontent in the History of Hasidism*, translated by Dena Ordan. Waltham, MA: Brandeis University Press, 2010.

Atkin, Abraham. *The Beth Jacob Movement in Poland (1917–1939)*. PhD thesis, Yeshiva University, 1959.

Bacon, Gershon. *The Politics of Tradition: Agudat Yisrael in Poland, 1916–1939*. Jerusalem: Magnes Press, 1996.

———. "Enduring Prestige, Eroded Authority: The Warsaw Rabbinate in the Interwar Period." In *Warsaw. The Jewish Metropolis: Essays in Honor of the 75th Birthday of Professor Antony Polonsky*, edited by Glenn Dynner and François Guesnet. Leiden: Brill, 2015, 347–369.

Bader, Gershom. *Mayne zikhroynes*. Buenos Aires: Tsentral-farband fun Poylishe Yidn in Argentine, 1953.

Bamberger, Seckel. "Torah Study for Women." *Oẓar ha- ḥayim* 4 (1928): 146–148. [Hebrew]

Bar-El, Adina. *Bein ha-'eẓim ha-yerakrakin: 'itonei yeladim be-yidish uve-'ivrit be-folin 1918–1939*. Jerusalem: ha-Sifriyah ha-Ẓiyonit, 2006.

Barth-Scalmani, Gunda. "Geschlecht: weiblich, Stand: ledig, Beruf: Lehrerin: Grundzüge der Professionalisierung des weiblichen Lehrberufs im Primarschulbereich in Österreich bis zum Ersten Weltkrieg." In *Bürgerliche Frauenkultur im 19. Jahrhundert*, edited by Brigitte Mazohl-Wallnig. Vienna: Böhlau, 1995, 343–400.

Barzycka-Paździor, Agata. "The Kraków Kluger affair. A Galician Micro-History." *Rocznik Przemyski* 52 (2016): 35–54. [Polish]

Baumgarten, Jean. "Yiddish Ethical Texts and the Diffusion of the Kabbalah in the 17th and 18th Centuries." *Bulletin du Centre de Recherche Français à Jérusalem* 73–91 (2007): 73–91.

Beit-Ha-Levi, Israel David. *Toldot Yehudei Kalish*. Tel Aviv: Self-published, 1961.

Bender, Basya (Epstein). "The Life of a Beit Yaakov Girl." In *Daughters of Destiny: Women Who Revolutionized Jewish life and Torah Education*, edited by Devora Rubin. Brooklyn, NY: Mesorah Publication, 1988, 178–183.

Benisch, Pearl. *Carry Me in Your Heart: The Life and Legacy of Sarah Schenirer, Founder and Visionary of the Bais Yaakov Movement*. Jerusalem: Feldheim, 1991.

Bergner, Hinde. *On Long Winter Nights . . . : Memoirs of a Jewish Family in a Galician Township (1870–1900)*, translated by Justin Danial Cammy. Cambridge, MA: Harvard University Press, 2005.

Blankenagel, John C. "More Unacknowledged Borrowing by Jakob Wassermann." *Journal of English and Germanic Philology* 40.4 (1941): 555–557.

Bled, Jean Paul. *Franz Joseph*, translated by Teresa Bridgeman. Cambridge, MA: Blackwell, 1992.

Bloch, Moshe Chaim. *Maharsham—ha-posek ha-aḥaron.* New York: Majeski, 1955.

Bogusz, Robert. "The Felician Sisters' Convent in Kraków as the Center Catechumenate in the Years 1873–1914." *Krakowski Rocznik Archiwalny* 9 (2003): 149–156. [Polish]

Brandstaetter, Roman. *Ja jestem Żyd z "Wesela": z wielogłosem i dokumentacją na temat "Żyda" i "Racheli."* Kraków: Baran i Suszczyński, 1993.

Brawer, Michael. "Memories of a Father and Son." In *Ha-Ḥeder: meḥkarim, te'udot u-firkei zikhronot,* edited by Immanuel Etkes et al. Tel Aviv: Beit Shalom Aleichem: 2010, 495–514. [Hebrew]

Breuer, Mordechai. "Rabbis-Doctors in Poland-Lithuania during the German Occupation (1918–1914)." *Bar-Ilan Annual* 24/25 (1989): 117–153. [Hebrew]

———. *Modernity within Tradition: The Social History of Orthodox Jewry in Imperial Germany,* translated by Elizabeth Petuchowski. New York: Columbia University Press, 1992.

Bristow, Edward J. *Prostitution and Prejudice: The Jewish Fight against White Slavery, 1870–1939.* Oxford: Oxford University Press, 1982.

Bronowski, Yoram. "Poets, Peasants, and Jews in *The Wedding.*" *Moznaim* 1 (1981): 11–15. [Hebrew]

Bross, Anna. "Pestalozzi und der polnische Freiheitsheld Kosciuszko." *Schweizerische pädagogische Zeitschrift* 38 (1928): 241–245.

———. "Die pädagogischen Ideen Berthold Ottos: Zu seinem siebzigjährigen Geburtstag." *Schweizerische pädagogische Zeitschrift* 39: 9/10 (1929): 234–238.

———. "Quelques rapports à Metternich sur Charles-Albert de Savoie (1828–1832)." *Revue Historique* 163.1 (1930): 103–110.

———. *Józef Mazzini szermierz niepodległości Włoch i przyjaciel Polski.* Lwów: Filomata, 1939.

Buchen, Tim. "'Herkules im antisemitischen Augiasstall': Joseph Samuel Bloch und Galizien in der Reaktion auf den Antisemitismus in der Habsburgermonarchie." In *Einspruch und Abwehr: Die Reaktion des europäischen Judentums auf die Entstehung des Antisemitismus (1879–1914),* edited by Ulrich Wyrwa. Frankfurt am Main: Campus Verlag, 2010, 193–214.

———. *Antisemitismus in Galizien: Agitation, Gewalt und Politik gegen Juden in der Habsburgermonarchie um 1900.* Berlin: Metropol-Verlag, 2012.

Burstyn, Joan N. "Education and Sex: The Medical Case Against Higher Education for Women in England, 1870–1900." *American Philosophical Society* 117 (1973): 79–89.

Carlebach, Alexander. "A German Rabbi Goes East." *Leo Baeck Yearbook* 4 (1961): 60–121.

Cohen, Israel, ed. *Sefer Butshash.* Tel Aviv: Am Oved, 1956.

Czajecka, Bogusława. "Convent Schools in Galicia in the Years 1867–1914." *Nasza przeszłość* 61 (1984): 233–301. [Polish]

———. *"Z domu w szeroki świat . . .": Droga kobiet do niezależności w zaborze austriackim w latach 1890–1914.* Kraków: Wydawców Prac Nauk. Universitas, 1990.

Czub, Robert. "The Reading Society for Women in Gostyń." *Rocznik Gostyński* 2 (2015): 55–64. [Polish]

Dadej, Iwona. "The Reading Room for Women as a Place and Space for the Kraków Women's Movement: Salon or a Room of One's Own?" In *Krakowski szlak kobiet. Przewodniczka po Krakowie emancypantek,* edited by Ewa Furgał. Kraków: Fundacja Przestrzeń Kobiet, 2009, vol. 1, 32–38. [Polish]

Dadej, Iwona and Angelique Leszczawski-Schwerk. "Together and Apart: Polish Women's Rights Activists and the Beginnings of International Women's Day Around 1911," *Aspasia* 6 (2012): 25–42.

Deák, István. *Beyond Nationalism: A Social and Political History of the Habsburg Officer Corps*. New York: Oxford University Press, 1990.

Dekiert, Dariusz and Joanna Lisek, eds. *"Żydówką być to rzecz niemała": Pisma autobiograficzne Sary Szenirer*. Warsaw: Wydawnictwo PWN, forthcoming.

Dutkowa, Renata. *Żeńskie gimnazja Krakowa w procesie emancypacji kobiet (1896–1918)*. Kraków: Instytut Historii Uniwersytetu Jagiellońskiego, 1995.

Dynner, Glenn. *Yankel's Tavern: Jews, Liquor, & Life in the Kingdom of Poland*. New York: Oxford University Press, 2013.

Dziadzio, Andrzej. "Weltliche oder konfessionelle Schule? Der Streit um Religionsunterricht in der Donaumonarchie nach der Ära des Liberalismus." *Krakowskie Studia z Historii Państwa i Prawa* 10.1 (2017): 31–47.

Eisner, Isi Jacob. "Reminiscences of the Berlin Rabbinical Seminary." *Leo Baeck Year Book* 12 (1967): 32–52.

Elias, Markus. "The Educational Work of Rabbi S. R. Hirsch: Jewish Schools in Western Europe." In *Ateret Zvi Jubilee Volume Presented in Honor of the Eightieth Birthday of Rabbi Dr. Joseph Breuer*. New York: Philipp Feldheim, 1962.

Ellenson, David. "German Orthodox Rabbinical Writings on the Jewish Textual Education of Women: The Views of Rabbi Samson Raphael Hirsch and Rabbi Esriel Hildesheimer." In *Gender and Jewish History*, edited by Marion A. Kaplan and Deborah Dash Moore. Bloomington and Indianapolis: Indiana University Press, 2011.

Endelman, Todd M. *Leaving the Jewish Fold: Conversion and Radical Assimilation in Modern Jewish History*. Princeton and Oxford: Princeton University Press, 2015.

Engelbrecht, Helmut. *Geschichte des österreichischen Bildungswesens: Erziehung und Unterricht auf dem Boden Österreichs*. 5 vols. Vienna: Österreichischer Bundesverlag, 1986.

Eżyon (Holżberg), Yiżḥak-Refa'el. "The 'Yavneh' Educational System in Lithuania." In *Yahadut Lita*. Vol. 2, edited by Dov Lipeż et al. Tel Aviv: Igud Yożei Lita, 1972, 160–165. [Hebrew]

Faierstein, Morris M. *Ze'enah U-Re'enah: A Critical Translation into English*. Berlin: De Gruyter, 2017.

Fischer-Kowalski, Marina and Peter Seidl. *Von den Tugenden der Weiblichkeit: Mädchen und Frauen im österreichischen Bildungssystem*. Vienna: Verlag für Gesellschaftskritik, 1986.

Foner, Nancy and Joanna Dreby. "Relations Between the Generations in Immigrant Families." *Annual Review of Sociology* 37 (2011): 545–564.

Freeze, ChaeRan. *Jewish Marriage and Divorce in Imperial Russia*. Hanover, NH: University Press of New England, 2002.

———. "When Chava Left Home: Gender, Conversion, and the Jewish Family in Tsarist Russia." *Polin: Studies in Polish Jewry* 18 (2007): 153–188.

Friedmann, Filip. *Die galizischen Juden im Kampfe um ihre Gleichberechtigung (1848–1868)*. Frankfurt am Main: J. Kauffmann Verlag, 1929.

Friedrich, Margaret. *"Ein Paradies ist uns verschlossen…": Zur Geschichte der schulischen Mädchenerziehung in Österreich im "langen" 19. Jahrhundert*. Vienna: Böhlau, 1999.

Fuchs, Ilan. *Jewish Women's Torah Study: Orthodox Religious Education and Modernity*. Abingdon, Oxfordshire; New York: Routledge, 2015.

Fürst, A. "Die jüdischen Realschulen Deutschlands." *Monatsschrift fur Geschichte und Wissenschaft des Judenthums* 7/8 (1914): 430–453.

Gawron, Edyta. "Salo W. Baron at Jagiellonian University." In *The Enduring Legacy of Salo W. Baron*, edited by Hava Tirosh-Samuelson and Edward Dąbrowa. Kraków: Jagiellonian University Press, 2017, 69–80.

Gifter, Mordechai. "The Telz Yeshiva." In *Mosdot Torah be-eropah be-vinyanam u-ve-ḥurbanam*, edited by Shmuel K. Mirski. New York: 'Ogen, 1956.

Glatzer, Nahum N., ed. *Franz Rosenzweig: His Life and Thought*. 2nd rev. ed. New York: Schocken Books, 1976.

Goldin, Simha. *Apostasy and Jewish Identity in High Middle Ages Northern Europe: "Are You Still My Brother?"* Manchester: Manchester University Press, 2014.

Granot, Tamir. "Women's Status and the Education of Girls according to the Ḥassidic Rebbe (Admor) Rabbi Yekutiel Yehudah Halberstam of Sanz-Klausenburg." *Hagut: Studies in Jewish Educational Thought* 8 (2008): 37–86. [Hebrew]

Grill, Tobias. *Der Westen im Osten: Deutsches Judentum und jüdische Bildungsreform in Osteuropa (1783–1939)*. Göttingen: Vandenhoeck & Ruprecht, 2013.

Grossman, Avraham. *Pious and Rebellious: Jewish Women in Medieval Europe*, translated by Jonathan Chipman. Waltham, MA: Brandeis University Press, 2004.

Grunfeld, Judith (Rosenfeld). "Growing Up in Frankfort." In *Daughters of Destiny: Women Who Revolutionized Jewish Life and Torah Education*, edited by Devora Rubin. Brooklyn, NY: Mesorah Publication, 1988, 119–147.

Halberstamm, Israel Dov (Berl). *Sefer mi-beit avotai ve-rabotai*. Brooklyn: [?], 2007.

Harmat, Ulrike. "'Till Death Do You Part': Catholicism, Marriage and Culture War in Austria(-Hungary)." In *Marriage, Law and Modernity: Global Histories*, edited by Julia Moses. London: Bloomsbury Academic, 2018, 109–128.

Hauptmann, Walter. "Die Entwicklung der Religionsmündigkeitsgrenze im Deutschen und im Österreichischen Recht." *Österreichisches Archiv für Kirchenrecht* (1968): 133–173.

Heindl, Waltraud and Marina Tichy. *"Durch Erkenntnis zu Freiheit und Glück—": Frauen an der Universität Wien (ab 1897)*. Vienna: WUV-Universitätsverlag, 1993.

———. "Die konfessionellen Verhältnisse. Jüdische und katholische Studentinnen." In *Durch Erkenntnis*, edited by Heindl and Tichy, 1993, 139–149.

———. "Regionale und nationale Herkunft." In *Durch Erkenntnis*, edited by Heindl and Tichy, 1993, 100–128.

Hess, Jonathan M. *Middlebrow Literature and the Making of German-Jewish Identity*. Stanford, CA: Stanford University Press, 2010.

Hildesheimer, Meir. "Religious Education in Response to Changing Times: Congregation Adass-Isroel Religious School in Berlin." *Zeitschrift für Religions- und Geistesgeschichte* 60.2 (2008): 111–130.

Homola-Skąpska. "Galicia: Initiatives for Emancipation of Polish Women." In *Women in Polish Society*, edited by Rudolf Jaworski. New York: Distributed by Columbia University Press, 1992, 71–89.

Hyman, Paula E. *Gender and Assimilation in Modern Jewish History: The Roles and Representation of Women.* Seattle and London: University of Washington Press, 1995.

Jenks, William A. *Austria Under the Iron Ring 1870–1893.* Charlottesville: University Press of Virginia, 1965.

Judson, Pieter M. *The Habsburg Empire: A New History.* Cambridge, MA: Belknap Press of Harvard University Press, 2016.

Juśko, Edmund. "Organizational Structure of Primary Schools in the Tarnów County in the Years 1918–1939." *Roczniki Nauk Społecznych* 32.2 (2004): 113–143. [Polish]

Kalish, Ita. *A rebishe heym in amolikn poyln.* Tel Aviv: Y. L. Perets, 1963.

Karmeli, Moshe et al., eds. *Sefer Kalish.* 2 vols. Tel-Aviv: Daʻat, 1967.

Karniel, Josef. "Das Toleranzpatent Kaiser Josephs II. für die Juden Galiziens und Lodomeriens." *Jahrbuch des Instituts für Deutsche Geschichte* 11 (1982): 55–89.

Kazdan, Chaim Solomon. *Di geschichte fun yidishe shulvesen in umophenigikn Poyln.* Mexico City: Kultur und Hilf, 1947.

Kertzer, David I. *The Kidnapping of Edgardo Mortara.* New York: Vintage Books, 1998.

Kohn, Pinchas. "Eine würdige Jubiläumserinnerung." *Nach'lath Z'wi: Eine Monatsschrift für Judentum in Lehre und Tat* 6 (1935/1936): 152–158.

Kołodziejska-Smagała, Zuzanna. "'Nature Has Created a Woman to Be a Wife and Mother': The Role of Women in the Eyes of Polish-Jewish Writers." In *Literatura polsko-żydowska 1861–1918: Studia i szkice,* edited by Zuzanna Kołodziejska-Smagała and Maria Antosik-Piela. Kraków: Wydawnictwo Uniwersytetu Jagiellońskiego, 2017, 147–187. [Polish]

Kras, Janina. *Wyższe kursy dla kobiet im. A. Baranieckiego w Krakowie 1868–1924.* Kraków: Wydawnictwo Literackie, 1972.

Kulczykowski, Mariusz. *Żydzi—studenci Uniwersytetu Jagiellońskiego w dobie autonomicznej Galicji (1867–1918).* Kraków: Księgarnia Akademicka, 1995.

Kutrzeba, Justyna. "Jewish Converts in Kraków at the Turn of the 19th and 20th Centuries." *Krzysztofory. Zeszyty Naukowe Muzeum Historycznego Miasta Krakowa* 35 (2018): 203–214. [Polish]

Lang, Beatrice Caplan. "Orthodox Yiddish Literature in Interwar Poland." PhD dissertation, Columbia University, 2005.

Łapot, Mirosław. "Female Teachers of the Mosaic Religion in Public Schools in Galicia in the Years 1867–1939." *Prace Naukowe Akademii im. Jana Długosza w Częstochowie. Seria Pedagogika* 20 (2011): 407–418. [Polish]

Lazar, Shlomo. *Beit ha-sefer ha-ʻivri bi-krakov 1908–1936.* Haifa: Vaʻadat ha-hanṣaḥah shel Yoẓʻei Krakov be-Ḥeifa, 1989.

Leiter, Moshe. "A Few Aspects of the Figure of the Maharshm." *Or ha-Mizraḥ* 3–4 (1964): 10–15. [Hebrew]

Leszczawski-Schwerk, Angelique. "*Die umkämpften Tore zur Gleichberechtigung": Frauenbewegungen in Galizien (1867–1918).* Vienna: LIT, 2015.

Leventahl, Moshe. "A Biography of R. Moshe David Flesch." [Hebrew] http://www.daat.ac.il/daat/history/tkufot/biyografya-2.htm#1, 2006, accessed February 2, 2020.

Lezzi, Eva. "Secularism and Neo-Orthodoxy: Conflicting Strategies in Modern Orthodox Fiction." In *Secularism in Question: Jews and Judaism in Modern Times,* edited by Ari Joskowicz and Ethan B. Katz. Philadelphia: University of Pennsylvania Press, 2015, 208–231.

Lieberman, Saul. *Greek in Jewish Palestine: Studies in the Life and Manners of Jewish Palestine in the II–IV Centuries C.E.* 2nd ed. New York: Feldheim, 1965.

Lisek, Joanna. "Orthodox Yiddishism in Beys Yakov Magazine in the Context of Religious Jewish Feminism." In *Ashkenazim and Sephardim: A European Persepctive*, edited by Andrzej Kątny et al. Frankfurt am Main: Peter Lang, 2013.

———. "Sara Schenirer: Diary (excerpts)." *Cwiszn: Żydowski kwartalnik o literaturze i sztuce* 3/4 (2014): 68–70. [Polish]

Manekin, Rachel. "'Something Completely New': The Development of the Idea of Female Religious Education in the Modern Period." *Masechet* 2 (2004): 63–85. [Hebrew]

———. "The Lost Generation: Education and Female Conversion in Fin-de-Siècle Cracow." *Polin: Studies in Polish Jewry* 18 (2005): 189–219.

———. "Orthodox Jewry in Kraków at the Turn of the Twentieth Century." *Polin: Studies in Polish Jewry* 23 (2011): 165–198.

———. *Yehudei Galizyah ve-ha-ḥukah ha-ostrit: reishitah shel politikah yehudit modernit.* Jerusalem: the Zalman Shazar Center for Jewish History, 2015.

———. "Being Jewish in *Fin de siècle* Galicia: The View from Salo Baron's Memoir." In *The Enduring Legacy of Salo W. Baron*, edited by Hava Tirosh-Samuelson and Edward Dąbrowa. Kraków: Jagiellonian University Press, 2017, 81–98.

———. "The Laws of Moses and the Laws of the Emperor: Austrian Marriage Laws and the Jews of Galicia." *Polin: Studies in Polish Jewry* 33. Forthcoming.

Margalit, Yehezkel. *The Jewish Family: Between Family Law and Contract Law.* Cambridge, UK: Cambridge University Press, 2017.

Mark, Rudolf A. *Galizien unter österreichischer Herrschaft: Verwaltung—Kirche—Bevölkerung.* Marburg: Herder Institut, 1994.

Markowski, Artur. "State Policies Concerning Jewish Conversions in the Kingdom of Poland During the First Half of the Nineteenth Century." *Gal-Ed* 25 (2017): 15–40.

Martin, Sean. *Jewish Life in Cracow 1918–1939.* London: Vallentine-Mitchell, 2004.

Maślak-Maciejewska, Alicja. *Modlili się w Templu: Krakowscy Żydzi postępowi w XIX wieku. Studium społeczno-religijne.* Kraków: Wydawnictwo Uniwersytetu Jagiellońskiego, 2018.

Meiri, Shmuel, ed. *Kehilat vilitchkah: sefer zikaron.* Tel Aviv: Irgun yo'ẓei vilitchka, 1980.

Oleszak, Agnieszka. "The Beit Ya'akov School in Kraków as an Encounter between East and West." *Polin: Studies in Polish Jewry* 23 (2011): 277–290.

Opalski, Magda. "Feldman, Wilhem." *The YIVO Encyclopedia of Jews in Eastern Europe.* Online edition, http://www.yivoencyclopedia.org/article.aspx/Feldman_Wilhelm. Accessed February 5, 2020.

Pappenheim, Bertha. *Zekhutah shel ishah: Mivḥar ketavim 'al feminizm ve-yahadut*, edited by Natalie Naimark-Goldberg. Ramat Gan: Bar-Ilan University Press, 2019.

Parush, Iris. *Reading Jewish Women: Marginality and Modernization in Nineteenth-Century Eastern European Jewish Society*, translated by Saadya Sternberg. Waltham, MA: Brandeis University Press, 2004.

———. *Ha-ḥot'im bi-khtivah: Mahapekhat ha-ktivah ba-ḥevrah ha-yehudit be-mizraḥ eropah ba-me'ah ha-tesha'-'esreh.* Jerusalem: Karmel, 2017.

Plach, Eva. "Botticelli Woman: Rachel Singer and the Jewish Theme in Stanisław Wyspiański's *The Wedding.*" *Polish Review* 41 (1996): 309–327.

Prokop-Janiec, Eugenia. *Pogranicze polsko-żydowskie: Topografie i teksty.* Kraków: Wydawnictwo Uniwersytetu Jagiellońskiego, 2013.

———. "A Woman Assimilationist and the Great War: The Case of Aniela Kallas." *Medaon* 10 (2016): 1–11. https://www.medaon.de/en/artikel/a-woman-assimilationist-and-the-great -war-the-case-of-aniela-kallas/.

Rakover, Nahum. "Coercive Marital Relations Between a Man and His Wife." *Shnaton ha-Mishpat ha-'Ivri* 6/7 (1979): 295–317. [Hebrew]

Religyose techter shul Khavatseles. *Khavatseles oysgabe gevidmet di feyerliche derefenung fun der relig. techter-shul "Khavatseles", Lodzsh.* Łódź: Fajner, 1932.

Rosenheim, Jacob. *Erinnerungen 1870–1920.* Frankfurt am Main: Waldemar Kramer, 1970.

Rozenblit, Marsha L. *The Jews of Vienna, 1867–1914: Assimilation and Identity.* Albany: State University of New York Press, 1983.

Rympel, Manuel. "A Word about Kraków Jews in the Interwar Period 1918–1939." In *Kopiec wspomnień,* edited by Władysław Bodnicki et al. Kraków: Wydawnictwo Literackie, 1964, 555–588. [Polish]

Sadan, Dov. *Mi-meḥoz ha-yaldut.* Tel Aviv: Am Oved, 1981.

Sadowski, Dirk. *Haskala und Lebenswelt. Herz Homberg und die jüdischen deutschen Schulen in Galizien 1782–1806.* Göttingen: Vandenhoeck & Ruprecht, 2010.

Samsonowska, Krystyna. "The Hebrew Secondary School and the Jewish Educational System in Kraków." In *This Was the Hebrew School of Kraków: The Hebrew Secondary School 1918–1939,* edited by Maciej Władysław Belda et al., 15–38. Kraków: Muzeum Historyczne Miasta Krakowa, 2011.

Sapir, A. "Anti-Semitism in Western Galicia." *Luaḥ sha'ashu'im shimushi ve-sifruti li-shnat tarsag* (1902): 148–155. [Hebrew]

Sarna Araten, Rachel. *Michalina: Daughter of Israel.* Jerusalem: Am Yisrael Chai Press, 1986.

Schainker, Ellie R. *Confessions of the Shtetl: Converts from Judaism in Imperial Russia, 1817–1906.* Stanford, CA: Stanford University Press, 2017.

Seidman, Hillel, ed. *Żydowskie szkolnictwo religijne w ramach ustawodawstwa polskiego.* Warsaw: Chorew, 1937.

Seidman, Naomi. "A Revolution in the Name of Tradition; Orthodoxy and Torah Study for Girls." *Polin: Studies in Polish Jewry* 30 (2018): 321–340.

———. *Sarah Schenirer and the Bais Yaakov Movement: A Revolution in the Name of Tradition.* Liverpool: Liverpool University Press, 2019.

Shanes, Joshua. "Ahron Marcus: Portrait of a Zionist Hasid." *Jewish Social Studies* 16.3 (2010): 116–160.

———. *Diaspora Nationalism and Jewish Identity in Habsburg Galicia.* New York: Cambridge University Press, 2012.

Singer, Isidore and L. Ysaye. "Kareis, Josef." *Jewish Encyclopedia.* Online edition, http://www. jewishencyclopedia.com/articles/9213-kareis-josef. Accessed February 5, 2020.

Sliozberg, Genrikh. "A Boy's Gymnasium Life: The Memoirs of Genrikh Sliozberg." In *Everyday Jewish Life in Imperial Russia: Select Documents, 1772–1914,* edited by ChaeRan Y. Freeze and Jay M. Harris, 403–411. Waltham, MA: Brandeis University Press, 2013.

Stampfer, Shaul. "Gender Differentiation and Education of the Jewish Woman in Nineteenth-Century Eastern Europe." *Polin: Studies in Polish Jewry* 7 (1992): 63–87.

Stauter-Halsted, Keely. *The Devil's Chain: Prostitution and Social Control in Partitioned Poland.* Ithaca, NY: Cornell University Press, 2015.

Sternbuch, Gutta and David Kranzler. *Gutta: Memories of a Vanished World. A Bais Yaakov Teacher's Poignant Account of the War Years with a Historical Overview.* Jerusalem: Feldheim, 2005.

Tarnowski, Andrew. *The Last Mazurka: A Tale of War, Passion and Loss.* London: Aurum Press, 2006.

Thon, Jakob. *Die Juden in Oesterreich.* Berlin: Louis Lamm, 1908.

Toury, Jacob. "Troubled Beginnings: The Emergence of the Österreichisch-Israelitische Union." *Leo Baeck Institute Year Book* 30 (1985): 457–475.

Trunk, Yehiel Yeshaia. *Poyln: My Life within Jewish Life in Poland: Sketches and Images,* translated by Anna Clarke and edited by Piotr Wróbel and Robert M. Shapiro. Toronto/ Buffalo/ London: University of Toronto Press, 2007.

Tuma, Renate. "Studienwahl—Fächerwahl—Studienabschlüsse." In *Durch Erkenntnis,* edited by Heindl and Tichy, 1993, 79–91.

Unowsky, Daniel. *The Plunder: The 1898 Anti-Jewish Riots in Habsburg Galicia.* Stanford, CA: Stanford University Press, 2018.

Verdiger, Yaakov, ed. *Sefer Zekhuta de-Avraham.* Tel-Aviv: Y. Laslau, 1970.

Verhoeven, Timothy. "The Sad Tale of Sister Barbara Ubryk: A Case Study in Convent Captivity." In *Case Studies and the Dissemination of Knowledge,* edited by Joy Damousi et al. New York: Routledge, 2015.

Warnke, Nina and Jeffrey Shandler. "Yiddish Shylocks in Theater and Literature." In *Wrestling with Shylock: Jewish Responses to the Merchant of Venice,* edited by Edna Nahshon and Michael Shapiro. Cambridge: Cambridge University Press, 2017.

Wassermann, Jakob. *Der Moloch.* 3rd and 4th eds. Berlin: S. Fischer, 1908.

Weissman, Deborah R. "Bais Ya'akov: A Women's Educational Movement in the Polish Jewish Community. A Case Study in Tradition and Modernity." Master's thesis. New York University, 1977.

Wistrich, Robert S. *The Jews of Vienna in the Age of Franz Joseph.* Oxford/ New York: Littman Library of Jewish Civilization, 1990.

Wodziński, Marcin. *Hasidism: Key Questions.* New York: Oxford University Press, 2017.

Wood, Nathaniel D. *Becoming Metropolitan: Urban Selfhood and the Making of Modern Cracow.* DeKalb: Northern Illinois University Press, 2010.

Ya'akobzon, Binyamin Zeev [=Wolf Jacobson]. *Zikhronot.* Jerusalem: Center for Haredi Literature, 1953.

Zalkin, Mordechai. "'Let It Be Entirely Hebraic': The Yavneh Educational Sytem in Lithuania Between 'Haredi Education' and 'Hebrew Education.'" In *Zekhor davar le-'avdekha: Asufat ma'amarim le-zekher Dov Rapel,* edited by Shmuel Glick. Jerusalem: Mikhlelet Lifshiẓ, 2007, 143–121. [Hebrew]

———. "Heder." *The YIVO Encyclopedia of Jews in Eastern Europe.* Online edition, http://www.yivoencyclopedia.org/article.aspx/Heder. Accessed February 5, 2020.

Żbikowski, Andrzej. *Żydzi krakowscy i ich gmina w latach 1869–1919.* Warsaw: Żydowski Instytut Historyczny, 1994.

Żeleński (Boy), Tadeusz. "Plauderei über Wyspiańskis 'Hochzeit' (Auszüge)." In Stanisław Wyspiański, *Die Hochzeit: Drama in drei Akten,* translated by Karl Dedecius. Frankfurt am Main: Suhrkamp Verlag, 1992, 266–285.

Żyndul, Jolanta. "Conversion of Jews in Łódz in the Interwar Period." In *W poszukiwaniu religii doskonałej? Konwersja a Żydzi,* edited by Agnieszka Jagodzińska. Wrocław: Wydawnictwo Uniwersytetu Wrocławskiego, 2012, 213–225. [Polish]

INDEX

Abbahu, Rabbi, 23–24

abduction narrative, 3

abductions, 77–78, 97, 131; accusations against Jews, 82n92; Araten case, 56, 74, 95, 103–4; Lewkowicz case, 114–15. *See also* kidnapping

abuse, 46; of Anna Kluger, 254–55; in convents, 93; of Michalina Araten, 63, 64, 65–66

age of majority, 114, 138; for religion, 42, 43, 57, 182; in Russia, 3; after World War I, 182

Agnon, Shmuel Yosef (S. Y. Czaczkes), 133
  —WRITINGS OF: *The Bridal Canopy,* 171–74; "Out of Hate," 133; "Tehilla," 167–71

Agudat Yeshurun, 50, 199n53

Agudat Yisrael, 51, 136, 181, 189, 190, 242; Alexander Zysha Frydman, 205; Beit Yaakov schools, 202–3, 206–7; Chaim Israel Eiss, 204; *Diglenu,* 217n108, 222n119, 233n155; founding conference, 217n110; Mordechai Luksenberg, 199–200; Wolf S. Jacobson, 197

Alter, Abraham Mordechai, 188, 223, 231n145

Alter, Yehudah Aryeh Leib, 57

'Amudei ha-golah (Stern), 233

anti-Semitism, 57, 78, 167; in fictional representation, 176; newspapers, 85

Arak (Arik), Zacharias, 138, 142, 145–47, 149, 161, 253, 254

Arak, Meir, 138

Araten affair, wide knowledge of, 6, 56–57, 88–89, 111, 137, 166n3, 192, 240

Araten, Cywia (Dvoira-Tsivye) (mother), 55, 58, 66, 68, 73, 87, 94–95, 245

Araten, Israel (father): basis for fiction, 166–67, 168–69; death of, 102; disciple of Waks, 67; blaming washerwoman, 81, 192
  —INTERACTIONS WITH CHURCH: accusations of convent kidnapping, 2, 55, 56, 88n111, 91, 103n152; blamed for false information, 56; and Kęty convent entry, 84, 86, 87;
  —INTERACTIONS WITH MICHA-LINA: announcement of engagement by, 66, 246; beating of daughter, 64–65; letters to, 75, 100, 246–51; meeting daughter again, 102; Michalina refuses to meet, 68; Michalina's age, 71–74, 247
  —LEGAL ACTIONS: and doctor visits to convent, 70–71; interrogation of, 95; Kronawetter interpellation, 91–92; and private investigation, 76, 78–79; testimony of, 89, 94, 95

Araten, Marcus (grandfather), 62, 63, 68, 76, 92n125, 92n127

Araten, Michalina, 6, 167; age of, 55–56, 63, 67, 71–74, 192
  —HOME LIFE: abuse of, 64–65, 66, 91; desire to leave home, 246; education, 58–60; engagement, 66–67, 246; friendships, 60;

JEWS, CHRISTIANS, AND MUSLIMS FROM THE ANCIENT TO THE MODERN WORLD

*Edited by Michael Cook, William Chester Jordan,
and Peter Schäfer*

A NOTE ON THE TYPE

This book has been composed in Arno, an Old-style serif typeface in the classic Venetian tradition, designed by Robert Slimbach at Adobe.